Capitalism and the World Economy

T0331408

Globalization is a phenomenon that has attracted much attention in the past, but there are still many questions that remain unanswered.

This book categorizes globalization into three types: financial globalization; the collapse of the Cold War order and the ensuing convergence toward the capitalistic system; and the rise of the emerging nations. The globalization of capitalism has two implications. One is trust in the market economy system and support for a minimal state while another is an aspect of the Casino Capitalism as typically seen by the rampant emergence of hedge funds.

This book explores both the light and shadow cast by globalization, endeavoring to identify both positive and problematic effects of the globalization process on the world economy. For this purpose we first examine the nature and the features of world capitalism in relation to globalization. Then we discuss and investigate the path along which important nations—first the developed nations (the USA, EU and Japan), followed by the emerging nations (BRICs)—have proceeded under the influence of globalization.

This collection, from a selection of leading international contributors, will not only shed light on world capitalism as it is now, but will also offer pointers as to its future directions.

Toshiaki Hirai is Emeritus Professor at Sophia University, Tokyo.

Routledge studies in the modern world economy

1 **Interest Rates and Budget Deficits**
A study of the advanced economies
Kanhaya L. Gupta and Bakhtiar Moazzami

2 **World Trade after the Uruguay Round**
Prospects and policy options for the twenty-first century
Edited by Harald Sander and András Inotai

3 **The Flow Analysis of Labour Markets**
Edited by Ronald Schettkat

4 **Inflation and Unemployment**
Contributions to a new macroeconomic approach
Edited by Alvaro Cencini and Mauro Baranzini

5 **Macroeconomic Dimensions of Public Finance**
Essays in honour of Vito Tanzi
Edited by Mario I. Blejer and Teresa M. Ter-Minassian

6 **Fiscal Policy and Economic Reforms**
Essays in honour of Vito Tanzi
Edited by Mario I. Blejer and Teresa M. Ter-Minassian

7 **Competition Policy in the Global Economy**
Modalities for co-operation
Edited by Leonard Waverman, William S. Comanor and Akira Goto

8 **Working in the Macro Economy**
A study of the US labor market
Martin F. J. Prachowny

9 **How Does Privatization Work?**
Edited by Anthony Bennett

10 **The Economics and Politics of International Trade**
Freedom and trade: volume II
Edited by Gary Cook

11 **The Legal and Moral Aspects of International Trade**
Freedom and trade: volume III
Edited by Asif Qureshi, Hillel Steiner and Geraint Parry

12 **Capital Markets and Corporate Governance in Japan, Germany and the United States**
Organizational response to market inefficiencies
Helmut M. Dietl

13 **Competition and Trade Policies**
Coherence or conflict
Edited by Einar Hope

14 **Rice**
The primary commodity
A. J. H. Latham

15 **Trade, Theory and Econometrics**
Essays in honour of
John S. Chipman
*Edited by James C. Moore,
Raymond Riezman,
James R. Melvin*

16 **Who benefits from Privatisation?**
*Edited by Moazzem Hossain and
Justin Malbon*

17 **Towards a Fair Global Labour Market**
Avoiding the new slave trade
*Ozay Mehmet, Errol Mendes and
Robert Sinding*

18 **Models of Futures Markets**
Edited by Barry Goss

19 **Venture Capital Investment**
An agency analysis of UK
practice
Gavin C. Reid

20 **Macroeconomic Forecasting**
A sociological appraisal
Robert Evans

21 **Multimedia and Regional Economic Restructuring**
*Edited by Hans-Joachim
Braczyk, Gerhard Fuchs and
Hans-Georg Wolf*

22 **The New Industrial Geography**
Regions, regulation and
institutions
*Edited by Trevor J. Barnes and
Meric S. Gertler*

23 **The Employment Impact of Innovation**
Evidence and policy
*Edited by Marco Vivarelli and
Mario Pianta*

24 **International Health Care Reform**
A legal, economic and political
analysis
Colleen Flood

25 **Competition Policy Analysis**
Edited by Einar Hope

26 **Culture and Enterprise**
The development, representation
and morality of business
*Don Lavoie and
Emily Chamlee-Wright*

27 **Global Financial Crises and Reforms**
Cases and caveats
B. N. Ghosh

28 **Geography of Production and Economic Integration**
Miroslav N. Jovanović

29 **Technology, Trade and Growth in OECD Countries**
Does specialisation matter?
Valentina Meliciani

30 **Post-Industrial Labour Markets**
Profiles of North America and
Scandinavia
*Edited by Thomas P. Boje and
Bengt Furaker*

31 **Capital Flows without Crisis**
Reconciling capital mobility and
economic stability
Edited by Dipak Dasgupta,
Marc Uzan and Dominic Wilson

32 **International Trade and**
National Welfare
Murray C. Kemp

33 **Global Trading Systems at**
Crossroads
A post-Seattle perspective
Dilip K. Das

34 **The Economics and**
Management of Technological
Diversification
Edited by John Cantwell,
Alfonso Gambardella and
Ove Granstrand

35 **Before and Beyond EMU**
Historical lessons and future
prospects
Edited by Patrick Crowley

36 **Fiscal Decentralization**
Ehtisham Ahmad and
Vito Tanzi

37 **Regionalisation of Globalised**
Innovation
Locations for advanced industrial
development and disparities in
participation
Edited by Ulrich Hilpert

38 **Gold and the Modern World**
Economy
Edited by MoonJoong Tcha

39 **Global Economic Institutions**
Willem Molle

40 **Global Governance and**
Financial Crises
Edited by Meghnad Desai and
Yahia Said

41 **Linking Local and Global**
Economies
The ties that bind
Edited by Carlo Pietrobelli and
Arni Sverrisson

42 **Tax Systems and Tax Reforms**
in Europe
Edited by Luigi Bernardi and
Paola Profeta

43 **Trade Liberalization and**
APEC
Edited by Jiro Okamoto

44 **Fiscal Deficits in the Pacific**
Region
Edited by Akira Kohsaka

45 **Financial Globalization and the**
Emerging Market Economies
Dilip K. Das

46 **International Labor Mobility**
Unemployment and increasing
returns to scale
Bharati Basu

47 **Good Governance in the Era of**
Global Neoliberalism
Conflict and depolitization in
Latin America, Eastern Europe,
Asia and Africa
Edited by Jolle Demmers,
Alex E. Fernández Jilberto and
Barbara Hogenboom

48 **The International Trade**
System
Alice Landau

49 **International Perspectives on Temporary Work and Workers**
Edited by John Burgess and Julia Connell

50 **Working Time and Workers' Preferences in Industrialized Countries**
Finding the balance
Edited by Jon C. Messenger

51 **Tax Systems and Tax Reforms in New EU Members**
Edited by Luigi Bernardi, Mark Chandler and Luca Gandullia

52 **Globalization and the Nation State**
The impact of the IMF and the World Bank
Edited by Gustav Ranis, James Vreeland and Stephen Kosak

53 **Macroeconomic Policies and Poverty Reduction**
Edited by Ashoka Mody and Catherine Pattillo

54 **Regional Monetary Policy**
Carlos J. Rodríguez-Fuentez

55 **Trade and Migration in the Modern World**
Carl Mosk

56 **Globalisation and the Labour Market**
Trade, technology and less-skilled workers in Europe and the United States
Edited by Robert Anderton, Paul Brenton and John Whalley

57 **Financial Crises**
Socio-economic causes and institutional context
Brenda Spotton Visano

58 **Globalization and Self Determination**
Is the nation-state under siege?
Edited by David R. Cameron, Gustav Ranis and Annalisa Zinn

59 **Developing Countries and the Doha Development Round of the WTO**
Edited by Pitou van Dijck and Gerrit Faber

60 **Immigrant Enterprise in Europe and the USA**
Prodromos Panayiotopoulos

61 **Solving the Riddle of Globalization and Development**
Edited by Manuel Agosín, David Bloom, George Chapelier and Jagdish Saigal

62 **Foreign Direct Investment and the World Economy**
Ashoka Mody

63 **The World Economy**
A global analysis
Horst Siebert

64 **Production Organizations in Japanese Economic Development**
Edited by Tetsuji Okazaki

65 **The Economics of Language**
International analyses
Edited by Barry R. Chiswick and Paul W. Miller

66 **Street Entrepreneurs**
People, place and politics in local
and global perspective
*Edited by John Cross and
Alfonso Morales*

67 **Global Challenges and Local
Responses**
The East Asian experience
Edited by Jang-Sup Shin

68 **Globalization and Regional
Integration**
The origins, development and
impact of the single European
aviation market
Alan Dobson

69 **Russia Moves into the Global
Economy**
Breaking out
John M. Letiche

70 **The European Economy in an
American Mirror**
*Barry Eichengreen,
Michael Landesmann and
Dieter Stiefel*

71 **Working Time Around the
World**
Trends in working hours, laws,
and policies in a global
comparative perspective
*Jon C. Messenger, Sangheon Lee
and Deidre McCann*

72 **International Water Treaties**
Negotiation and cooperation
along transboundary rivers
Shlomi Dinar

73 **Economic Integration in the
Americas**
*Edited by Joseph A. McKinney
and H. Stephen Gardner*

74 **Expanding Frontiers of Global
Trade Rules**
The political economy dynamics
of the international trading system
Nitya Nanda

75 **The Macroeconomics of Global
Imbalances**
European and Asian perspectives
Edited by Marc Uzan

76 **China and Asia**
Economic and financial
interactions
*Edited by Yin-Wong Cheung and
Kar-Yiu Wong*

77 **Regional Inequality in China**
Trends, explanations and policy
responses
*Edited by Shenggen Fan,
Ravi Kanbur and Xiaobo Zhang*

78 **Governing Rapid Growth in
China**
Equity and institutions
*Edited by Ravi Kanbur and
Xiaobo Zhang*

79 **The Indonesian Labour Market**
*Shafiq Dhanani, Iyanatul Islam
and Anis Chowdhury*

80 **Cost-Benefit Analysis in Multi-
level Government in Europe
and the USA**
The case of EU cohesion policy
and of US federal investment
policies
Alessandro Ferrara

81 **The Economic Geography of
Air Transportation**
Space, time, and the freedom of
the sky
John Bowen

82 Cartelization, Antitrust and
    Globalization in the US and
    Europe
    Mark LeClair

83 The Political Economy of
    Integration
    Jeffrey Cason

84 Critical Issues in Air Transport
    Economics and Business
    *Rosario Macario and
    Eddy Van de Voorde*

85 Financial Liberalisation and
    Economic Performance
    Luiz Fernando de Paula

86 A General Theory of
    Institutional Change
    Shiping Tang

87 The Dynamics of Asian
    Financial Integration
    *Edited by Michael Devereux,
    Philip Lane, Park Cyn-young
    and Wei Shang-jin*

88 Innovative Fiscal Policy and
    Economic Development in
    Transition Economies
    Aleksandr Gevorkyan

89 Foreign Direct Investments in
    Asia
    *Edited by
    Chalongphob Sussangkarn,
    Yung Chul Park and
    Sung Jin Kang*

90 Time Zones, Communications
    Networks, and International
    Trade
    Toru Kikuchi

91 Miraculous Growth and
    Stagnation in Post-War Japan
    *Edited by Koichi Hamada,
    Keijiro Otsuka, Gustav Ranis,
    and Ken Togo*

92 Multilateralism and
    Regionalism in Global
    Economic Governance
    Trade, investment and finance
    Edited by Junji Nakagawa

93 Economic Growth and Income
    Inequality in China, India and
    Singapore
    Trends and policy implications
    *Pundarik Mukhopadhaya,
    G. Shantakumar and
    Bhanoji Rao*

94 Foreign Direct Investment in
    China
    Spillover effects on domestic
    enterprises
    Deng Ziliang

95 Enterprise Forms and
    Economic Efficiency
    Capitalist, cooperative and
    government firms
    Kazuhiko Mikami

96 Diversity and Transformations
    of Asian Capitalism
    *Edited by Boyer, Uemura and
    Isogai*

97 Knowledge Transfer in the
    Automobile Industry
    Global–local production networks
    Dessy Irawati

98 Exchange Rates and Foreign
    Direct Investment in Emerging
    Asia
    Selected issues and policy
    options
    Ramkishen S. Rajan

99 **Singapore, the Energy Economy**
From the first refinery to the end
of cheap oil, 1960–2010
Ng Weng Hoong

100 **China–India Economics**
Challenges, competition and
collaboration
Amitendu Palit

101 **Case Studies on Chinese
Enterprises**
Edited by Donglin Xia

102 **Argentina's Economic Growth
and Recovery**
Michael Cohen

103 **The Korean Labour Market
After the 1997 Economic Crisis**
*Edited by Joonmo Cho,
Richard B. Freeman,
Jaeho Keum and Sunwoong Kim*

104 **China and India**
The quest for energy resources in
the 21st century
Zhao Hong

105 **Beyond the Global Crisis**
Structural adjustments and
regional integration in Europe
and Latin America
*Edited by Lionello Punzo,
Carmen Aparecida Feio and
Martin Putchet Anyui*

106 **The Global Economic Crisis in
Latin America**
Impacts and responses
Edited by Michael Cohen

107 **The Processes and Practices of
Fair Trade**
Trust, ethics and governance
*Edited by Brigitte Granville and
Janet Dine*

108 **Regional Development through
Ecological Business**
Unique cases in Japanese rural
regions
Makoto Hirano

109 **Aging and Economic Growth
Potentials in the Pacific Region**
Edited by Akira Kohsaka

110 **Crises of Global Economy and
the Future of Capitalism**
An insight into the Marx's crisis
theory
*Edited by Kiichiro Yagi,
Nobuharu Yokokawa,
Shinjiro Hagiwara and
Gary A. Dymski*

111 **The Financial History of the
Bank for International
Settlements**
Kazuhiko Yago

112 **Freight Transport and the
Modern Economy**
Michel Savy and June Burnham

113 **Thoughts on Economic
Development in China**
*Edited by Ma Ying and Hans-
Michael Trautwein*

114 **China's Ethnic Minorities**
Social and economic indicators
Rongxing Guo

115 **Globalization, Outsourcing and
Labour Development in ASEAN**
*Shandre Thangavelu and
Aekapol Chongvilaivan*

116 **The Role of Informal Economies
in the Post-Soviet World**
The end of transition?
*Colin C. Williams, John Round
and Peter Rodgers*

117 **Demystifying the Chinese Economy Miracle**
The rise and future of relational capitalism
Yongqin Wang

118 **Globalism and Regional Economy**
Edited by Susumu Egashira

119 **Russia's Changing Economic and Political Regimes**
The Putin years and afterwards
Andrey Makarychev and André Mommen

120 **Innovation and Regional Development in China**
Edited by Ingo Liefner and Yehua Dennis Wei

121 **International Trade Negotiations and Domestic Politics**
The intermestic politics of trade liberalization
Edited by Oluf Langhelle

122 **Emerging Knowledge Economies in Asia**
Current trends in ASEAN 5
Edited by Dessy Irawati and Roel Rutten

123 **The Internationalization of the Renminbi**
International Monetary Institute, Renmin University of China

124 **Financial Globalization and Regionalism in East Asia**
Edited by Takuji Kinkyo, Yoichi Matsubayashi and Shigeyuki Hamori

125 **Successful Business Dealings and Management with China Oil, Gas and Chemical Giants**
EurIng. Henry K. H. Wang

126 **State Building and Development**
Edited by Keijiro Otsuka and Takashi Shiraishi

127 **International Economic Development**
Leading issues and challenges
Edited by Fu Lai Tony Yu, Wai Kee Yuen and Diana S. Kwan

128 **Innovation, Globalization and Firm Dynamics**
Lessons for enterprise policy
Edited by Anna Ferragina, Erol Taymoz and Kamil Yilmaz

129 **International Remittance Payments and the Global Economy**
Bharati Basu with James T. Bang

130 **The Open Society and its Enemies in East Asia**
The relevance of the Popperian framework
Edited by Gregory C. G. Moore

131 **The Economics of Knowledge Generation and Distribution**
The role of interactions in the system dynamics of innovation and growth
Edited by Pier Paolo Patrucco

132 **Japan's Aid**
Lessons for economic growth, development and political economy
Edward M. Feasel

133 **The Geographical Transformation of China**
Edited by Michael Dunford and Weidong Lui

134 **The Economics of Cooperative Education**
A practitioners' guide to the theoretical framework and empirical assessment of cooperative education
Yasushi Tanaka

135 **Comparing Post War Japanese and Finnish Economies and Societies**
Edited by Yasushi Tanaka, Toshiaki Tamaki, Jari Ojala, and Jari Eloranta

136 **Measuring National Income in the Centrally Planned Economies**
Why the West underestimated the transition to capitalism
William Jefferies

137 **Crises in Europe in the Transatlantic Context**
Economic and political appraisals
Edited by Bruno Dallago and John McGowan

138 **The International Monetary System, Energy and Sustainable Development**
Edited by Sung Jin Kang and Yung Chul Park

139 **Capitalism and the World Economy**
The light and shadow of globalization
Edited by Toshiaki Hirai

140 **Irish Economic Development**
Serial under-achievement or high-performing EU state?
Eoin O'Leary

Capitalism and the World Economy

Economy

The light and shadow of globalization

Edited by Toshiaki Hirai

Routledge
Taylor & Francis Group

LONDON AND NEW YORK

First published 2015
by Routledge
2 Park Square, Milton Park, Abingdon, Oxon OX14 4RN

and by Routledge
52 Vanderbilt Avenue, New York, NY 10017

First issued in paperback 2020

Routledge is an imprint of the Taylor & Francis Group, an informa business

British Library Cataloguing in Publication Data
A catalogue record for this book is available from the British Library

Library of Congress Cataloging in Publication Data
Capitalism and the world economy : the light and shadow of globalization / edited by Toshiaki Hirai.
    pages cm
    1. Globalization–Economic aspects. 2. Capitalism. 3. International finance. 4. International economic relations. I. Hirai, Toshiaki
    HF1365.C37 2015
    330.12'2–dc23   2014035032

ISBN 13: 978-0-367-66895-2 (pbk)
ISBN 13: 978-0-415-73391-5 (hbk)
ISBN 13: 978-1-315-83278-4 (ebk)

Typeset in Times New Roman
by Wearset Ltd, Boldon, Tyne and Wear

Contents

List of figures   xv
List of tables   xvi
List of contributors   xvii
Preface   xviii

PART I
Bird's-eye view   1

1   **Capitalism and globalization**   3
    TOSHIAKI HIRAI

2   **Financial globalization and the instability of the world
    economy**   27
    TOSHIAKI HIRAI

3   **Globalization and Keynes's ideal of a "sounder political
    economy between all nations"**   46
    ANNA M. CRABELLI AND MARIO A. CEDRINI

4   **Globalization and the ladder of comparative advantage**   71
    ROGER J. SANDILANDS

PART II
Developed nations—USA, EU and Japan   87

5   **The crisis, the bailout and financial reform: a Minskian
    approach to improving crisis response**   89
    L. RANDALL WRAY

 6 Economic crisis and globalization in the European Union   115
    COSIMO PERROTTA

 7 "Eurocrisis": origins, the present and perspectives   128
    PAOLO PIACENTINI

 8 "We are all Keynesians now": the paradox of British fiscal
    policy in the aftermath of the global financial crisis
    2007–2009   149
    WILLIAM REDVERS GARSIDE

 9 Beyond de-globalization in Japan   165
    YUTAKA HARADA

10 Trade friction with no foundation: a review of US–Japanese
    economic relations in the 1980s and the 1990s   184
    ASAHI NOGUCHI

PART III
Emerging nations—BRICs   201

11 Globalization, policy autonomy and economic development:
    the case of Brazil   203
    FERNANDO J. CARDIM DE CARVALHO

12 The Indian economy under economic reforms: responses
    from society and the state   219
    SUNANDA SEN

13 A mixed effect of globalization on China's economic growth   234
    HIDEO OHASHI

14 Dynamics of state–business relations and the evolution of
    capitalism in Russia in an age of globalization   254
    YUKO ADACHI

    Index   278

Figures

5.1 Primary Dealer Credit Facility (PDCF) weekly amounts lent
    and outstanding   97
5.2 Facility percentage of bailout total   99
5.3 Disaggregated consolidated Federal Reserve assets, in
    millions, 2007–2013   102
7.1 The decline in the share of income going to labor in advanced
    countries   143
8.1 Government budget surpluses in the OECD, 2007–2009   154
8.2 Annual change in public sector net borrowing, 1997–2009   155
8.3 Real interest rate on index-linked gilts, 1990–2009   160
9.1 Trends of GDP (exchange rate) of major countries and areas   168
9.2 Trends of GDP (purchasing power parity) of major countries
    and areas   169
9.3 Trends of exports volumes of major countries and areas   170
9.4 Trends of exports volumes of major countries and areas
    excluding China and Developing Asia   171
9.5 Shares of exports and imports of major countries, 1960–2012   172
9.6 Net capital outflows of major countries, 1960–2011   173
9.7 Foreign direct investment of major countries, 1960–2012   174
9.8 Japanese students in the US and foreign students in Japan   176
9.9 Terms of trade, 1960–2012   178
10.1 The current account in the US and Japan, 1980–2007   192
13.1 Rising inequality in China (Gini Coefficient)   239
13.2 Saving-investment balance in China   248
13.3 Child and old-age dependency ratios to working population in
    China   249

Tables

1.1	Annual average rate of growth of GDP	18
1.2	GDP ranking in terms of purchasing power parity	18
5.1	Five largest Primary Dealer Credit Facility borrowers	98
5.2	Cumulative facility totals	99
7.1	GDP growth rates, 2008–2013	141
8.1	Public spending totals	158
11.1	Share of exports and imports in the value of domestic manufacture	212
11.2	Balance of payments – Brazil	213
14.1	The ten big groups in 1997	256
14.2	Russia, company ranking, 2003 and 2013	257
14.3	Major groups in 2008	258
14.4	Forbes Russia list, 2004 and 2013	260
14.5	Private sector share of GDP	266
14.6	State ownership by sectors, 2011	267
14.7	The extent of state control	267

Contributors

Toshiaki Hirai Emeritus Professor, Sophia University, Japan.

Anna M. Crabelli Professor, University of Eastern Piedmont, Italy.

Mario A. Cedrini Associate Professor, University of Turin, Italy.

Roger J. Sandilands Professor, University of Strathclyde, UK.

L. Randall Wray Professor, University of Missouri—Kansas City, USA.

Cosimo Perrotta Professor, University of Salento, Italy.

Paolo Piacentini Professor, University of Rome "La Sapienza," Italy.

William Redvers Garside Professor, Waseda University, Japan.

Yutaka Harada Professor, Waseda University, Japan.

Asahi Noguchi Professor, Senshu University, Japan.

Fernando J. Cardim de Carvalho Emeritus Professor, Federal University of Rio de Janeiro, Brazil.

Sunanda Sen Former Professor, Jawaharlal Nehru University, India.

Hideo Ohashi Professor, Senshu University, Japan.

Yuko Adachi Professor, Sophia University, Japan.

Preface

1 The aim of this book

The aim of this book is to identify what globalization has brought about over the last three decades, examine how world capitalism has evolved and changed through globalization, and evaluate globalization (focusing on its light and shadow) through representative nations—both developed and emerging nations.

Focusing on this phenomenon from diverse points of view should prove fruitful for an understanding not only of world capitalism as it is but also of the direction in which it will be moving.

A word about the general design of this book might be helpful for readers approaching it. What follows is entirely attributable to the editor, although we have discussed it together (further details are elucidated in Chapter 1).

Since the mid-1980s the world economy has seen the evolution of globalization, which can be characterized as the "phenomenon moving toward a market economy on a global scale."

Globalization can be considered from two viewpoints—the factors that favored it and the phenomena that occurred as a result of those factors.

With regard to the factors, we will single out the following five:

1   neoliberalism;
2   financial liberalization;
3   liberalization of capital transaction;
4   New Industrial Revolution; and
5   the collapse of the socialistic system.

More in detail, (1) is the fruit of developments in thought in the broad sense, (2) and (3) are steps intentionally taken by governments and financial institutions in the direction of financial liberalization, (4) is a conquest of the IT revolution, initiated by many young US entrepreneurs, and (5) is the collapse of a rival to the capitalistic system, for a number of reasons.

As for the phenomena, four types of globalization could be identified as constituting the great transformation of the world economic system:

1 Financial Globalization;
2 Market System I—Globalization, with the collapse of the Cold War order and the ensuing convergence toward the capitalistic system;
3 Market System II—Globalization, with the rise of the emerging nations—the so-called BRICs; and
4 Globalization of Market Integration—the EU (or the euro system).

Globalization, in a nutshell, has offered great opportunities for the emerging nations to attain high rates of economic growth—so high, indeed, as to qualify them for membership of the G20 (although Russia suffered severely from the so-called Shock Therapy). For the US and the UK, globalization has contributed to their regaining economic power from Japan, especially through financial globalization. Financial globalization, on the other hand, has proved so excessive as to make the world economy increasingly fragile and unstable.

We cannot and need not prevent the advent of globalization. But we need to know what capitalism is and how it should be managed in order to prevent excesses, especially in financial globalization.

2 Contents explained

The book is composed of three parts.

Part I, "Bird's-eye view," addresses the following problems broadly and theoretically: What is globalization? How should we evaluate it in relation to world capitalism?

Chapter 1 explores the light and shadow of globalization in a broad perspective, serving as a general introduction to the whole book. Chapter 2 examines how financial globalization has made the world economy increasingly unstable and volatile in the course of time, focusing on the Dodd–Frank Act (July 2010) and its implementation in the US. Chapter 3 offers a qualified analysis of the recent global economic disorder and sheds light on Keynes's legacy in terms of international economic relations. Chapter 4 explains how openness to world trade and investment has fostered both faster growth and greater income equality between and within countries in terms of dynamic comparative advantage.

Part II, "Developed nations—USA, EU and Japan" examines how the developed nations have been affected by globalization.

Chapter 5 states, based on a Minskian approach, that when markets do not work to promote the public interest, a system of constraints and interventions can work better, and we need to make "industry" dominate over "speculation" for meeting the crisis.

Chapter 6 insists that the European crisis is mainly due to the tendency of the traditional market toward saturation. This is not sufficiently counteracted—neither with the new inventions nor with great development projects supported by the state. Chapter 7 maintains that the institutional and structural flaws of the "eurosystem" are still there in spite of the European Central Bank's policy, and the crisis in the real economies, facing austerity measures, appears to be getting worse.

Chapter 8 seeks to explore the extent to which British developments reflected a return to Keynesian doctrines in the conduct of public policy—Britain which, as from 2008, embraced fiscal policy after the prolonged reaction against Keynesianism.

Chapter 9 argues that Japan's ratio of exports and imports to GDP showed practically no increase in 1990s, while other countries' ratios increased significantly. Why did de-globalization come about in Japan? Chapter 10 examines the trade friction that existed between the US and Japan during the 1980s and the 1990s and the associated economic policies that contributed to this friction, with a deep-rooted misguided belief.

Part III, "Emerging nations—BRICs," deals with how they have been able to exploit globalization and achieve high rates of economic growth, to the extent of taking on increasingly important roles in the world economy.

Chapter 11 examines how, in Brazil, globalization constrained policy decision-making in the period, including the definition of growth policies, and what the result of the process was in terms of economic growth. Chapter 12, following Karl Polanyi's theory, examines the four stages of a sequence in the Indian economy: economic reforms and liberalization; impact on economy with regressive consequences; resistance by people-centered organizations; and limited measures by the state.

Chapter 13 turns the focus towards China. It has greatly benefited from globalization, attaining high economic growth through trade and foreign direct investment. However, this has also caused growing disparity. Thus globalization has produced a mixed effect on China. Chapter 14 examines the effect of globalization on the development of the corporate sector in Russia, focusing on its mixed impact on the rise and functioning of Russia's major natural resource corporations.

3 How did this project emerge?

The present project originated with a project funded by Sophia University (2009–2012). The findings of these three years' activities, including the international symposia at the University of Graz (Austria, January 2010) and Sophia University (Japan, October 2010), were submitted to the Repository [Sophia-R] in August 2012.

Then an idea emerged: why not concentrate our focus on the present globalization and continue our study? We then worked out how to organize a new project, the findings of which are presented here.

We wish to express our gratitude to the collaborators on the former project (Prof. Linda Grove [Sophia University], and Prof. Noriko Hataya [Sophia University]) as well as Sophia University for providing funds, and the University of Graz for holding a superb conference (thanks to Prof. Heinz Kurz [University of Graz]).

We have organized this project in the belief that globalization is an important object of study in the social sciences and in understanding the present world. We will have fulfilled our ambition if readers are able to gain some insight into the light and shadow of globalization and world capitalism.

Tokyo, May 2014

Part I
Bird's-eye view

1 Capitalism and globalization

Toshiaki Hirai

1 Introduction

This chapter aims to address the following themes fairly broadly and theoretically, reflecting a general perspective on the whole book: What is the present state of globalization? How should we evaluate it in relation to capitalism?

If we try to characterize the development of the world economy from the latter half of the 1980s to the present day with a single word, there could be none more appropriate than "globalization," which may be defined as the "phenomenon moving toward market economy (or capitalism) on a global scale."

We may then go on to single out three points to characterize the present state of globalization: (1) As a principle of operating the economy, capitalism has been globally adopted, while socialism has been abandoned; (2) financial globalization has developed to an extreme degree; and (3) several countries that had been regarded as developing countries have attained remarkable economic growth, to such a degree that they have come to occupy an important role in the world economy. (1) is an epoch-making phenomenon in the postwar world economy, never before seen on the worldwide scale, although it found a place in the Pax Britannica. (2) is remarkable in terms of scale and the multiplicity of financial products. (3) is a new phenomenon that is throwing the North–South dichotomy awry.

This chapter runs as follows. First, we look into the nature of capitalism, for the present globalization constitutes a development of it. Here the essential characteristics of the capitalistic system are pointed out, followed by its problematics.

Second, globalization is examined. It can be approached from two sides—five factors which caused it, and four types of globalization which occurred as a result.

The five factors are: (1) neoliberalism; (2) financial liberalization; (3) liberalization of capital transactions; (4) the New Industrial Revolution; and (5) the collapse of socialistic systems. The four types of globalization lie in: (1) financial globalization; (2) capitalism in the ex-communist bloc; (3) the emerging countries; and (4) the EU. An important point is that globalization can be classified under the broad headings of financial globalization (1) and market system globalization, which includes (2), (3) and (4). The salient tendency has been for the former to promote the latter; while bringing about a huge glut of financial capital, the former has left the world economy more fragile.

2 The capitalistic system

2.1 Essentials

We may mention six points worth noting as essentials of capitalism: (1) dynamics, (2) markets, (3) capital, (4) firms, (5) uncertainty, (6) ambiguities. The first four are connected with the strong points in a capitalistic system, the last two with the weak points.

1   Dynamics—The essential nature of a capitalistic system is embodiment of an impulse toward growth. A capitalistic system generates increase in production and growth through the development of division of labor, competition and technology while it plows down the existing systems. Thus the capitalistic system is a dynamic system which also embodies instability. Its "dynamics" operates through "markets" and "capital."

2   Markets—They have two salient characteristics: (a) that of "turning everything into commodities" and (b) "the monetary economy."

    a   A capitalistic society might even be summed up as a society in which the most important elements of the economy come to be transacted, being turned into commodities. These include not only labor but also, in recent years, securitized products, the emission trading system, etc.

    b   In the markets, almost all the transactions are carried out by means of money. That is, in a capitalistic society barter is not an essential form of transaction.

3   Capital—Capital, which is divided broadly into "real capital" and "finance capital," is an important wheel which sets markets in motion. Finance capital, among other things, keeping a lookout over all the markets on the globe, enters those deemed most profitable, making some markets active, others inactive. Firms and industries that cannot procure finance capital face grim prospects. As a result, the industrial structure undergoes sweeping transformation and the capitalistic system sees growth.

4   Firms—Firms play an absolutely vital role in "dynamics" of capitalism. They must develop, looking to the uncertain future, new goods and new markets, injecting huge amounts of capital and human resources.

The above-mentioned four features are strong points. Through a gigantic network of markets, economic activities are developed and economic agents are allowed to behave on a self-driven basis. Through the mechanism of numerous markets a great many economic agents produce and exchange vast quantities of goods and services. Moreover, through the activities of firms the economy as a whole can enjoy dynamic development.

The capitalistic system operates through the activities of economic agents who are free to choose their rational behaviors, bringing about desirable results from the point of view of economic efficiency. It is superior to socialistic systems in terms of freedom, for it is through the markets—to a great extent "autonomous," not depending on decrees by some particular persons—that the production and exchange of goods and services are carried out.

In contrast with the above (1)–(4), the following show the capitalistic system as subject to various uncertainties and ambiguities.

5   Uncertainties—the capitalistic system faces various kinds of uncertainties. Firms need to go on producing goods forecasting sales in the markets. They need to make great efforts to develop new goods. Once they succeed in doing so, they need to build capital equipment, seeking to boost profits. And yet forecasting is a very difficult art because the sales of the goods depend on demand.

Moreover, present-day capitalism has tended to get involved in "self-augmentation of finance capital," so that firms in the real economy are forced to produce and sell goods while coping with the behavior of finance capital, which makes forecasting more difficult.

6   Ambiguities—Economics has assumed "rationality" in regard to markets and economic agents and maintained that the unfettered market system can bring about the Pareto optimum. To some extent, this system has superior features in that independent individuals can make their own decisions in the market, and many goods and services are determined without any intentional interference from outside.

This assumption, however, entails big problems. It relies excessively on "rationality." If the capitalistic system was conceived exclusively in terms of rationality, cognitive errors would be inevitable. One example lies in the "ambiguities" characterizing capitalism, as distinct from uncertainties. We will illustrate this point with three cases.[1]

Market price: Economics teaches us that the relative price is determined at the intersection between demand and supply in each market, regarding money as a veil. However, it should be an absolute price which is actually determined at the intersection, with money always working as a counterparty. This has important consequences, quite different from barter transactions.

Suppose that a certain good has enjoyed extremely high sales due to, say, word of mouth or advertising. The absolute price goes up and the firms concerned can make a huge profit. In this situation financial institutions can enter this market, creating money. As this phenomenon encroaches on the goods concerned, the possibility looms up that the price as determined by demand and supply is not the result of optimal behaviors of economic agents. Could the market mechanism, greatly influenced as it is by credit creation, really determine a "fair" price? We need to keep an eye on the market, with some idea of fairness in mind.

Accounting: The amount of profit a firm can make depends entirely on the accounting system, for complicated everyday business activities cannot provide it with concrete information. Thus every transaction is kept on a balance sheet. And once or twice a year a firm makes performance public in the form of the balance sheet and the earnings statement.

However, this system has a shortcoming. Among other things, depreciation allowance and inflation/deflation are serious matters. Depreciation allowance is not exempt from some degree of arbitrariness. Inflation/deflation is more serious, for if it went to extremes, accounting would lose its significance. The figures thus kept for, say, half a year, show a bias and do not convey correct information, and yet firms have no other choice. In this case, nominal GDP does not constitute correct information. In order to avoid the problem, social accounting calculates real GDP by dividing it by the GDP deflator, although even this method cannot prevent the essential ambiguity.[2]

Debt contract: In a capitalistic system various kinds of debt contracts are made, using money as unit of account. In this case, debts cannot avoid the influence of inflation/deflation, and yet people cannot help but enter upon debt contracts based on money as unit of account. In spite of the fact that in a capitalistic system contracts in terms of money are absolutely fundamental, "ambiguities" always crop up there.

2.2 *Issues involved*

We saw in section 2.1 that a capitalistic system, in principle, has strong points in terms of "dynamism," "market," "capital," and "firms" while it has weak points in terms of "uncertainties" and "ambiguities." In this section we will see three issues—(1) the bubble phenomenon; (2) corruption and injustice; and (3) the disparity problem—as constituting headaches for the system, which are, more or less, related to the weak points.

2.2.1 *The bubble phenomenon*

Reference here is to a situation in which the economy overheats due to some factor, to such a degree that the government tries in vain to control it, finally leading to the bubble bursting. These phenomena have occurred repeatedly over the centuries (e.g., the Tulip Bubble and the Stock Bubble associated with John Law).

In economics, however, the bubble phenomenon has been dealt with as an exceptional case. The principal task of economics has resided, rather, in analyzing normal processes. Most economists placed profound trust in the "classical dichotomy" and "Say's Law," thereby failing to address an issue like unemployment in a capitalistic society until Keynes appeared on the scene.

The trend in these last two decades has been to revert to the tenets prior to Keynes. The new classical macroeconomics has defended the "classical dichotomy" and Say's Law, and yet it allowed for economic fluctuations. Worse still, this has become the mainstream.

Strangely enough, these two decades have seen increase in the degree of instability of the capitalistic system with repeated bubble phenomena—e.g., the Japanese bubble and its burst from the end of the 1980s to the early 1990s, the US dot.com bubble and its burst from the mid-1990s to 2000, and the housing and subprime bubble and its burst in the early 2000s, all of which occurred due to speculative activities with an abnormal bloat of money. Moreover, our modern-day governments have been unable to prevent these bubbles from reaching a bursting point. The reason why the bubble is a serious issue for the economic system is that it could drive people excessively into money-making activities. When rival firms are making huge profits on a bubble, the CEO of any particular company will not be allowed to sit and wait, stating that the bubble will burst soon. Employees are put in a similar position. This sort of climate comes from human nature itself, underlying society—people cannot sit and wait while rivals are making profits.

Human beings are consciously or potentially driven by the desire to obtain wealth and fortune. Once the bubble occurs, increasing numbers of people grow eager to pursue profit—even those who had hitherto been composed—and sooner or later join in, driven by such an instinct. As a result, the economy eventually plunges into the engulfing foam of the bubble, the real economy being neglected.

Thus the responsibility to prevent bubbles should be taken on by governments, and yet repeatedly we see them incapable of containing the burgeoning bubble. This is indicative of a malfunction of the capitalistic system and the respective system of government, thus constituting a problem we need to diagnose, and so reform the structure.

2.2.2 Corruption and injustice

When the excellence of the capitalistic system is evoked, free exchanges among agencies in the market are argued to be efficient and reasonable, with freedom and fairness being guaranteed.

Compared with a socialistic system, this is true, and yet this system has a weak point—corruption and injustice.[3]

Mainstream classical and neoclassical economics take the classical dichotomy for granted. They analyze the real economy in terms of relative prices, and then take money as determining absolute prices. However, this method is a static and non-monetary approach to the actual economy. Let us focus on the "monetary" aspect here.

Capitalism is a system which is inconceivable without money. As the real economy grows, the degree to which it depends on outside capital for production and service activities grows larger. Finance has its own existence value, for it enables smooth growth of the real economy. At the same time, however, finance is a sphere in which there is ample room for fraudulence. When finance enjoys unlimited freedom, the room for fraud grows disproportionately large. Today's world has been witnessing the money game conducted by means of "securitized products" together with the technique of "leverage" on a global level. These activities, unless some regulations are imposed, tend toward excessive speculation wrapped with a veil, and the scope for fraudulence is vast.

There are several types of corruption as well as dishonesty on the part of the financial institutions.

Forced saving: This is a behavior of financial institutions that buy goods ahead of the public with money they create. As a result, the amount of goods left for the public decreases proportionately. Thus the public is forced to save. This shows that they can procure money and get whatever goods they want at will. The market system could thus be misappropriated.

Stock market malpractice: The stock market is a market representing the capitalistic system. It is an important means by which firms can procure the money they require. And yet it is a place that enables many wrongdoings. From illegal operations to suspicious borderline dealing, including insider trading, stock price manipulations by means of disinformation and so forth by means of which unjustifiable profits are obtained.

Way of usurping profits through non-existence, or opacity of markets: We can in many cases point out the transparency of capitalism as a strength. In the financial markets, however, this virtue may be lacking.

In recent years "securitized products" have multiplied at an amazing rate, but many have been transacted in a disturbingly opaque way, without markets. Moreover, hedge funds, which have played a major role here, have not been subject to oversight by any governmental organization. The financial institutions have had a tendency to emphasize the importance of independence. However, the funds have carried out operations with huge amounts of money, to such an extent as to endanger the world economy, as exemplified by the LTCM in 1998. The runaway effect in the form of "market non-existence" and "opacity" of the financial system threatens to disintegrate capitalism.

2.2.3 The disparity problem

Capitalism bases the foundations of economic activities on the markets. Economists seeking to work out its mechanism have placed their trust in the general equilibrium theory. However, there is one point which is left out—distribution of income and/or wealth.

Moreover, in economics there is a proposition to the effect that "perfect competition brings about Pareto optimality." We are not told at which point on the so-called contract curve the exchange will be determined.

Mainstream economics interprets "justice" in terms of "commutative justice." This is an idea that the market mechanism attains "justice" through exchange behavior. It precludes value judgment of the state of distribution of stock— "distributive justice" is excluded.

When economists applaud market efficiency, they tend to emphasize an equality in the premise. This is also problematic, for in a capitalistic system there is no "equality in the premise." There exists the conviction that, left to the free market, the economic system will be efficient. However, in a society in which there exists a great disparity in the ways of obtaining wealth or incomes, there is a possibility that if left to the free market great disparity could result.

The world, which has been driven by market fundamentalism, has seen, as a result, a very great disparity in income and wealth in many countries, notably in the US, and even more notably in the emerging nations.

Let us take the US as an example (the distribution trend in family incomes from 1979 to 2007 reported by the CBO in October 2011); in 2007 the top 1 percent showed three times as much as 1979. Contrastingly, the other classes have remained stagnant. The 81–99 percent group showed a 50 percent increase, and the 21–80 percent group a 25 percent increase. The lowest class has shown little increase. Thus this period is called "the Period of Great Disparity."

3 Globalization

3.1 Five factors which have caused globalization

We have already seen five points constituting the cause which has brought about globalization. "Neoliberalism" is a development in thought in the wider sense. "Financial liberalization" and "liberalization of capital transaction" are a conscious movement on the part of governments and financial institutions aiming at promoting financial liberalization. The "New Industrial Revolution" occurred due to the IT revolution, initiated by many young US entrepreneurs. The "collapse of a socialistic system" is the fall of a rival to the capitalistic system.

3.1.1 Neoliberalism

Like many terminologies in political philosophy, historically the term neoliberalism has been used with different meanings.[4] Here we take it as used from the 1980s on with Hayek and Friedman as representatives, and indeed as also understood among the general public as well as the politicians.[5]

The main claims of neoliberalism run as follows:

- respect the free activities of individual to the maximum degree;
- governments should not interfere with the market;
- governments should not adopt discretionary economic policies;
- structures should be reformed in such a way that as many regulations as possible be discarded.

Neoliberalism thus identified has been dominant since the 1980s.

There is no hiding the fact that there are great differences among the scholars representative of neoliberalism—for example, in the perception of liberty, and the market. We can distinguish great differences between, say, Hayek and Friedman, or Hayek and Robbins/Knight. However, this is not the place to make comparisons at this level.

First, neoliberalism enjoyed overwhelming support from Thatcher and Reagan, among others—Hayek in the case of Thatcher, Friedman in the case of Reagan. As both governments aimed at strengthening military power, they never succeeded in attaining "small government." However, what matters here is that both advocated neoliberalism as political thought.[6] Thatcher invoked neoliberalism as social philosophy against the strong trade unions, governmental enterprises, and the old-fashioned City, while Reagan invoked it to favor the entrepreneurs, with a sharp reduction in income tax for the upper class and a sharp reduction in corporate tax, while raising income tax for the middle and lower classes.

Second, neoliberalism enjoyed the convinced support of economists. In the US, through monetarism, the new classical school as represented by Lucas, Kydland and Prescot became mainstream macroeconomics, with scathing criticism of Keynesian economics. Their economic models assumed rational expectations on the part of economic agents, instantaneous equilibrium in the market and Say's Law. The so-called "policy ineffectiveness proposition" and financial engineering based on the efficient market hypothesis can be said to be along the same line.

Mainstream economics had previously been represented by "the neoclassical synthesis," which consisted of Keynesian economics and Walrasian general equilibrium theory. In this framework, discretionary economic policy was essential in situations of underemployment, while general equilibrium theory was also regarded as essential for describing the full employment. The social philosophy was built on this synthesis.

Neoliberalism, in a nutshell, might be said to have been built on the framework in which neoclassical microeconomics is preserved, and new macroeconomic theories such as monetarism and the new classical theory are advocated as alternative to Keynesian economics. Thus over these three decades economic theory and social philosophy could be said to have gone hand in hand[7,8]—an entirely new phenomenon in the history of economic thought.

Thus neoliberalism has made a great contribution to globalization over the three decades since the 1980s.[9]

3.1.2 Financial liberalization

Financial liberalization was initiated by the financial institutions, aiming at abolishing regulations in order to widen the scope for procurement of capital and investment. Above all, extraordinary persistence was to be seen in the activities aiming at attenuation of the Glass–Steagall Act.

These activities led to a rapid increase in hedge funds, structured investment vehicles (SIV) and private equity funds (PEF) together with a rapid increase in securitized commodities such as MBS (mortgage backed security), CDO (collateralized debt obligation), CDS (credit default swap).[10]

3.1.3 Liberalization of capital transaction

An international movement aiming at liberalization of capital transactions was advocated by the IMF in the 1990s—"liberalization of capital account." The central figure here was Stanley Fischer.[11] After the Breton Woods system collapsed in the early 1970s, the IMF's function had remained unclear. Then it came to find its way into financing the developing countries. The 1980s saw the debt crisis of the Latin American countries, greatly afflicted by the oil shocks. Faced with these phenomena, the IMF took on the liberalization of capital account as its major task.

However, the articles of agreement of the IMF did not include the liberalization of capital account from the outset, so the IMF needed to work on it. The pressure to reform the articles of agreement peaked in 1997, when the South East Asian financial crisis broke out and the movement ended up in failure. That said, this movement ran together with the movement for attenuation of the Glass–Steagall Act.

The latter half of the 1980s saw a great increase in foreign direct investment (FDI) by Japanese firms in China and the South East Asian countries due to appreciation of yen, which contributed to a high economic growth there through exports. But this is not the whole story. In the early 1990s, India and Brazil came to adopt a policy of capital liberalization, which brought about economic development through FDI.

It is worth noting that the Japanese government had been critical of the IMF and the World Bank, both of which promoted capital liberalization, and among other things a speculative international monetary system, as exemplified by the idea of the Asian Monetary Fund, and the Miyazawa Proposal. The Japanese proposals were not able to bear fruit due to the staunch opposition of Rubin and Summers.

3.1.4 The New Industrial Revolution

The IT industry was initiated in the US in the 1980s. Initially, Japanese firms could continue to lead the world by setting up sections which adopted the technology developed there. However, it was not long before the situation changed dramatically. The IT revolution in the US was to achieve startling growth due to the originality of young entrepreneurs creating enterprises such as Microsoft, Apple, Yahoo and Google while established Japanese firms were to suffer from competition with the newborn US firms.

While until the 1980s the Japanese firms had led the world economy in terms of industrial technology, the US took over the lead in the 1990s. Moreover, the IT revolution was to offer great economic opportunities to countries like India in the form of outsourcing.

3.1.5 Collapse of a socialistic system—why did the Soviet Union collapse?

Here let us see how the Soviet Union came to collapse, focusing on the 1970s on, leaving aside discussion of the nature of the system.

Sharp drop in petroleum price and the defeat of the Afghan War: The 1970s saw a sharp increase in the price of petroleum due to the oil shocks. The developed countries, which plunged into serious depression in consequence, succeeded not only in exploring new oil fields, as a result of which oil production saw a great increase, but also in using alternative energy sources. Moreover, the industries that consumed much petroleum worked out efficient ways of using it. In consequence the situation dramatically changed in the mid-1980s, which saw a sharp drop in oil price.

Thus, the Soviet Union, which largely depended on oil revenue, suffered a severe drop in fiscal revenue. To make matters worse, it had undertaken huge military expenditure for the Afghan War (1979–1989), and was finally forced to pull out.

The rise of Gorbachev: It was then Gorbachev's turn to come to the front (General Secretary in 1985) and he promoted a great reform in the sphere of politics rather than the economy. He approved political freedoms never seen before with the idea of "Europe as a Common House"—including approval of the democratic movement in Eastern Europe, which finally led to the reunification of Germany.

In 1990 Gorbachev introduced the presidential system as well as a pluralistic political party system, becoming the first president himself.

These political trends, however, eventually weakened his power of leadership. A coup took place in August of 1991. Yeltsin, who was given credit for the suppression, grabbed political power. He came to conclude the Belavezha Accords with the leaders of Belarus and Ukraine, proclaiming the collapse of the Soviet Union. It was quite natural for capitalism to enter the vacuum thus created.

3.2 Four types of globalization

Globalization can be broadly classified in terms of "financial globalization" and "market system globalization."

Financial globalization is caused by financial liberalization and liberalization of capital transactions in which financial business can conduct operations without any oversight from any government in the world. Financial business has procured huge amounts of capital through various methods and entered various financial markets, thus achieving global unification of the financial markets.

Let us turn to "market system globalization." The market system is one in which goods and services are freely transacted among firms and consumers in the market. This type of market system adopted throughout the world constitutes market system globalization.

Speaking of the relation between the two globalizations, the salient tendency has been for the progress of financial globalization to promote market system globalization. Financial business has actively invested funds in the areas of the globe which are judged to yield profit. This tendency has given great momentum to many developing countries.

On the other hand, as the development of financial globalization brought about an extraordinary glut of financial capital, it became increasingly difficult for governments to oversee the behavior of financial institutions (the bloated Shadow Banking System—SBS), which has made the world economy ever more unstable.

Four types of globalization can be identified as constituting the great transformation of the world political economy system: (1) financial globalization; (2) market system I—relating to the collapse of the Soviet Union; (3) market system II—the rise of the emerging nations; and (4) globalization of market integration—the euro system (or EU).

3.2.1 *Financial globalization—usurpation of leadership by US–UK financial capital*

In the 1970s and 1980s the world capitalistic system, in which the US economy had so far ruled the roost, saw a great transformation. The Breton Woods regime suffered from recurrent dollar crises and finally ended up with the "Nixon Doctrine" in 1971. Then, following the Smithsonian agreement, the major countries agreed to shift to the floating system.

This transformation was greatly related to the economic development of the Japanese and West German economies. This tendency has led, among other things, to continual trade friction between the US and Japan.

Two oil shocks in the 1970s caused an exorbitant rise in the price of oil, plunging the world economy into serious depression. Then Thatcher (1979–1990) and Reagan (1981–1989) appeared on the scene. In order to revive the stagnant economy, they advocated the market system, unrestrained economic activities on the part of the entrepreneurs, deregulation, and so forth. These meant switching from the Keynes–Beveridge approach to that of Hayek–Friedman.

With these developments, a "financial globalization" strategy was adopted by the two politicians as the way of claiming back their position in the world economy.

The US and the UK governments made efforts to create greater scope for operations through financial institutions. In the first half of the 1980s, however, no particularly conspicuous effect had been achieved in terms of the US and the UK regaining their position. It was, rather, the Plaza Accord in 1985 that was to bring about a truly notable effect, in turn provoking an abrupt appreciation of the yen.

In the 1990s, under the leadership of the US and the UK, "financial globalization" developed at an ever-faster pace. This has contributed to recovery of control of the world financial market by the US and the UK. In addition, US business activities have also picked up thanks to the IT revolution.

By contrast, Japan—the only winner in the world economy up until the early 1990s—failed to adapt to the Plaza Accord well, failed to deal with the bubble economy, and was plunged into the "Lost Two Decades" of self-trapped failure.

In the latter half of the 1990s, Japanese financial institutions were forced to withdraw from the world market due to the domestic financial crisis. Moreover, the Japanese firms were left far behind even in respect of entrepreneurial spirit, and the Japanese economy fell short of GDP growth.

Although it remains unclear how far the US and the UK governments and their financial industries had foreseen this development, financial globalization was to define the line along which the world economy would be running.

3.2.2 Market System I—the end of the Cold War and convergence to the capitalistic system

In this section we will consider the former Soviet bloc (together with China), which came to adopt the market system subsequent to the collapse of the Cold War regime.

EMERGENCE AND DECLINE OF THE SOCIALISTIC SYSTEM

The post-World War II period saw the US–Soviet Cold War, with the two antagonistic economic systems struggling for mastery. In the socialistic system, markets, firms and the price mechanism were almost non-existent. Goods and services were bought and sold, but the prices were not determined in the markets. Production activities were programmed by the central planning bureau, while the lower organizations carried out production following the planning. Thus in this system there was no room for entrepreneurs to pursue whatever activities they liked.

The Cold War regime came to an end due to the abrupt collapse of the Soviet bloc in 1991.Was the socialistic system doomed to collapse by its very nature? It is easy to judge so with hindsight. However, until just before the collapse, no one could have foreseen such an abrupt and total end. For better or worse, most of us have short memories. While the world capitalistic system had almost collapsed in the 1930s, it was the Soviet Union that was enjoying economic growth. Moreover, in economic performance it did not lag behind the US in the 1960s.

TRANSITIONAL PROCESS TOWARD THE CAPITALISTIC SYSTEM

Here we will see how the former Soviet Union system turned into a capitalistic system after collapse (China, which is an exception, gradually adopted capitalistic elements under the sway of the Communist Party). Let us see the steps Russia and China took toward the capitalistic system.

Russia: After the coup by Yanayev and its suppression, the Belavezha Accord was concluded in December 1991, with declaration of the Commonwealth of Independent States (CIS) and abolition of the Soviet Union. Russia was the largest nation in the CIS.

Yeltsin aimed at making Russia a capitalistic society, adopting the so-called "shock therapy" recommended by the IMF. His presidency (1991–1999) had two distinct periods.

The first half saw rapid transformation into a capitalistic society through shock therapy, led by Gaidal and Chubais with Sachs and Schleifer (Summers was his protégé) as advisers. Their methods were price liberalization, privatization of state-owned companies through the "voucher method" and establishment of the stock market. Their performance proved miserable. In 1992 the Russian economy suffered hyperinflation at 2,510 percent and −14.5 percent in terms of GDP per annum. The hyperinflation together with the collapse of the social security system drove a considerable part of the population into destitution while the voucher method was to beget the oligarchy.

The second half saw political and economic turmoil. It started with the Moscow Turmoil in 1993, which resulted in Yeltsin's victory. His popularity, however, dropped sharply due to the miserable economic performance. He was forced to ask the oligarchy for help in the election campaign. He was re-elected but the influence of the oligarchy was conspicuous. They had possessed many state-owned companies through loans with the equity as collateral.

In 1998 Russia plunged into national debt default. This was a result of a sharp drop in revenues, capital flight and so forth. Officials and the military had been left unpaid, while confidence in the ruble plummeted and the barter system became prevalent. The default caused a collapse of hedge funds such as the LTCM, which came close to plunging the world economy into serious financial crisis.

In 1999 Yeltsin resigned from the presidency, appointing Putin as acting president; he was elected president in 2000. Around this period the Russian economy began to show miraculous recovery due to the hike in oil prices. In the first period Putin was earnest in reforming Russia politically as well as economically. In the second period he came to change the course in such a way as to strengthen state control, and expelled the oligarchs who did not bow to his power. While the Lehman shock also hit Russia, the influence of the sovereign state over firms became all the stronger.

Thus the path adopted to transform Russia into a capitalistic society resulted in the gratuitous concentration of wealth in the hands of the oligarchy, and in the destitution of the masses. And yet since 2000 Russia has succeeded in forming a middle class due to the strong economic growth, while wealth shifted to the state from the oligarchy.

China: "The Great Leap Forward" policy (1958–1960) advocated by Mao Zedong resulted in a calamitous economic situation (sharp decline in agricultural production and the death of some billions of people due to starvation).

In 1965–1977, then, China saw the "Great Cultural Revolution." Learning being negated, intellectuals and students were expelled into remote areas. This was initiated by Mao to regain power. The revolution soon kindled internal strife among the leaders as the economy plunged into a miserable state. After complicated and perverse struggles, the revolution finally ended with the arrest and conviction of the "Gang of Four."

In 1978 the "Economic Reform" policy was launched by Deng Xiaoping, who came back from the dead like a phoenix. This was a starting point toward the miraculous economic development of the Chinese economy. This policy aimed, in substance, at transforming the Chinese economy into a capitalistic system, although it was dubbed the "Socialist Market Economy." It was a gradual reform, in sharp contrast to Russia's shock therapy.

Initially the Chinese economy recovered from its miserable situation due to an increase in agricultural output through the introduction of land privatization in rural areas, as well as the growth of the so-called "township and village enterprises." Then followed a policy of attracting foreign firms to the "special economic zones," which saw the beginning of miraculous economic growth in China.

In 1985 Deng advocated the so-called "Xian Fu [Wealth as Prioritized]" doctrine. And the rapid growth of the Chinese economy was accomplished mainly by private firms. In 1992 he delivered his "South Tour Speeches," insisting on speeding up reform policy against the conservative group. This contributed to bringing the Chinese economy back onto capitalistic tracks amid political and economic confusion subsequent to the Tiananmen Square incident (1989). The guiding principle in the mid-1990s was to privatize small state-owned enterprises while maintaining big ones under the control of the government. It was reconfirmed in the Fifteenth National Congress of the Chinese Communist Party in 1997 with the decision that economic growth should be left to private firms while confining state-owned enterprises to the four fields. In consequence the share of the state-owned enterprises in the economy steadily continued to decline. Thereafter the government allowed local governments in the inland areas to attract foreign firms to newly developed zones, which was to spark off economic development there.

In December 2001 China entered the WTO, which has treatment of foreign capital equal to domestic capital, liberalization of tariffs and a considerable degree of liberalization of labor mobility as necessary requirements.

3.2.3 Market System II—the rise of the emerging countries

The global operations of business activities contributed to bringing about large-scale economic development in some "developing" countries. This was ascribed not only to the business activities of the developed countries but also to those of the developing countries. The result was the rise of the emerging countries as represented by the B[R]ICs—Brazil, [Russia], India and China.

What matters here, especially after the Lehman shock, is that the world economy has been greatly transformed from the growing developed countries vs. the stagnant developing countries to the stagnant developed countries vs. the growing emerging countries. Above all, the Asian area has attained a high rate of economic growth. Moreover, economic growth in the South American area has also gained attention. This is, to a large extent, due to the fact that economic growth in China and India caused a huge demand for minerals and agricultural products, while the areas had a relatively stable financial system. In consequence, the US ambition, entertained in the early 1990s, to control the world economy alone has been shattered.

Over these two decades the economic growth of the developed countries has been slow or stagnant, while the emerging countries have consistently attained high rates of economic growth (in the case of Russia this is true of the last decade only). Consequently the BRICs have not only been rapidly catching up with the developed countries, but also rapidly looming larger in the world economy. Indeed, China has often been ranked as one of the G2. The future of the world economy is expected quite certainly to revolve around them. The world map in terms of economy and geopolitics has dramatically changed.

We will outline the cases of Brazil and India before going on to consider the role of the BRICs in the world economy in more concrete terms.

Brazil: In the 1980s and the first half of the 1990s, Brazil had suffered from bloated debt and hyperinflation. In 1990 President Collor (1990–1992) adopted a policy of promoting the market economy, opening the door to abroad and privatizing the state-owned firms: all this would greatly change the course for Brazil. In 1994 President Franco (1992–1995) created the *real* under the dollar-pegged system, which helped bring down hyperinflation dramatically. Then President Cardoso (1995–2003) achieved sound fiscal status through the Fiscal Responsibility Law and the Fiscal Crimes Law. President Lula (2003–2011) followed the same line. When the twenty-first century dawned, Brazil was able to accomplish a high rate of economic growth due to the rapid growth of demand for agricultural products from China, and has since asserted its status in the world economy as a resource-rich country.

India: India had long operated on a socialistic economic system and remained stagnant. In 1991 Prime Minister Rao (1991–1996) adopted a new economic policy to meet economic stagnation—a liberal policy which includes (1) liberalization of trade, foreign exchange and capital; (2) deregulation; (3) privatization of state-owned firms; and (4) financial system reform. This line was to be followed by the successive prime ministers including Singh (2004–2014).

India has been able to attain a high rate of economic growth due to the growth of the IT industry, among other things, which began with outsourcing business thanks to increased orders from US firms. In India the literacy rate remains low, and yet the country has produced a vast number of young people endowed with IT knowledge.

THE PRESENCE OF THE BRICs IN THE WORLD ECONOMY

Up until the end of the 1980s Brazil, India and Russia had suffered serious economic stagnation or turmoil. In the early 1990s, however, Brazil and India succeeded in attaining a high rate of economic growth through liberalization of the market and sharp increase in demand for agricultural products in Brazil and for IT services in India from abroad (in China, economic liberalization started in 1978).

In Russia, the shock therapy brought about only destruction and confusion. At the dawn of the 2000s, however, it succeeded in attaining economic growth thanks to the hike in the price of oil and natural gas. Putin succeeded in rectifying the market economy system while stepping up the power of control by the sovereign state.

The economic destiny of the BRICs has been greatly influenced by the events which have occurred since the latter half of the 1980s.

First, the collapse of the Soviet bloc. A movement for political and economic liberalization was initiated by Poland, followed by other East European countries, finally leading to the demise of the Soviet Union.

Second, financial globalization. As it developed in the 1990s, BRI[C]s came round to a policy of liberalization in general (China had already adopted it in 1978). Financial globalization was to contribute to a high rate of economic growth for the BRICs thereafter through the influx of capital. To sum up, they were able to attain high economic growth, reaping benefit from both "Market System II" and "Financial Globalization."[12]

Table 1.1 lists average annual GDP growth, Table 1.2 GDP of the top 11 in terms of purchasing power parity (PPP) in 2013. The BRICs are included here. Above all, China's figures are amazing. We could say that in terms of national powers the BRICs have achieved an equal footing. What is certain is that China is soon going to be No. 1.

Table 1.1 Annual average rate of growth of GDP (%)

China	10.46	1991–2010
India	7.54	2001–2010
Russia	6.58	2001–2010
Brazil	3.61	2001–2010
US	2.55	1991–2010
Germany	1.47	1991–2010
Japan	0.97	1991–2010

Original source: http://ecodb.net/.

Table 1.2 GDP ranking in terms of purchasing power parity (US$ billion)

	Nation	2013	2010	2000	1990
1	US	16,800	14,958	10,290	5,980
2	China	13,395	10,040	3,020 (3)	914 (7)
3	India	5,069	4,130 (4)	1,607 (5)	762 (9)
4	Japan	4,699	4,351 (3)	3,261 (2)	2,379 (2)
5	Germany	3,233	2,926	2,148 (4)	1,452 (3)
6	Russia	2,556	2,222	1,213 (10)	unavailable
7	Brazil	2,423	2,167 (8)	1,236 (9)	789 (8)
8	UK	2,391	2,201 (7)	1,515 (7)	915 (6)
9	France	2,278	2,114	1,535 (6)	1,031 (4)
10	Mexico	1,843	1,603 (11)	1,082 (11)	631 (10)
11	Italy	1,808	1,784 (10)	1,406 (8)	980 (5)

Original sources: http://ecodb.net/, based on IMF, *World Economic Outlook Databases*, April 2014.

Note
Values in parentheses are world rankings.

3.2.4 Market system integration—euro system (or EU)

The euro system (or the EU) might be described as a sort of globalization which has continued over a long period, for it has aimed at a common market, mobility of labor and capital, and a common currency. The movement started immediately after World War II, and has by now accomplished these objectives.

The EU and the euro system were set up in the 1990s when the current globalization saw acceleration and the socialistic system collapsed. The EU adopted a policy of bringing the ex-Soviet members into the EU. In this respect, the EU or the euro system can be said to constitute Market System Integration, which includes a partial Financial Globalization (in the form of the euro) and Market System I.

The euro system, however, which had been applauded with a touch of envy in the early twenty-first century, became prone to great drawbacks soon after the Lehman shock.

The policy adopted to address the euro crises which started in May 2010 has been bailout cum an ultra-austerity budget for the PI[I]G[S]—Portugal, Ireland, [Italy], Greece and [Spain]—and the European Central Bank (ECB) monetary policy (initially a low-rate interest policy, and then the Long Term Refinancing Operations). The underlying idea was that with an ultra-austerity budget and structural reform (such as liberalization of the labor market, privatization of the public sector), the afflicted country can enhance its international competitive power and achieve economic recovery.

The consequence, however, was even greater crisis within the PI[I]G[S]. An ultra-austerity budget implies an ultra-deflationary policy. Continued restructuring, increased taxes and pension cuts brought about a sharp drop in effective demand, high rates of unemployment, and further deterioration of the budget situation.

The afflicted members, with no monetary policy or exchange rate policy to fall back on, were again obliged to implement an ultra-austerity budget. Consequently the economies saw further deterioration, trapped in a deflationary spiral.

Moreover, the bailout is used only to stabilize the euro system, thereby saving the German and French megabanks as lenders to the PIIGS, while the populations are called upon only to shoulder the heavy burden.

The European leadership has never addressed the fundamental causes which should reside in "the widening intra-regional disequilibrium" and "the situation of the member states." Consequently the euro system has often been driven close to collapse.

The widening intra-regional disequilibrium can be typically expressed as the economic imbalance between Germany and the PI[I]GS. The initial ECB monetary policy allowed Germany to expand exports while the PI[I]GS made huge investments in real estate by exploiting low rates of interest. Or, to put it another way, surplus savings which had accrued in Germany had been lent to the PI[I]GS—a regional version of the so-called global imbalance.[13] This imbalance has continued since the birth of the euro. However, with the Lehman shock as triggering event, it brought about the euro crisis as the PI[I]IGS bubbles burst.

What is more problematic is the survival of the EU per se, for it is now losing its founding spirit—the Schuman spirit—while nationalism is becoming prevalent. The risk is growing of a divided Europe. The EU is ironically losing the ability to override nationalism, although it was set up for the very purpose. The EU as well as the euro system is facing a major turning point.

4 The Lehman shock and the present

4.1 Collapse of neoliberalism and resurgence of Keynes

The Lehman shock, which struck in September 2008, caused the meltdown of the US financial system and abruptly drove almost all the nations into critical condition. Many financial institutions as well as manufacturing firms went bankrupt, which set the number of unemployed soaring. Various governments made strenuous efforts to surmount the crisis, injecting huge amounts of money and implementing drastic fiscal policies.

This was a state of affairs that marked a great turning point in the world economy. Neoliberalism and new classical economics collapsed in the midst of this calamity, with governments being forced to surmount the crisis with instinct. "The market economy should be a self-discipline system. Success or failure should be attributable to one's own responsibility. The government should not interfere with the market economy"—such were the credo and motto of the neoliberals.

What happened in reality? Almost all the US megabanks and investment banks pleaded with the government for bailout. And yet the management personnel received exorbitant salaries from the bailout, justifying it as due to "redemption of contract." Here we see abandonment of the self-discipline principle and the collapse of business ethics by the CEOs. By contrast, many people faced foreclosure, being unable to repay their mortgage loans, with much debt being left. The masses alone were forced to observe the self-discipline principle.

As the world economic crisis went from bad to worse, reference to Keynes became ever more widespread. While hardly any of the economists were able to do anything about the Great Depression in the 1930s, Keynes deftly put forward his own economic theory and policy proposals. Now the same phenomenon emerged in the face of the impotence of the established macroeconomics.

Noted economists declared abandonment of their belief in the neoliberalism. Many economists urged Keynesian fiscal policies. In October 2008, the (UK) Chancellor of the Exchequer insisted on the need for fiscal policy. The economic policy staff of the Obama Administration advocated fiscal policy which became the backbone of his economic policy.

4.2 Thereafter—austerity measures

Until May 2010, the Keynesian policy line had been predominant in the world, putting the Obama Administration at the top. Around June 2010, however, the world was to see a great turn in the economic policy stance (except for China).

In the spring of 2010 the Greek crisis abruptly extended into a euro crisis. Faced with this situation, a huge bailout (€110 billion) to Greece by the EU/IMF was decided on condition that austerity measures were implemented. Thereafter the EU went on persisting with this policy.

Reflecting this state of affairs, the Toronto G20 (June 2010) showed an outlook quite different from the London G20 (April 2009). Although Obama advocated a fiscal policy to tackle the depression, the Toronto G20 ended with a grand chorus invoking austerity measures.

In the US criticism of Obama's budget line had become louder and louder. The fiscal policies such as the Job Act (June 2009), the Hire Act (February 2010), a large-scale fiscal stimulus policy (May 2010) were foiled, due not only to the rising "Tea Party" movement but also the increasingly passive tendency even among the Democrats. The decision of the Toronto G20 gave impetus to criticism, and contributed to the fatal defeat of the president's Democratic Party in the midterm election (November 2011). Thereafter Obama had a difficult path to follow to implement all sorts of economic policies. Among other things, Obama was forced to accept the Budget Control Act (austerity measures) in the debt ceiling crisis of July 2011. Following this, the Super Committee in November determined to cut $120 billion from defense and social security annually as from the end of 2012.

Thus since June 2010 the US and the EU (including the UK) have been pursuing austerity measure policies, abandoning economic policies to address the depression. With the governments implementing big spending cuts, effective demand is in steady decline, which will only make the fiscal situation worse. The only economic policy adopted to address the depression seems to be the quantitative easing (QE) policy. But effectively, the result is to bail out and then encourage the megabanks to make room for financial investment, without substantial effect on the real economy.

4.3 The Shadow Banking System remains intact

The Dodd–Frank Act was enacted in July 2010. However, the implementation process took a very long time due mainly to the Republicans' opposition and the banking lobby activities. It was not until early 2014 that most, but not all, of the implementation process was somehow finished.

What will this long delay imply? The financial institutions, having successfully bounced back from the brink of failure due to huge bailout from the government,[14] have been obstructing the establishment of organizations set up to oversee their speculative activities. They have also tried to weaken the Act with their lobbying activities. In consequence, the SBS has remained intact, which probably implies a huge financial crisis in the near future.

So far only the US has put through a financial regulatory act. Unless other countries including the UK and the EU bring in similar acts, the world will be left with a huge loophole.

In the UK, in December 2013, the Financial Services (Banking Reform) Act was enacted, adopting the ring-fence method advocated by the Vickers Report.

In France the Banking Reform Act was enacted in March 2013, again with a ring-fencing method. In Germany the Ring-Fencing and Recovery and Resolution Planning of Credit Institutions Act was enacted in May 2013, based on the Liikanen Report. The implementation process in these countries is yet to come underway.

5 Conclusion

We began by discussing the essentials and issues involved in the capitalistic system. Second, we examined globalization, selecting five factors which caused it and illustrating four types of globalization. Third, we explained what the Lehman shock brought about in relation to globalization and what occurred thereafter. The conclusion runs as follows.

Globalization has helped the US and the UK regain economic power from Japan, especially through financial globalization.

Globalization has offered great opportunities for the emerging nations to attain high rates of economic growth, to the extent that they have qualified as members of the G20 (though Russia suffered from shock therapy severely).

Globalization, however, has made the world economy increasingly fragile due to its excesses.

We cannot and need not prevent the advance of globalization. But we need to know what capitalism is and how it should be managed in order to prevent excesses, especially in financial globalization.

Now there are several important points to make about globalization. The economic crisis subsequent to the Lehman shock was the consequence of excessive financial liberalization, supported and promoted by neoliberals and the neoclassicals. This produced the unregulated problem of multilayered securitized papers and induced moral hazard on the part of the CEOs. Ironically enough, in the midst of feverish market fundamentalism, the world also witnessed the phenomena of market non-existence and market opaqueness.

In what direction will the market society be moving? What is clear at the moment is the collapse of neoliberalism, and movement of market society in a very different direction. To tackle the phenomena of market non-existence and market opaqueness and the SBS, many governments are taking steps to improve the financial system so as to render it controllable.

And yet, as we saw above, this movement is proceeding extremely slowly, and the slowness has allowed the financial institutions to behave just as they did before the Lehman shock. This could bring about another financial meltdown in the not-too-distant future.

Another important problem concerns business ethics. In these crises we saw that many business leaders who had been advocating the self-discipline principle were the first to plead with the government for financial help, bearing the "too big to fail" principle in mind. Amazingly enough, having got huge bailouts, they have displayed shameless behavior in awarding themselves handsome bonuses. The fact that this kind of injustice, corruption and selfishness has been prevalent in the US business community is eloquent evidence of the need for a new business model for the market society. If it were not created, the market society would face an even more serious problem in the not-too-distant future.

The world is still navigating without a mariner's compass.

Notes

1 On accounting and debt contract, see Akerlof and Shiller (2009).
2 Lately "current value accounting" has received attention. The problem raised here, however, cannot be solved with this method.
3 The points raised below cannot be dealt with in the framework of corporate social responsibility, for capitalism cannot eliminate all the scope for fraudulence.
4 In the 1930s when the term "neoliberalism" was first coined, it was tinged with "Ordo-Liberalism." It was against it that Hayek and others were determined to set up the Mont Pelerin Society.
5 Although the term "The Washington Consensus" was first coined by J. Williamson in 1989, it came to be used with a different meaning, which is tinged with neoliberalism as adopted here. The term is not used in this chapter to avoid this confusion.
6 It would be misleading if Thatcherism and Reaganomics were to be interpreted exclusively from the point of view of neoliberalism, for both were characterized by strong nationalism as well.
7 It should be noted that the "New Keynesianism"—another dominant school of macroeconomics—does not belong to neoliberalism. It sees the fundamental flaw in the market economy in some rigidities of prices, and advocates discretionary economic policy in addressing unemployment. What makes the matter complicated, however, is that while it shares a social philosophy similar to that in the age of the neoclassical synthesis, it accepts important theoretical ideas from the newclassicals.
8 Libertarianism is quite often argued in relation to neoliberalism. However, it might be wiser not to use it here because it has many different meanings. The most popular is advocated by Rothbard, who concedes no place for nation and government.
9 It should be noted that during this period government activities greatly increased, betraying neoliberalism (during the Reagan Administration, for example, the US turned from the largest foreign creditor into the largest foreign debtor).
10 For further details, see Section 2 of Chapter 2.
11 He held senior positions in the Citi Group during 2002–2005.
12 As a result of this, a great geopolitical shift has taken place in recent years which nobody had imagined in the early 1990s—from the US predominance system to the tripolar system (the US, Russia and China). The Ukraine crisis is emblematic of this shift. Incidentally, Rodrik (2007) sees globalization in terms of political economy—trilemma.
13 Eichengreen (2006) introduces four theories for global imbalance. First, the standard analysis by Bernanke. Here great attention is paid to excessive savings, above all, in China. Maintaining that the US current account deficits at the present level cannot be sustained, this theory argues that substantial adjustment of asset prices for spending and substantial change in relative prices for balance of trade should be required on both sides. Unlike this, the following three ("New Economy" theory; "Dark Matter" theory and "Savvy Investor" theory) argue that correction of the present global imbalance should not be required. For critical views of these theories, see Carabelli and Cedrini (2010) which stands on Keynes's 1945 memorandum "Overseas Financial Policy in Stage III."
14 The Federal Reserve Bank (FRB) then helped the megabanks through a series of QE policies, which means that they are in the same boat. Very strong connections in personal terms between the FRB, the megabanks (and the Treasury Department) are to be seen.

Bibliography

Akerlof, G. A. and Shiller, R. J. (2009) *Animal Spirits: How Human Psychology Drives the Economy, and Why It Matters for Global Capitalism*, Princeton, NJ: Princeton University Press.

Baer, W. (2013) *The Brazilian Economy: Growth and Development*, Boulder, CO: Lynne Rienner Publishers.

Bateman, B., Hirai, T. and Marcuzzo, M. C. (2010) *The Return to Keynes*, Cambridge, MA: The Belknap Press of Harvard University Press.

Bernanke, B. S. (2005) "The Global Saving Glut and the U.S. Current Account Deficit," remarks at the Sandridge Lecture, Virginia Association of Economics, Richmond, Virginia, March 10, available at: www.federalreserve.gov/boarddocs/speeches/2005/200503102/default.htm.

Blinder, A. S. (1997) "Is There a Core of Practical Macroeconomics That We Should All Believe?" *American Economic Review*, 87(2): 230–246.

Buiter, W. (2009) "The Unfortunate Uselessness of Most 'State of the Art' Academic Monetary Economics," *Economist's View*, March 3, available at: http://economists-view.typepad.com/economistsview/2009/03/the-unfortunate-uselessness-of-most-state-of-the-art-academic-monetary-economics.html.

Buttonwood (2009) "The Grand Illusion: How Efficient-Market Theory Has Been Proved Both Wrong and Right," *Economist Print Edition*, March 5, available at: www.economist.com/node/13240822.

Carabelli, A. and Cedrini, M. (2010) "Current Global Imbalances: Might Keynes Be of Help?" in B. Bateman, T. Hirai and M. C. Marcuzzo (eds.) *The Return to Keynes*, Cambridge, MA: The Belknap Press of Harvard University Press.

Clarida, R., Gali, J. and Gertler, M. (1999) "The Science of Monetary Policy: A New-Keynesian Perspective" *Journal of Economic Literature*, 37(4): 1661–707.

Collard, D. (2004) "IS-LM Persistence," in M. De Vroey and K. D. Hoover (eds.) "The IS-LM Model: Its Rise, Fall and Strange Persistence," *History of Political Economy*, 36(Suppl.1).

De Grauwe, P. (2003) *The Economics of European Monetary Union*, 5th edition, Oxford: Oxford University Press.

Economist, The (2010) "The Future of Europe: Staring into the Abyss," July 8, available at: www.economist.com/node/16536898.

Eichengreen, B. J. (2006) "Global Imbalances: The New Economy, the Dark Matter, the Savvy Investor, and the Standard Analysis," *Journal of Policy Modeling*, 28(6): 645–652.

Feldstein, M. (2008) "Resolving the Global Imbalance: The Dollar and the U.S. Saving Rate," *Journal of Economic Perspectives* 22(3): 113–125.

Fischer, S. (1997) "Capital Account Liberalization and the Role of the IMF," paper presented at the IMF Seminar "Asia and the IMF," September 19, available at: www.iie.com/fischer/pdf/Fischer144.pdf.

Friedman, M. and Friedman, R. (1990) *Free to Choose: A Personal Statement*, San Diego: Harvest Books.

Greenwald, B. and Stiglitz J. (1993) "New and Old Keynesians," *Journal of Economic Perspectives*, 7(1): 23–34.

Hirai, T. (2009) "Whither Capitalism (the Market Society)?" *Modern Thought*, May (in Japanese).

Hirai, T. (2009) "Whither Economics?" *Modern Thought*, August (in Japanese).

Hirai, T. (2012) *Can Keynes Save Capitalism? The World Economy in Crisis*, Kyoto: Showado (in Japanese).

Hirai, T. (ed.) (2007) *What Is the Market Society*, Tokyo: Sophia University Press (in Japanese).

Hirai, T., Marcuzzo, M. C. and Mehrling, P. (eds.) (2013) *Keynesian Reflections: Effective Demand, Money, Finance, and Policies in the Crisis*, New Delhi: Oxford University Press.

IMF (2014) *World Economic Outlook Databases*, April, available at: www.imf.org/external/ns/cs.aspx?id=28.

Independent Commission on Banking (2011) *Final Report Recommendations* (The Vickers Report), available at: www.ecgi.org/documents/icb_final_report_ 12sep2011. pdf.

Kan, S. (2002) *Re-introduction of the Chinese Economy*, Tokyo: Toyo Keizai Shinposha (in Japanese).

Keynes, J. M. (1936) *The General Theory of Employment, Interest and Money*, London: Macmillan.

Kimura, H. (2009) *On Modern Russian State*, Tokyo: Chuo Kouron Shinsha (in Japanese).

Krugman, P. (2008a) "Depression Economics Returns," *New York Times*, November 14.

Krugman, P. (2008b) *The Return of Depression Economics and the Crisis of 2008*, New York: Norton.

Kydland, F. E. and Prescott, C. (1982) "Time to Build and Aggregate Fluctuations," *Econometrica*, 50(6): 1345–1370

Liikanen, E. (2012) "Report of the European Commission's High-level Expert Group on Bank Structural Reform," October, available at: http://ec.europa.eu/internal_market/bank/docs/high-level_expert_group/report_en. pdf#search='Report+of+the+European+Commission%27s+Highlevel+Expert+Group+on+Bank+Structural+Reform'.

London Summit (2009) "Global Plan for Recovery and Reform: The Communiqué from the London Summit," April, available at: www.state.gov/e/eb/ecosum/ pittsburgh2009/resources/165077.htm.

Lucas, R. (1975) "An Equilibrium Model of the Business Cycle," *Journal of Political Economy*, 83(6): 1113–1144.

Lyne, R., Talbott, S. and Watanabe, K. (2006) "Engaging with Russia—The Next Phase," in The Trilateral Commission (eds.) *Challenges to Trilateral Cooperation, The Trilateral Commission Tokyo Plenary Meeting 2006*, Washington, DC: The Trilateral Commission, pp. 87–99.

Mankiw, N. G. and Romer, D. (eds.) (1991) *New Keynesian Economics*, Cambridge, MA: MIT Press.

Mizuho Research Institute (2007) *The Subprime*, Tokyo: Nihon Keizai Shinbun Shuppansha (in Japanese).

Morris, C. (2008) *The Trillion Dollar Meltdown*, New York: Public Affairs.

Rodrik, D. (2007) "The Inescapable Trilemma of the World Economy," June 27, available at: http://rodrik.typepad.com/dani_rodriks_weblog/2007/06/the-inescapable.html.

Romer, C. and Bernstein, J. (2009) "The Job Impact of the American Recovery and Reinvestment Plan," January 9, available at: www.thompson.com/images/ thompson/nclb/openresources/obamaeconplanjan9.pdf.

Romer, D. (1993) "The New Keynesian Synthesis," *Journal of Economic Perspectives*, 7(1): 5–22.

Sen, S. (2007) *Globalisation and Development*, New Delhi: National Book Trust of India.

Soejima, T. (1995) *A Great Study of Contemporary American Political Thought*, Tokyo: Chikuma Shobou (in Japanese).

Solow R. (2005) "Dumb and Dumber in Macroeconomics," available at: https://www0. gsb.columbia.edu/faculty/jstiglitz/new_web/festschrift/Papers/Stig-Solow.pdf.

Sonoda, S. (2008) *Whither the Chinese Society*, Tokyo: Iwanami (in Japanese).

Stadler, G. (1994) "Real Business Cycles," *Journal of Economic Literature*, 32(4): 1750–1783.

Stiglitz, J. (2003) *Globalization and Its Discontents*, New York: Norton.

Stiglitz, J. and Greenwald, B. (2006) "A Modest Proposal for International Monetary Reform," Columbia University, January 4, available at: www2.gsb.columbia.edu/ faculty/jstiglitz/download/2006_Intl_Monetary_Reform.pdf.

Williamson, J. (1990) "What Washington Means by Policy Reform," in J. Williamson (ed.) *Latin American Adjustment: How Much Has Happened?* Washington, DC: Institute for International Economics, available at: www.iie.com/publications/ papers/paper. cfm?researchid=486.

Yoshioka, K. (2008) *Globalization of China*, Tokyo: Asahi Shinbun Shuppan (in Japanese).

2 Financial globalization and the instability of the world economy[1]

Toshiaki Hirai

1 Introduction—globalization

We can divide globalization into two types: "financial globalization" (FG), on the one hand, and "market system (or capitalist) globalization" (MG) on the other. FG is the global unification or liberalization of the financial market, while MG is the multiplication of nations, on the global level, which favor adopting the market system as the fundamental economic mechanism.

In this chapter we will focus mainly on how FG has been making the world economy increasingly unstable and volatile as time goes by. In Section 2 we will explain how financial liberalization has proceeded in the US, while in Section 3 we will see how the world financial system has become unstable and vulnerable, leading up to instability in the world economy, as a result of FG. In Section 4 we will reflect upon what financial liberalization has implied in relation to the world economy, and in Section 5 go on to explain how the US administration grappled with the meltdown caused by the Lehman shock and barely managed to enact the Financial Regulatory Reform Act in July 2010, still being hard-pressed to implement it. Finally, in Section 6, we will consider the need for financial regulation reform and concluding remarks appear in Section 7.

2 US financial liberalization—attenuation of the Glass–Steagall Act and enactment of the Gramm–Leach–Bliley Act

2.1 The outline

The Glass–Steagall Act (the GS Act hereafter) enacted in 1933 had long been a dominant measure for regulating and overseeing the US financial system. The USA of the 1920s saw financial fraudulence rampant, to the extent that President Roosevelt ascribed the Great Depression to it.[2] Thus the GS Act was enacted, aiming at imposing strict regulations on the financial institutions. It is composed of three pillars: (1) regulation of interest rates ("Regulation Q"); (2) separation of commercial banking from investment banking; and (3) regulation of interstate banking.

As early as the 1960s a movement calling for softer regulation was launched through the lobbying activities of banks, eager to enter the municipal bond market. But the GS Act had worked well enough up until the 1970s, when the situation took a new turn.

In the 1970s the investment banks tried to edge into the sphere of commercial banking, providing customers with money accounts (with interest paid), and check and credit services. The role that the DTCC (Depository Trust and Clearing Corporation) played here was significant. Throughout the 1970s and 1980s computerization went ahead only in mega investment banks, where individuals came to make transactions by means of the so-called "street names," which worked as a sort of reserve ratio in the case of commercial banks. Investment banks were able to obtain new funds by exploiting these "street names," which aggravated the commercial banks' growing impatience.

In the 1980s bills aiming at relaxing the GS Act had often been submitted to Congress. Abolition of Regulation Q came first in 1986, followed by the bill for deregulation of interstate banking in 1995 (the Riegle–Neal Act). Lastly, the separation of commercial banking from investment banking was unlocked by the Gramm–Leach–Bliley Act (the GLB Act hereafter) in 1999.

2.2 Relaxation of the separation of commercial banking from investment banking

Here we will see how the GS Act came to be alleviated and finally abolished, focusing on the separation of commercial banking from investment banking.

The progress toward relaxation might be said to have proceeded through a sequence of extended interpretations of Section 20 of the GS Act by the Federal Reserve Bank (FRB). In December of 1986 the FRB interpreted a clause in the Section—which prohibits "in principle" a commercial bank from dealing in investment banking—in such a way that it is allowed to do so for up to 5 percent of the total revenue, followed by the FRB's decision (spring of 1987) that a commercial bank may underwrite some securities.

Since the appointment of Alan Greenspan, a former executive of JP Morgan, as chairman of the FRB in 1987, relaxation of the GS Act has been expedited through the following stages:

1   In 1989 the FRB permitted commercial banks to engage in underwriting securities for up to 10 percent of the total revenue (the first bank allowed was the JP Morgan).
2   In December 1996 the FRB authorized bank holding companies to have investment banks as subsidiaries for up to 25 percent of the total revenue.
3   February 1998 saw a merger deal between the Travelers Insurance Company (the CEO was Sanford Weill) and the Citicorp (the president was John Reed). This should have been impossible under the GS Act, but vigorous lobbying activities developed, targeting top figures such as Clinton, Greenspan and Rubin, resulting in the FRB's approval of the merger in September.
4   The final blow came with pressure from hardliners calling for abolition of the GS Act, resulting in the enactment of the GLB Act in November 1999.

2.3 Promulgators for the GLB Act

It was financiers such as Weill and Reed, and politicians and/or academics such as Robert Rubin, Lawrence Summers (a protégé of Rubin), Alan Greenspan and Phil Gramm (Republican senator) who worked on the GLB Act.

Summers and Greenspan were responsible for drawing up the GLB Act, alias "the Citi-Group Approval Act." Rubin, who resigned as Secretary of the Treasury in July 2000, was welcomed as CEO of Citi Group. While he was there, he induced Citi Group to embark on risky investments such as the CDO (Collateralized Debt Obligation).[3]

Gramm was also involved with enactment of the Commodity Futures Modernization Act of 2000 (the CFM Act hereafter), which gave momentum to moves to legalize the future trade of energy and credit default swaps (the CDS hereafter).

Prior to this, Brooksley Born, chair of the Commodity Futures Trading Committee (the CFTC), who was worried about OTC (Over-the-Counter) Derivatives (especially the CDS) being transacted on an ever-larger scale, evading control by the financial authorities, insisted on the need for supervision. Her move, however, came up against harsh opposition from Greenspan, Rubin (the then Secretary of the Treasury) and Summers, who had promoted relaxation of the GS Act. It was they who reversed the direction and succeeded in putting through the CFM Act. Wendy, Gramm's wife and chair of the CFTC under the Reagan and the G. H. Bush Administrations, also worked hard for the CMF Act, thanks to which she was to be welcomed by Enron.

The salient feature of the CFM Act, known as the so-called "Enron Loophole" (exemption from supervision for futures trading), lies in "the single stock future" being allowed; this was to enable higher leverage and more speculative activities (the Act is held responsible for the California Electricity Crisis in 2000–2001).

Enron had been very much involved in derivative dealings in the 1990s. In 1999 it set up "Enron Online" and greatly extended derivative dealings. It was subsequently to be exposed for continued fraudulent accounting and was forced into bankruptcy. Thus began the burst of the so-called "dot.com bubble."

Gramm[4] was thereafter welcomed as executive for the UBS,[5] where he is reputed to have played a central role in its extensive involvement with the CDS.

3 The instability of the world financial system

How are we to evaluate the influences on the world economy which financial liberalization or globalization has brought about? They can be approached from both affirmative and problematic positions.

Because FG has enabled capital to move to regions where it can obtain higher rates of profit, it has contributed to bringing about high economic growth which otherwise might have been impossible.

Leaving consideration from this affirmative viewpoint to Section 3.2 of Chapter 1, we will here focus on the problematic aspect—the instability of the world financial system as the cause of collapse of the world economy. First, we will take the rise of the Shadow Banking System, followed by the two turbulent examples.

3.1 The rise of the Shadow Banking System

FG, which gained momentum in the 1990s, generated the "Shadow Banking System" (SBS hereafter). The US financial system, which had so far been supervised by the FRB under the GS Act of 1933 with the purpose of keeping the speculative activities of banking business under control, came to be relaxed through the above-mentioned financial liberalization, bringing forth manifold new types of financial firms such as hedge funds and private equities that lend themselves freely to speculative dealings without supervision by the financial authorities. Devising various kinds of securitized papers such as the MBS, the CDO and the CDS and using leverage, these firms came to be involved in risky speculative dealings in the global financial markets. Observing their surprisingly high rates of return, the commercial banks, which had been kept under control by the FRB, found their way into the SBS by means of an off-balance technique, the product being "Special Investment Vehicles" (or SIVs).

Thus as the years went by the SBS grew bigger and bigger, squeezing the share of conventional banking to ever smaller dimensions, and making the world financial system increasingly unstable and volatile.

Excessive FG had often precipitated the world economy into critical conditions, and yet the world had managed to evade serious catastrophe. But it eventually led to the Lehman shock in September 2008, which set the world financial system, as well as the world economy, plunging precipitously.

This series of events prompts the following questions: Could the rise of the SBS have been desirable, and indeed indispensable to the development of the world economy? How are we to justify the layered securitized papers and the financial institutions' speculative activities free from any supervision? To what degree can the finance engineering be justified in terms of improvement and/or growth of the capitalistic system?

Leaving these questions to Section 4.2 below, here we will consider two examples of economic instability as caused by excessive FG: the Asian financial crisis in 1997–1998 and the subprime loan crisis of 2008, from which the US, the EU and Japan have yet to find the way out.[6]

3.2 Two examples

3.2.1 The Asian Financial Crisis

The crisis of 1997, which started in Thailand, was caused by speculative activities of hedge funds. Thailand, which adopted the dollar-pegged system, began to suffer from a sharp drop in exports due to appreciation of the dollar (and thus of the baht). Hedge funds, seeing the opportunity for speculation, continued to sell off the baht, which finally forced the Thai government to depreciate it. The Thai economy, which had so far continued to enjoy a high rate of economic growth thanks to dollars borrowed in the short term, plunged into serious depression with abruptly increased debt in terms of the dollar. The depression rapidly propagated to Malaysia, Indonesia and so forth.

Hedge fund speculative activities then turned to target Russia in 1998.

In 1991 the Soviet Union disintegrated into several nations, the largest being Russia. President Yeltsin went ahead with headlong transformation of the Russian economy into a capitalistic system—the so-called "shock-therapy method," accepting the IMF's advice. The result turned out to be devastating, causing high inflation and severe unemployment as well as the 1997 fiscal crisis. The Russian government was forced to collect the necessary revenues through issue of national bonds. Thus it was Russia, sunk in a very precarious and chaotic situation, that hedge funds targeted. Russia failed to maintain the ruble, and was forced to declare its default on the national bonds.

Now came the turn of a hedge fund named "Long Term Capital Management" (LTCM hereafter), which continued to buy the Russian bonds. It gloried in two Nobel Laureates for Economics (for the "Black-Scholes Equation" determining option prices) as co-founders. Although it had only 200 employees, it gained such a high reputation with its startling initial success that major banks from all over the world were willing to hand out blank checks. Around 1998 the LTCM, a neutral-type hedge fund, came to manipulate $100 billion and take a position of $1,000 billion.

Due to the default of the Russian bonds, however, the LTCM suffered heavy loss. Suddenly there emerged a serious possibility[7] that, if the LTCM were left as it was, the world would plunge into a formidable financial crisis, and in September 1998 the Federal Reserve Bank of New York (the then president was Timothy Geithner), asked the Wall Street megabanks to bail out the LTCM. Thanks to this prompt action the world economy managed to evade an impending crisis.

3.2.2 The Subprime Loan Crisis

The crisis erupted in September 2008. Since 2005 high interest rate mortgage loans had been made targeting low-income earners (the so-called "subprime loans"). The financial institutions bought them up, and issued MBSs (Mortgage-Backed Securities) with them as collateral. A spate of new types of securities was then unleashed, mingling other loans such as car loans, credit card loans and so forth as collateral. Thus the US economy came to be filled with multilayered securities ("securitized papers"), which came to be certified by rating agencies such as Moody's as definitely safe securities (80 percent of the securitized papers based on the subprime mortgage loans were ranked AAA), and were sold all over the world. The financial institutions eventually started to issue subprime mortgage loans without any assessment (the so-called "ninja loans") and, based on them, set about structuring layered securitized papers.... Thus the negative catenation went on. The Lehman shock occasioned this fragile monetary and credit structure to collapse, plunging the world economy into the deep depression we have been experiencing.

4 "Financial liberalization" considered

As explained above, financial liberalization proceeded with the impulsion of financial capital as catalyst. It was a movement led by the US commercial banks—eager to break out of conditions imposed by the GS Act in competition with the US investment banks which, free from regulation, saw rapid development—and by the US government, which again wanted to hold the world financial market as well as the world economy in the palm of its hands.

In sympathy with this impulsion, the big figures such as Rubin, Greenspan, Summers and politicians like Gramm made great efforts to attenuate the GS through extended interpretations of Section 20, finally succeeding in enacting the GLB Act as well as the CMF Act.

4.1 The geopolitical significance

Financial liberalization accorded well with the US government's desire to regain world hegemony in the economic scene. The US administrations that had suffered miserable economic performance throughout the 1980s came to think that finance could be a key to regain and extend US influence over the world economy. The "Washington Consensus" line taken by the IMF and the World Bank as well as the "shock therapy" method adopted by the former members of the Soviet Bloc with US economists as advisers[8] also accorded with the financial liberalization movement.

These movements, moreover, derived strong support and credibility from the intellectual authority associated with neoliberalism, finance theory and the new classical school, as well as ideologies like neoconservatism and Deep South Christian fundamentalism. To say nothing of these ideologies, neoliberalism also took on a very authoritarian stance, quite different from its ostensible attitude. As champions of "freedom," the neoliberals did not hesitate to interfere with foreign countries where freedom as they conceived it was judged to be lacking, either through the "structural adjustment programs" or with military operations. In this sense, neoliberalism contains a sort of "power-ism."

In terms of political dynamics, furthermore, these movements can be said to have proceeded hand in hand with kleptocracy—the "quid pro quo" ties between financiers and the financial authorities.

4.2 The economic significance

What kind of economic significance will financial liberalization be seen to have? It is an extension of the markets in which the financial institutions can raise funds at their own disposal (where securitized papers are structured, accompanying leverage), ever pursuing speculative profits by means of the funds thus obtained. The pursuit of profit has been engaged in to such a degree, at times, as to incur moral hazard.

Hedge funds have targeted weak and fragile countries, mounting speculative attacks to make huge gains with no concern for the considerable damage to the countries concerned, ascribing the defects and failures to their economic system. In recent years these attitudes have become blatantly evident. "Finance for the sake of finance," or speculative activities without any regard for the real economy, can be characterized as "autotelism" on the part of financial capital, far from the original role which finance should play—the role of providing the finance required to make the real economy grow, and making the market economy run smoothly. Thus we see the phenomenon of the real economy caught up in speculative waves.

The enlargement of the SBS was also a product of the activities of governments under the leadership of the US administration, entailing some divergence from the original role which each government should be playing—the pursuit of its own economic growth. All governments should be independent of the financial community, implementing their own policies and placing top priority on the well-being of their people. On the road to financial liberalization, in fact, various governments including the US government have gone hand in hand with the financial community at the cost of a stampede of hedge funds, the emergence of multilayered securitized papers and a catastrophic meltdown.

4.3 Significance for Japan and the BRICs (Brazil, Russia, India and China)

Financial globalization and the multiplication of financial products achieved with financial engineering under the leadership of the US and the UK in the 1990s has revived the hegemony of the world market by US and UK financial capital. In the same period, moreover, it was young US entrepreneurs who led the world market through IT innovation, placing the US as world leader even in the real economy, where Japan and West Germany had been leaders.[9]

In the same period many Japanese banks, which had expanded their operations globally, were driven to pull out from the world financial market due to their own financial crisis (on top of the requirement to observe the Basel Capital Accord). Moreover, Japanese firms were left behind US firms in terms of entrepreneurial spirit, showing a sharp contrast with the 1980s, when established Japanese firms had succeeded in operations by absorbing new innovatory technologies. In consequence, the Japanese economy was unable to raise its nominal GDP (although the real GDP did not fall).

On the other hand, financial globalization was to contribute, in consequence, to boosting the emerging nations such as the BRICs to great economic growth. The rise of the BRICs is not only a matter of the developing countries attaining economic growth, but a phenomenon of historical significance on a worldwide scale in that they have become important economic and political players in the world of the twenty-first century.

As for China, it has attained high economic growth over a long period such as no other country has shown in human history, making use of foreign capital.

In the case of Russia, the situation is quite different, for (as the Soviet Union) it had been the leader of the Communist Bloc and a major power in terms of its economy. It suffered a serious meltdown (devastating capitalism) through "shock therapy" in the 1990s. However, since the early twenty-first century it has made a miraculous recovery due to the momentum given by the surge in prices of natural resources. Two circumstances also proved lucky for Russia: (1) commodities themselves became a target of "index speculation" and (2) the economic growth of China raised the demand for commodities.

In the case of India, which had suffered from an inferiority in infrastructure detrimental to economic development, the IT revolution, which began in the US, has since the early 1990s created the right conditions for the economic exploitation of brainpower, which was a great factor in qualifying India as a member of the BRICs.

In the case of Brazil, contributing in no small measure to the country's economic development is the miraculous economic growth of China, generating a high demand for all sorts of commodities.

Thus during these two decades the presence of the Japanese economy on the world scene has shown a dramatic decline in terms of every index, while the BRICs have shown the opposite tendency. Moreover, Russia and China are consciously grabbing back their position as hegemon,[10] and this is rapidly transforming the geopolitical scene in the world.

5   The Financial Regulatory Reform Act

The instability of the world economy recently experienced appears to be attributable to the growth of the SBS so, in order to stabilize the world economy, we need to bring it under the control of the financial authorities. This is a point recognized by the Obama Administration.

5.1   *How things went in the US*

5.1.1   *Obama's Financial regulatory reform proposals*

In June 2009 President Obama made public the outline of his financial regulatory reform proposals, aiming at repeal of the GLB and modern-day resurrection of the GS Act.

The central pillars are: (1) enlargement of the FRB, which is to work not only as a central bank but also as an institution to oversee systemic risk, and (2) creation of the Consumer Financial Protection Agency (CFPA), to safeguard consumers against financial abuse and fraudulence.

Through these institutions, securitized papers, financial derivatives, futures and so forth should be dealt in on open and clear markets, while the activities of hedge funds, investment banks, rating agencies and so forth could be overseen. Thus the proposal aims at scaling down, if not abolishing, the SBS.

5.1.2 The bailout and early recovery of the megabanks

The Wall Street megabanks were rescued first and foremost through bailout with huge sums of public money.[11] But the story does not end here. They were soon able to make immense profits by investing gigantic volumes of money, obtainable thanks to both the FRB's zero interest rate and its quantitative easing (QE) policy, in the emerging nations (such as China, Brazil and India)—the so-called "zero carry trade." Having repaid the public money to the government, the megabanks were then to engage in a fierce battle aiming at blocking Obama's financial regulatory reform.[12]

5.1.3 The growing perception of unfairness

Contrastingly, in spite of the FRB's easy-money policy the US real economy cannot be said to have made much progress toward recovery. What has concerned the US people are, among other things, the continued high unemployment rate and the rapid increase in arrears and foreclosure due to the housing market bust, which has also driven many local banks into bankruptcy (the number reaching a record high subsequent to the S&L crisis in 1992). The credit crunch brought in by the local banks has, in turn, aggravated conditions in the real economy.

The perception of unfairness has grown among the public, for Wall Street was instantly bailed out (by the Bush Administration) while Main Street remained stagnant (in spite of the Obama Administration's strenuous efforts).

5.2 The Dodd–Frank Act

5.2.1 The process

After public announcement of Obama's financial regulatory reform proposals in June 2009, deliberations in the two Houses proceeded very slowly.

On December 11, 2009 the financial regulatory reform act (the Wall Street Reform and Consumer Protection Act) got through in the House of Representatives. However, the Senate version which was first elaborated as a discussion draft in November 2009 was to proceed along a very difficult road thereafter. Leaving the details to my other paper,[13] let us here summarize the process in the Senate:

1   In May 2010 the Dodd Act (the Restoring American Financial Stability Act) was deliberated.
2   The deliberations continued for three weeks. On May 21 at long last the Dodd Act was passed with some slight modification.
3   The Conference Committee was then set up to unify the House and Senate versions. After a few weeks' deliberations, the committee report was adopted.
4   On June 30 the Dodd–Frank Act was passed in the House, while on July 15 it finally got through the Senate.
5   On July 21 the Act was enacted with President Obama's signature.

5.2.2 The gist of the Act

The Dodd–Frank Act covers the following items.

1   The Consumer Financial Protection Agency (CFPA)

   This is to be set up within the FRB, but should remain independent. The head is to be nominated by the president (this reflects some compromise with the House version and the president's view). During the subprime boom many financial institutions made mortgage loans to people on low incomes without any serious screening. In consequence, when the bubble burst great numbers of people were rapidly driven into default and foreclosure. In order to prevent this state of affairs from recurring (that is, to prevent consumers from being cheated and forced to conclude unfair contracts), the CFPA is to be set up.

2   The Volcker Rule

   This was first advocated by Paul Volcker in January 2010 and supported by Obama, and subsequently incorporated into the Act. The rule aims at prohibiting commercial banks from dealing in so-called "proprietary trading for their own account" and at imposing limits on the commercial banks' investments in hedge funds and private equity funds, for it would expose the depositors' money to risk through speculative activities engaged in by the banks.[14]

3   The Lincoln Provision

   This provision was first adopted by the Senate Agriculture Committee chaired by Blanche Lincoln in April 2010 and was incorporated into the Act. It aims at making derivative transactions fair and transparent by abolishing Over-the-Counter (OTC) derivatives and creating an open market.[15]

4   Creation of a committee for prevention of possible systemic risk

   The committee is to be composed of nine members headed by the Secretary of the Treasury.

5   The president of the FRB of New York is to be appointed by the US president.

   This condition aims at blocking Wall Street influence.

6   In the case of megabank bankruptcy, clearing and dissolution should be carried out smoothly with the funds collected from the financial industry.

   In short, the "TBTF" (Too Big To Fail) idea should be swept away. The megabanks have got used to assuming that because they are huge the government will never fail to rescue them in the event of their failure. Otherwise the economy as a whole, they think, would be exposed to serious crisis. Thus they are likely to run into impossible speculative activities—with serious moral hazard.

   Challenging the TBTF notion, the provision aims at clearing financial institutions on the brink of failure through the self-responsibility of the financial sector rather than taxes.

5.2.3 The implementation of the Act

It was at first estimated that it would take a year and a half for the Dodd–Frank Act to be implemented. Each section needs interpretation, so there will be confrontation on it. The lobbying activities are very influential and might change the nature and/or direction of the Act (for the actual process, see 5.3 below).

Moreover, should other countries—including the EU (with the UK)—fail to follow suit, the aim of the Dodd–Frank Act will be thwarted, for finance has been developed on the global scale, so loopholes will remain gaping. If the US intensified regulation but other countries did not follow suit, the financial institutions would continue risky speculative activities, shifting their headquarters elsewhere.

And yet the Dodd–Frank Act should be welcomed, for this will be the only feasible and effective road which could lead to financial regulation on the global level.

5.3 Tough path for implementation

President Obama finally succeeded in enacting the Dodd–Frank Act, of epoch-making importance in the US history, getting through many difficulties. Three years have passed since then to the time of this writing, and yet it is still far from becoming effective. The concrete process for implementation has been very tough, as illustrated below.

5.3.1 Up until August 2011

In January 2011, a Republican of the Tea Party persuasion brought in a motion to repeal the Dodd–Frank Act (July 2010) in the House to the effect that the Act entails excessive authority of the administration over the banking sector, while it does not deal with government-sponsored enterprises such as Fannie Mae and Freddie Mac. It will also bring about unemployment. The Dodd–Frank Act is against the Constitution. It got through in the House, but not in the Senate.

A dispute arose over the organizational form of the Consumer Financial Protection Bureau (CFPB). First came the problem of appointing its director. Obama strongly endorsed Elizabeth Warren, the founder of the CFPB, whom the Republicans fiercely opposed (thereafter Obama gave her up, and went on to nominate Richard Cordray in July 2011).

The Republicans, instead, proposed to change the organization of the CFPB. They first demanded adoption of a collegiate system composed of five members appointed by the leadership of the two parties rather than one director; second, they demanded that its budget be drawn up not from within the FRB but as a matter requiring the approval of Congress[16] (these tactics aimed at weakening the activities of the CFPB by excluding an influential director and curtailing the budget); third, they demanded that the activities of the CFPB be subject to the Banking Overseeing Committee majority rule.

Thereafter the Republican Party tried to obstruct the Dodd–Frank Act. To take just one example, it presented the Consumer Financial Protection Safety and Soundness Improvement Act (H. R.1315, Republican Sean Duffy) to the House. This Act, far from keeping the promise of the title, aims at pulling the teeth of the Dodd–Frank Act, in particular hamstringing the CFPB by changing Article 1023 and buying time to make loopholes for Wall Street. It passed in the House in July 2011, but not in the Senate.

Together with the CFPB, the Republicans made the CFTC (Commodity Futures Trading Commission) and the SEC (Securities and Exchange Commission) major targets for attack. The important posts for these commissions also proved impossible to determine due to obstruction by the Republicans. They made it clear that unless their argument was accepted, they would refuse to approve the people recommended by the president.

Then came the victory of the Republican Party in the midterm election in November, which naturally intensified their opposition activities.

5.3.2 As of July 2013 and February 2014

As mentioned above, in July 2011 Obama appointed Cordray as director of the CFPB, having given up on Warren. As the Republicans continued to oppose him, Obama made Cordray director in January 2012 by means of "Recess Appointment." Thus it was one year and a half after enactment of the Dodd–Frank Act that the CFPB started to work with Cordray at its head. The story of the director does not end here, however. For another year and a half the Senate would not approve Cordray due to the harsh opposition of the Republicans. In July 2013, in order to break out of this state of affairs, the leader of the Senate, Harry Reid, threatened to bring in the so-called "Atomic Option," which finally brought the Republican Party round to approving Cordray—the end of a problem that had meant long delay in implementing financial regulation reform.

Let us now see the present situation of implementation of the Dodd–Frank Act, based on the testimony of Daniel Tarullo,[17] director of the FRB, to the committee in the Senate in July 11, 2013 and February 6, 2014 (in the following, (i) indicates testimony in July, (ii) in February).

1 Request for greater "prudence" toward megabanks:

   i   The rule for the dissolution plan and stress test has already been established.
   ii   The FRB issued proposed rules that would establish enhanced prudential standards for megabanks. The FRB is making efforts for regulatory proposals which aim at reducing the probability of failure of a GSIB (Global Systematically Important Bank).

2 Requirement of stress test and capital planning for major banks:

   i   Full-scale stress test is scheduled to be extended to more than ten megabanks with $50 billion in assets this fall.
   ii   In July the FRB, OCC (Office of the Comptroller of the Currency) and FDIC (Federal Deposit Insurance Corporation) reached an agreement

on the final plan to be carried out in the US for implementing capital rule in accordance with Basel III.

iii The FRB issued proposed supervisory guidance for stress testing by big banks and issued interim final rules clarifying how banks should incorporate the revised Basel III capital framework into their capital projections.

iv The FRB and other US banking agencies have proposed imposing leverage surcharges on GSIBs.

v The FRB is considering imposing risk-based capital surcharges on GSIBs.

3 Improvement of the method for liquidation of megabanks:

i The Orderly Liquidation Authority (OLA) was set up, under which it was decided that the FDIC has the authority to ask shareholders and creditors to cover loss, change the management personnel, and liquidate a financial institution except for its robust sections.

ii The FRB is making efforts to improve GSIBs' resolvability, proposing relevant rules, consulting with the FDIC and OLA.

4 The FRB, CFPB, FDIC, FHFA (Federal Housing Financial Agency), NCUA (National Credit Union Agency), and OCC issued the final rule for implementing assessment of high-risk mortgage loans.

5 Article for Excluding Derivatives (Derivatives push-out):

i This became effective in July 2013. It was applied to the American branches of foreign banks lacking deposit guarantee, while the banks with deposit guarantee can apply for two years' suspension.

ii In December 2013 the FRB approved a final rule which clarifies the treatment of uninsured US branches and agencies of foreign banks.

6 The Measure for the Shadow Banking System:

i This is a measure to prevent financial institutions which use extreme levels of leverage from reaping huge amounts of short-term capital. In July two non-banks (including AIG) were selected as its targets.

ii Since the crisis, regulators have collectively made progress in addressing some of the close linkages between shadow banking and traditional banking organizations, and have addressed risks resulting from derivatives transactions. In August 2013, the Financial Stability Board issued a consultative document that outlined a framework of minimum margin requirements for securities financing transactions. Still, regulators have yet to address head-on the financial stability risks from securities financing transactions and other forms of short-term wholesale funding that lie at the heart of shadow banking.

7 The Volcker Rule:

i In the fall of 2011 the FRB and the SEC proposed a rule implementing the Volcker Rule, followed by a similar rule by the CFTC a few months

later. The Volcker Rule is yet to be finalized, due mainly to the difficulty of distinguishing between the proprietary trading and the hedging
and market-making activities.

ii   In December 2013 the US banking agencies, the SEC and the CFTC
finalized the Volker Rule.

8   Problem of regulating the amount of credit to single OTCs:

i   It is under review.

9   Liquidity rules for megabanks:

i   In October 2013 the FRB and other US banking agencies proposed a
rule for quantitative liquidity requirement for megabanks.

10   FRB emergency lending authority:

i   In December the FRB proposed amendments to Emergency Lending
Authority to protect taxpayers from loss and provide liquidity to the financial system.

11   Supervisory Assessment Fees:

i   In August 2013 the FRB issued a final rule for Supervisory Assessment
Fees. This rule became effective in October. Payments for the 2012
assessment period were made by 72 companies worth $433 million.

12   Risk retention responsibility provision:

i   In August 2013 the US banking agencies, the Federal Housing Finance
Agency, the Department of Housing and Urban Development, and the
SEC revised a rule proposed in 2011 to implement the risk retention
responsibility provision.

What is clear from the above is that, although more than four years have passed
since the Dodd–Frank Act was enacted, while some of the items are, at last, set
to start, the most important have yet to be finalized. Long delay seems to be the
prospect on all sides.

What will this delay mean? The financial institutions, with the help of the
Republican Party, having successfully bounced back from the brink of failure due
to huge bailout from the government, have been trying to obstruct the creation of
organizations designed to oversee their speculative activities. They have also been
making great efforts to have the Act softened and weakened with big loopholes,
lavishing huge sums of money on the political arena and engaging in lobbying
activities with some success. Thus the SBS has remained intact, which suggests
the serious risk of a huge financial crisis hitting the world again in the near future.

It needs to be borne in mind that so far it is only the US that has put through a
financial regulatory act. Unless other countries, including the UK and the EU,
enact the same sort of acts, the world will be left with a great loophole. The financial field is, for better or worse, now global.

5.4 Appendix: the UK and the EU

The following is the present state (at the time of this writing) of the UK and EU action in tackling financial instability. As compared with the US, implementation of the measures is much slower.

5.4.1 The UK

The Vickers Report, which was published by the Independent Commission on Banking (ICB) in September 2011,[18] is an important document proposing the appropriate approach to financial regulatory reform.

The most salient feature of the report is the creation of a ring-fence between commercial banks and investment banks so that money deposited at the former be protected from being used speculatively by the latter. In spirit, it is similar to the Glass–Steagall Act, but different in that a fence is built rather than two types of banks being separated. Another feature is a device for raising the British banks' "loss absorbing power."

In December 2013, the Financial Services (Banking Reform) Act was enacted, adopting the ring-fence method advocated by the Vickers Report. The government called on the banks to reform their structure along this line immediately. Moreover, it clarified that "the loss absorbing power" should be in place by 2019.

5.4.2 The EU

The Euro group is considering whether it should adopt the Volcker rule and/or ring-fence method. In Germany the Ring-Fencing and Recovery and Resolution Planning of Credit Institutions Act, based on the Liikanen Report, was enacted in May 2013. In France the Banking Reform Act, adopting a ring-fence method, was enacted in March 2013.

Per contra, the ECB is skeptical about the ring-fence method while the European Commission (EC) is planning a law to prohibit prop trading.

Moreover, there is the Banking Union plan (which the EU most prefers, but is difficult to implement) and the financial transaction tax (FTT: a kind of Tobin tax). Let us take a look at the FTT, which is making the most progress.

The FTT was first discussed in June 2010. However, it did not go down so well in the EU as a whole. Then, in October 2012, the European Commission (EC) changed the plan in such a way that would-be member countries should be authorized to enjoy "enhanced cooperation." In December 2012 the plan, which 11 member countries had endorsed, was approved in the European parliament. In February 2013 the EC again submitted the plan, in a revised form, to the European parliament, and it was approved in July. The plan agreed among ten members, due to the withdrawal of Slovenia, is that 0.1 percent is imposed on transaction of equities and debts, and 0.01 percent on transaction of derivatives, to come into effect on January 1, 2016. (This is different from the bank levy, which is to be imposed on banks ready for possible bailouts in the future.)

It should be noted that financial regulation reform is not a priority for the EU. The euro system crisis continues, rooted in its inherent characteristics.

6 The need for financial regulation reform

We now turn to the fundamental question: Why is financial regulation reform needed? Two points are worth noting in particular. One is "distorted capitalism," the other reconsideration of "freedom and market" as concepts.

6.1 The distorted capitalistic system

Finance is an essential element for the modern capitalistic system. Without it, the smooth working and development of the economy would be inconceivable. The problem is, however, the relation between financial liberalization and the "sound" development of capitalism. If the financial sector is left unchecked, those involved seek to gain as large a share of GDP as they can for their own advantage. In consequence, they are tempted to distort income distribution to a considerable degree; hence the emergence of distorted capitalism.

It should be noted that regulation or overseeing is not inconsistent with liberalization. What the financial institutions have done in recent decades in the name of "liberalization" is to bring about the phenomena of market "non-existence" and "opaqueness." Non-existence emerged as a result of multilayered securitized products, while opaqueness characterizes the financial market in which many hedge funds can deal in huge amounts of money without any obligation to report their dealings to the authority.

It is very important to make a rule for the financial market. It is wrong to identify lack of rules with financial liberalization. To take one example, Wall Street has, with lobbying activities, shown fierce resistance to the transaction rule for derivatives, on the ground that it is an unjust intervention in the market. This is not the case, however. The measure aims at observance of the rule of the market, and as a framework to guarantee this, puts forward a proposal to construct a system which is as fair and transparent as equity market. Here we need to work out "what the market is, and how the market should be."

6.2 Freedom and market as concepts that must be rethought

Neoliberalism has vociferously maintained that the capitalistic economy is a system of self-responsibility, so the need is to challenge the future under one's own responsibility, not depending on the government, while the government should not interfere with the market.

The transfer of short-term capital has been liberalized to an extreme degree, and the multilayered securitized products have gone to extremes in the name of the triumph of financial engineering.

Many international financial banks which had been leading in the race then found themselves in serious jeopardy. They then asked the governments for financial help, abandoning the "self-responsibility" gospel.

This phenomenon should, to a considerable degree, be attributed to an extreme belief in the "pure market economy." Liberalization without due prudence has set extremely short-run speculative activities completely free, and business ethics and social ethics have been dropped.

On the other hand, the people who went bankrupt due to subprime loans have lost their homes in foreclosure, with the loans left. It is on them that the principle of self-responsibility is enforced. Neoliberalism collapses of itself in the face of the nitty-gritty.

7 Conclusion

This chapter has addressed the problems of financial liberalization which have been developing over these 30 years and the increasing instability it has brought about in the capitalistic system, focusing on the US. If finance is set free, there is the risk of more serious economic meltdown in the near future. However, the administration has been extremely slow in implementing financial regulation, leaving the SBS as it was before the Lehman shock. At present, the world has no means at its disposal to prevent a second Lehman shock.

This chapter also warns against the dogma that regulation is incompatible with freedom. The market and the freedom which neoliberalism has advocated contain self-conflicting elements such as the phenomena of market non-existence and opaqueness. To resolve them and determine what the market should be, and what freedom should mean in this context—the need is immediate and urgent.

Notes

1 This is an updated and extended version of my paper (Ch.1) in Perrotta and Sunna (2013)—with Sections 5.3, 5.4 and 6 newly added. The final rewriting in March 2014.
2 The Pecora Commission made a great contribution to revealing this fact.
3 Incidentally, Timothy Geithner, the Secretary of the Treasury (Summers was a mentor), was president of the FRB of New York. In September 2008 he forced the Lehman Brothers into bankruptcy, and yet bailed out Citi Group with the TARP fund.
4 Gramm ran for Republican nomination in the 1966 presidential election. In the 2008 campaign for the presidency he was among McCain's principal supporters. According to some sources, he would have been Secretary of the Treasury if McCain had been elected president.
5 In October 2008 the UBS, which suffered a huge loss, not only received public money (amounting to six billion Swiss francs) from the Swiss government, but also handed over the bad assets (worth 72 billion Swiss francs) to it.
6 As examples of serious financial crises which occurred in the US (though it had no influence on the international scene), we may mention the S&L crisis (around 1990) and the bust of the dot.com bubble (around 2001; Enron is emblematic here).
7 For this dramatic story, see an interview with Brooksley Born, Chair, Commodity Futures Trading Commission (1996–1999). www.pbs.org/wgbh/pages/frontline/warning/interviews/born.html.

8 The most famous, and indeed, notorious was Andrei Schleifer, Professor at Harvard University (a protégé of Lawrence Summers), in the case of Russia.
9 As a prelude to this, we need to mention the Plaza Accord of 1985. This was to mean a great ordeal for Japan, and, due to the failure in appropriately dealing with subsequent events, led to the "Lost Decade" of the 1990s.
10 China goes on playing a sort of imperialistic role in vast parts of the globe, including the African continent, much as the Western powers had formerly done.
11 Funded by the TARP (the Troubled Asset Relief Program), which was hastily proposed, and was to be used in a very ambiguous way by the Bush Administration.
12 As representative of the lobbyists criticizing financial regulation, we may mention the American Bankers Association, and in support of it the US Public Interest Research Group.
13 See Hirai (2012, Chapter 7).
14 In September 2010 JP Morgan and Goldman Sachs decided to close the proprietary trading section, considering the Volcker Rule.
15 Recently the yields gained by hedge funds have shown some decline. Wary of risks, investors are now tending to concentrate their resources in large funds rather than small ones.
16 The FRB, the FDIC (Federal Deposit Insurance Corporation) and the OCC (Office of the Comptroller of the Currency) are allowed to carry out operations with independent funds while the SEC (Securities and Exchange Commission) and the CFTC (Commodities Futures Trading Commission) are incorporated in the budget system, which requires the approval of Congress.
17 See Tarullo (2013, 2014).
18 See the Independent Commission on Banking (2011).

References

Dodd–Frank (2010) *Dodd–Frank Wall Street Reform and Consumer Protection Act*, H. R. 4173, July, available at: www.sec.gov/about/laws/wallstreetreform-cpa.pdf.
Dodd–Frank Update, available at: www.doddfrankupdate.com/DFU/ArticlesDFU.aspx?issueid=b954a64f-c4b9–4f2f-b1de-ae61da584c15.
Egawa, Y. (2007) *The Lessons of the Subprime Problem*, Tokyo: Shouji-Houmu (in Japanese).
European Commission (2011) European Union Financial Transaction Tax (EU FTT), September, available at: http://en.wikipedia.org/wiki/European_Union_financial_transaction_tax.
Hirai, T. (2010) "The Two Institutional Reforms of President Obama," *Statistics*, November (in Japanese).
Hirai, T. (2012) *Can Keynes Save Capitalism?* Kyoto: Showado (in Japanese).
Independent Commission on Banking (2011) *Final Report Recommendations* (The Vickers Report), available at: www.ecgi.org/documents/icb_final_report_ 12sep2011.pdf.
Krugman, P. (2009) "The Market Mystique," *New York Times*, April 1.
Kurahashi, T. and Kobayashi, M. (2008) *The Right Way of Thinking of the Subprime Problem*, Tokyo: Chuko-Shinsho (in Japanese).
Liikanen, E. (2012) "Report of the European Commission's High-level Expert Group on Bank Structural Reform," October, available at: http://ec.europa.eu/internal_market/bank/docs/high-level_expert_group/report_ en.pdf#search='Report+of+the+European+Commission%27s+Highlevel+Expert+Group+on+Bank+Structural+Reform'.
Ogura, M. and Yasuda, Y. (2008) *The Subprime Problem and the U.S. Housing and Mortgage Market*, Tokyo: Jutaku Sinposha (in Japanese).

Perrotta, C. and Sunna, C. (eds.) (2013) *Globalization and Economic Crisis*, Lecce, Italy: Salento University Press.

Polk, D. (2013) "Dodd–Frank Progress Report," available at: www.davispolk.com/sites/default/files/Sep2013_Dodd.Frank_.Progress.Report_0.pdf.

Shiller, R. (2008) *Subprime Solution*, Princeton, NJ: Princeton University Press.

Soros, G. (2008) *The New Paradigm for Financial Markets*, New York, NY: Public Affairs.

Spiegel (2010) "No More Naked: Germany and France Call for an EU Ban on Financial Speculation," *Spiegel Online*, June 9, available at: www.spiegel.de/ international/europe/no-more-naked-germany-and-france-call-for-an-eu-ban-on-financial-speculation-a-699615.html.

Stiglitz, J. (2009) "Obama's Ersatz Capitalism," *New York Times*, April 1.

Takita, Y. (2008) *The World Financial Crisis*, Tokyo: Nihon Keizai Shinbun Shuppansha (in Japanese).

Talbott, J. R. (2008) *Obamanomics*, New York, NY: Seven Stories Press.

Tarpley, W. G. (2010) "Euro Momentarily Stabilized: German Ban on Naked Credit Default Swaps Is Working," May 21, available at: http://tarpley.net/2010/05/ 22/euro-momentarily-stabilized/.

Tarullo, D. K. (2013, 2014) "Dodd–Frank Implementation, Before the Committee on Banking, Housing, and Urban Affairs, US Senate, Washington, DC," Board of Governors of the Federal Reserve System, July 11, 2013 and February 6, 2014, available at, respectively www.federalreserve.gov/newsevents/testimony/tarullo20130711a.htm and www.federalreserve.gov/newsevents/testimony/ tarullo20140206a.htm.

Turner, G. (2008) *The Credit Crunch*, London: Pluto Press.

Wikipedia (2013) "Financial Transaction Tax," available at: http://en.wikipedia.org/wiki/Financial_transaction_tax.

3 Globalization and Keynes's ideal of a "sounder political economy between all nations"

Anna M. Carabelli and Mario A. Cedrini

1 Introduction: gated globalization

Ours is a "gated globe," according to the report of *The Economist* (2013) on world economy.

> After two decades in which people, capital and goods were moving ever more freely across borders, walls have been going up, albeit ones with gates. Governments increasingly pick and choose whom they trade with, what sort of capital they welcome and how much freedom they allow for doing business abroad
>
> (*The Economist* 2013)

This would have produced a new kind of globalization, a "gated globalization," whose appeal is "closely tied to state capitalism" (ibid.), at a time when this latter is currently enjoying greater popularity than its main competitor, liberal capitalism. In the liberal view of *The Economist*, we are currently living in a world wherein globalization has "paused." This might confirm Eric Helleiner's (2010) speculations about the future of the international economic order: the 2007–2008 crisis should be regarded as a "legitimacy crisis"[1] for the neoliberal order which followed the collapse of Bretton Woods, as well as an important stimulus to elaborate an international reform agenda. But this does not necessarily mean that the process will end with a "constitutive phase" of the Bretton Woods kind; rather, the lack of consensus concerning the content of the reform agenda induces us to interpret the current one as a phase of "interregnum" between two global orders, of which the future one remains unpredictable. "The more plausible scenario," writes Helleiner, "is one in which states increasingly attempt to carve out greater degrees of autonomy to pursue distinctive national and regional practices within the context of a still quite integrated global economy."[2]

The world seems to desire a new Bretton Woods order, but such expectations are likely to be disappointed. Still, an "interregnum" will not, by definition, last forever, and contains, in all probability, the seeds of the future order. Today's gated globalization allows a certain dose of pluralism, as shown by the increasing autonomization of Southern developing countries, the widespread use of capital controls and the inconsistency of International Monetary Fund's conditionality programs.[3] No transnational policy paradigm such as the Washington Consensus has already replaced, or is likely to replace this latter in the near future.[4] This might be a first sign of transition to that "form of embedded communitarian liberalism, which seeks to reconcile the achievement of national, regional and global objectives, and to marry universal values with a respect for diversity" which Gore saw,[5] as the likely outcome of the Washington Consensus parable. Curiously enough, the "more heterogeneous international regime"[6] of the future might in truth rest on a "return" to Bretton Woods and its "embedded liberalism."[7] Hence the current discussion about the possibility to recreate the historical conditions which favored the establishment of an international system which, James warns, among others, runs the risk of being interpreted in the light of "what happened *after* as well as *before*"[8] its birth in 1942.

From this, two consequences follow. First, the attack of contemporary "embedded liberals" on the neoliberal globalization of the Nineties might appear to have a backward-looking character.[9] Second, the current nostalgia for Bretton Woods might in truth rest on a "positive mythology"[10] which overestimates the actual relevance of the 1944 conference and overlooks that the system was "the outcome of a much more extended historical process."[11] More subtly, this induces us to reinterpret Bretton Woods as "a solution, not just to the question of post-war reconstruction, but to the problem of recasting capitalism in such a way that it would not permanently destabilize both itself and the international political and legal order."[12] Dani Rodrik has passionately contributed to the cause of a new Bretton Woods compromise, as he calls his preferred option in the "political trilemma of the world economy." Democracy, national sovereignty and global economic integration are mutually incompatible, Rodrik argues. Globalization requires the elimination of transaction costs produced by national borders: either it becomes the concern of a world government ("global federalism" model) taking care of a world market, or it totally determines the political agenda of nation states whose main, if not unique task would be to attract the confidence of foreign investors ("golden straitjacket"). The only alternative left is a new "compromise of Bretton Woods," significantly narrowing the scope of globalization to leave adequate policy space available to developing countries. Under the Bretton Woods order, writes Rodrik, "countries were free to dance to their own tune as long as they removed a number of board restrictions on trade and generally did not discriminate among their trade partners ... [and] were allowed to maintain restrictions on capital flows."[13]

Among other reasons, the mythicization of both the conference of Bretton Woods and the merits of the regime it established may explain why Rodrik's far-reaching criticism of the neoliberal globalization of the Nineties makes no use of the peculiar vision of international economic relations elaborated by one of the two theoretical fathers of Bretton Woods, the one who finally lost. The post-Bretton Woods era "continually regenerates the myth of Bretton Woods"[14] but not necessarily the one of John Maynard Keynes. There is a widespread trend in the international relations literature[15] to identify in the "intellectual consensus," as John Williamson named it,[16] forged by Keynes in the interwar years the main driving force behind the birth of the Bretton Woods order. Once the embedded liberalism (multilateral liberalism predicated upon domestic intervention, in Ruggie's words) of Bretton Woods is defined as a "neoclassical synthesis"[17] of microeconomic liberalism and macroeconomic management, it becomes easy to explain why this theoretical consensus excluded Keynes himself, despite the role he played in shaping it. Still, Williamson's observation, 30 years ago, that a post-Bretton Woods international order worthy of this name requires a new intellectual consensus of this kind still holds today, provided the attention is focused not on the consensus that Keynes defended despite the final rejection of his reform plans at Bretton Woods, but on the deep sense of the intellectual consensus that he *wished* to create for the postwar world. That is, on the possible legacy of that same rejected proposal, which wanted to establish a consensus on freedom and policy space, rather than on the sacrifice of national autonomy on the altar of market discipline and aggressive globalization.

Keynes's *desired* consensus may serve two distinct but interrelated purposes. First, the theoretical foundations of Keynes's project of "sounder political economy between all nations"[18] can be a valuable asset in constructing a historical narrative of the international economic disorder. Having in the Washington Consensus[19] saga and the rise of the global imbalances of the so-called "Bretton Woods II" (non-)system[20] its salient episodes, the narrative should resist the temptation to give the "normality" of the lack of legitimated order for granted. It should rather present the current crisis as the sad epilogue of the attempt, in the Nineties, to impose a neoliberal order structured around the concept of market discipline, symbolizing not only the abandonment, but the complete abjuration of Keynes's work of international economics. Second, Keynes's desired consensus can contribute to identify the possible pillars of the new narrative explicitly and rightly called for by Rodrik (2011), among others, to shape the future of globalization. Keynes's mature vision of global economic integration "was rooted in his longstanding effort to understand both the strength and weaknesses of the pre-1914 era of globalization under the gold standard,"[21] as Dimand aptly puts it. Keynes's reform plans of the Forties are the result of a long theoretical journey, shaped by changing times and circumstances, which deepened his skepticism about the possibility of recreating the lost paradise without a revolution in international management. And it is exactly this skepticism—Keynes's growing doubts about the apparent certainties of the gold-standard globalization—to demonstrate the relevance of Keynes's reasoning to today's world.

2 The Washington Consensus: discipline without freedom

The final suggestion to dethrone gold and build an international system freeing nation states from its "golden fetters" strikes the imagination also because it came from an early supporter of the gold standard. Likewise, it was a thinker of global economic integration, who had offered an enthusiastic picture of prewar globalization in the opening pages of *The Economic Consequences of the Peace* (1919), to opt for national self-sufficiency in the most acute phase of the Great Depression. Although one naturally tends to overvalue such radical positions when trying to grasp the essence of Keynes's work of international economics, a much more representative example of his way of reasoning about international economic relations is provided by the "dilemma of the international system"[22] he discussed at length in the *Treatise on Money*. The dilemma opposes the advantages of the stability of national currencies in terms of the international standard to the benefit of national autonomy over domestic rate of interest, which the gold standard tends to the contrary to equalize in all countries, and foreign lending. In analyzing the impact of financial globalization on domestic economies, Keynes therefore referred to an apparently ineliminable tension between international discipline (as regards exchange rates and capital movements) and domestic autonomy (as regards policy to attain and maintain full employment). As Kregel notes, "in today's jargon this would be called a discussion of the 'national policy space' available to developing countries in designing their domestic economic policy."[23]

A possible solution to these tensions is to externally finance policy space,[24] that is to finance it through external capital flows. If Keynes had previously praised the virtue of the gold standard, this was because the system ensured its reserve countries the possibility of facing their short-term balance-of-payments deficits while investing long-term in peripheral countries. Britain's ability to make the Empire finance its deficit with Europe and the US, but also her "responsible" behavior toward the "new" countries (limiting the strict discipline of the classical mechanism and allowing member countries the possibility of living and developing in a global multilateral economy) guaranteed multilateralism and dynamism.[25] In the postwar period, however, foreign lending, namely the "process by which rich countries spread the proceeds of their wealth over the world" could not "be strongly supported on nationalist grounds" any longer.[26] The old relationship between foreign lending and exports—capital inflows being used by borrowing countries to finance imports from the lender—was in fact no longer valid in the twentieth century. In discussing the dilemma of the international system, Keynes warned about the risks of allowing "a disproportionate degree of mobility" to capital only, in an economic system which is "extremely rigid in several other respects."[27]

When Latin America implemented the Washington Consensus recipes under the promise of financial support on the part of the United States, it managed to reduce inflation through external capital flows. Still, these latter "produced by-products that were crucial to [the strategy's] success—overvalued exchange rates, open capital markets, high levels of capital inflows—but ... created domestic incentives that impeded the domestic restructuring required to provide improved growth and employment."[28] Adjustment policies produced current account surpluses and a tendency to currency appreciation, and favored financial assets and rentiers[29] over domestic corporate restructuring; productivity gains were simply wasted in the process.[30] Capital market liberalization was therefore a necessary condition for the initial success of stabilization policies, but ran against developing countries' desire to position themselves on a growth path, and forcedly established, somehow ironically, the seeds of future financial crises, which the Consensus was meant to prevent. But capital market liberalization was the password (and main tool) of a bigger overall project of universal convergence toward a specific model of capitalism, destined to reaffirm the principle of "monoeconomics."[31] It should pose an end to the era of "global apartheid"[32] which had allowed developing countries to (attempt to) reduce their income gap by unorthodox means such as inflation, state-led industrialization, and import substitution. And, in truth, the Consensus rapidly became something more than a blueprint for development. If critics of the "neoliberal" theory of globalization[33] identify the Washington Consensus paradigm as the main culprit for the socio-economic disasters of the past decades, it is mainly because it became the theoretical foundation of an aggressive neoliberal agenda imposed by the two Bretton Woods institutions to crisis-hit and developing countries.

As is known, the Consensus failed both as set of policy prescriptions for development and as a structural adjustment reform package for countries presenting unsustainable balance-of-payment disequilibria. The agenda of capital market liberalization implemented in East Asia throughout the Nineties had pushed up the value of the region's currencies and produced large current account deficits; IMF austerity policies during the crisis, which were meant to restore investors' confidence, soon revealed their "beggar-thy-neighbor," and, worse, "beggar-thyself" character. The crisis itself was taken as an opportunity to remodel Asian "crony capitalisms" into free market economies worthy of the name. In Stiglitz's words, the collapse cast doubt on the presumedly superior model of capitalism embedded in the Washington Consensus, so that:

> the IMF and the U.S. Treasury had to argue that the problem was not with the reforms ... but with the fact that the reforms had not been carried far enough. By focusing on the weaknesses of the crisis countries, they not only shifted blame away from their own failures—both the failures of policy and the failures in lending—but they attempted to use the experience to push their agenda still further.[34]

Hence the "Augmented Washington Consensus,"[35] with the shift from "getting prices right" to "getting the institutions right." Establishing a tautological relationship between the augmented list and economic development, "second generation" reforms made it simply too easy to ascribe failures to developing countries' scarce political courage. Above all, they transformed the predominant Western model of socioeconomic organization into the unique reference for international institutions' policy reforms.[36] Conditionalities imposed by the IMF and the World Bank on fundamentally sound Asian countries were based on what the technocratic Washington believed to be the "universal norms of a proper economy"[37]—capital market liberalization was supplemented by Anglo-Saxon financial regulation, reforms of business–government relations and of labor market institutions. Structural adjustment policies, currency board regime (dollarization of the economy) and full integration into the Free Trade Area of Americas made Argentina the poster child for the neoliberal economics of the Washington Consensus as understood by the international financial institutions. Economic policy in developing countries was shaped by the rules of a "confidence game"[38] played by the IMF in the attempt to restore market confidence in crisis-hit economies. Argentina's default, in particular, served to demonstrate at the same time the circularity of the argument—"If market confidence comes only after sound policies are followed and sound policies are defined as policies that trigger confidence, financial markets and the IMF can in principle converge on any arbitrary set of policies."[39]

The Washington Consensus, Rodrik argues at the end of the saga, too easily neglects the "need for humility, for policy diversity, for selective and modest reforms, and for experimentation."[40] As Stiglitz observes, the only possible "Post Washington Consensus" can be on the fact that there should be no consensus about growth strategies. Policy space is required to exercise autonomy in the choice—"the essence of freedom is the right to make a choice—and to accept the responsibility that comes with it."[41] There is here an interesting parallel with Keynes's work of international economics. For critics of the Washington Consensus tend to believe that it is not possible to satisfy the demand for enhanced policy space generated by the application of the paradigm by other means than a reform of the international architecture.

This brings us back to Williamson's 1983 work on Keynes's work on international economics, where the father of the Washington Consensus complained about the lack of an intellectual consensus on "a set of generally accepted rules and conventions regarding the proper way for countries to conduct those of their economic policies that have significant repercussions outside their own borders."[42] Williamson was quite convinced, at the epoch, that there was no chance of building "a framework that significantly constrains countries' policies in the general interest."[43] In a way, the Consensus aimed at remedying this state of affairs. The paradigm truly created an international economic order, although its evolution over time, until the final collapse, demonstrates the intrinsic fragility that necessarily characterizes fully technocratic constructions lacking veritable democratic support. It therefore becomes necessary to investigate the peculiar nature of the "general interest" of the Consensus international order. As Gore maintains, contrary to the structuralist view, the Washington Consensus employs a "national explanatory framework" to analyze the specific development situation of each emerging nation, and adopts a "global normative framework" which asks countries to conform with the norms of a liberal international economic order. Such conformity, it was argued, would lead to better performances for both global economy and individual countries, whereas deviations would be self-defeating, heterodox countries ending up with being excluded from the "global field of flows"[44] and the distribution of the benefits of globalization. In truth, globalization itself was the "general interest" of the liberal international economic order established by the Consensus. Technocratic in nature, the attempted order included the political project, as Bourdieu (1998) called it, of neoliberalism: the only freedom allowed in and by the order was that of market forces. Its final aim was to make the world a safe place for free trade in goods and capital,[45] which required, though disguised under the promise of allowing countries to borrow it from abroad, the suppression of policy space, and what Chang (2006) defines as the "right to be wrong" with it.

3 Keynes's desired consensus: in defense of policy space

What precedes casts light on the deep anti-Keynesian nature of the Consensus (attempted) order. The author of a fundamental essay on probability as the most general form of knowledge and a guide for human action in conditions of uncertainty ("A Treatise on Probability"),[46] Keynes was a thinker of the complexity of international economic relations. To these he applied his conception of economics as "a method rather than a doctrine, an apparatus of the mind, a technique of thinking, which helps its possessor to draw correct conclusions."[47] The object of economics being to provide ourselves not with "settled conclusions"[48] or "infallible" answers, but rather "with an organised and orderly method of thinking out particular problems."[49] Aware of the complexity of the material under consideration, Keynes opposed the introduction and use of the "atomic hypothesis"[50] in the analysis of economic issues, a rule to which his international economics makes no exception. As Vines points out, Keynes's way of reasoning about the international environment was shaped by an "extraordinarily clear understanding of how pieces of the global economy interact, driven by the policies of autonomous nations, in an only partly coherent manner."[51]

The above-recalled dilemma of the international system truly occupies a central position in Keynes's work. In the *Treatise on Money*, Keynes draws attention to the (open-economy) problems of Britain, the former leader of the system, now (in 1930) a debtor country facing the enormous costs of the return to gold and creditor countries' anti-social attitude. The Great Depression and the "international" disease which accompanied it brought Keynes to elaborate a view of economic history as a permanent conflict between creditors and debtors which readers of the *Treatise* find exposed at length in the famous chapter on the "historical illustrations."[52] As Cairncross puts it,

> in an anarchic world [Keynes] accepted the need for each country to preserve its freedom of action.... Without international management, however, the task of individual governments would become indefinitely more difficult ... individual countries would find it hard to keep in internal and external balance and maintain full employment unless they operated within a framework of international institutions planned and managed for the common good.[53]

Keynes's early proposals of global reform (the more rational gold exchange standard of *Indian Currency and Finance*; the suggestion of reshaping the global monetary system, in *A Tract on Monetary Reform*, so as to free monetary policy to point at price stability; the "maximum" plan of the *Treatise on Money*, whereby an international central bank should issue new global money and provide liquidity to crisis-hit countries) aimed "to weaken the pressures on deficit countries and slow down the process of adjustment in the hope that surplus countries would allow the adjustment mechanism to operate."[54] The plan for the creation of an International Clearing Union (ICU) is the accomplishment of the more ambitious task of sketching a model of national behavior consistent with the general interests of the system.[55]

Keynes brought forth this model in the *General Theory*: it was the "twice blessed"[56] policies of regaining control over the interest rate, whereby countries could reach and maintain full employment and help their neighbors, at the same time, to achieve this same result. Still, only the "simultaneous pursuit of these policies by all countries together"[57] could transform international trade, up to then "a desperate expedient to maintain employment at home by forcing sales on foreign markets and restricting purchases," into "a willing and unimpeded exchange of goods and services in conditions of mutual advantage."[58] A revolution in global management was key to avoid having to recur to the isolationism of national self-sufficiency, which Keynes advocated as second-best solution to, and just before, sterling devaluation and departure from the gold standard. This did not prevent him from partially borrowing from his heretical proposal of national self-sufficiency in preparing the ICU project: undesired capital flows from debtor to creditor countries, hitherto "the major cause of instability,"[59] should be subject to strict controls in the proposed flexible exchange rate system. As he stressed in a speech to the House of Lords on May 23, 1944,

> the external value of sterling should conform to its internal value as set by our own domestic policies … we intend to retain control of our domestic rate of interest, so that we can keep it as low as suits our own purposes, without interference from the ebb and flow of international capital movements or flights of hot money … whilst we intend to prevent inflation at home, we will not accept deflation at the dictates of influences from outside.[60]

Another main influence to the ICU was the interwar "Schachtian" experiment, which Keynes saw as a straightforward device to cope with the "secular international problem"[61] of international balance-of-payment imbalances. Whereas a "freely convertible international standard"[62] usually throws the adjustment burden on debtor countries, the ICU plan rested on a principle of shared responsibilities for global imbalances, asking creditors to take their part. In Keynes's scheme, the Clearing Union issues a newly created bank money (bancor) functioning as the new international standard. Deficits and surpluses in the balance of payments are settled through the use of clearing accounts at the ICU denominated in bancor; and the institution can create reserves in the amount required to satisfy the needs of international trade. Members are granted an overdraft facility corresponding to half the average trade size over the five last prewar years. To counteract the formation of surplus positions in excess of a quarter of their quota, creditors would be allowed and, the case being, required to revalue their currencies and unblock foreign investments, as well as to pay rising interests on excess credits. Symmetrical obligations are imposed on debtor countries. It is to be noted that Keynes opposed the interpretation of his plan as an "automatic surrender of surpluses."[63] Creditors were simply asked not to hoard those resources which they could choose "to leave idle"[64] and left free to choose how to employ them—expansion of credit and domestic demand, currency appreciation or wages increase, abatement of trade restrictions or foreign lending for development—exactly as in the absence of the ICU. This way, creditors would no longer fear the "automatic tendency towards a general slump in international trade"[65] produced by the exhaustion of debtors' means of repayment. The plan presents therefore a "built-in expansionary bias," and configures a "free lunch for all," as Davidson (2009) calls it.

In the light of what precedes, that Keynes developed "a theory of how the system *as a whole* would behave"[66] though starting from a national perspective[67] is less surprising than it may appear. The ICU plan was meant to transform adherence to international discipline into a choice of freedom: policy space lies at the core of the project, as the analysis of the ethics of international economic relations embedded in Keynes's vision allows us to understand. The parallel with the *General Theory* is, in a way, direct. It is in fact to be noted that Keynes's late global reform plans aim at the euthanasia of rentier countries. Keynes criticizes domestic rentiers, first, for exercising a demand for money rather than for goods or labor; second, for producing deflation and thereby unemployment; third, for their being functionless investors, exploiting the purely artificial scarcity of capital.[68] Now, in the closed world of the ICU project, the "dead hand" of debt cannot impose its burden on deficit countries. Credits cannot be removed outside the system but only transferred within it, while facilities available to debtor countries "do not involve particular indebtedness between one member state and another ... [they] are not a real burden to others."[69] Second, the system's clearing principle evidently makes the possession of capital an asset of "insignificant importance,"[70] and prevents a repetition of the interwar "competitive struggle for liquidity"[71] from happening. Third, the expansionist bias of the plan severely reduces the incentives to become a "functionless investor" on the model of France and the United States in the early Thirties.

A fundamental aim of the plan was to enhance member states' policy space. Somehow paradoxically, this is what the "patchwork solution"—one of those "the post-war world must not be content with,"[72] wrote Keynes when still convinced that the United States could comply with his suggestion of a "system of general and collective responsibility, applying to all countries alike"[73]—of the American gift he proposed after the rejection the ICU plan helps us to understand. As is known, Keynes asked for an American gift, rather than a business loan, to Britain, to solve international imbalances further and dramatically nurtured by the war. The rejection of the ICU plan had left the newborn international institutions with scarce resources to deal with the transition to the new order. Global trade was threatened by Britain's deficit position toward the sterling area, since this latter was the only actor, itself indebted toward the US, that could stimulate American exports in the postwar period. During the first three years of war, before negotiating the Lend-Lease agreement with the United States, Britain had "held the fort alone"[74] and financed the common cause of the Allies' war against Germany; the sterling area countries had accepted centralizing their gold and foreign exchange reserves in London in exchange for sterling. Revamping the approach he had already used in 1919 when dealing with German reparations and the burden of Inter-Allied debts,[75] Keynes insisted on the freedom-enhancing effects that a shared-responsibilities approach to the imbalances, implying a strong involvement of the world creditor power, would have on debtor countries' policy space.[76]

His solution for unsustainable international imbalances relied on the "psychological atmosphere of the free gift,"[77] as he explained in the correspondence with the Treasury representative in Washington Robert H. Brand while preparing the negotiation of American assistance to London. He believed that an American gift (to be given as a sort of retrospective Lend-Lease) could assist Britain in approaching the sterling area countries with an equally generous program of debt restructuring. By helping Britain to return to sterling convertibility, sterling countries (highly indebted to the United States) would have regained the possibility of revitalizing their trade with the United States, and world trade in general with it. Only a gift could help enlarge the spectrum of countries disposed to take part in a "shared responsibilities" international adjustment to a more balanced order, debtor countries being otherwise compelled either to return to distasteful isolationist interwar policies or to accept the rules of a new multilateral order of free trade for which they were financially unprepared.

The proposal aimed at convincing the Americans, as Keynes observed in the correspondence with Brand, to use

> their financial strength not as an instrument to force us to their will, but as a means of making it possible for us to participate in arrangements which we ourselves prefer on their merits if only they can be made practicable for us.[78]

Otherwise, "they would fail to get, here and now,"[79] the multilateral world of free trade the Americans themselves desired. The plan was thus a sort of test of the leader's willingness to comply with the rules of Keynes's desired new system despite its final rejection at Bretton Woods. The "American Gift" embodied the spirit of the ICU plan: by granting the gift, the United States would have allowed Britain the freedom to choose and proactively help to shape the multilateral option, whereas a loan would have compelled her to accept the "American conception of the international economic system"[80] through market adjustment and austerity. The "shared responsibilities" approach of the American gift proposal, relying on a preliminary generous attitude on the part of the world creditor power, was first and foremost a defense of policy space.

It is Keynes himself to support the (though partially disappointing) results of the Anglo-American negotiations as the

> first great attempt at organizing international order out of the chaos of the war in a way which will not interfere with the *diversity of national policy* yet which will minimize the causes of friction and ill will between nations.[81]

While the unrestricted laissez-faire of the late gold standard and interwar period had "mistake[n] private licence for public liberty,"[82] he wanted the new system to protect freedom to choose, that is to manage the cohabitation of different varieties of national capitalism, instead of imposing them from outside a one-size-fits-all set of right policies. The ICU shared-responsibilities principle was intended to perform the same function of the "central controls"[83] invoked in the *General Theory* as a solution to unemployment, that is to protect the "traditional advantages of individualism." In Keynes's Aristotelian, anti-utilitarian but individualistic ethics,[84] individualism is

> the best safeguard of personal liberty in the sense that, compared with any other system, it greatly widens the field for the exercise of personal choice. It is also the best safeguard of the variety of life, which emerges precisely from this extended field of personal choice.[85]

4 The "global imbalances" world

Instead of the "genuine organ of truly international government"[86] envisaged by Keynes, the United States provided the world with a guardian of world monetary stability. The Marshall Plan and rather happy historical circumstances prevented the Bretton Woods system, in its 30 glorious years, from assuming the quite pronounced disciplinary traits of Harry Dexter White's plan. It is no coincidence that the "integrationist agenda"[87] of the Nineties could be easily described as the attempt to revive the pre-1914 era of globalization by means of disciplinary mechanisms which follow closely those of the gold standard, finally abandoned exactly by reason of the excessive suppression of policy space they necessarily implied (see Polanyi-Levitt 2006). Those, to put it differently, whom Keynes strenuously opposed, ending up with elaborating a global reform plan expressly designed to dethrone gold and its dangerous automatisms. But Keynes's legacy might be of the utmost importance even for today's (post-Washington Consensus) world. Before the crisis, it had become commonplace to describe this latter as the "Bretton Woods II" (BWII) world, after a highly influential paper by Dooley, Folkerts-Landau and Garber (2003). The Bretton Woods order was still in place, the three economists argued, for Asian countries in particular, with a long line of countries destined to follow, were covering the same road traced in the Sixties by the then peripheral Europe in the successful attempt to regain a central position in the global order. Their development strategy—export-led growth with undervalued exchange rates, capital controls and reserve accumulation (mostly dollars)—acted as a long-term, always operating safety clause for dollar stability, despite the widening of unprecedented global imbalances.

Due to the weaknesses of the theoretical hypothesis on which it rests, the label BWII is a camouflage of what could be more correctly referred to as the "global imbalances" world, despite that disequilibria of this kind are in truth the norm rather than the exception in the history of global economy. The Washington Consensus taught developing countries that foreign borrowing is a risky strategy. In the international non-system post-Bretton Woods, the more a developing country is successful in attracting foreign capital to finance its growth, the larger its foreign imbalances, which reduces the chances of retaining the desired level of capital inflows.[88] Hence the widespread adoption of costly but effective strategies of "self-protection through increased liquidity."[89] As Cruz and Walters argue, such strategies were developed "in the context of the decision to adopt or reinforce the neoliberal strategy of rapid financial liberalization, unrelated to the development of either deep financial markets or mature and effective regulatory structures."[90] In general, developing countries' reserve accumulation finds its rationale in a combination of precautionary motives—the need for protection from procyclical capital inflows, even more so when a country is unable to adopt countercyclical policies[91]—and a desire to compete in a mercantilist hoarding game to win access to Western markets.[92]

Global imbalances were the engine of global growth (under the tacit assumption of ever-growing American demand for foreign goods and with the help of China's growing demand for commodities and raw materials from the South) in the Noughties. Nevertheless, they result from fearful behaviors (either aggressive or defensive) adopted in a neoliberal environment which is in its turn a legacy of the Washington Consensus decade. This runs against arguments justifying inactivity with regard to their persistence, such as those stressing that global imbalances should not be counted among the causes of the crisis. In truth, a significant majority of economists consider them as a "handmaiden" to the crisis,[93] and they will in all probability be a relevant feature also of the post-crisis global economic environment. Remarkably, all this is strongly connected with the Washington Consensus attempted order. For, as Davidson points out, the Consensus philosophy—independently of concrete applications of the paradigm—presupposes "a global environment where *each* nation independently sees significant national advantages in a policy of export-led growth,"[94] despite the evident resulting fallacy of composition.

> The Washington Consensus has created perverse incentives that set nation against nation in a process that perpetuates a world of slow growth (if not stagnation) ... [the] continuing U.S. Trade deficit has been, in recent decades, the primary (sole?) engine of growth for the rest of the global economy as the other nations of the world focus on policies that promote export-led growth as a solution to each nation's unemployment rates and stagnating rates of growth.[95]

Hence the importance of so-called "co-dependence" views about global imbalances, emphasizing the ongoing dependence of the rest of the world on net exports to the United States.[96]

As Kregel (2006) maintains, financial flows accompanying global imbalances derive from global investment and production decisions that determine the global pattern of trade. Surplus countries invest in the United States to finance their exports, as was the case with pre-World War I Britain's foreign lending, which promoted exports of capital goods to new countries. Though aiming at different national or regional targets, therefore, pre-crisis Europe, Asia and Latin America adopted the same current account surplus-cum-foreign lending strategy as a substitute for, respectively, the unusable or dangerous device of external and government borrowing. In other words, global imbalances result from national policy choices—reflecting attempts by emerging countries to integrate into international trade and finance, and efforts by European firms to acquire American assets and technology. Hence the paradox of global imbalances: although their orderly unwinding, given the systemic risk they produce, should be in the interest of all countries concerned, multilateral coordination remains an insurmountable problem. Structural reasons—not only the stimulus provided by American growth to raising incomes abroad, but also China's role as major engine of growth in Asia and a promoter of increased trade among developing countries—explain their persistence, with the result that, due to lack of policy coordination in the times of a severe recession, adjustment will be more likely imposed to world economy by developed countries' waning appetite for imports from developing countries.[97]

5 Keynes and today's globalization

We have shown elsewhere that Keynes's reasoning in international economics offers a powerful analytical instrument to identify the shortcomings of the global imbalances world and detect solutions to overcome the current impasse. Keynes would likely support the case of coordination. He would probably join the Stiglitz Commission of the United Nations in pointing at the risks inherent to the building up of global imbalances, and recommend new rules to counteract the asymmetric character of international adjustment. In so doing, he would perhaps use that same theoretical framework that supported the case of an American gift to Britain at the end of World War II.[98] But he would also reflect on reserve accumulation and ambiguous creditor–debtor relationships as the two main features of our international non-system.[99] He would note that we are still unable to cope with the spectacular effects of "a change of ideas in Asia,"[100] to borrow words from *Indian Currency and Finance* (1913), namely, the passage to the "undervaluation-cum-intervention" strategies after the 1997 collapse, and the fact that Asia has by now "turned the tables on the West."[101] Keynes would likely condemn the "expensiveness with instability" character of the non-system—as opposed to the "cheapness with stability"[102] order he wanted to establish on the eve of the war—and reiterate his plea to adopt a "reserves are to be used not shown" principle, but would not fail to note that economic anxieties lie behind reserve hoarding.

In sum, Keynes would evidently attempt reforming the system. Still, as Kregel[103] points out in his report on the proposals advanced by the Stiglitz Commission, it would be an error to look at the shortcomings of the current disorder as if they could be remedied through the use of a new international currency alone. The challenge is to discover a new international adjustment mechanism, and one that is "also sufficiently compatible with global aggregate demand to provide full employment and support the national development strategies of developing countries."[104] Keynes was not a development economist, nor had a specific interest, however defined, in the problems of economic development, poverty alleviation and so on.[105] However, Keynes might really be of help to create an international climate revamping the "guiding philosophy behind the Bretton Woods regime," as Rodrik defines it, that is "that nations—not only the advanced nations but also the newly independent ones—needed the policy space within which they could manage their economies and protect their social contracts,"[106] for in present times, Keynes's notion of a "sounder political economy between all nations" would rest with all probability on a criticism of developed countries that adopt export-led rather than internal-demand growth policies: a well-managed system should help developing countries fill the gap with already developed nations.[107]

Now, it has been observed that Keynes developed the ICU plan having in mind a world of already developed countries, and that the plan requires a high degree of economic cooperation.[108] Keynes himself knew that, conceived "in a spirit of hopefulness which may be disappointed," his proposals assumed a high measure of "international discipline and good neighbourliness and, in general, a readiness of governments to accept proper standards of international behaviour."[109] To complicate matters, the very fact that developing countries may deliberately opt, in principle as in the current practice, for growth policies based on net exports would require "not only a coordinated policy to distribute surpluses and deficits but also an appropriate allocation of the costs of this distribution, as well as the required liquidity provision to finance them."[110] Keynes's plan should therefore be updated so as to be able to distinguish between different stages of development in applying sanctioning for the creation of excessive surpluses. And, in general, it might be an easy victim of the lack of global monetary cooperation and of willingness to proceed with constructive efforts of this kind. Still, it is to be noted that an essential feature of Keynes's plan, namely capital controls, is also a main feature of today's international economy, exactly because of the absence of an international monetary order.

In the current international non-system, the developing world is therefore trying to achieve what Keynes considered as a fundamental expected outcome of his plans of global reform. In assessing the relevance of Keynes to today's globalization, therefore, this paper has subscribed to Hans W. Singer's[111] reading of this legacy as one of "philosophy and methodology." The point is stressed with force in Newton's analysis of Keynes's World War II diplomacy, which he finds representative of a "fundamental difference of philosophy"[112] with respect to the American delegation. As is known, Keynes "wanted the two institutions to be a-political, deciding matters on technical criteria."[113] For this reason, he believed that they should be located in New York instead of Washington, that the IMF managing director should exercise unencumbered control over the institution, while its executive directors (representing their own countries) should be part-time and receive part-time salaries. This latter wanted the Fund

> to exercise constant pressure on members in the direction of currency convertibility, fixed exchange rates and non discriminatory in trade … [whereas] Keynes on the other hand, had believed that the Fund's deliberations would always be led by national policy programmes rather than the other way around. It followed that he envisaged a neutral organization which would allow the automatic use of drawing rights and meet to consider changes in exchange rates.[114]

And while Keynes had initially favored the authority of the ICU in the trade-off with members' discretion,[115] already in 1943 had he pointed out that:

> there should be the least possible interference with internal national policies and the plan should not wander from the international *terrain*. Since such policies may have important repercussions on international relations, they cannot be left out of account. Nevertheless in the realm of internal policy the authority of the Governing Board of the proposed institution should be limited to recommendations, or at the most to imposing conditions for the more extended enjoyment of the facilities which the institution offers.[116]

Helleiner has recently emphasized White's contribution to a "'development' orientation of the Bretton Woods vision,"[117] and concluded that "White and other US officials were far ahead of Keynes in mapping out an international financial order based on embedded liberal principles."[118] But Skidelsky notes that the attention posed by the Americans on Latin American countries (that is, on the "monetary indiscipline" of the area's debtor nations) is responsible for the more disciplinary character of White's plans.[119] Keynes, on the contrary, wanted the euthanasia of rentier nations to establish a principle of shared-responsibilities, but also to save policy space and variety. As Kirshner argues, Keynes believed it "a fallacy to think that every country should pursue the same macroeconomic policies."[120] Capital controls were simply necessary, in Keynes's scheme, to the aim of protecting policy heterogeneity from the push to conformity, so to speak, exercised by profit-seeking investors.[121] And it is in this sense that Keynes's "pragmatism"[122] about protection, his "practical protectionism,"[123] as Radice calls it, are to be explained. When Keynes advocated protectionism, he did so in reaction to an international system functioning in such a way as to repress, rather than safeguard, policy space:[124] he did so in reaction to the interwar gold standard, whose error, he claimed, "lay in submitting national wage-policies to outside dictation."[125]

Singer observes that when Hirschman refers to the "mutual benefit claim" of development economics, as well as to the possibility of creating a global order bringing developing countries "into a network of international relations to the mutual benefit of both themselves and the industrial countries,"[126] Keynes's "role in proposing just such a global system inevitably comes to mind."[127] This drives attention toward the holistic approach to the problems of international economic relations embedded in Keynes's plan for the creation of a "global macromanager."[128] The original ICU scheme included a series of ancillary international institutions destined to combat the evils of the trade cycle, to be financed by extra overdraft facilities, transfers from the Reserve Fund of the ICU, and, as seen, through direct contributions by surplus countries. These included a relief and reconstruction authority, a board for international investment or development corporation, a supernational policing body, and a scheme for commodity controls. This last[129] was destined to counteract a deflationary bias of the same kind of the one exercised by rentier nations.

Dating back to 1942, the "Commod Control" proposal was to be an important element of the ICU plan, and one which shared the essence of the monetary reform proposal. Here too, Keynes wrote, "we have ... a plan for international co-operation which can be safely adopted in the common interest by every country alike irrespective of its national economic policy."[130] Setting up an international body representing both producing and consuming countries should have stabilized commodity prices within a reasonable band around the normal price, and the international trade cycle with them. Fully aware of the extremely harmful effects of commodity price volatility in a context of global interdependence, Keynes argued that:

> a falling off in effective demand in the industrial consuming countries causes a price collapse which means a corresponding break in the level of income and of effective demand in the raw material producing countries, with a further adverse reaction, by repercussion, on effective demand in the industrial countries; and so, in a familiar way, the slump proceeds from bad to worse. And when the recovery comes, the rebound of excessive demand through the stimulus of inflated price promotes, in the same evil manner, the excesses of the boom.[131]

Curiously enough, Skidelsky believed it safe to argue that the urgency of such schemes "has gone out of the issue,"[132] for deterioration in developing countries' terms of trade and primary commodities volatility had proved to be less dramatic than expected. It is obviously less safe, now, to argue that "financial hedging ... offer a better alternative to physical storage."[133] As Fantacci et al. have recently pointed out, "the dogma of 'unfettered competition' has been shaken by the global financial crisis. Even commodity trading, which typically occurs on the broadest and most sophisticated futures markets, has suffered unprecedented strains."[134] In the light of this, today's world might therefore have an incentive to revisit "the remedy proposed by Keynes, as an ideal complement to the International Clearing

Union, and in the same spirit of a regulation not designed to contrast, to impede or to substitute, but rather to facilitate private transactions in commodities,"[135] in the interest of both developed and developing countries.

6 Conclusion: the vitality of Keynes's reasoning in the times of gated globalization

To offer a concrete demonstration of the vitality of Keynes's reasoning to today's world, let us consider UNCTAD's *Trade and Development Report 1981–2011*, where the "integrationist agenda" is found responsible for posing both de jure (multilateral trade and investment agreements) and de facto (capital movement and financial liberalization) constraints to policy space. Here follows a summary of each of the *Report*'s chapters, read in the light of Keynes's international economics. First, the *Report* detects the theoretical basis for the analysis of the problems of economic development in the notion of "interdependence," that is in the impact of the performances, as well as of the macroeconomic, trade and financial policies on the developing world. From the beginning (the monetarist turn in the US) to the end (revealing the dangers of borrowing policy space from abroad), the Washington Consensus saga demonstrates that Keynes was right to insist on the dilemma of the international system. The only truly disciplinary aspect of a global order that wants to defend policy space must concern undesired policies on the part of wealthier countries, which should not be free to mistake "private license" for "public liberty."

Second, the *Report* correctly ascribes the loss of policy space available to developing countries to the mix of deflationary fiscal policies included in loan conditionalities imposed by the international financial institutions and of restrictive monetary policy to counteract the emergence of inflation. On the other hand, it points to the detrimental effects of such neglect on the key variable of global demand to explain the build-up of global imbalances and the zero-sum mercantilist game played by both developed and developing countries. Keynes taught us that a successful global order must include an expansionary built-in mechanism: exactly the contrary of today's expensiveness-with-instability international nonsystem of global imbalances, nurturing these latter in the unreasonable hope that they can indefinitely persist without threatening global growth.

Third, "global economic governance." The legacy of Keynes in this regard is simply obvious. Still, two points should be noted. One is the interesting parallel between Keynes's case against capital-account liberalization, which introduces a "mobile element, highly sensitive to outside influences, as a connected part of a machine of which the other parts are much more rigid,"[136] and UNCTAD's complaint about the lack of "coherence" between today's international trade, monetary and financial systems. The other point to raise is that Keynes's "holistic approach" to international economic relations covered practically all aspects touched on by UNCTAD's *Report*: trade multilateralism and commodity price stabilization, on one side; financial instability, conditionalities, exchange rate disorder and debt problems, on the other. The *Report* itself adopts an holistic approach à la Keynes in explaining the loss of policy space available to developing countries in pursuing their national strategies. This loss derives from insufficient coherence first, "in the design of national policies across countries"; second, "between national policies and international arrangements"; third, "in the assignment and performances of international institutions."[137]

The final chapter of the *Report* includes an assessment of development strategies and policy recommendations, and concludes with a discussion of policy space in the times of the hyperglobalization. The chapter joins Rodrik in stressing that development needs experimentation:

> The most successful societies of the future will leave room for experimentation and allow for further evolution of institutions over time. A global economy that recognizes the need and value of institutional diversity would foster rather than stifle such experimentation and evolution.[138]

Now, if Rodrik is right, we do not need a new development agenda, but a new global order. One that leaves room for experimentation, and manages the cohabitation of different varieties of national capitalisms without attempting to reduce them to the only "right" model. If Rodrik is right, Keynes should come back.

Notes

 1 Helleiner (2010, p. 620).
 2 Helleiner (2010, p. 635).
 3 See Grabel (2011).
 4 See Babb (2013).
 5 See Gore (2000, p. 801).
 6 Babb (2013, p. 291).
 7 See Ruggie (1982).
 8 James (2012, p. 412).
 9 See Helleiner (2003).
10 James (2012, p. 428).
11 Helleiner (2010, p. 620).
12 James (2012, p. 412).
13 Rodrik (2000, p. 183).
14 James (2012, p. 428).
15 Among others, see Ikenberry (1993) and Boughton (2002).
16 Williamson (1983, p. 107).
17 Williamson (1983, p. 88).
18 Keynes (1980a, p. 43).
19 See Cedrini (2008).
20 See Carabelli and Cedrini (2010–2011).
21 Dimand (2006, p. 175).
22 Keynes (1971 [1930], p. 272).
23 Kregel (2008a, p. 168).
24 Kregel (2008a, p. 169).
25 See De Cecco (1974).
26 Reported in Fleming (2000, p. 142).
27 Keynes (1971 [1930], p. 335).
28 Kregel (2008b, pp. 553–554).

29 See Câmara Neto and Vernengo (2002–2003).
30 See Ocampo (2004–2005).
31 Hirschman (1981).
32 Williamson (2002).
33 See Quiggin (2005).
34 Stiglitz (2002, p. 213).
35 Rodrik (2004).
36 Ocampo (2004–2005).
37 Vestergaard (2004, p. 818).
38 Krugman (1998).
39 Rodrik (1999, p. 118).
40 Rodrik (2006, p. 974).
41 Stiglitz (2002, p. 88).
42 Williamson (1983, p. 87).
43 Williamson (1983, p. 109).
44 Gore (2000, p. 793).
45 See Rodrik (1998).
46 See Carabelli (1988).
47 Keynes (1983, p. 856).
48 Keynes (1983, p. 856).
49 Keynes (1973 [1936], p. 297).
50 Keynes (1972 [1933], p. 262).
51 Vines (2003, p. 339).
52 De Cecco (2001).
53 Cairncross (1978, p. 46).
54 Moggridge (1986, p. 71).
55 Moggridge (1986, p. 71).
56 Keynes (1973 [1936], p. 349).
57 Keynes (1973 [1936], p. 349).
58 Keynes (1973 [1936], pp. 382–383).
59 Keynes (1980a, p. 31).
60 Keynes (1980b, pp. 16–17). See Dimand (2006).
61 Keynes (1980a, p. 21).
62 Keynes (1980a, p. 27).
63 Reported in Skidelsky (2000, p. 213).
64 Keynes (1980a, p. 74).
65 Keynes (1980a, p. 457).
66 Vines (2003, p. 349).
67 See Newton (2000).
68 See Elliott and Jensen (1997).
69 Keynes (1980a, p. 74).
70 Keynes (1980a, p. 210).
71 Keynes (1982, p. 42).
72 Keynes (1980a, p. 26).
73 Keynes (1980a, p. 47).
74 Keynes (1979, p. 609).
75 Carabelli and Cedrini (2010a).
76 Carabelli and Cedrini (2010b).
77 Keynes (1979, p. 340).
78 Keynes (1979, p. 272).
79 Keynes (1979, p. 328).
80 Keynes (1979, p. 61).
81 Keynes (1979, p. 608).
82 Keynes (1979, p. 622).

 83 Keynes (1973 [1936], p. 380).
 84 See Carabelli and Cedrini (2011).
 85 Keynes (1973 [1936], p. 380).
 86 Keynes (1980a, p. 193).
 87 Rodrik (2007).
 88 Kregel (1999).
 89 Feldstein (1999).
 90 Cruz and Walters (2008, pp. 666–667).
 91 Ocampo (2007).
 92 Aizenman (2008).
 93 Suominen (2010).
 94 Davidson (2004–2005, p. 213).
 95 Davidson (2004–2005, p. 217).
 96 Mann (2005).
 97 Frieden et al. (2011).
 98 Carabelli and Cedrini (2010b).
 99 Carabelli and Cedrini (2011).
100 Keynes (1971 [1913], p. 71).
101 Keynes (1971 [1913], p. 71).
102 Keynes (1971 [1913], p. 91).
103 Kregel (2009, p. 5).
104 Kregel (2009, p. 5).
105 See Chandavarkar (1986) and Toye (2006).
106 Rodrik (2013, p. 8).
107 Kregel (2006).
108 See Davidson (2009).
109 Keynes (1980c, pp. 13–38).
110 Kregel (2009, p. 5).
111 Singer (1987, p. 70).
112 Newton (2000, p. 202).
113 Skidelsky (2000, p. 465).
114 Skidelsky (2000, p. 465).
115 Moggridge (1986).
116 Keynes (1980a, p. 234).
117 Helleiner (2006, p. 964).
118 Helleiner (2006, p. 963).
119 Skidelsky (2005, p. 21).
120 Kirshner (1999, p. 316). See also Kirshner 2009.
121 See also Kregel (2008a).
122 Kirshner (1999, p. 322).
123 Radice (1988).
124 See also Eichengreen (1984).
125 Keynes (1980b, p. 33).
126 Singer (1987, p. 71).
127 Singer (1985, p. 141).
128 Skidelsky (2005, p. 21).
129 See Thirlwall (2007, 1987) and Fantacci et al. (2012).
130 Keynes (1980c, p. 162).
131 Keynes (1980c, p. 121).
132 Skidelsky (2005, pp. 24–25).
133 Skidelsky (2005, pp. 24–25).
134 Fantacci et al. (2012, p. 469).
135 Fantacci et al. (2012, p. 470).
136 Keynes (1971 [1930], pp. 334–335).

137 UNCTAD (2012, p. 37).
138 Rodrik (2011, pp. 239–240).

References

Aizenman, J. (2008) "Large Hoarding of International Reserves and the Emerging Global Economic Architecture," *The Manchester School*, 76(5): 487–503.

Babb, S. (2013) "The Washington Consensus as Transnational Policy Paradigm: Its Origins, Trajectory and Likely Successor," *Review of International Political Economy*, 20(2): 286–297.

Boughton, J. M. (2002) "Why White, Not Keynes? Inventing the Postwar International Monetary System," in A. Arnon and W. Young (eds.) *The Open Economy Macromodel: Past, Present and Future*, Norwell, MA/Dordrecht: Kluwer, pp. 73–102.

Bourdieu, P. (1998) "The Essence of Neoliberalism," *Le Monde Diplomatique*, December, available at: http://mondediplo.com/1998/12/08bourdieu.

Cairncross, A. (1978) "Keynes and the Planned Economy," in A. Thirlwall (ed.) *Keynes and Laissez-Faire*, London: Macmillan, pp. 36–58.

Câmara Neto, A. F. and Vernengo, M. (2002–2003) "Globalization, A Dangerous Obsession: Latin America in the Post-Washington Consensus Era," *International Journal of Political Economy*, 32(4): 4–21.

Carabelli, A. M. (1988) *On Keynes's Method*, London: Macmillan.

Carabelli, A. M. and Cedrini, M. A. (2010–2011) "Indian Currency and Beyond: The Legacy of the Early Economics of Keynes in the Times of Bretton Woods II," *Journal of Post Keynesian Economics*, 33(2): 255–279.

Carabelli, A. M. and Cedrini, M. A. (2010a) "Keynes and the Complexity of International Economic Relations in the Aftermath of World War I," *Journal of Economic Issues*, 44(4): 1009–1027.

Carabelli, A. M. and Cedrini, M. A. (2010b) "Current Global Imbalances, Might Keynes Be of Help?" in M. C. Marcuzzo, T. Hirai and B. Bateman (eds.) *The Return to Keynes*, Cambridge, MA: Harvard University Press, pp. 257–274.

Carabelli, A. M. and Cedrini, M. A. (2011) "The Economic Problem of Happiness. Keynes on Happiness and Economics," *Forum for Social Economics*, 40(3): 335–339.

Cedrini, M. A. (2008) "Consensus Versus Freedom or Consensus Upon Freedom? From Washington Disorder to the Rediscovery of Keynes," *Journal of Post Keynesian Economics*, 30(4): 499–522.

Chandavarkar, A. G. (1986) "Was Keynes a Development Economist?" *Economic and Political Weekly*, 21(7): 304–307.

Chang, H.-J. (2006) "Policy Space in Historical Perspective—with Special Reference to Trade and Industrial Policies," *Economic and Political Weekly*, 41(7): 627–633.

Cruz, M. and Walters, B. (2008) "Is the Accumulation of International Reserves Good for Development?" *Cambridge Journal of Economics*, 32(5): 665–681.

Davidson, P. (2004–2005) "A Post Keynesian View of the Washington Consensus and How to Improve It," *Journal of Post Keynesian Economics*, 27(2): 207–230.

Davidson, P. (2009) *The Keynes Solution: The Path to Global Economic Prosperity*, New York, NY: Palgrave Macmillan.

De Cecco, M. (1974) *Money and Empire: The International Gold Standard, 1890–1914*, Oxford: Basil Blackwell.

De Cecco, M. (2001) "John Maynard Keynes," *Rivista di storia economica*, 17(3): 373–382.

Dimand, R. W. (2006) "Keynes and Global Economic Integration," *Atlantic Economic Journal*, 34(2): 175–182.

Dooley, M. P., Folkerts-Landau, D. and Garber, P. (2003) "An Essay on the Revived Bretton Woods System," National Bureau of Economic Research Working Paper No. 9971.

Eichengreen, B. (1984) "Keynes and Protection," *The Journal of Economic History*, 44(2): 363–373.

Elliott, J. E. and Jensen, H. E. (1997) "John Maynard Keynes on Socio-Economic Classes in Twentieth-Century Capitalism," in J. P. Henderson (ed.) *The State of the History of Economics*, London/New York: Routledge, pp. 105–129.

Fantacci, L., Marcuzzo, M. C., Rosselli, A. and Sanfilippo, E. (2012) "Speculation and Commodities: The Legacy of Keynes and Kahn," *European Journal of the History of Economic Thought*, 19(3): 453–473.

Feldstein, M. A. (1999) "Self-Help Guide for Emerging Markets," *Foreign Affairs*, 78(2): 93–109.

Fleming, G. (2000) "Foreign Investment, Reparations and the Proposal for an International Bank: Notes on the Lectures of J. M. Keynes in Geneva, July 1929," *Cambridge Journal of Economics*, 24(2): 139–151.

Frieden, J., Pettis, M. and Rodrik, D. (2011) "After the Fall: The Future of Global Cooperation," *Geneva Reports on the World Economy*, 14, London: Centre for Economic Policy Research.

Gore, C. (2000) "The Rise and Fall of the Washington Consensus as a Paradigm for Developing Countries," *World Development*, 28(5): 789–804.

Grabel, I. (2011) "Not Your Grandfather's IMF: Global Crisis, 'Productive Incoherence' and Developmental Policy Space," *Cambridge Journal of Economics*, 35(5): 805–830.

Helleiner, E. (2003) "Economic Liberalism and its Critics: The Past as Prologue?" *Review of International Political Economy*, 10(4): 685–696.

Helleiner, E. (2006) "Reinterpreting Bretton Woods: International Development and the Neglected Origins of Embedded Liberalism," *Development and Change*, 37(5): 943–967.

Helleiner, E. (2010) "A Bretton Woods Moment? The 2007–2008 Crisis and the Future of Global Finance," *International Affairs*, 86(3): 619–636.

Hirschman, A. O. (1981) "The Rise and Decline of Development Economics," in A. O. Hirschman (ed.) *Essays in Trespassing: Economics to Politics & Beyond*, Cambridge: Cambridge University Press, pp. 1–24.

Ikenberry, G. J. (1993) "Creating Yesterday's New World Order: Keynesian 'New Thinking' and the Anglo-American Postwar Settlement," in J. Goldstein and R. O. Keohane (eds.) *Ideas and Foreign Policy. Beliefs, Institutions, and Political Change*, Ithaca, NY/London: Cornell University Press, pp. 57–86.

James, H. (2012) "The Multiple Contexts of Bretton Woods," *Oxford Review of Economic Policy*, 28(3): 411–430.

Keynes, J. M. (1971 [1913]) *Indian Currency and Finance*, Vol. 1 in E. Johnson and D. E. Moggridge (eds.) *The Collected Writings of John Maynard Keynes*, London: Macmillan.

Keynes, J. M. (1971 [1919]) *The Economic Consequences of Peace*, Vol. 2 in E. Johnson and D. E. Moggridge (eds.) *The Collected Writings of John Maynard Keynes*, London: Macmillan.

Keynes, J. M. (1971 [1930]) *A Treatise on Money: II. The Applied Theory of Money*, Vol. 6 in E. Johnson and D. E. Moggridge (eds.) *The Collected Writings of John Maynard Keynes*, London: Macmillan.

Keynes, J. M. (1972 [1933]) *Essays in Biography*, Vol. 10 in E. Johnson and D. E. Moggridge (eds.) *The Collected Writings of John Maynard Keynes*, London: Macmillan.

Keynes, J. M. (1973 [1936]) *The General Theory of Employment, Interest and Money*, Vol. 7 in E. Johnson and D. E. Moggridge (eds.) *The Collected Writings of John Maynard Keynes*, London: Macmillan.

Keynes, J. M. (1979) *Activities 1944–1946: The Transition to Peace*, Vol. 24 in E. Johnson and D. E. Moggridge (eds.) *The Collected Writings of John Maynard Keynes*, London: Macmillan.

Keynes, J. M. (1980a) *Activities 1940–44: Shaping the Post-War World: The Clearing Union*, Vol. 25 in E. Johnson and D. E. Moggridge (eds.) *The Collected Writings of John Maynard Keynes*, London: Macmillan.

Keynes, J. M. (1980b) *Activities 1941–46: Shaping the Post-War World: Bretton Woods and Reparations*, Vol. 26 in E. Johnson and D. E. Moggridge (eds.) *The Collected Writings of John Maynard Keynes*, London: Macmillan.

Keynes, J. M. (1980c) *Activities 1940–46: Shaping the Post-War World: Employment and Commodities*, Vol. 27 in E. Johnson and D. E. Moggridge (eds.) *The Collected Writings of John Maynard Keynes*, London: Macmillan.

Keynes, J. M. (1982) *Activities 1931–39: World Crisis and Policies in Britain and America*, Vol. 21 in E. Johnson and D. E. Moggridge (eds.) *The Collected Writings of John Maynard Keynes*, London: Macmillan.

Keynes, J. M. (1983) *Economic Articles and Correspondence: Investment and Editorial*, Vol. 12 in E. Johnson and D. E. Moggridge (eds.) *The Collected Writings of John Maynard Keynes*, London: Macmillan.

Kirshner, J. (1999) "Keynes, Capital Mobility and the Crisis of Embedded Liberalism." *Review of International Political Economy*, 6(3): 313–337.

Kirshner, J. (2009) "Keynes, Legacies and Inquiries," *Theory and Society*, 38(5): 527–541.

Kregel, J. A. (1999) "A New Triffin Paradox for the Global Economy," remarks prepared for the Federal Council of Economists and the Regional Council of Economists of Rio de Janeiro meeting of the 13th Brazilian Congress of Economists and the 7th Congress of the Association of Economists from Latin-America and the Caribbean, September 15, available at: http://cas.umkc.edu/econ/economics/faculty/Kregel/Econ%20512/.

Kregel, J. A. (2006) "Understanding Imbalances in a Globalised International Economic System," in J. J. Teunissen and A. Akkerman (eds.) *Global Imbalances and the US Debt Problem: Should Developing Countries Support the US Dollar?* The Hague: Fondad, pp. 149–173

Kregel, J. A. (2008a) "What Can Keynes Tell Us About Policies to Reduce Unemployment and Financial Instability in a Globalised International Economy?" *METU Studies in Development*, 35: 161–176.

Kregel, J. A. (2009) "Some Simple Observations on the Reform of the International Monetary System," Levy Economics Institute of Bard College Policy Note No. 8.

Kregel, J. A. (2008b) "The Discrete Charm of the Washington Consensus." *Journal of Post Keynesian Economics*, 30(4): 541–560.

Krugman, P. (1998) "The Confidence Game: How Washington Worsened Asia's Crash," *New Republic*, October 5, 219(14): 23–25.

Mann, C. L. (2005) "Breaking Up Is Hard to Do: Global Co-Dependency, Collective Action, and the Challenges of Global Adjustment," *CESifo Forum*, 1: 16–23.

Moggridge, D. E. (1986) "Keynes and the International Monetary System 1909–46," in J. S. Cohen and G. C. Harcourt (eds.) *International Monetary Problems and Supply-Side Economics: Essays in Honour of Lorie Tarshis*, London: Macmillan, pp. 56–83.

Newton, S. (2000) "A 'Visionary Hope' Frustrated: J. M. Keynes and the Origins of the Postwar International Monetary Order," *Diplomacy and Statecraft*, 11(1): 189–210.

Ocampo, J. A. (2004–2005) "Beyond the Washington Consensus: What Do We Mean?" *Journal of Post Keynesian Economics*, 27(2): 293–314.

Ocampo, J. A. (2007) "The Instability and Inequities of the Global Reserve System," *International Journal of Political Economy*, 36(4): 71–96.

Polanyi-Levitt, K. (2006) "Keynes and Polanyi: The 1920s and the 1990s," *Review of International Political Economy*, 13(1): 152–177.

Quiggin, J. (2005) "Interpreting Globalization. Neoliberal and Internationalist Views of Changing Patterns of the Global Trade and Financial System," Overarching Concern Programme Paper number 7, United Nations Research Institute for Social Development, available at: www.unrisd.org/80256b3c005bccf9/%28httpauxpages%29/6080e2e 34d6e8934c12570b4004b2a71/$file/quiggin.pdf.

Radice, H. (1988) "Keynes and the Policy of Practical Protectionism," in J. Hillard (ed.) *J. M. Keynes in Retrospect: The Legacy of the Keynesian Revolution*, Aldershot: Edward Elgar, pp. 152–171.

Rodrik, D. (1998) "The Global Fix: A Plan to Save the World Economy," *New Republic*, November 2, 219(18): 17–20.

Rodrik, D. (1999) "Governing the Global Economy: Does One Architectural Style Fit All?" in S. Collins and R. Lawrence (eds.) (2000) *Brookings Trade Forum: 1999*, Brookings Institution, Washington, DC, pp. 105–126.

Rodrik, D. (2000) "How Far Will International Economic Integration Go?" *Journal of Economic Perspectives*, 14(1): 177–186.

Rodrik, D. (2004) "Rethinking Economic Growth in Developing Countries," Second Luca d'Agliano Lecture in Development Economics, Fondazione Luigi Einaudi, Turin, October 8, available at: http://ksghome.harvard.edu/~drodrik/Luca_d_Agliano_ Lecture_Oct_2004.pdf.

Rodrik, D. (2006) "Goodbye Washington Consensus, Hello Washington Confusion? A Review of the World Bank's 'Economic Growth in the 1990s: Learning from a Decade of Reform'," *Journal of Economic Literature*, 44(4): 973–987.

Rodrik, D. (2007) *One Economics, Many Recipes: Globalization, Institutions, and Economic Growth*, Princeton, NJ: Princeton University Press.

Rodrik, D. (2011) *The Globalization Paradox. Democracy and the Future of the World Economy*, New York, NY/London: W. W. Norton.

Rodrik, D. (2013) "Roepke Lecture in Economic Geography: Who Needs the Nation State?" *Economic Geography*, 89(1): 1–19.

Ruggie, J. G. (1982) "International Regimes, Transactions, and Change: Embedded Liberalism in the Postwar Economic Order," *International Organization*, 36(2): 379–415.

Singer, H. W. (1985) "Relevance of Keynes for Developing Countries," in H. L. Wattel (ed.) *The Policy Consequences of John Maynard Keynes*, Armonk, NY: Sharpe, pp. 128–143.

Singer, H. W. (1987) "What Keynes and Keynesianism Can Teach Us About Less Developed Countries," in A. Thirlwall (ed.) *Keynes and Economic Development: The Seventh Keynes Seminar Held at the University of Kent at Canterbury, 1985*, London: Macmillan, pp. 70–89.

Skidelsky, R. (2000) *John Maynard Keynes. Vol. 3: Fighting for Britain, 1937–1946*, London: Macmillan.

Skidelsky, R. (2005) "Keynes, Globalisation and the Bretton Woods Institutions in the Light of Changing Ideas About Markets," *World Economics*, 6(1): 15–30.

Stiglitz, J. E. (2002) *Globalization and Its Discontents*, New York, NY: W. W. Norton.

Suominen, K. (2010) "Did Global Imbalances Cause the Crisis?" *Vox*, June 14, available at: www.voxeu.org/article/did-global-imbalances-cause-crisis.

The Economist (2013) *Special Report: World Economy*, October 12, available at: www.economist.com/printedition/2013-10-12.

Thirlwall, A. P. (1987) "Keynes, Economic Development and the Developing Countries," in A. Thirlwall (ed.) *Keynes and Economic Development: The Seventh Keynes Seminar Held at the University of Kent at Canterbury, 1985*, London: Macmillan, pp. 3–35.

Thirlwall, A. P. (2007) "Keynes and Economic Development," *Economia Aplicada*, 11(3): 447–457.

Toye, J. (2006) "Keynes and Development Economics: A Sixty-Years Perspective," *Journal of International Development*, 18(7): 983–995.

UNCTAD (2012) *Trade and Development Report, 1981–2011: Three Decades of Thinking Development*, New York, NY/Geneva: UNCTAD.

Vestergaard, J. (2004) "The Asian Crisis and the Shaping of 'Proper' Economies," *Cambridge Journal of Economics*, 28(6): 809–827.

Vines, D. (2003) "John Maynard Keynes 1937–1946: The Creation of International Macroeconomics," *Economic Journal*, 113(488): 338–361.

Williamson, J. (1983) "Keynes and the International Economic Order," in D. Worswick and J. Trevithick (eds.) *Keynes and the Modern World*, Cambridge: Cambridge University Press, pp. 87–113.

Williamson, J. (2002) "Did the Washington Consensus Fail?" outline of speech at the Center for Strategic & International Studies Washington, DC, November 6, available at: www.iie.com/publications/papers/paper.cfm?ResearchID=488.

4 Globalization and the ladder of comparative advantage

Roger J. Sandilands

"The division of labour is limited by the size of the market."

(Adam Smith, 1776)

1 Introduction

With Asian and Latin American examples, this paper examines the conditions under which openness to world trade and investment can foster both faster growth and greater income equality between and within countries. The theory of comparative advantage is explained from a dynamic point of view. This highlights the need for outward-oriented development strategies to be accompanied by complementary measures to enhance the geographic and occupational mobility of labor as the growth process alters countries' comparative advantage. Growth and income distribution benefits are maximized when factors of production are helped to move smoothly from activities where comparative advantage is being eroded (for example because rising real wages undermine the ability to export labor-intensive products) to those where new opportunities emerge. The complementary role of foreign investment in this process is also indicated. As countries develop though trade-induced industrialization and urbanization, land values escalate in metropolises such as Shanghai, Bombay, Singapore and Bogota (albeit interrupted with some sharp, disruptive downturns) with adverse effects on income distribution and stability. These negative features of globalization require policies that direct these unearned increments away from landowners and toward the wider community.

2 Productivity and market size

Adam Smith's famous aphorism above is the fundamental insight that drove him to protest against the dominant mercantilist philosophy of his time. He is best understood not as the advocate of unbridled laissez-faire—which may lead producers to defend protectionism and monopoly—but rather as the champion of competition and openness on behalf of the consumer, not least the worker as consumer. Thus the opening chapters of his *opus magnum* stress how important for the wealth of nations is the "power of exchanging" (Smith 1976 [1776]: 21).

He explains that this power is greatest where markets are most open and that the greater the opportunity to exchange, the greater is labor's productivity. To give this central idea maximum impact, he opens his treatise thus: "The greatest improvement in the productive powers of labour, and the greatest part of the skill, dexterity and judgment with which it is anywhere directed, or applied, seem to have been the effects of the division of labour."

As stressed elsewhere (Sandilands 2009; Chandra and Sandilands 2005), one of the most fertile extensions of Smith's aphorism on the importance of open markets, nationally and internationally, was by Allyn Young (1928) in his seminal paper on "Increasing Returns and Economic Progress." He complained that most of Smith's successors were:

> disappointingly vague with respect to the origins and the precise nature of the "improvements" which they counted upon to retard somewhat the operation of the tendency toward diminishing returns in agriculture and to secure a progressively more effective use of labor in manufactures.
>
> (Young 1928, p. 529)

Thus Young's intention was to convert Smith's insights into a broader theory of increasing returns or self-sustaining growth that depended on the growth of increasingly capital-intensive methods and the division of labor among increasingly specialized firms, as and when the size of the market grew.

Market size could grow because of the elimination of mercantilist and monopolistic barriers to entry. Also, because the organizational and technical changes that larger markets make economical are themselves the cause of price reductions that further extend consumers' purchasing power in a process of cumulative circular causation.

Young explained this theory of self-sustaining growth in terms of reciprocal real exchange in the marketplace, abstracting from the money and finance that intermediate the vast bulk of these transactions. But while money and finance are an essential element in the extension of the market, they can also be a barrier to progress and a cause of national and global business cycles if mismanaged, nationally or internationally (as stressed by Wolf 2009). It was a tragedy that Young, one of the world's most prominent monetary theorists and policy advisers, met an early death in 1929 on the eve of the Great Depression of the 1930s. In view of the prominence at this workshop of scholars who have studied both the world economy and more specifically the place of Colombia as an "emerging economy" over the past 50 years, my chapter will conclude by referring to ways in which one of Young's most prominent Harvard students, Lauchlin Currie (1902–1993), developed his ideas on money and growth as a top economic adviser, first in the Roosevelt Administration, 1934–1945, and then as a development economist in Colombia from 1949 until his death in 1993, and his continuing influence in that country thereafter.

3 The ladder of comparative advantage

Another of Young's students at Harvard (in 1922–1923) was Bertil Ohlin who would later win a Nobel prize for his work on trade theory. Ohlin wrote:

> I am inclined to believe that [Young] was a man, who knew and thoroughly understood his subject—economics—better than anyone else I have met. I tested him by means of a question about the "Wicksell effect," i.e. the special aspects of the marginal productivity of capital, which at that time was practically unknown in most countries outside of Scandinavia. He immediately gave a fine account in a five minutes speech before the students.
>
> (Sandilands 1999, p. 473)

The Wicksell effect, or effects, as Heinz Kurz (2008) explains, concern ways in which alterations in the distribution of income between labor and capital (and ignoring land as a separate factor) affect (1) relative product prices (especially between consumer and producer goods)—the "price Wicksell effect"; and (2) the choice of techniques (the labor–capital ratio)—the "real Wicksell effect." Both effects are generally held to be positive, although interesting caveats were hotly debated during the capital controversies of the 1950s and 1960s that pitted Cambridge England against Cambridge Massachusetts in their evaluation of neo-classical marginal productivity theory of efficient resource allocation and ethically defensible income distribution under putative free-market capitalism. Ohlin was the co-author of the famous Heckscher–Ohlin theory of comparative advantage. He related each nation's set of relative factor prices to their relative factor supplies which in turn explained their relative product prices, hence their comparative advantage in international trade.

This took trade theory beyond David Ricardo's theory of comparative advantage which was an extension of Smith's explanation of the wealth of nations based on the above dictum that the *absolute* productivity of labor depends on the division of labor and the size of the market. Ricardo explained that even the poorest nations, with very low productivity in all lines of production, could still engage advantageously in trade so long as there was some line in which their absolute disadvantage was less than elsewhere, and so long as low overall productivity was reflected in a similarly low going wage rate.

Ricardo's theory thus greatly increased the extent to which nations could profitably engage in mutually advantageous trade through productivity-enhancing specialization. But Ricardo is also regarded as the originator of the modern theory of diminishing returns (or diminishing marginal productivity) and the related theory of rent. As one factor of production (such as labor or capital) increases relative to other factors (notably land, the "free gift of Nature" but whose supply is fixed), its marginal productivity and price tend to decline (and vice versa). In modern textbooks, Ricardo's theory of trade has been caricatured as a one-factor (labor) theory of value and price. But his theory of rent, based on diminishing marginal product of labor as population increases relative to the fixed supply of natural resources, indicates a more sophisticated understanding of the basis of comparative advantage than he is commonly allowed. His celebrated example of Portugal with a comparative advantage in wine while England's was in cloth, despite England having a lower absolute advantage in both, was based on Portugal having a greater abundance of natural resources (including sunshine) relative to its population, and because wine is relatively more land-intensive than cloth. However, Eli Heckscher and Bertil Ohlin spelled out a factor-proportions (and related factor-abundance) explanation of comparative advantage that was more explicit than Ricardo's.

Nevertheless, Ricardo's classical theory of comparative costs provides other insights that are often obscured by modern neoclassical theory. First, his was a labor theory of value (as was Smith's) that highlighted that capital goods could be regarded as "stored-up" or "indirect" labor, so that relative product prices could be determined as the present value of direct and indirect labor, with the cost of land (in the form of Ricardian rents) being a transfer payment, or surplus, hence not a cost of production from the social point of view.[1] In modern theory, land tends to be lumped in with capital, and so-called $2 \times 2 \times 2$ models are constructed with two countries trading two commodities that embody (in different proportions) just two factors of production, "capital" and labor. This somewhat vitiates the comprehensiveness of Ohlin's neoclassical trade theory insofar as it is in line with, and may have evolved from, Wicksell's two-factor (direct and indirect labor) approach to the effect of changing relative factor prices upon the evolution of product prices, hence comparative advantage through time and in different countries.

Second, Ricardo's static or snapshot analysis of the example of the comparative cost differences that drove the pattern of trade of wine for cloth between Portugal and England, and how this represented an advance over Smith's explanation of trade, should not distract us from a more important motive behind Ricardo's analysis, namely, to stress the role of specialization in offsetting his own so-called "law" of diminishing returns by extending the size of the market. Comparative advantage drives specialization, and specialization drives productivity. But as it drives productivity, it also drives the accumulation of different factors at different rates. This in turn helps determine the distribution of income—not only between the rate of interest and the wage rate, as in the analysis of Wicksell effects, but also between these and the rent of land and natural resources whose overall supply is fixed, even if access to them is affected by the application of labor and capital to the opening up of cultivable land or exploitation of mineral reserves.

4 Growth, globalization, and the dynamic ladder of comparative advantage

Allyn Young's most notable contribution was his analysis of specialization in the theory of growth and, by extension, in trade theory also. Dissatisfaction with neoclassical growth and trade theories has recently spawned new interest in Young's theory of increasing returns. The result is modern endogenous growth theory (with Paul Romer perhaps the best-known contributor; e.g., Romer 1994) and "new" trade theory (with Paul Krugman's work perhaps the best known; e.g., Krugman 1990).

The new growth theory has been driven by attempts to explain, or endogenize, the unexplained or exogenous productivity growth that characterizes long-run growth in the seminal neoclassical growth models of Robert Solow (1956) and Trevor Swan (1956). Empirical tests of these models (in which the rewards to labor and capital were taken as a measure of their marginal product) seemed to reveal that additional inputs of labor and capital have often played a minor role in growth as compared to the increased productivity of these inputs. Yet the early models offered little explanation of this so-called "total factor productivity growth," or "technical progress," or "residual," or "measure of our ignorance" (Moses Abramovitz 1956, p. 11, 1989, p. 15). If the aggregate production function could be characterized as exhibiting constant returns to scale but diminishing marginal product to each factor taken separately, countries could be expected to converge toward a similar level of per capita income if international trade and capital flows were liberalized.

This would, in theory, have two main effects: First, the opening up of international trade would mean that poor countries could increase their export of relatively labor-intensive goods and services (including the direct export of low-wage labor) in exchange for imports of relatively capital-intensive goods and services (including human capital), thereby tending to drive up wage rates in poor countries while restraining the wages of lower-skilled workers in rich countries. However, the expected benign effect of increased trade on wages in low-wage countries would be disguised if rapid population growth increased the supply of labor faster than trade increased the demand, as has often been the case.

Second, the neoclassical models suggested that international capital flows would reinforce the benign effect of trade on poor-country wages and restrain the growth of wages in high-wage countries.[2] This was explained by the expectation that rich, capital-abundant countries would have relatively low marginal rates of return on investment (because of the "law" of diminishing returns), inducing a flow of capital from rich to poor countries where return on capital is greater, so that workers would have more capital and technology to work with, thus boosting their productivity and wages (again assuming the effect is not diluted by population growth).

In view of the relative lack of economic convergence between rich and poor countries, modern endogenous growth and trade theories have sought to explain this by reference to the way in which innovation—new ideas embodied in technical processes and new products—yield special kinds of external benefits that maintain the return on capital in rich countries beyond what neoclassical theory predicts. New ideas are non-rivalrous (in the sense that firms may acquire new knowledge without taking that knowledge away from those who already possess it) and only partially excludable (because it is hard to keep trade secrets, and patents offer only limited protection).

Allyn Young also stressed these features of new ideas, and drew two important implications that differentiate his ideas on increasing returns from some of the recent endogenous growth theorists. First, he agreed that because new ideas are largely non-excludable the return to innovators is much less than their social productivity. Therefore what conventional factors are paid may greatly exaggerate their contributions to growth. But this did not, in his view, justify strong patent protection nor tariffs that promote "industrial policy" to internalize the externalities associated with innovative industries. He regarded pecuniary externalities as inherent in the market process, which means their elimination would, by keeping taxes and/or prices high, also reduce the gains from expansion of reciprocal trade.

Second, the productivity gains arising from increased market size were not so much gains from increased size of firm—or economies of scale in the microeconomic sense—but rather gains from specialization due to a larger overall market size. For, "with the extension of the division of labor among industries the representative firm, like the industry of which it is a part, loses its identity" (Young 1928, p. 538), and may be larger or smaller than its predecessors. Any internal economies of scale will tend to

> dissolve into the internal and external economies of the more highly specialized undertakings which are its successors, and are supplemented by new economies. Insofar as it is an adjustment to a new situation created by the growth of the market for the final products of industry the division of labor among industries is a vehicle of increasing returns. It is more than a change of form incidental to the full securing of the advantages of capitalistic methods of production—although it is largely that—for it has some advantages of its own which are independent of changes in productive technique.
>
> (ibid.)

Thus capital is important for the aggregate degree of roundaboutness, though the individual firm may not need more capital than its less specialized predecessor. But the greater the degree of overall roundaboutness, the greater the productivity in the economy; and it is this that can explain why the underlying trend of endogenous growth may be self-sustaining rather than self-exhausting as in the Solow (1956) model. Dynamically, the "law" of diminishing returns is offset by the economies of specialization.

This may partly explain why capital may flow "uphill" internationally or, rather, why it flows two ways between rich and poor countries in search of heterogeneous returns that depend on differing factor prices in different industries. The $2 \times 2 \times 2$ models of trade and investment cannot explain the rich tapestry of modern trade relations. The great bulk of global trade in recent decades has taken the form of "intra-industry" trade between rich industrialized countries rather than "inter-industry" trade between rich and poor countries. The latter type is the focus of the Heckscher–Ohlin theory and the related Stolper–Samuelson theorem that predicts factor-price equalization from trade in products whose factor intensities differ greatly.[3]

Nevertheless, the theory of increasing returns from increasing market size (a theory that has been characterized, non-tautologically, as explaining growth largely by growth itself) predicts that both kinds of international trade promote a more rapid growth of the global economy, inducing more rapid accumulation of capital and innovation that have the potential to boost global wages, especially for workers in low-wage countries. The main offsets again would be the drag of population growth and the related rise in land and natural resource rents as global growth boosts demand for these resources (even as technical progress can mitigate these pressures on cost).

In this process of global growth—inherently self-sustaining (in the absence of exogenous shocks or binding resource constraints) through increasing specialization—changes in international relative wages, interest rates and resource rents, plus changes in patterns of demand, will dictate continuous changes in the global pattern and ladder of comparative advantage. These changes are disruptive in that they impose a greater burden on the mobility mechanism, especially labor mobility. To take full advantage of the new opportunities that these changes offer requires a high degree of occupational and geographical mobility of labor and capital to those sectors and locations where actual and potential returns are growing most rapidly. In developing countries this implies a faster rate of rural–urban migration. This has huge cultural, political and sociological implications that may not be comfortable. But the alternatives—lower economic growth, per capita income, standards of health and education, and high birth rates—may be even less comfortable.

5 The ladder of comparative advantage: a Singaporean example

Those countries that most successfully embrace and promote competition and mobility will tend to enjoy relatively fast growth through progressive cost and (real) price reductions, with associated increases in real purchasing power. This goes hand in hand with (1) relatively fast erosion of these countries' traditional areas of comparative advantage, plus (2) relatively fast opening up of new opportunities in sectors that become newly competitive internationally as their productivity improves with the progressive accumulation of physical and human capital and technology.

Thus, to give one dramatic example from which much can be generalized, Singapore in the 1960s and early 1970s had a strong comparative advantage in simple, labor-intensive products such as textiles, and these sectors attracted considerable foreign investment. Per capita growth averaged more than 8 percent a year between 1965–1975, and as wages rose so labor-intensive manufacturing and services (especially in the busy port) rapidly gave way to more capital- and skill-intensive products and activities (Sandilands and Tan 1986).

Firms complained of "disloyal" job-hopping but the government ignored these complaints. If firms lost their competitive edge their resources were to flow to sectors where demand and rewards were greater. Overall, the country's real costs and prices fell continuously, and monetary inflation was lower than anywhere in the world. With the growth of the market many firms failed, only to be replaced by new firms specializing in activities where new comparative advantages were emerging. The firms that disappeared reappeared in new forms in Malaysia, then China, Vietnam and Cambodia, with Singapore happily importing labor-intensive products from there instead of wasting her own resources on them. Singapore meanwhile increasingly exported in exchange pharmaceuticals, specialist optical instruments and refined oil, or high-quality health, education, legal and architectural services.

From 1965 to 1987, Singapore ran a trade deficit every year (Lloyd and Sandilands 1986; Sandilands 1992). Though her exports grew at more than twice the rate as GDP, imports grew even faster. The difference was covered by foreign investment inflows that financed the importation of the raw materials and component parts that were processed by multinational firms prior to being re-exported in finished products. Some of the capital inflows were also used to accumulate official foreign exchange reserves. But Singapore did not allow the domestic currency counterparts to grow much in excess of the growth of the domestic demand for money to finance the growth of real GDP, and inflation seldom exceeded 2 percent a year. After 1987 Singapore became a net exporter of capital as her own entrepreneurs sought to expand overseas. Thus a negative capital account began to be matched by a positive current account balance (increasingly through high-quality services and more sophisticated consumer and capital goods).

6 Global imbalances and distortions to comparative advantage

Singapore's experience differs from China's on foreign reserves and inflation control. Whereas Singapore's reserves reflect the precautionary motive—to cushion the country from unusual exchange rate volatility associated with capital flight (as during the 1997 Asian financial crisis)—China's reserves seem to far exceed any precautionary need, and are more motivated by desire to maintain an undervalued currency in the pursuit of export-led growth. But having accumulated such a large stock of dollar assets, China is now on the horns of a dilemma: if it allows the renmimbi to appreciate this would help correct global imbalances by reducing her own net exports, but would also diminish the value of her US dollar assets.

How apportion blame for this egregious bilateral global imbalance? Martin Wolf (2009) blames China while Terry McKinley (2009), for example, blames the United States for prolonged loose fiscal and monetary policy (helped by its reserve currency status). So long as the US runs fiscal deficits that exceed the surplus of domestic saving over private investment, it must finance them through foreign borrowing. This in turn involves a balance-of-payments deficit on current account that requires a surplus on capital account; and since much of this is Chinese money it also explains the build-up of China's reserves. Official Chinese purchases of US dollar assets greatly exceed Chinese private sector investment in the US (Wolf 2009, pp. 86, 123).

Whoever is to blame, global imbalances of this magnitude (with international capital flows greatly exceeding the amounts needed to finance profitable investments, or being wrongly directed) move exchange rates away from "fundamental equilibrium" rates which in turn distorts the pattern of international comparative advantage.

In light of the superior performance of outwardly oriented developing countries that fostered industrialization through an export-promotion (XP) strategy supported by freer importing (notably the "Asian Tigers") compared with inwardly oriented, protectionist countries (such as Pakistan, India and most countries in Africa and Latin America) that followed an import-substituting industrialization (ISI) strategy, China likewise chose the liberal XP path as soon as reformers were able to discard the shackles of Maoism in the late 1970s. ISI strategies raised costs for potential exporters, causing real exchange rate appreciation that exacerbated the bias against trade. As Jagdish Bhagwati (1978) explained, countries can go too far in their enthusiasm for export-led growth.

Although the distortion associated with XP strategies is usually less than with ISI (see David Dollar 1992), nonetheless a heavily undervalued exchange rate also creates a bias in favor of too much exporting and too little importing. In the case of China's current account surpluses, much of the counterpart has been an excessive payments deficit for the United States. The result has been excessive US public and household debt (leading to the subprime housing crisis with its dire international repercussions), and repression of Chinese wages and domestic consumption. The difference between China's recent growth and that of the earlier Asian Tigers is that the latter allowed the growth of their imports to be almost as impressive as the growth of their exports, with *both* greatly exceeding growth of GDP, with imports not only complementing the export effort but also allowing a faster growth of wages and consumption. Though many millions have been lifted out of absolute poverty in China in the last 20 years (Dollar 2007; Sandilands 2008), many millions still subsist in this state than is likely if a less extreme XP strategy had been pursued.

The articles of agreement at the 1944 Bretton Woods conference that established the International Monetary Fund included the famous but very rarely invoked "scarce-currency clause." This imposed an obligation on surplus as well as deficit countries to share the burden of adjustment in the face of disruptive "fundamental disequilibrium" in international payments. Failing appropriate action by countries in chronic surplus, the IMF has the power to invoke the scarce-currency clause to approve discrimination against the exports of such countries. It is surprising that China has so far escaped this sanction.

Since the collapse in 1971 of the Bretton Woods "adjustable peg" exchange rate system, most of the world has adopted a floating rate regime, though this has often been "dirty" floating through currency manipulations by central banks—not least by the People's Bank of China. However, much of the increased exchange-rate volatility since the 1970s has been associated with private hot money flows, most notoriously prior to the 1997 Asian financial crisis. That was largely due to the speculative carry trade with money borrowed at low interest rates in Japan to invest in short-term bank deposits in Bangkok, for example, where rates were much higher, and where they fueled an unsustainable real estate boom. But the rates were higher because the risk of depreciation was also higher. When the Thai baht could no longer be supported by central bank intervention, the real estate market began to turn sour, leading to massive flight of hot money from Thailand—and from its neighbors too.

A nation's money supply and spending is closely linked with the exchange rate and/or changes in official reserves. Hot money flows can therefore be very disruptive of domestic stability. So a case can be made for sterilizing the monetary implications of short-term international finance, or for a "Tobin tax." It is clear that money is not neutral, for failure to control monetary inflation has profound implications for the efficient allocation of resources. There are two main ways in which inflation carries this danger: (1) through its impact on the real exchange rate, hence on the volume and direction of international trade; and (2) through its effect on interest rates which can harm the volume of savings and investment, and cause large distortions in the allocation of loanable funds between long- and short-term debt. This has important effects on housing finance which is an especially grave problem for developing countries that need to accelerate rural–urban migration if they are to capture the full benefits of the Youngian increasing returns that arise from greater integration into the global economy.

Colombia offers an instructive case study of these effects and the policy responses. In view of the prominence given to Colombia by other participants at this conference, the following is a review of an influential critique of recent development strategies in Colombia by a former director of its National Planning Department, Juan Carlos Echeverry. Notable among these strategies was one known as "The Plan of the Four Strategies," 1972–1974, drawn up by Colombia's prominent economic adviser, Lauchlin Currie, and defended by him vigorously, in the face of much opposition, over the next 20 years until his death in 1993. Currie was a student of Allyn Young at Harvard in the 1920s and was greatly influenced by Young's writing on money and growth, as explained below.

7 The case of Colombia: a review of Juan Carlos Echeverry's "Keys to the Future" (2002)

Juan Carlos Echeverry directed the National Planning Department during the crisis years of 1998–2002. His book under review surveyed the evolution of the Colombian economy over the previous 30 years, with a focus on the 1990s during which time Colombia embarked upon an ambitious program of *apertura*, or openness. He negotiated with the IMF and was sympathetic to the "Washington Consensus" that stressed "fiscal health," privatization, financial liberalization and central bank independence, and tax, pension and labor-market reforms. He laments that the vicious "narco-guerrilla war" that Colombia suffered during this "reform" period greatly offset the benefits of sound economic policy, and that this gave liberalization an undeserved bad name.

The appearance of his book was timely, coinciding with much publicity surrounding the centenary of the birth (in 1902) of Lauchlin Currie. After a distinguished career at Harvard, the Federal Reserve Board and in the White House as Franklin Roosevelt's economic adviser from 1939–1945, Currie headed a World Bank mission to Colombia in 1949 (see Sandilands 1990b; Laidler and Sandilands 2002). He then stayed on as an adviser to successive governments for the next 40 years. Most notably, in 1972 he founded a unique index-linked housing finance system (known by its Spanish acronym, UPAC, for "unit of constant purchasing power") as part of the above-mentioned "Plan of the Four Strategies" (for urban housing, export diversification, agricultural productivity and improved income distribution).

Echeverry gave considerable space to an analysis of Currie's innovative but controversial housing finance system. He notes that its original aim was to make construction a "leading" sector that could permanently boost the overall economic growth rate (see details in Currie 1974). In 2002 the system lay in ruins, the victim of countless debilitating modifications. Construction had for the previous four years been leading the economy down instead of up. Many thousands had lost their jobs, both directly and as a result of depression in industries that supply the construction sector. Urban unemployment stood at 18 percent (with urban underemployment officially 33 percent). In other words, only half of the workforce was fully employed (rural underemployment was even worse.)

The two directors of the National Planning Department who implemented Currie's Plan of the Four Strategies between 1971 and 1974 were Roberto Arenas and Luis Eduardo Rosas. At the Currie centenary in October 2002 both recalled the great impulse that "UPAC" had given to construction and overall growth in the 1970s, together with full employment and improved distribution. Comparing the dynamism of the 1970s with the stagnation of 1998–2002, Rosas remarked, in his tribute to Currie: "Como nos hace de falta en estos momentos!" ("How we have need of him now!")

Echeverry concedes that in the 1970s and 1980s construction played a positive role: it created jobs and was a contra-cyclical influence. But he claims that in the 1990s, with *apertura* and the great influx of external credits and drug money, construction became a pro-cyclical speculative activity that was bound to collapse, as collapse it did in 1998—though he stressed that the problem was compounded by the worsening civil war. His main complaint was that construction had diverted resources from traded goods and that it relies on unskilled workers whereas the future depends on skills and an allocation of resources more in tune with market forces. Let us rely on Adam Smith, he insisted, not on protectionist "models of development" and privileged "leading sectors."

However, Currie's ideas were also heavily influenced by Smith. As noted above, Currie's mentor at Harvard was Allyn Young, whose famous paper (1928) on "Increasing Returns and Economic Progress" inspired modern development theory, to which Currie was a prominent contributor (for example,

Currie 1997). Echeverry did not refer to this endogenous growth theory, perhaps because of his profound skepticism of "models of development." But Young and Currie were inspired by the opening chapters of *The Wealth of Nations* where Smith emphasized specialization or the division of labor which in turn depended upon the size of the market, or upon real demand.

Today demand management is generally associated with Keynesian policies to tackle short-run business cycles around a secular trend. These cycles are closely associated with interruptions to the flow of monetary incomes and expenditures (or monetary demand). But Smith and Young focused on competition, openness and the mobility of labor to increase the underlying trend of real demand and market size (or what Smith also called "the power of exchanging"), hence specialization, hence productivity.

Young explained that in the modern economy specialization takes the form of new, more specialized firms and industries that compete against the old. They introduce new forms of organization and technology, but only as and when it pays to do so. The larger the market, the greater the incentive to innovate. Currie extended this idea to show that the existing growth rate (of the overall market, or GDP) had a tendency to perpetuate itself. But in Colombia where resources were abundant but grossly misallocated and underutilized, and where labor mobility was very poor, growth fell far short of potential. This self-perpetuating (or endogenous) growth rate was a vicious circle best broken by institutional measures to mobilize the great potential supply by liberating the great potential demand.

This is where Currie's vision of construction's potential role differs from Echeverry's. As a "leading sector" it is valuable not so much as a contra-cyclical, stabilizing force (though it could also serve that purpose). Rather, it could help Colombia (and other countries) to break free of its historically slow, endogenous growth path. It is a leading sector because (1) it is an important direct and indirect component of GDP, so its growth has a significant effect on overall growth; (2) it moves independently of movements in the rest of the economy, and can be moved exogenously through discretionary policies; (3) it plays a vital role in promoting labor mobility; and (4) it is a sector with enormous latent demand.

But in the past this latent demand had been severely repressed. Potential homeowners can usually only buy a home with the help of substantial mortgages. Thus effective demand required a rapidly expanding flow of credit on convenient terms. This was not available because chronic inflation discriminated against it. High inflation requires high interest rates to attract savings. But for people borrowing large sums high interest rates impose a severe cash-flow problem (the "front-end loading problem"). This curtails effective demand. By contrast, "constant value" savings and loans made it both more attractive to save and easier to borrow.

Echeverry is a stout opponent of inflationary finance. But in Colombia chronic inflation has been a reality. Echeverry failed to highlight its main distortionary effects. In practice some sectors suffer far greater harm than others. The disadvantaged sectors—mainly construction and exports—are not "privileged" when measures are introduced that protect them from harmful inflation. Furthermore, conventional policies to squeeze inflation out of the system (through temporarily higher interest rates on government bonds) and to reduce fiscal deficits (partly due to depressed incomes) can also damage the housing sector by making it less attractive to place savings there.

Currie sought to combine tight monetary and fiscal policies with policies to reactivate the real economy by redirecting incomes and expenditures toward leading sectors that rely not on the printing press but upon genuine savings. The great economist Harry G. Johnson (1958) similarly distinguished between "expenditure-reducing" and "expenditure-switching" policies. A blueprint for such a combination, with detailed quantitative estimates of the size of the required "compensatory" effect required of the leading sectors, was drawn up by Currie and Alvaro Montenegro (1984) as advice for President Belisario Betancur in the mid-1980s. The advice was not taken and the country suffered severe instability and capital flight.

The construction sector's indispensable role in the labor mobility mechanism was also ignored by Echeverry. It promotes not only faster growth but also better distribution. In Colombia there is still a great imbalance in the allocation of labor, notably between low-paying agriculture and high-paying urban activities. And in cities like Bogota there is urgent need for better balance between where people live and where they work, and for improved housing for all.

Echeverry claims there is a conflict between investment in internationally traded goods and investment in housing. Yet in countries such as Singapore, noted for spectacular export growth, investment in housing has also been enormous, and far greater than in Colombia. Despite rehousing almost the entire population in the last 35 years its construction sector still booms. There has been no saturation of demand.[4] As incomes increased so Singaporeans demanded better accommodation and related infrastructure. This has been aided by low inflation and large pension fund contributions that can be released for down payments on homes and the servicing of mortgages at low nominal interest rates. Building is concentrated on well-built conventional high-rise blocks for the middle classes. As these families move into new homes lower-income families move into the ones vacated. This "escalation" process enables poorer families to enjoy far better accommodation than the type of subsidized "vivienda de interés social" (popular housing) that Colombia is desperately trying to provide today out of limited fiscal resources.

Housing and exports are complements, not substitutes. Both are capable of expanding on the basis of a stimulus to and redirection of real savings, rather than via inflationary finance or subsidies. Here are the real *"claves del futuro."*

By contrast, Echeverry's overview of the Colombian economy and economic policies focused mainly on the structure and balance of the national budget and the rate of growth of money and credit. This is rather typical too of the focus of the international lending agencies when drawing up conditions for further foreign loans. Its key limitation is that it gives insufficient weight to the dynamic changes in the composition of real incomes and expenditures over time in developing countries like Colombia, and of the need to ensure that a country's abundant natural and human resources are allocated—and reallocated—accordingly. Herein the supreme importance of the mobility mechanism, and of the related role of a dynamic and well-funded construction sector as a necessary adjunct to greater industrialization and integration into the global economy.

8 Conclusion

We have explained how openness to world trade and investment can foster both faster growth and greater income equality between and within countries. However, theory and the case studies reviewed here have shown that dynamic comparative advantage highlights the need for trade strategies to be accompanied by greater mobility of labor and capital as comparative advantages change. Experience also shows that land values escalate with increased urbanization, and this negative aspect of globalization requires that these unearned increments be recaptured for the wider community if growth is not to be vitiated by increasing inequality.

Notes

1 Cf. Allyn Young's comment in his LSE lectures 1927–1929, as reproduced in Sandilands (1990a, p. 99): "From the individual point of view, one can 'invest' in either land or capital. But, socially, investment in land merely transfers ownership, while capital investment produces capital." Thus rent is a cost to the individual but not to society. Young also distinguished the static from the dynamic view. In the static view, with given amounts of land, labor and capital, the return to each may be regarded as a rent (or surplus over "normal" returns). But for dynamic long-run tendencies—which most interested Ricardo—land rent never enters into social cost but does affect the distribution of income. For, unlike the price of capital, "rent cannot control the process of land accumulation; there is no such process" (ibid.: 100). Young (1999 [1908]) had already shown how this clarifies the ambiguous concept of "productivity" and the value of the "social dividend" within a "continually recurring cycle of income and outgo" as final products emerge from a long sequence of past investments in intermediate products—and dependent on differential changes in the supply of and demand for the various factors. This is helpful in understanding his later paper (Young 1928) on increasing returns.

2 A more optimistic view of the effect on rich-country wages would be that international capital flows would increase the global efficiency of capital, hence global growth, and that the resultant increased spending power of poorer countries would spill over on to demand for rich countries' products.

3 This theorem abstracts from transport and other transactions costs (as well as tariffs) that interfere with free trade. These prevent complete factor-price equalization.

4 Colombia has not relied heavily on global finance for its private housing programs, and that was not the intention for the system introduced in the early 1970s. Instead it relied on non-inflationary domestic saving. This may have helped insulate Colombia from the kind of fallout from the US subprime debacle that engulfed Britain, for example, after 2007. However, its housing sector has been subject to recession whenever incentives to saving in the system were cut. "Valorization" taxes have also helped curb inflationary booms, and have returned some of the Ricardian rents to the community whose taxes have financed the urban infrastructure that helps create those rents. In China, where "house" (read "land") prices have recently risen spectacularly (partly due to reckless

use of inflationary finance rather than real saving), there are calls for an annual property tax to moderate her boom–bust cycles. China obviously requires a dynamic urban housing program (the urbanized proportion of its population is still far below that needed for greater equality), but it also needs a far less cyclical character.

References

Abramovitz, Moses (1956) *Resource and Output Trends in the United States Since 1870*, Cambridge, MA: National Bureau of Economic Research.

Abramovitz, Moses (1989) *Thinking About Growth*, Cambridge: Cambridge University Press.

Bhagwati, Jagdish (1978) *Anatomy and Consequences of Exchange Control Regimes*, Cambridge, MA: Ballinger Publishing Co.

Chandra, Ramesh and Sandilands, Roger J. (2005) "Does Modern Endogenous Growth Theory Adequately Represent Allyn Young?" *Cambridge Journal of Economics*, 29(3): 463–473.

Currie, Lauchlin (1974) "The 'Leading Sector' Model of Growth in Developing Countries," *Journal of Economic Studies*, 1(1): 1–16.

Currie, Lauchlin (1997) "Implications of an Endogenous Theory of Growth in Allyn Young's Macroeconomic Concept of Increasing Returns," *History of Political Economy*, 29(3): 413–443.

Currie, Lauchlin and Montenegro, Alvaro (1984) *Crecimiento con Estabilidad: Un Modelo*, Bogotá: Fundación Simon Bolívar.

Dollar, David (1992) "Outward-Oriented Developing Economies Really Do Grow More Rapidly: Evidence from 95 LDCs, 1976–1985," *Economic Development and Cultural Change*, 40(3): 523–544.

Dollar, David (2007) "Poverty, Inequality and Social Disparities During China's Economic Reform," Policy, Research Working Paper No. WPS 4253, Beijing: World Bank.

Echeverry, Juan Carlos (2002) *Las Claves del Futuro: Economía y Conflicto en Colombia* [Keys to the Future: Economics and Conflict in Colombia], Bogotá: Editorial Oveja Negra.

Johnson, Harry G. (1958) "Towards a General Theory of the Balance of Payments," *International Trade and Economic Growth: Studies in Pure Theory*, London: Unwin.

Krugman, Paul (1990) *Rethinking International Trade*, Cambridge, MA: MIT Press.

Kurz, Heinz (2008) "Wicksell Effects," in William J. Darity Jr. (ed.) *International Encyclopedia of Social Sciences*, second edition, New York, NY: Macmillan, pp. 94–96.

Laidler, David and Sandilands, Roger J. (2002) "An Early Harvard Memorandum on Anti-depression Policy: An Introduction," *History of Political Economy*, 34(3): 515–552.

Lloyd, Peter J. and Sandilands, Roger J. (1986) "The Trade Sector in a Very Open Re-export Economy: The Case of Singapore," in P. J. Lloyd and C. Y. Lim (eds.) *Singapore: Resources and Growth*, Singapore: Oxford University Press.

McKinley, Terry (2009) "Will Pinning the Blame on China Help Correct Global Imbalances?" Policy Brief No. 2, June, London: School of Oriental and African Studies.

Romer, Paul M. (1994) "The Origins of Endogenous Growth," *Journal of Economic Perspectives*, 8(1): 3–22.

Sandilands, Roger J. (1990a) "Nicholas Kaldor's Notes on Allyn Young's LSE lectures, 1927–29," *Journal of Economic Studies*, 17(3/4).

Sandilands, Roger J. (1990b) *The Life and Political Economy of Lauchlin Currie: New Dealer, Presidential Adviser, and Development Economist*, Durham, NC: Duke University Press.

Sandilands, Roger J. (1992) "Savings, Investment and Housing in Singapore's Growth, 1965–90," *Savings and Development*, 16(2): 119–143.

Sandilands, Roger J. (1999) "New Evidence on Allyn Young's Style and Influence as a Teacher," *Journal of Economic Studies*, 26(6): 453–480.

Sandilands, Roger J. (2008) "China: The Role of Rural–Urban Migration in Economic Development under Capitalism," in Roger Clarke (ed.) *The Future of Capitalism after the Collapse of Communism*, London: Centre for Research into Post-Communist Economies.

Sandilands, Roger J. (2009) "Solovian and New Growth Theory from the Perspective of Allyn Young on Macroeconomic Increasing Returns," *History of Political Economy*, 41(Suppl. 1): 285–303.

Sandilands, Roger J. and Tan, Ling Hui (1986) "Comparative Advantage in a Re-export Economy: the Case of Singapore," *Singapore Economic Review*, 31(2): 34–56.

Smith, Adam (1976 [1776]) *An Enquiry into the Nature and Causes of the Wealth of Nations*, Chicago, IL: Chicago University Press.

Solow, Robert M. (1956) "A Contribution to the Theory of Economic Growth," *Quarterly Journal of Economics*, 70(1): 65–94.

Swan, Trevor W. (1956) "Economic Growth and Capital Accumulation," *Economic Record*, 32(2): 334–361.

Wolf, Martin (2009) *Fixing Global Finance*, New Haven, CT: Yale University Press.

Young, Allyn A. (1928) "Increasing Returns and Economic Progress," *The Economic Journal*, 38: 527–542.

Young, Allyn A. (1999 [1908]) "The Social Dividend," reproduced in Perry G. Mehrling and Roger J. Sandilands (eds.) *Money and Growth: Selected Papers of Allyn Abbott Young*, London: Routledge.

Part II

Developed nations—USA, EU and Japan

5 The crisis, the bailout and financial reform

A Minskian approach to improving crisis response[1]

L. Randall Wray[2]

1 Introduction

"Never waste a crisis." Those words were often invoked by reformers who wanted to tighten regulations and financial supervision in the aftermath of the Global Financial Crisis (GFC) that began in late 2007.[3] Many of them have been disappointed because the relatively weak reforms adopted (for example in Dodd–Frank) appear to have fallen far short of what is needed. But the same words can be and should have been invoked in reference to the policy response to the crisis—that is, to the rescue of the financial system. To date, the crisis was also wasted in that area, too. If anything, the crisis response largely restored the financial system that existed in 2007 on the eve of the crisis. Risky practices are already returning. The economic system is still burdened with excessive "financialization," with "Wall Street" sucking economic rents from the economy, hindering recovery.

But it may not be too late to use the crisis and the response itself to formulate a different approach to dealing with the next financial crisis. If we are correct in our analysis, because the response last time simply propped up a deeply flawed financial structure and because financial system reform will do little to prevent financial institutions from continuing risky practices, another crisis is inevitable—and indeed will likely occur far sooner than most analysts expect. In any event, we recall Hyman Minsky's belief that "stability is destabilizing"—implying that even if we had successfully stabilized the financial system, that would change behavior in a manner to make another crisis more likely. So no matter what one believes about the previous response and the reforms now in place, policymakers of the future will have to deal with another financial crisis. We need to prepare for that policy response by learning from our policy mistakes made in reaction to the last crisis.

From our perspective, there were two problems with the response as undertaken mostly by the Federal Reserve Bank (Fed) with assistance from the Treasury. First, the rescue actually creates potentially strong adverse incentives. This is widely conceded by analysts. If government rescues an institution that had engaged in risky and even fraudulent behavior, without imposing huge costs on those responsible, then the lesson that is learned is perverse. While a few institutions were forcibly closed or merged, for the most part, the punishment across the biggest institutions (those most responsible for the crisis) was light. Early financial losses (for example equities prices) were large but over time have largely been recouped. No top executives and few traders from the biggest institutions were prosecuted for fraud. Some lost their jobs but generally received large compensation anyway. In recent months, Washington has finally gone after the biggest institutions for fraudulent activity, but it has only slapped them with fines—not with criminal indictments.

Second, the rescue was mostly formulated and conducted in virtual secrecy. Even after the fact, the Fed refused to release information related to its actions. It took a major effort by Congress (led by Senator Bernie Sanders and Representative Alan Grayson) plus a Freedom of Information Act lawsuit (by Bloomberg) to get the data released. When the Fed finally provided the data, it was in a form that made analysis extremely difficult. Only a tremendous amount of work by Bloomberg and by our team of researchers at the Levy Economics Institute[4] made it possible to get a complete accounting of the Fed's actions. The crisis response was truly unprecedented. It was done behind closed doors. There was almost no involvement by elected representatives, almost no public discussion (before or even immediately after the fact) and little accountability. All of this subverts democratic governance.

In response to criticism, one finds that the policymakers who formulated the crisis response argue that while even *they* were troubled by what they "had" to do, they had no alternative. The system faced a complete meltdown. Even though what they did "stinks" (several of those involved have used such words to describe the feelings they had at the time), they saw no other possibility.

These claims are questionable. What the Fed (and Treasury) did after 2008 is quite unlike any previous US response—including both the savings and loan crisis response and, more importantly, the approach taken under President Roosevelt. Further, other countries (or regions) that have faced financial meltdowns in more recent years have also taken alternative approaches. More importantly, it is crucial to understand why the financial system as currently constructed is not only prone to crisis, but also why it is so hard to resolve the crises that occur. In short, we believe that it is because financial institutions are highly leveraged, highly layered and highly interconnected. By understanding the nature of the crisis and the nature of our financial system, we can move toward a coordinated reform of the system that not only makes it safer but also easier to rescue in crisis. In the view of the project team[5] at the Levy Economics Institute, Minsky's work points toward reform that accomplishes both goals.

In this chapter we will address three issues in detail: the nature of the crisis, the nature of the "bailout," and Minsky's views on "reconstructing" the financial system to promote the capital development of the economy. The goal is to develop an understanding that would allow us to transform the financial system in a manner that would make it more stable and easier to resolve in the event of crisis.

We focus our critique on the role the Fed played as "lender of last resort" in the aftermath of the financial crisis. For more than a century and a half it has been recognized that a central bank *must* act as lender of last resort in a crisis. A body of thought to guide practice has been well established over that period, and central banks have used those guidelines many, many times to deal with countless financial crises around the globe. As we explain in this chapter, however, the Fed's intervention this time stands out for three reasons: the sheer size of its intervention, the duration of its intervention and its deviation from standard practice in terms of interest rates charged and collateral required against loans. Even as the Fed's lender of last resort interventions finally came to an end, it began another unprecedented intervention with "quantitative easing." We will present an alternative view of the impacts of that policy—which is purported to have been undertaken to encourage lending in order to "jumpstart" recovery on Main Street. Instead, we see this as a continuation of the misguided effort to prop up *money manager capitalism*. We conclude with a discussion of Minsky's views on *reconstruction* of the financial system.

2 Overview of the unprecedented nature of the response to the crisis

2.1 Background

In its response to the expanding financial crisis touched off in the spring of 2007 the Federal Reserve engaged in actions well beyond its traditional lender of last resort support to insured deposit taking institutions that were members of the Federal Reserve System. Support was eventually extended to non-insured investment banks, broker-dealers, insurance companies, and automobile and other nonfinancial corporations. By the end of this process the Fed owned a wide range of real and financial assets, both in the United States and abroad. While most of this support was lending against collateral, the Fed also provided unsecured dollar support to foreign central banks directly through swaps facilities that indirectly provided dollar funding to foreign banks and businesses.

This was not the first time such generalized support has been provided to the economic system in the face of financial crisis. In the crisis that emerged after the German declaration of war in 1914, even before the Fed was formally in operation, the Aldrich–Vreeland Emergency Currency Act provided for the advance of currency to banks against financial and commercial assets. The Act, which was to cease in 1913, but was extended in the original Federal Reserve Act, expired on June 30, 1915. As a result, similar support to the general system was provided in the Great Depression by the "emergency banking act" of 1933 and eventually became Section 13c of the Reserve Act.

In a sense, any action by the Fed, for example when it sets interest rates, usurps the market process. This is one of the reasons that the Fed stopped intervening in the long-term money market, since it was thought that this would have an impact on investment allocation decisions thought to be determined by long-term interest rates. In the current crisis, the Fed has once again taken up intervention in longer-term securities markets in the form of the policy of quantitative easing.

As a result of these extensive interventions and its supplanting of normal economic processes, both the Congress and the public at large have become increasingly concerned not only about the size of the financial commitments that have been assumed by the Fed on their behalf, but also about the lack of transparency and normal governmental oversight surrounding these actions. For the most part, the Fed has refused requests for greater access to information. This is indeed ironic for the initial request for rescue funds by Secretary Paulson was rejected precisely because it lacked details and a mechanism to give Congress oversight on the spending. Eventually a detailed stimulus package that totaled nearly $800 billion gained Congressional approval.[6] But the Fed has spent, lent or promised far more money than Congress has so far approved for direct government intervention in response to the crisis. Most of these actions have been negotiated in secret, often at the New York Fed with the participation of Treasury officials. The justification is that such secrecy is needed to prevent increasing uncertainty over the stability of financial institutions and generating uncertainty that could lead to a collapse of troubled institutions, which would only increase the government's costs of resolution. There is, of course, a legitimate reason to fear sparking a panic.

Yet, even when relative calm returned to financial markets, the Fed continued to resist requests to explain its actions even ex post. This finally led Congress to call for an audit of the Fed in a nearly unanimous vote. Some in Congress are now questioning the legitimacy of the Fed's independence. In particular, given the importance of the NYFed (New York Reserve Bank—responsible for Wall Street institutions) some are worried that it is too close to the Wall Street banks it is supposed to oversee and that it has in many cases been forced to rescue. The president of the NYFed met frequently with top management of Wall Street institutions throughout the crisis, and reportedly pushed deals that favored one institution over another. However, like the other presidents of district banks, the president of the NYFed is selected by the regulated banks. This led critics to call for a change to allow appointment by the president of the nation. Critics note that while the Fed has become much more open since the early 1990s, the crisis has highlighted how little oversight the congressional and executive branches have over the Fed, and how little transparency there is even today.

There is an inherent conflict between the need for transparency and oversight when public spending is involved and the need for independence and secrecy in formulating monetary policy and in supervising regulated financial institutions. A democratic government cannot formulate its budget in secrecy. Except when it comes to national defense, budgetary policy must be openly debated and all spending must be subject to open audits. That is exactly what was done in the case of the stimulus package. However, it is argued that monetary policy cannot be formulated in the open—a long and drawn out open debate by the Federal Open Market Committee (FOMC) about when and by how much interest rates ought to be raised would generate chaos in financial markets. Similarly, an open discussion by regulators about which financial institutions might be insolvent would guarantee a run out of their liabilities and force a government take-over.

Even if these arguments are overstated and even if a bit more transparency could be allowed in such deliberations by the Fed, it is clear that the normal operations of a central bank will involve more deliberation behind closed doors than is expected of the budgetary process for government spending. Further, even if the governance of the Fed were to be substantially reformed to allow for presidential appointments of all top officials, this would not reduce the need for closed deliberations.

The question is whether the Fed should be able to commit the Congress and citizens in times of national crisis. Was it appropriate for the Fed to commit the US government to trillions of dollars of funds to rescue US financial institutions, as well as foreign institutions and governments?[7] When Chairman Bernanke testified before Congress about whether he had committed the "taxpayers' money" he responded "no," it is simply entries on balance sheets. While this response is operationally correct, it is also misleading. There is no difference between a Treasury guarantee of a private liability and a Fed guarantee. When the Fed buys an asset by means of "crediting" the recipient's balance sheet, this is not significantly different from the US Treasury financing the purchase of an asset by "crediting" the recipient's balance sheet. The only difference is that in the former case the debit is on the Fed's balance sheet and in the latter it is on the Treasury's balance sheet. But the impact is the same in either case—it represents the creation of dollars of government liabilities in support of a private sector entity.

The fact that the Fed does keep a separate balance sheet should not mask the identical nature of the operation. It is true that the Fed normally runs a profit on its activities since its assets earn more than it pays on its liabilities, while the Treasury does not usually aim to make a profit on its spending. Yet Fed profits above 6 percent are turned over to the Treasury. If its actions in support of the financial system reduce the Fed's profitability, Treasury revenues will suffer. If the Fed were to accumulate massive losses, the Treasury would have to bail it out—with Congress budgeting for the losses. It is not likely that this will be the case, but the point remains that in practice the Fed's obligations and commitments are ultimately the same as the Treasury's, and these promises are made without Congressional approval, or even its knowledge many months after the fact.

Some will object that there is a fundamental difference between spending by the Fed and spending by the Treasury. The Fed's actions are limited to purchasing financial assets, lending against collateral and guaranteeing private liabilities. While the Treasury also operates some lending programs and guarantees private liabilities (for example, through the FDIC—Federal Deposit Insurance Corporation—and Sallie Mae—student loan—programs), and while it has purchased private equities in recent bailouts (of General Motors, for example), most of its spending takes the form of transfer payments and purchases of real output. Yet, when Treasury engages in lending or guarantees, its funds must be provided by Congress. The Fed does not face such a budgetary constraint—it can commit to trillions of dollars of obligations without going to Congress.

Further, when the Treasury provides a transfer payment to a social security recipient, a credit to the recipient's bank account will be made (and the bank's reserves are credited by the same amount). If the Fed were to buy a private financial asset from that same retiree (let us say it is a mortgage-backed security), the bank account would be credited in exactly the same manner (and the bank's reserves would also be credited). In the first case, Congress has approved the payment to the social security beneficiary; in the second case, no Congressional approval was obtained. While these two operations are likely to lead to very different outcomes (the social security recipient is likely to spend the receipt; the sale of a mortgage-backed security simply increases the seller's liquidity and may not induce spending by the seller), so far as creating a government commitment they are equivalent because each leads to the creation of a bank deposit as well as bank reserves.

Again, this equivalence is masked by the way the Fed's and the Treasury's balance sheets are constructed. Spending by the Treasury that is not offset by tax revenue will lead to a reported budget deficit and (normally) to an increase in the outstanding government debt stock. By contrast, spending by the Fed leads to an increase of outstanding bank reserves (an IOU of the Fed) that is not counted as part of deficit spending or as government debt and is off the government balance sheet. While this could be seen as an advantage because it effectively keeps the support of the financial system in crisis "off balance sheet," it comes at the cost of reduced accountability and diminished democratic deliberation. This is unfortunate because operationally there is no difference between support for a financial or non-financial entity taken by the Treasury "on the balance sheet" and one that is undertaken by the Fed "off the balance sheet" thus, largely unaccountable.

There is a recognition that financial crisis support necessarily results in winners and losers, and socialization of losses. At the end of the 1980s when it became necessary to rescue and restructure the thrift (Saving and Loan institutions) industry, Congress created an authority and budgeted funds for the resolution. It was recognized that losses would be socialized—with a final accounting in the neighborhood of $200 billion. Government officials involved in the resolution were held accountable for their actions, and more than 1,000 top management officers of thrifts went to prison. While undoubtedly imperfect, the resolution was properly funded, implemented and managed to completion. In general outline, it followed the procedures adopted to deal with bank resolutions in the 1930s.

By contrast, the bailouts in the much more serious recent crisis have been uncoordinated, mostly off budget and done largely in secret—and mostly by the Fed. There were exceptions, of course. There was a spirited public debate about whether government ought to rescue the auto industry. In the end, funds were budgeted while government took an equity share and an active role in decision-making, and openly picked winners and losers. Again, the rescue was imperfect but, as at the time of this writing, it seems to have been successful. Whether it will still look successful a decade from now we cannot know, but at least we do know that Congress decided the industry was worth saving as a matter of public policy. No such public debate occurred in the case of the rescue of Bear Stearns, the bankruptcy of Lehman brothers, the rescue of AIG or the support for Goldman Sachs.

2.2 Review of the nature of the crisis and the Fed's response

Here we quickly summarize five key issues: the nature of the crisis (liquidity or solvency problems), the nature of the response ("deal-making" largely in secret), a detailed accounting of the Fed's response, problematic incentives created by the response and policy implications.

2.2.1 Liquidity or solvency crisis?

It has been recognized for well over a century that the central bank must intervene as "lender of last resort" in a crisis. Walter Bagehot explained this as a policy of stopping a run on banks by lending without limit, against good collateral, at a penalty interest rate. This would allow the banks to cover withdrawals so the run would stop. Once deposit insurance was added to the assurance of emergency lending, runs on demand deposits virtually stopped. However, banks have increasingly financed their positions in assets by issuing a combination of uninsured deposits plus very short-term non-deposit liabilities. Hence, the GFC (Global Financial Crisis) actually began as a run on these non-deposit liabilities, which were largely held by other financial institutions. Suspicions about insolvency led to refusal to roll-over short-term liabilities, which then forced institutions to sell assets. In truth, it was not simply a liquidity crisis but rather a solvency crisis brought on by risky and, in many cases, fraudulent practices.

Government response to a failing, insolvent bank is supposed to be much different than its response to a liquidity crisis: government is supposed to step in, seize the institution, fire the management and begin a resolution. Indeed, in the case of the US, there is a mandate to minimize costs to the Treasury (the FDIC maintains a fund to cover some of the losses so that insured depositors are paid dollar-for-dollar) as specified by the Federal Deposit Insurance Corporation Improvement Act (FDICIA) of 1991.[8] Normally, stockholders lose, as do the uninsured creditors—which would have included other financial institutions. It is the Treasury (through the FDIC) that is responsible for resolution. However, rather than resolving institutions that were probably insolvent, the Fed, working with the Treasury, tried to save them—by purchasing troubled assets and recapitalizing them, and by providing loans for long periods. Yet, the crisis continued to escalate—with problems spilling over to insurers of securities, including the "monolines" (that specialized in providing private mortgage insurance), to AIG, to all of the investment banks, and finally to the biggest commercial banks.

2.2.2 Deal-making and special purpose vehicles

With Congress reluctant to provide more funding, the Fed and Treasury gradually worked out an alternative. The "bailout" can be characterized as "deal-making through contracts" as the Treasury and Fed stretched the boundaries of law with behind-closed-doors hard-headed negotiations. Whereas markets would shut down an insolvent financial institution, the government would find a way to keep it operating. This "deal-making" approach that was favored over a resolution by "authority" approach is troubling from the perspectives of transparency and accountability as well for its creation of "moral hazard" (see below).

The other aspect of this approach was the unprecedented assistance through the Fed's special facilities created to provide loans as well as to purchase troubled assets (and to lend to institutions and even individuals who would purchase troubled assets). The Fed's actions went far beyond "normal" lending. First, it is probable that the biggest recipients of funds were insolvent. Second, the Fed provided funding for financial institutions (and to financial markets in an attempt to support particular financial instruments) that went far beyond the member banks that it is supposed to support. It had to make use of special sections of the Federal Reserve Act (FRA), some of which had not been used since the Great Depression. And as in the case of the deal-making, the Fed appears to have stretched its interpretation of those sections beyond the boundaries of the law.

Further, the Fed engaged in massive "quantitative easing" (QE, discussed below), which saw its balance sheet grow from well under $1 trillion before the crisis to nearly $3 trillion; bank reserves increase by a similar amount as the Fed's balance sheet grows. QE included asset purchases by the Fed that went well beyond treasuries—as the Fed bought mortgage-backed securities (MBSs), some of which were "private label" MBSs (not government-backed). In the beginning of 2008, the Fed's balance sheet was $926 billion, of which 80 percent of its assets were US Treasury bonds; in November 2010, its balance sheet had reached $2.3 trillion, of which almost half of its assets were MBSs. To the extent that the Fed paid more than market price to buy "trashy" assets from financial institutions, that could be construed as a "bailout."

2.2.3 Accounting for the response

There are two main measures of the Fed's intervention. The first is "peak outstanding" Fed lending summed across each special facility (at a point in time), which reached approximately $1.5 trillion in December 2008—the maximum outstanding loans made through the Fed's special facilities on any day, providing an idea of the maximum "effort" to save the financial system at a point in time and also some indication of the Fed's exposure to risk of loss.

The second method is to add up Fed lending and asset purchases through special facilities over time to obtain a cumulative measure of the Fed's response, counting every new loan origination and asset purchase made over the course of the life of each special facility. This indicates just how unprecedented the Fed's intervention was in terms of both volume and time—more than $29 trillion through November 2011. Much of this activity required invocation of "unusual and exigent" circumstances that permit extraordinary activity under Section 13(3) of the FRA. However, the volume of Fed assistance of questionable legality under 13(3) was very large. Its four special purpose vehicles (SPVs) lent approximately $1.75 trillion (almost 12 percent of the total Fed cumulative intervention) under questionable circumstances. In addition, its problematic loan programs that either lent against ineligible assets or lent to parties that were not troubled total $9.2 trillion (30 percent of the total intervention). In sum, of the $29 trillion lent and spent by fall 2011, over 40 percent was perhaps improperly justified under Section 13(3) of the FRA. Beneficiaries included member banks, investment banks and the rest of the Shadow Banking System, industrial firms, foreign banks and central banks, and even individuals such as the "Real Housewives of Wall Street" identified by *Rolling Stone*'s Matt Taibbi.

For example, as reported in Felkerson[9] we can look at three measures of the Primary Dealer Credit Facility (PDCF) that was created on March 16, 2008 in response to the troubles at Bear Stearns. The PDCF was effectively a "discount window for primary dealers" to ease strains in the repo market by lending reserves on an overnight basis to primary dealers at their initiative. As Felkerson writes, "PDCF credit was secured by eligible collateral; with haircuts applied to provide the Fed with a degree of protection from risk. Initial collateral accepted in transactions under the PDCF were investment grade securities" but that was relaxed "to include all forms of securities normally used in private sector repo transactions." If we use the cumulative measure, we find the "PDCF issued 1,376 loans totaling $8,950.99 billion." By contrast, the peak weekly amounts outstanding and lent (both occurred on October 1, 2008) were $156.57 billion and $728.64 billion, respectively. Figure 5.1 shows the peak weekly lending and peak outstanding loaned graphs.

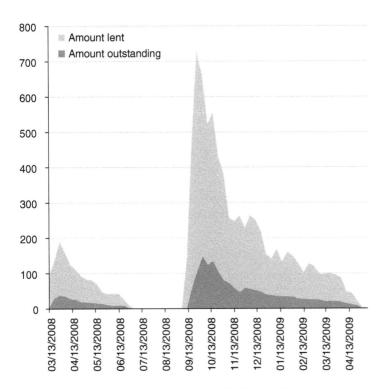

Figure 5.1 Primary Dealer Credit Facility (PDCF) weekly amounts lent and outstanding, in billions (source: Federal Reserve; see Felkerson 2011, Figure 10, p. 19).

Matthews and Felkerson also provide estimates of the users of each facility—allowing us to see that the vast majority of the Fed's commitments were made to the biggest banks. For example, most of the $9 trillion cumulative borrowing in the PDCF can be attributed to just five banks, as shown in Table 5.1.

Clearly, these were troubled institutions—two (Merrill and Bear) disappeared as independent banks, Citi came perilously close to the cliff, and Morgan and Bank of America remained in some distress. The cumulative lending by the Fed contributes to our understanding of the depths of their problems.

When all individual transactions are summed across all facilities created to deal with the crisis, the Fed committed a total of $29,616.4 billion. This includes direct lending plus asset purchases. Table 5.2 and Figure 5.2 depict the cumulative amounts for all facilities; in Table 5.2, any amount outstanding as of November 10, 2011 is in parentheses below the total. Three facilities—CBLS, PDCF and TAF—overshadow all other facilities, and make up 71.1 percent ($22,826.8 billion) of all assistance.

The extraordinary scope and magnitude of the financial crisis of 2007–2009 induced an extraordinary response by the Fed in the fulfillment of its lender of last resort function. Once we know what the Fed did, we can begin to assess the Fed's approach to crisis and to understand the consequences.

2.2.4 Incentives following the rescue

With the "deal-making" and "bailout" approaches of the Fed and Treasury, it is unlikely that financial institutions have learned much from the crisis—except that risky behavior will lead to a bailout. Continued expansion of government's "safety net" to protect "too big to fail" institutions not only runs afoul of established legal tradition but also produces perverse incentives and competitive advantages. The largest institutions enjoy "subsidized" interest rates—their uninsured liabilities have de facto protection because of the way the government (Fed, FDIC, OCC—Office of the Comptroller of the Currency, and Treasury) props them up, eliminating risk of default on their liabilities (usually only stockholders lose). These "too big to fail" institutions are really "systemically dangerous institutions"—often engaged in risky and even fraudulent practices that endanger the entire financial system.

Table 5.1 Five largest Primary Dealer Credit Facility borrowers (US$ billion)

Borrower	Total
Merrill Lynch	2,081.4
Citigroup	2,020.2
Morgan Stanley	1,912.6
Bear Stearns	960.1
Bank of America	638.9

Source: Felkerson 2011, Table 9, p. 19.

Table 5.2 Cumulative facility totals (US$ billion)

Facility	Total	Percentage of total
Term Auction Facility	3,818.41	12.89
Central Bank Liquidity Swaps	10,057.4 (1.96)	33.96
Single Tranche Open Market Operation	855	2.89
Terms Securities Lending Facility and Term Options Program	2,005.7	6.77
Bear Stearns Bridge Loan	12.9	0.04
Maiden Lane I	28.82 (12.98)	0.10
Primary Dealer Credit Facility	8,950.99	30.22
Asset-Backed Commercial Paper Money Market Mutual Fund Liquidity Facility	217.45	0.73
Commercial Paper Funding Facility	737.07	2.49
Term Asset-Backed Securities Loan Facility	71.09 (10.57)	0.24
Agency Mortgage-Backed Security Purchase Program	1,850.14 (849.26)	6.25
AIG Revolving Credit Facility	140.316	0.47
AIG Securities Borrowing Facility	802.316	2.71
Maiden Lane II	19.5 (9.33)	0.07
Maiden Lane III	24.3 (18.15)	0.08
AIA/ALICO	25	0.08
Totals	29,616.4	100.0

Source: Felkerson 2011, Table 16, p. 32.

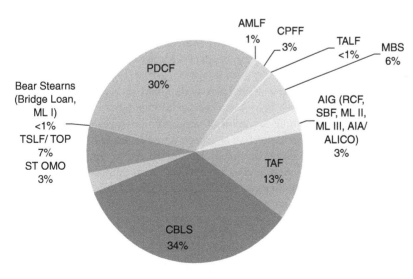

Figure 5.2 Facility percentage of bailout total (source: Felkerson 2011, Figure 21, p. 32).

No significant financial reforms made it through Congress (we will not address in detail Dodd–Frank, but its measures are too weak and have already been weakened further upon implementation).[10] In short, the "bailout" promoted moral hazard.

2.2.5 Policy implications

The Fed's bailouts of Wall Street certainly stretched and might have violated both the law as established in the Federal Reserve Act (and its amendments) and well-established procedure. Some might object that while there was some questionable, possibly illegal, activity by our nation's central bank, was it not justified by the circumstances?

The problem is that this "bailout" validated the questionable, risky and, in some cases illegal, activities of top management on Wall Street. Most researchers agree that the effect of the bailout has been to continue if not increase the distribution of income and wealth flowing to the top. It has kept the same management in control of the biggest institutions whose practices brought on the crisis, even as they paid record bonuses to top management. Some of their activity has been exposed, and the top banks have paid numerous fines for bad behavior. Yet, Washington has been seemingly paralyzed—there has not been significant investigation of possibly criminal behavior by top management.

What should have been done? Bagehot's recommendations are sound but must be amended. If we had followed normal US practice, we would have taken troubled banks into "resolution." The FDIC should have been called in (in the case of institutions with insured deposits), but in any case the institutions should have been dissolved according to existing law: at least cost to Treasury and to avoid increasing concentration in the financial sector. Dodd–Frank does, in some respects, codify such a procedure (for example, with "living wills," that require that systemically important institutions have a resolution plan), but it now appears unlikely that these measures will ever be implemented—and it is not clear that they would be the best way to deal with the crisis even if they were fully implemented.

Still, financial crises have appeared across the globe on a relatively frequent basis. Some resolutions have been more successful than others. Our goal going forward should be to examine examples of successful crisis resolutions to learn what works to formulate an alternative approach based on successful experiences around the world. The alternative should be constructed to improve transparency, accountability and democratic governance. It is important to involve citizens and their representatives in formulating, implementing and overseeing the response to the next crisis.

2.2.6 Coda: quantitative easing

In September 2012 the Fed announced a full-speed-ahead procession with QE3. This time, the Fed promised to buy $40 billion worth of mortgage-backed securities (MBSs) every month through the end of the year, and to keep what is essentially a zero interest-rate policy (ZIRP) in place through mid-2015. The Fed also announced that it will purchase other long-maturity assets to bring the total monthly purchases up to $85 billion, with the bias toward the long end expected to put downward pressure on long-term interest rates. The Fed made clear that QE3 is open-ended, to continue as long as necessary to stimulate to a robust economic recovery.

There are two reasons why economic stimulus has come down to reliance on the Fed's QE. First, policymakers have adopted the view that fiscal policy is out of bounds; some believe it does not work, others believe government has "run out of money." Both of those views are wrong, but beyond the scope of this section. The second reason is that Chairman Bernanke is enamored with the view that proper monetary policy could have avoided the American Great Depression as well as the Japanese lost decade(s)—two and counting. Essentially, his argument is that there is more that the central bank can do, beyond pushing its overnight rate (federal funds rate in the US) to zero (ZIRP—zero interest rate policy).

When the crisis hit the US in 2007, Bernanke followed the Japanese example by quickly relaxing monetary policy, rapidly pushing down the policy interest rate. After some fumbling around, the Fed also gradually opened its discount window and created a number of special lending facilities to lend an unprecedented amount of reserves to troubled institutions. The Fed's balance sheet literally exploded—which worries quantity theory Monetarists as well as many Austrians and Ron Paul followers who fear this could spark hyperinflation. But that did not put the economy on the road to recovery. So the Fed would go beyond ZIRP to try unconventional policy; namely, it would continue to buy assets even after it had driven short-term interest rates to the zero lower bound. Over the course of the three rounds of QE, the Fed has bought prodigious amounts of Treasuries and MBSs, as Figure 5.3 shows.

When the Fed buys assets, it purchases them by crediting banks with reserves. The result of QE is that the Fed's balance sheet grows rapidly—to, literally, trillions of dollars. At the same time, banks exchange the assets they are selling (the Treasuries and MBSs that the Fed is buying) for credits to their reserves held at the Fed. Normally, banks try to minimize reserve holdings—to what they need to cover payments clearing (banks clear accounts with one another using reserves) as well as Fed-imposed required reserve ratios. With QE, the banks accumulate large quantities of excess reserves.

Normally, banks would not hold excess reserves voluntarily—reserves used to earn zero, so banks would try to lend them out in the federal funds market (to other banks). But in the ZIRP environment, they cannot get much return on lending reserves. Further, the Fed switched policy in the aftermath of the crisis so that it now pays a small, positive return on reserves. Banks are holding the excess reserves and the Fed credits them with interest. They are not thrilled with the low interest rate, but there is nothing they can do: the Fed offers them an attractive price on the Treasuries and MBSs it wants to buy, and they trade Treasuries for excess reserves that earn less interest.

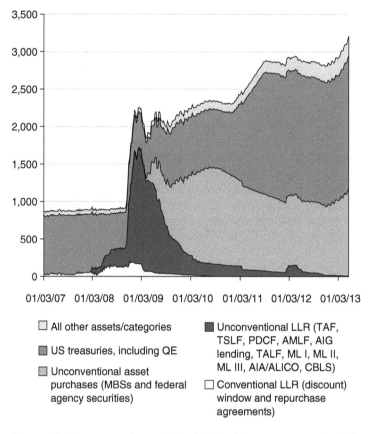

Figure 5.3 Disaggregated consolidated Federal Reserve assets, in millions, January 1, 2007–March 21, 2013 (source: Federal Reserve H.4.1 Statistical Release).

A lot of people—including policymakers—exhort the banks to "lend out the reserves" on the notion that this would "get the economy going." There are two problems with that thinking. First, banks can lend reserves only to other banks— and all the other banks have exactly the same problem: too many reserves. A bank cannot lend reserves to households or firms because they do not have accounts at the Fed; indeed, there is no operational maneuver that would allow anyone but a bank to borrow the reserves (when a bank lends reserves to another bank, the Fed debits the lending bank's reserves and credits the borrowing bank's reserves).

The second problem with the argument is that banks do not need reserves in order to lend. What they need is good, willing and credit-worthy borrowers. That is what is sadly lacking. Those who are credit-worthy are not willing; those who are willing are mostly not credit-worthy. Actually, we should be glad that banks are not currently lending to the non-credit-worthy—that is what got us into this mess in the first place. Indeed, given the mountain of debt under which US households are buried, the notion that we need to get banks lending again is ludicrous. We should not want banks to lend or households to borrow. What we need is to work off the private debt—pay it down or default on it.

Some believe that the path to recovery is to get firms to borrow. Again, that is problematic. US firms are actually wallowing in cash—they have cut costs, fired workers and stopped spending in order to shore up their cash reserves. They do not need banks. Indeed, they mostly stopped using banks to finance their spending a long time ago, as they shifted to commercial paper and other non-bank funding. The story is probably different for small firms—they do not have cash flow and they are not considered credit-worthy so they cannot borrow. They are, in a sense, collateral damage of the crisis, paying the price of Wall Street's excesses. However, the solution is not more debt for them. If anything, small firms need to do the same thing that most households need to do: reduce debt.

So, we have banks that do not want to lend and households and small firms that should not borrow. We have got bigger firms hoarding cash. In short, we have what Richard Koo calls a "balance sheet recession": too much debt and a strong incentive to de-lever. Firms and households are not only cutting spending, they are also trying to sell assets to pay back debt. Some asset prices are falling—especially real estate in many cities—which is the reason why banks do not want to lend: the assets that could serve as collateral are falling in value.

Is there a way out? Yes, there is. There is only one entity in the US that can directly spend more in a balance-sheet recession: Uncle Sam. But Washington will not do it, so we will not recover. That is the lesson we can learn from Japan: if government does not ramp up the fiscal stimulus, and keep it ramped up until a full-blown recovery has occurred, the economy will remain trapped in recession. To be sure, it is not the Fed's fault that Washington will not spend more; it is playing with the only hand it was dealt: monetary policy. In a balance-sheet recession that hand is impotent.

What QE comes down to, really, is a substitution of reserve deposits at the Fed in place of Treasuries and MBSs on the asset side of banks. In the case of Fed purchases of Treasuries, this reduces bank interest income—making them less profitable. Some held out the unjustifiable hope that less profits for banks would equate to more inducement to increase lending. That did not work, and would have been a bad idea even if it did. Policy should encourage banks to make good loans to willing and credit-worthy borrowers. It should not seek to make banks so desperate for profits that they make crazy loans (again!).

On the other hand, there could be some benefits to banks that manage to unload risky MBSs by selling them to the Fed. If a bank were full of the NINJA mortgages (no income, no job, no assets) made back in 2006, it would be quite willing to sell those to the Fed. It is likely that as a result of the bailout plus three rounds of QE, a lot of the bad assets have been moved to the Fed's balance sheet. Effectively, the banks are moving losers off their balance sheets in order to get safe reserves that earn next to nothing. That is a good trade! But, again, it does not induce banks to make more loans, does little to stimulate Main Street and creates moral hazard in the financial system as it teaches banks an invaluable lesson: too dumb to fail.

In the Fed's defense, many of the mortgages behind the MBSs are guaranteed by the government-sponsored enterprises, so Uncle Sam is on the hook whether they are held by the Fed or by banks. Still, it is questionable public policy to shift them to the Fed's balance sheet. And the worst mortgages were packaged into "private label" securities. We do not know how many private label securities the Fed has taken off their balance sheets, but we are investigating. In short, we might summarize QE in this way: it essentially amounts to shifting funds from a bank's saving account at the Fed (Treasuries) to its checking account at the Fed (Reserves), reducing bank earnings. And this is supposed to simulate the economy?

3 A Minskian view on reforming the financial system with a view to crisis response

3.1 The stages approach[11]

While Minsky's Financial Instability Hypothesis (FIH) is usually interpreted as a theory of the business cycle, he also developed a theory of the long-term transformation of the economy. Briefly, capitalism evolves through several stages, each marked by a different financial structure. The nineteenth century saw "commercial capitalism" where commercial banking dominated—banks made short-term commercial loans and issued deposits. This was replaced by the beginning of the twentieth century, with "finance capitalism," after Rudolf Hilferding, where investment banks ruled. The distinguishing characteristic was the use of long-term external finance to purchase expensive capital assets. The financial structure was riskier, and collapsed into the Great Depression—which Minsky saw as the failure of finance capitalism. We emerged from World War II with a new form of capitalism, "managerial welfare-state capitalism" in which financial institutions were constrained by New Deal reforms, and with large oligopolistic corporations that financed investment out of retained earnings. Private sector debt was small, but government debt left over from war finance was large—providing safe assets for households, firms and banks. This system was financially robust, unlikely to experience deep recession because of the Big Government (Treasury's countercyclical budget) and Big Bank (Fed's lender of last resort actions) constraints.

However, the relative stability of the first few decades after World War II encouraged ever-greater risk-taking as the financial system was transformed into "money manager capitalism," where the dominant financial players are "managed money"—lightly regulated "shadow banks" like pension funds, hedge funds, sovereign wealth funds and university endowments—with huge pools of funds in search of the highest returns. Innovations by financial engineers encouraged growth of private debt relative to income, and increased reliance on volatile short-term finance.

The first US postwar financial crisis occurred in 1966 but it was quickly resolved by swift government intervention. This set a pattern: crises came more frequently but government saved the day each time. As a result, ever more risky financial arrangements were "validated," leading to more experimentation. The crises became more severe, requiring greater rescue efforts by governments. Finally, the entire global financial system crashed in fall 2008—with many calling it the "Minsky Moment" or "Minsky Crisis." Unfortunately, most analyses relied on his FIH rather than on his "stages" approach. If, as Minsky believed, the financial system had experienced a long-term transformation toward fragility then recovery would only presage an even bigger collapse—on a scale such as the 1929 crash that ended the finance capitalism stage. In that case, what will be necessary is fundamental—New Deal style—reforms.

Money Manager Capitalism is an inherently unstable form of capitalism with managed money largely unregulated, and with competitive advantages over the regulated banks. It played a role in the rise of what came to be called "shadow banks" and many have pointed to that portion of the financial system as an important contributor to the crisis. Indeed, much of the deregulation of banks was designed to allow them to compete with the less regulated, lower cost and more highly leveraged shadow banks. By tapping managed money, they helped to bubble up stocks, then real estate and finally commodities markets. To compete, banks created off-balance sheet entities (such as SPVs) that took huge risks without supervision. Those risks came back to banks when the crisis hit. It is difficult to imagine how we could have had the global financial crisis without the rise of money managers and the shadow banks.

In a very important sense, our current stage of capitalism, Money Manager Capitalism, was a resurrection of early twentieth century Finance Capitalism—an economic system in which finance is the tail that wags the dog. It is characterized by complex layering of financial commitments on top of real assets that generate income—a kind of capitalism in which ownership positions need to be continually validated. According to Minsky, that first phase of finance capitalism imploded in the Great Depression. The government was too small to offset the collapse of gross capital income that followed the Great Crash of 1929. After World War II, we emerged with a government so large that its deficit could expand sufficiently in a downturn to offset the swing of investment. This maintained incomes, allowing debts to be serviced. In addition, an array of New Deal reforms had strengthened the financial system, separating investment banks from commercial banks and putting in place government guarantees such as deposit insurance. But, as Minsky observed, stability is destabilizing. The relatively high rate of economic growth, plus the relative stability of the financial system, over time encouraged innovations that subverted the New Deal constraints. In addition, the financial wealth (and private debt) grew on trend, producing huge sums of money under professional management. Minsky called this stage the "money manager" phase of capitalism.

3.2 What do banks do? What should they do?

Let us turn to a summary of Minsky's view of money and banking. In many of his writings he emphasized six main points:

1 a capitalist economy is a financial system;
2 neoclassical economics is not useful because it denies that the financial system matters;
3 the financial structure has become much more fragile;
4 this fragility makes it likely that stagnation or even a deep depression is possible;
5 a stagnant capitalist economy will not promote capital development;
6 however, this can be avoided by apt reform of the financial structure in conjunction with apt use of fiscal powers of the government.

Central to his argument is the understanding of banking that he developed over his career; the development of his approach paralleled the transformation of the financial system toward the money manager stage. The banker holds the key—he is the "ephor of capitalism," as Minsky's original dissertation adviser, Josef Schumpeter, put it—because not only do entrepreneurs have to be sufficiently optimistic to invest, they must also find a banker willing to advance the wage bill to produce investment output. For Schumpeter, and for Minsky, the "ephor" breaks the simple circuit of production and consumption of wage goods—in which banks simply finance production of consumer goods by workers whose consumption exactly exhausts the wage bill required to produce them. In other words, the ephor allows generation of profits by financing spending of those not directly involved in producing consumption goods.

To go further would get us into complicated matters, but the next step would be to discuss the role of the investment banker, who finances the long-term positions in capital assets. This is a quite different activity, which allows savers to choose between holding liquid (financial) assets or positions in real assets (either directly by owning a firm, or indirectly through ownership of shares). Glass–Steagall maintained a separation of the investment banking and commercial banking functions. Lines were blurred when we first allowed bank holding companies to own both types of banks, and then gutted and finally repealed Glass–Steagall.[12]

Let us recap Minsky's views:

1 Banking should not be described as a process of accepting deposits in order to make loans.
2 Rather, banks accept the IOUs of borrowers then create bank deposit IOUs that the borrowers can spend.
3 Indeed, often the bank simply accepts the IOU of the borrower and then makes the payment for the borrower—cutting a check in the name of the car dealer, for example.

4   Like all economic units, banks finance positions in their assets (including IOUs of borrowers) by issuing their own IOUs (including demand deposits).
5   Banks use reserves for clearing with other banks (and with the government). Banks also use reserves to meet cash withdrawals by customers. Bank reserves at the central bank are debited when they need cash for withdrawal.
6   In some systems, including the US's, the central bank sets a required reserve ratio. But this does not provide the central bank with any quantitative controls over bank loans and deposits. Rather, the central bank supplies reserves on demand but sets the "price" at which it supplies reserves when it targets the overnight interest rate. In the US the main target is the federal funds rate. Fed control over banks is all about price, not quantity, of reserves.

Over the two decades prior to the GFC, financial institutions relied increasingly on extremely short-term non-deposit liabilities to finance their positions in assets. Over the final decade leading up to the crisis, they took positions in increasingly risky—indeed, ephemeral—assets that were divorced from the "real" economy. The proto-typical position would be in a derivative (an asset whose value is "derived from" another asset that is linked to an income flow or asset), say, a CDO or a CDO-squared (collateralized debt obligation), with that position financed by overnight borrowing from another financial institution. This is the notion of layering: a household's income flow is used to service a mortgage, which is packaged into a security that is further layered as a CDO "bet" that the household can make the promised payments. On the other side of the balance sheet, the holder of the CDO may have issued commercial paper to a Money Market Mutual Fund (MMMF) that issued a "deposit-like" liability that is supposed to "never break the buck." And of course it gets more complex because others used credit default swaps to "bet" that the mortgage, the MBS and the CDO (and CDOs squared and cubed) will go bad. When mortgage delinquencies rose, the MBS was downgraded, the CDO failed and the CDSs (credit default swaps) came into the money—often triggering default by the counterparties—while the MMMF refused to roll-over the commercial paper, triggering a liquidity problem for the issuer. The combination of leverage and layering meant that a highly interconnected financial system would almost instantly fall into crisis.

Since the crisis of one highly connected institution (Lehman, Bear) would cause problems to race through the entire system, the Fed—the global lender of last resort—felt there was no alternative to mount its unprecedented response. In retrospect, while it is true that an immediate but temporary intervention could not be avoided, it does not appear to be true that the Fed needed to continue the intervention for years—which cannot be interpreted as lender of last resort activity but rather as an attempt to make "bad banks" whole. Still to reduce the scope and size of response, it is necessary to address the excessive leverage, layering and interconnectedness of financial institutions under money manager capitalism. To understand how the financial system needs to be reformed to make crisis response easier, we need to understand what financial institutions *ought* to do, then aim to reform them along those lines. This is quite different from current approaches to reform that aim at reducing "systemic risk" by attempting to identify particularly risky behaviors. This does not ensure that remaining behaviors actually provide the services that ought to be provided, nor does it eliminate those that serve no social purpose.

Minsky recognized that Glass–Steagall (that separated commercial and investment banking) had already become anachronistic by the early 1990s. He insisted that any new reforms must take into account the accelerated innovations in both financial intermediation and the payments mechanism. He believed these changes were largely market driven, and not due to deregulation. The demise of commercial banking and the rise of shadow banking was largely a consequence of the transition to money manager capitalism.

In his proposal for development of the newly independent Eastern European nations, Minsky argued that the critical problem was to "create a monetary and financial system which will facilitate economic development, the emergence of democracy and the integration with the capitalist world."[13] Except for the latter goal, this statement applies equally well to promotion of capital development of the Western nations.[14] In Minsky's view, capital development of the economy can be "ill done" in two main ways: the "Smithian" and the "Keynesian." The first refers to what might be called "misallocation": the wrong investments are financed. The second refers to an insufficiency of investment, which leads to a level of aggregate demand that is too low to promote high employment. The 1980s suffered from both, but mostly from inappropriate investment—especially in commercial real estate investment. We could say that the 2000s again suffered from ill-done, Smithian capital development, since far too much finance flowed into the residential real estate sector. In both cases, Minsky pointed the finger at securitization. In the 1980s, the thrifts that had lowered underwriting standards had funding capacity that flowed into commercial real estate; in the 2000s, the mania for risky (high return) asset-backed securities fueled subprime lending.

In a discerning 1987 analysis,[15] Minsky argued that because of the way the mortgages were packaged it was possible to sell off a package of mortgages at a premium so that the originator and the investment banking firms walked away from the deal with a net income and no recourse from the holders. The instrument originators and the security underwriters did not hazard any of their wealth on the longer-term viability of the underlying projects. Obviously in such packaged financing the selection and supervisory functions of lenders and underwriters are not as well done as they might be when the fortunes of the originators are at hazard over the longer term. The implication is rather obvious: good underwriting is promoted when the underwriter is exposed to the longer-term risks. This brings us to Minsky's skeptical banker:

> When we go to the theater we enter into a conspiracy with the players to suspend disbelief. The financial developments of the 1980's can be viewed as theater: promoters and portfolio managers suspended disbelief with respect to where the cash would come from that would [validate] the projects being

financed. Bankers, the designated sceptic in the financial structure, placed their critical faculties on hold. As a result the capital development was not done well. Decentralization of finance may well be the way to reintroduce the necessary scepticism.[16]

Decentralization plus maintaining exposure to risk could reorient institutions back toward relationship banking.

Unfortunately, most trends in recent years have favored concentration. The "too big to fail" doctrine that dates back to the problems of Continental Illinois in the early 1970s gives an obvious advantage to the biggest banks. These are able to finance positions at the lowest cost because the government stands behind them. Small local banks face higher costs as they try to attract local deposits by opening more offices than necessary; it also costs them more to attract "wholesale" deposits in national markets. Even in the case of FDIC-insured deposits (which have no default risk), smaller banks pay more simply because of the market's perception that they are riskier (i.e., the government does not backstop them). Investment banks (Goldman Sachs) are now allowed to operate like hedge funds, but they can obtain FDIC-insured deposits and can rely on Fed and Treasury protection should risky trades go bad.

How can the system be reformed to favor relationship banking that seems to be more conducive to promoting the capital development of the economy? First, reduce government protections for less-desirable banking activities. The government currently provides two important kinds of protection: liquidity and solvency. Liquidity is mostly provided by the Fed, which lends reserves at the discount window and buys assets (in the past, mostly government debt, but in recent years the Fed has bought private debt as well). Refusing to provide liquidity is not the right way to discipline the financial system. Minsky always advocated extending discount window operations to include a wide range of financial institutions. If the Fed had lent reserves without limit to all financial institutions when the crisis first hit, the liquidity crisis probably could have been resolved more quickly. Hence, this kind of government protection should not be restrained.

The second kind of protection, against default, is more problematic. Deposit insurance guarantees no default risk on certain classes of deposits—now up to $250,000. This guarantee is essential for clearing at par and for maintaining a safe and secure payments system. There is no good reason to limit FDIC insurance, so the cap should be lifted. The question is which types of institutions should be allowed to offer such deposits, or rather, which types of assets would be eligible for financing using insured deposits. Some considerations would include riskiness of assets, maturity of assets, and whether purchase of the assets fulfills the public purpose: the capital development of the economy. The major argument for limiting the ability of financial institutions to finance asset positions by issuing insured deposits is that government has a legitimate interest in promoting the public purpose. Banks should be prevented from issuing insured deposits in a manner that causes the capital development of the country to be "ill done." Banks that receive government protection in the form of liquidity and (partial) solvency guarantees are essentially public–private partnerships. They promote the public purpose by specializing in activities that they can perform more competently than the government can. One of these is underwriting: assessing credit-worthiness and building relations with borrowers that enhance their willingness to repay.

Since the mid-1990s, a belief that underwriting is unnecessary flowered and then collapsed. Financial institutions discovered that credit rating scores could not substitute for underwriting, in part because those scores can be manipulated, but also because the elimination of relationship banking changes the behavior of borrowers and lenders. This means that past default rates become irrelevant to assessing risk. If banks are not underwriting, why would the government need them as partners? The government could just finance directly activities that it perceives to be in the public interest: home mortgages, student loans, state and local government infrastructure, and even small-business activities (commercial real estate and working capital expenses). Where underwriting is not seen to fulfill a public purpose, then the government can simply cut out the middleman. Indeed, there has been a movement in that direction, with the government taking back control of student loans. When the government guarantees deposits as well as loans (e.g., mortgages and student loans), the banks' role becomes merely to provide underwriting. On the other hand, where underwriting is critical—say, in commercial lending—then the government needs the middleman to select those firms deserving of credit.

Solving the Smithian problem requires direct oversight of bank activity, mostly on the asset side of their balance sheet. Financial activities that further the capital development of the economy need to be encouraged; those that cause it to be "ill done" need to be discouraged. One of the reasons that Minsky wanted the Fed to lend reserves to all comers was so that private institutions would be indebted to the Fed. As a creditor, the Fed would be able to ask the banker the question, "How will you repay me?" The Federal Reserve's powers to examine are inherent in its ability to lend to banks through the discount window. Examination of a bank's books also allows the Fed to look for risky practices and keep abreast of developments. The Fed was caught with its pants down, so to speak, by the crisis that began in 2007, in part because it generally supplied reserves in open market operations rather than at the discount window. Forcing private banks "into the bank" can give the Fed more leverage over their activities. The Fed would be better informed to the extent that it supervised and examined banks—leading, one hopes, to better policy formation. Minsky worried that the trend toward megabanks

> may well allow the weakest part of the system, the giant banks, to expand, not because they are efficient but because they can use the clout of their large asset base and cash flows to make life uncomfortable for local banks: predatory pricing and corners [of the market] cannot be ruled out in the American context.[17]

Further, since the size of loans depends on the capital base, big banks have a natural affinity for the "big deals," while small banks service smaller clients. For this reason, Minsky advocated a proactive government policy to create and support small community development banks (CDBs).[18] The proposal would have created a network of small community development banks to provide a full range of services (a sort of universal bank for underserved communities):

1   A payment system for check cashing and clearing, and for credit and debit cards.
2   Secure depositories for savings and transaction balances.
3   Household financing for housing, consumer debts, and student loans.
4   Commercial banking services for loans, payroll services, and advice.
5   Investment banking services for determining the appropriate liability structure for the assets of a firm, and placing those liabilities.
6   Asset management and advice for households.[19]

It will be obvious that Minsky would have these perform the main functions expected for a financial system. The institutions would be kept small, local and profitable. They would be public–private partnerships, with a new Federal Bank for Community Development Banks created to provide equity and to charter and supervise the CDBs. Each CDB would be organized as a bank holding company. Examples of its composition would be: a narrow bank to provide payments services; a commercial bank to provide loans to firms and mortgages to households; an investment bank to intermediate equity issues and long-term debt of firms; and a trust bank to act as a trustee and to provide financial advice.

Reform of the financial system does need to address the "shadow banks" of money manager capitalism. Minsky believed that pension funds were largely responsible for the leveraged buyout boom (and bust) of the 1980s; similarly, strong evidence indicates that pension funds drove the commodities boom and bust of the mid-2000s. To be sure, this is just a part of managed money, but it is a government-protected-and-supported portion—both because it gets favorable tax treatment and because it has quasi-government backing through the Pension Benefit Guaranty Corporation.[20] Greater regulation of pension funds—to ensure they serve the public purpose—is also required. For example, there is no justification for letting pension funds speculate in commodities, such as food and energy products. Nor should pension funds be allowed to use CDSs to bet against firms, households or governments. The argument that such activities are potentially profitable should hold no water—even if it were true. As protected and tax-supported funds, these should not be allowed to engage in activities that run counter to the public purpose.

Finally, returning to Minsky's views on the role that financial institutions play in the capital development of the economy, he was appalled at recent trends. First, an important shift has taken place, away from wage share and toward gross capital income, and stagnant wages clearly played a part in promoting the growth of household indebtedness over the past three decades, with rapid acceleration since the mid-1990s. As many at the Levy Institute had been arguing since 1996, the shift toward a private sector deficit that was unprecedentedly large and persistent proved to be unsustainable. The mountain of debt still crushing households is in part due to the shift of national income away from wage income, as households try to maintain living standards through borrowing. Equally problematic is the allocation of profits toward the financial sector. Just before the crisis broke, in late 2007, 40 percent of all corporate profits accrued to the FIRE (finance, insurance, real estate) sector, and its share has returned to that level. This contrasts with a 10–15 percent share until the 1970s, and a 20 percent share until the 1990s. While value added by the FIRE sector also grew, from about 12 percent in the early postwar period to nearly 20 percent today, its share of profits was twice as high as its share of value added by the time of the 2000s bubble. Hence, we see three interrelated problems: the profit share is probably too large (the wage share is too small), the share of GDP coming from the financial sector is probably too large, and the share of profits allocated by the financial sector to itself is far too large. Downsizing finance is necessary to ensure that the capital development of the economy can be well done, not "ill done." With 40 percent of corporate profits going to finance, too little is left to other sectors, which encourages entrepreneurial effort and innovations to be directed (wrongly, in the Smithian sense) toward the financial sector.

4 Conclusion

Over past decades, the belief that "markets work to promote the public interest" gained in popularity. Minsky asked, *But what if they don't?* A system of constraints and interventions can work better. He also believed that we need to make "industry" dominate over "speculation" (recalling Keynes's famous dichotomy), and not vice versa, or the capital development of the economy will be ill done in two ways: the Smithian/Neoclassical way or the Keynes/Aggregate Demand way. If investment is misdirected, we not only waste resources but also get boom and bust. If investment is too low, we not only suffer from unemployment but also achieve profits too low to support commitments, leading to default. Further, when profits are low in "industry," problems arise in the financial sector, since commitments cannot be met. In that case, individual profit-seeking behavior leads to incoherent results as financial markets, labor markets and goods markets all react in a manner that causes wages and prices to fall, generating a debt deflation. Unfortunately, things are not better when investment is too high: it generates high profits that reward innovation, generating greater risk-taking and eventually producing a financial structure that is too fragile. As Minsky always argued, the really dangerous instability in a capitalist economy is in the upward direction—toward a euphoric boom. That is what makes a debt deflation possible, as asset prices become overvalued and too much unserviceable debt is issued.

The Smithian ideal is that debt deflations are not endogenous; rather, they must result from exogenous factors, including too much government regulation and intervention. So the solution is deregulation, downsizing government, tax cuts, and making markets more flexible. The Keynesian view is that the financial structure is transformed over a run of good times, from a robust to a fragile state, as a result of the natural reaction of agents to the successful operation of the economy. If policymakers understood this, they could formulate policy to attenuate the transformation—and then to deal with a crisis when it occurs.

Notes

1 This chapter is based on research supported by Ford Foundation Grant no. 1110-0184, administered by the University of Missouri—Kansas City for a project *Research and Policy Dialogue Project on Improving Governance of the Government Safety Net in Financial Crises*.
2 University of Missouri—Kansas City, and Levy Economics Institute of Bard College. I would like to acknowledge research support provided by the team that has contributed to this project: Robert Auerbach, Jan Kregel, Linwood Tauheed, Walker Todd, Frank Veneroso, Thomas Ferguson, Robert A. Johnson, Nicola Matthews, William Greider, Andy Felkerson, Bernard Shull, Thorvald Moe, Avi Barnes, Yeva Nersisyan, Thomas Humphrey, Daniel Alpert, Pavlina Tcherneva, and Scott Fullwiler.
3 The GFC was the worst financial crisis since the Great Depression and represented a dramatic failure of corporate governance and risk management.
4 The main researchers on this part of the project were James Felkerson and Nicola Mathews, both graduate students of the University of Missouri—Kansas City at the time. See www.levyinstitute.org/ford-levy/governance/.
5 See www.levyinstitute.org/ford-levy/governance/.
6 These funds were used in part to "recapitalize" selected financial institutions. Most of the capital injected was eventually repaid to the Treasury.
7 Note, again, that for the much smaller Treasury intervention—Paulson's $800 billion—Congressional approval was required.
8 FDICIA required the resolution of insolvent banks to be conducted by the *least costly* method available. See Shull (2010).
9 For detailed explanation, see Felkerson (2011). Quotations taken from p. 18.
10 See the Ford–Levy Institute Project on *Financial Instability and the Reregulation of Financial Institutions and Markets*, www.levyinstitute.org/ford-levy/.
11 See Tymoigne and Wray (2014).
12 For those interested in Minsky's views on all of this, see Wray (2010).
13 Minsky (1992c, p.28)
14 See also Minsky 1993.
15 Minsky (1987).
16 Minsky (1992b, p. 37).
17 Minsky (1992a, p. 12).
18 Minsky et al. (1993).
19 Minsky et al. (1993, pp. 10–11).
20 Yeva and Wray (2010).

References

Felkerson, J. A. (2011) "$29,000,000,000,000: A Detailed Look at the Fed's Bailout by Funding Facility and Recipient," Working Paper No. 698, December, Annandale-on-Hudson, NY: Levy Economics Institute of Bard College.

Minsky, H. P. (1987) "Securitization," mimeo, in Minsky Archives at the Levy Economics Institute of Bard College.

Minsky. H. P. (1992a) "Reconstituting the Financial Structure: The United States" (prospective chapter, four parts), May 13, in Minsky Archives at the Levy Economics Institute of Bard College.

Minsky, H. P. (1992b) "Reconstituting the United States' Financial Structure: Some fundamental issues," Working Paper No. 69, January, Annandale-on-Hudson, NY: Levy Economics Institute of Bard College.

Minsky, H. P. (1992c) "The Economic Problem at the End of the Second Millennium: Creating Capitalism, Reforming Capitalism and Making Capitalism Work," May 13, in Manuscripts in Minsky Archives at Levy Institute www.bard.edu/library/archive/minsky/.

Minsky, H. P. (1993) "Financial Structure and the Financing of the Capital Development of the Economy," The Jerome Levy Institute Presents Proposals for Reform of the Financial System, Corpus Christie, TX, April 23, in Minsky Archives at the Levy Economics Institute of Bard College.

Minsky, H. P., Papdimitriou, D. B., Phillips, R. J. and Wray, L. R. (1993) "Community Development Banking: A Proposal to Establish a Nationwide System of Community Development Banks," Public Policy Brief No. 3, Annandale-on-Hudson, NY: Levy Economics Institute of Bard College.

Shull, B. (2010) "Too Big To Fail in Financial Crisis: Motives, Countermeasures and Prospects," Working Paper No. 601, June, Annandale-on-Hudson, NY: Levy Economics Institute of Bard College.

Tymoigne, E. and Wray, L. R. (2014) *The Rise and Fall of Money Manager Capitalism: Minsky's half century from World War Two to the Great Recession*, New York, NY: Routledge.

Wray, L. R. (2010) "What Do Banks Do? What Should Banks Do?" Working Paper No. 612, August, Annandale-on-Hudson, NY: Levy Economics Institute of Bard College.

Yeva, N. and Wray, L. R. (2010) "The Trouble with Pensions," Public Policy Brief No. 109, March Annandale-on-Hudson, NY: Levy Economics Institute of Bard College.

6 Economic crisis and globalization in the European Union

Cosimo Perrotta

1 The nature of globalization

What has been called globalization is a set of economic processes, which derive from the tendency of markets to unify and form a single world market. Local markets progressively lose their specific features, and also their respective protection. They all become similar to each other.

Globalization does not have a straightforward, linear development. It depends on the policies of the various countries. Market unification is usually more advanced for industrial products, which are based more and more on automatized and standard production. Standardized goods lose the specific features of local products. They are cheap and can be easily sold in the local markets. This aspect of globalization almost always wins the praise of economists. In industrial production, standardization is the necessary step for an increase in productivity.[1]

Kindleberger observes that the unification of markets eliminates injustices and social disparities which can be found in the local markets. For example, it improves working conditions. It is actually true that when the labor market is segmented—at the national or local level, or for particular social structures—it allows discrimination and extreme exploitation. See for instance the usual treatment of immigrants and of ethnic, religious or cultural minorities.[2]

However, the opposite is often true. Market unification, when it is promoted by the multinationals, aims to limit social control over economic processes. This eliminates the protection of workers or of consumers, protections that had been managed within the local culture in various ways. The very process of standardization tends to eliminate niche markets, which typically provided protection for jobs, product quality and consumption styles.

In more general terms, there are three commonplaces about globalization we should question. The first is the belief that globalization simply consists in the liberalization of international trade (reduction of duties, elimination of import quotas, etc.). In actual fact globalization also depends on countries' internal demand, foreign debt, the exporting (or flight) of capital, the relocation abroad of factories and of new investments.

The second stereotype is the idea that liberalization and the other processes just mentioned are promoted by governments in the interests of the country. In fact they are almost always promoted by the multinationals or by the economic lobbies of the stronger countries, and are set in motion either directly or indirectly through the national governments.[3]

The third commonplace that needs to be corrected is the idea that globalization always causes development and gives benefits to all; and that local opposition to it is only due to the defense of certain particular interests. In fact globalization does not always produce development. Quite the opposite, it often damages weaker economies.[4] Local opposition movements sometimes do actually defend corporative privileges and inefficiencies. But in other instances they defend the positive elements that would get lost with globalization: the variety and quality of products; biodiversity; non-extreme competition and cooperative work, based on participation; less standardized and more refined consumption; a culture that is not obsessed by the maximization of profits and earnings.

Thus we can see that globalization is a more complex phenomenon than is usually thought, and shows contradictory tendencies. As far as Europe is concerned, the emergence of globalization derives from the crisis of the welfare state. We must therefore start our discussion with the welfare state.

2 The welfare state and the prospects for development

From 1950 to about 1975 the states of Western Europe witnessed the creation of the welfare state, one of the greatest experiences in the history of economic development. It was inspired by two intellectual traditions: the Keynesian idea of stimulating growth by increasing internal demand (supported by the state's "deficit spending") and the social-democratic idea of redistributing wealth, which is produced by development, in favor of the poorer classes.[5] For the first time, after nine centuries of development, there was a radical improvement in the living standard of these classes.

The huge hidden unemployment in agriculture was largely eliminated. The massive emigration from southern to central Europe fed a rapid industrialization. Hunger, illnesses connected to poverty, and illiteracy were reduced to a minimum, along with the subsistence economy and unproductive small businesses in the tertiary sector. Houses for all, pensions, schools, health care, roads and other infrastructure were created.

The spectacular rise in consumption was financed partly by public investments and government welfare spending, partly by the growth in private production. In turn, the increase in basic consumption generated a marked increase in labor productivity.[6]

Such a rapid and long growth period could not avoid some market gluts. The gluts were caused by the fantastic increase in productivity in all of the production sectors.[7] Contrary to what Malthus wrote, in theory an absolute market glut does not exist. There are always new needs to satisfy, which keep markets open. This is what development means. However, there can be a *tendency* to gluts. In such a case there are only two ways to sustain accumulation: extending the market to new consumers or creating new goods to satisfy new needs and desires.

An increase in consumption by the lower classes was one solution that Keynes suggested in the case of the 1930s crisis. But in the mid-Seventies this process was coming to an end.[8] Development could continue only if other structural changes intervened, to open new sectors of investment. However, in general, private investments are not enough to trigger or restart growth.[9] According to historical experience, when an economy moves from backwardness—or stagnation—toward development, state intervention is indispensable.

In the 1980s new markets were created, above all in the enormous sector of information technology, electronics and telecommunications. But it was not enough to relaunch development. The Western economy only managed, until 2008, to avoid an explosive crisis. It limped along without finding a clear vent for accumulation.

An organic policy to restart development should address problems such as: elimination of the remaining poverty, which in spite of the welfare state is still present in huge dimensions in western Europe; development of southern Europe, and then of eastern Europe. In addition, the Delors plan could be put in motion, to create great continent-wide infrastructure.[10] There could be a large-scale project to improve education and extend research. Great emphasis could be placed on collective goods, like transport systems, hydro-geologic reorganization, or restoration of the natural and artistic patrimony.

Then there could be a radical change in the relationships with the poorer countries. It is necessary to abandon neo-colonial policies that perpetuate poverty in those countries. Paradoxically, although neocolonial policies cause a huge drain on world resources toward Europe, in the long run they do not advantage European growth. The latter could be fostered by creating a market in the poor countries, to enable them to absorb some portion of European products.[11] Also strong support of the NGOs (non-governmental organizations) and in general of the third sector can be important.[12] This sector can fulfill needs (personal, cultural, social) that the profit sector is unable to cope with.

Lastly, it was necessary to implement integrated policies to rescue the environment and to develop renewable energy sources. This was already a pressing problem in the 1980s. Environmental policies refer to such a vast, variegated area of production that merely putting them into effect would suffice to restart development.[13] However, European policies in this field were introduced very late. Although they are the most advanced in the world, they have not been powerful enough to change production and consumption models and to create a new kind of growth.[14]

In conclusion, Europe has done very little for all these new types of demand. The building of large-scale infrastructure has been underway in the last few years; for instance high speed trains; oil and gas pipelines; information technology nets. There is now some timid policy of incentives for renewable energy. On the other hand the income distribution gap and the gap between northern and southeastern Europe increased enormously. There is still no real policy for the development of education and research. Relations with most of the poor countries are still at the level of neocolonialism. Environmental pollution is on the increase.

3 The prevalence of unproductive consumption

Why were none of the above paths to development taken? There are essentially two reasons. The first is that single states refused, and still refuse, to give Europe too great a decision-making power, which would weaken their own.

Europe was initially set up as a common market for coal and steel. It later developed a broad common agricultural policy, which absorbed, and still absorbs, the major share of the European common funds. As development has advanced, this agriculture policy has become seriously distorted. In fact in developed economies the productivity of industrialized agriculture has grown so much that less than 3 percent of the workforce is able to feed an entire country. Spending most of the common funds on such a small sector means renouncing strong policy options for the rest of the economy.

The second failure lies in the distortions of the welfare state. In its initial approach there were already glaring weaknesses.[15] Over time they became so serious that growth was hindered.

First, in the public sector there was not an adequate increase in productivity. During the periods of development the public sector has to grow, as society becomes more and more complex and requires new services. In the case of the European welfare state, public sectors—like administration, education, health care, research, infrastructure, transport, housing—grew enormously. The trade unions in these sectors, unlike those of the private sector, obtained various privileges; and above all, in many European countries, they prevented their productivity level from being monitored. In fact politicians have no interest in opposing such privileges. As a result, public spending became an increasing drain on the budget, instead of being an investment.

The same thing happened in the industries financed by public capital. They were set up for strategic sectors—like steel, electricity, freeways, coal, big shipping, chemicals, etc.—sectors in which private investment was difficult. But often they were run more in line with political and social criteria than with efficiency and profit criteria. This too became an increasing drain on the public coffers.

The most serious distortion was the following: thanks to development, the protected lower classes started to decline in number, as the younger generation of lower-class families were able to study and get better jobs. However, although the numbers of poor declined, for electoral reasons welfare spending did not decline. On the contrary, benefits were often extended to others not really involved in the protected sectors. The same happened in the cases of the disabled or jobless. Finally, although the average life-span was increasing, employees were allowed to retire when they were still relatively young and efficient. Pension payments generated a huge deficit in public spending.

Often welfare intervention has encouraged corporate protection. However, such a tendency did not protect the weaker members of society, rather it has protected the more numerous and stronger categories. A growing part of welfare spending went to the advantage of categories which were already protected, while the weaker categories (manual workers, young jobless, disabled individuals, immigrants, mothers, low-income elderly people) were given less protection.

This distorted welfare state has produced a high level of consumption; but a part is unproductive and hinders development. For example the welfare benefits which go to the privileged middle classes produce unproductive consumption. These kinds of payments have created a new form of hidden unemployment. These unproductive forms of payment no longer go to peasants in agriculture, but to some public employees, and also to the workers of the non-competitive factories supported by public capital.

4 The real meaning of the fiscal crisis

In analyzing the crisis of the welfare state, the distinction between productive and unproductive spending should be kept in mind. The crisis appeared in the mid-Seventies as a fiscal crisis of the state. The blame was immediately placed on welfare spending (with no distinctions), and on the state's "interference" in the economy.

The Keynesians were at a loss, because Keynes himself had made no distinction between productive and unproductive spending.[16] Keynes was interested in raising demand in the short run. But without a distinction between productive and unproductive public spending it was difficult to defend social spending in the long run.

This failure to make the distinction allowed the arguments of neoliberals to prevail. They claimed that welfare spending took wealth away from private investment; and that it had to be cut in order to restart growth. The welfare state, which had generated one of the longest booms in history, was targeted as a source of waste. In this view, only the private sector could generate wealth.

In fact this argument has been devastating for growth. Real waste in public spending has not been cut in any significant way, either that caused by inefficiency or that caused by corporate privileges. The classes that benefit from this waste have too much political influence to be affected. The only spending that has been cut consistently is productive spending, the kind that raises wages and the living standard of the lower working classes. Therefore what has been done is the opposite of what is claimed. Unproductive spending has been protected and productive spending has been cut. The taxable base has shrunk. Moreover in the private sector, tax evasion is very high. This has further restricted state revenue.

In sum, in the last 40 years unproductive spending has soared and productive spending has diminished in relative terms. This does not mean, however, that public spending is always unproductive, as neoliberals claim.

In fact the neoliberal cuts have worsened the crisis, instead of solving it. Their policy decisions played a major role in the recession of 2008.[17] Investments in the traditional markets did not absorb the growth of the surplus available. This has ended up in encouraging not only unproductive welfare spending, but also unproductive investments.

5 Market glut and repetitive goods

For mainstream economics it is senseless to speak of "unproductive investment," because private investment is always supposed to be productive. But experience disproves this claim. In the 1980s, since there were no large investments in new fields led by public spending, European private investment spread out in four directions. The first one, and quite obvious, concerned the new sectors created by the market. The second was directed toward saving, which soon began to encourage increasing financial speculation. The third continued to go toward traditional markets. Lastly, later on there was an increase in investments in backward economies.

Let us here look closely at the developments with regard to traditional markets. These markets already tended to glut. Therefore investments tried, and try, above all else, to keep the markets open, by creating extra demand. Many tools are used to achieve this goal. First of all, advertising, including campaigns of discounts, sales, public incentives, etc. Increasingly invasive, advertising absorbs a growing part of the budgets of big enterprises; and has a determining economic influence on all the mass media (which does not help freedom).

It must be stressed that an increase in advertising is not an increase in wealth. Advertising can have two different effects. One is that some consumers shift from one product to another of the same kind. This is often followed by an intensifying of competition, and may lead the market to become oligopolistic;[18] but the overall demand does not change. The other possibility is that consumers are driven to buy bigger quantities of a certain good. But the effect is the same as in the first case: incomes being equal, consumers will replace one kind of good with another. However we must note that there is also informative advertising.

The other strategies to keep traditional outlets open push consumers to buy new items while the old ones, of the same kind, are still useful. Examples are: fashion items; packaging variations; useless optional items; throwaway goods; the use of less durable materials in cases where the production costs are equal.

All these strategies flood the market with new goods that do not give the consumer an increase in utility; or only provide a minimum increase. For instance consumers fill their houses with television sets or clothes or books, etc. that they do not use. They act this way because the present structure of the market does not give them the chance to buy alternative goods that satisfy new and existing needs. For example, if the same sum could be used to pay for more efficient public transport or for more nurseries, instead of buying a third TV set, many consumers would probably prefer the first option.

Thus in traditional markets we have a frantic turnover of products without any increase in utility, or with decreasing marginal utility. Such goods can be called repetitive. They do not create new wealth.

Many people claim that while all the above may be true, at the minimum this production creates jobs, incomes and profits; that it causes growth and therefore creates wealth. But the production of repetitive goods is socially unproductive, even though it can provide profits and incomes. It is similar to the traditional hidden unemployment: it provides income to private individuals, but from the social point of view it is a loss of social wealth. On the other hand the production of a new kind of goods would increase utility and the productive capacity of individuals.

The increase in the unproductive employment of wealth within the European economy has created a cumulative process that reinforces these perverse tendencies. Unemployment rates rise. Incomes and protection of the middle and lower classes are falling. These tendencies progressively narrow the market and discourage investments. A great quantity of investment capital is transformed into rents. It goes to building (which has in general a low value added) or financial speculation; or to "refuge goods," like houses, land and gold. Meanwhile, the European economy is stagnating and getting poorer.

6 Financial globalization

Globalization was designed to be the liberalization of commerce. But in fact the market was unified primarily by financial speculation.[19] The difficulty of making productive investments drives capital toward finance. At present the world's finance capital is three times bigger than that invested in the production of goods and services.

The present structure of the European Union has accentuated this tendency. There is no organic economic policy, and only one financial institution has been set up, the European Central Bank. According to its statute, it has to check inflation but is not interested in development. This results in the discouragement of productive investments. European currency too has undergone this distortion. The euro could have been the basis for planning for new growth. But in fact it contributed to the increase in income inequality.

Mainstream economics does not distinguish between the formation of private income and the creation of social wealth. In consequence it was too slow in noticing that such an abnormal growth of finance capital was unhealthy. Financial investments normally give far higher short-term yields than productive investments. So there was an enormous transfer of savings from productive to speculative investments.[20] Public institutions, too, and even productive businesses were pushed to invest in financial speculation.

But, these investments being speculative, they give advantages only in the short term. In the long term the result was that weak or uninformed investors lost money, while speculators and stronger investors gained the advantage. Here too a cumulative process emerged. The financialization of the European economy, due to the lack of opportunities for productive investments, generated a further reduction of these opportunities. This tendency reduced taxable wealth. Moreover the liberalization of capital movements has boosted the tendency to relocate production abroad in search of lower wages.

To this situation neoliberalism applied a remedy that worsens the negative tendency. In order to facilitate investment, taxes on higher incomes were cut.

However the investment crisis depended, not on excessive taxation, but on the lack of positive expectations. So, the increase in higher incomes simply increased rents, luxury consumption and, once again, the speculative use of capital. This has been encouraged by the fact that financial speculation is taxed at a lower level.[21]

Another remedy offered by neoliberalism to solve the states' fiscal crisis is to cut costs by limiting welfare spending, that is, by narrowing the consumption of the lowest classes. The result was the same as that obtained by the IMF, which for 50 years has granted loans on the same conditions and has strangled the economies of poor countries, blocking their development.[22]

These policies have enormously accentuated the unequal distribution of wealth. In the last 30 years the gap between the highest and the lowest incomes has increased significantly compared to the preceding period.[23] The increasing gap has given rise to a chronic Keynesian shortage of demand, which blocks the profitability of investing, and encourages the use of capital in acquiring properties and in financial rents.

Today financial globalization has created such a strong concentration of speculative capital that it is able to attack national economies.[24] Europe is hardly able to oppose these speculative operations. Its weaker countries are under the constant threat of the so-called "market judgment," that is, the self-interested judgment of international financial speculation, often favored by the rating agencies.[25]

7 Commercial globalization

Europe encouraged only one great structural change, namely a massive increase of investments in the emerging countries. In the past decades the European states have supported the domination of the developing economies by Western multinationals. The latter continued the extraction of raw materials at monopolistic prices; monoculture, established during the colonial period to the benefit of the European importers; and bank loans to finance the purchase of Western industrial plants.[26] On the other hand China is now following the same path as Europe in Latin America and Africa, in efforts to gain control of raw materials and cultivable land.[27]

The outcome of these policies has been a massive drain on developing countries' wealth toward the West, growing debt and the failure of industrialization in developing countries.[28] However, in recent years there has been the take-off in development of some of the biggest developing countries, such as China, India and Brazil. These emerging countries seem to have at least in part overcome neocolonial subordination.

In China and India a dualistic economy has been created in which the model theorized by W. Arthur Lewis in the 1950s is working.[29] The development of these countries in fact is essentially based on the production of industrial goods for export; and, to a lesser degree, for the domestic market. These goods are very cheap because industrial workers—who come from the countryside—get wages not much higher than the wages of the agricultural workers (although industrial wages are now growing rapidly). The huge domestic market and Western investments have created in these countries the minimum conditions for the take-off.

The exporting of European capital to emerging countries is due to both the search for low wages and the difficulty of investing at home. This is an alternative outlet, other than the production of repetitive goods, rents or financial speculation. However these processes of globalization are coming about in the worst possible way.

First of all, in many poor countries (especially in Africa and Latin America), liberalization of trade has destroyed some of their infant industries.[30] Even worse is the situation in agriculture. European agriculture receives massive public aid through the EU common agricultural policy.[31] In international trade this leads to a dumping policy. European agricultural exports to Africa are extremely competitive; and undermine local production. Yet the growth of agricultural production could be the best way to start development in these countries. In general terms, many African and Latin American countries are seeing their commercial and productive conditions worsening due to globalization.[32]

But even for Europe, globalization is beginning to bring more damage than advantage. The export of capital and the delocalization of factories in the developing countries (Eastern Europe included) is making European unemployment soar. This fact is pulling wages down, and is worsening working conditions.[33] The whole set of workers' rights, which was a pillar of the welfare state, is collapsing. Maris is right in saying that globalization is nothing else than the disintegration of the welfare state.[34] If development does not restart, Europe risks losing not only its wealth, but also its greatest achievements: individual freedom, respect for human rights, solidarity.[35]

On the other hand, liberalization allows Chinese goods to flood Western markets with low prices such that many European producers are unable to compete. This fact worsens the crisis. Certainly, some of these phenomena are unavoidable. They prospect a new international division of labor, where traditional industrial production is increasingly delegated to emerging countries (as should also be the case for traditional agriculture). But Europe's problem is that this process does not go together with new kinds of investments.

8 Conclusions

Europe's economic strength lies in the fact that it has created in the past a development model inspired by the Enlightenment. In this model the growth of wealth was supported not only by accumulation but also by other social factors: reduction of income inequalities; individual rights; protection of weaker groups; and the search for social welfare. This model was confirmed and strengthened by Keynesian policies and by the welfare state, which aimed to ensure full employment and the increase in consumption for all. Today Europe has tacitly given up a significant part of this model, and is strongly influenced by the model of neoliberalism.

The two dominant models of development in the mid-2010s seem to be that of neoliberalism, under the leadership of the USA, and that of authoritarian capitalism, led by China. The first is responsible for the economic decline of the West and for the current crisis. The second puts economic growth and freedom in dramatic opposition.

If Europeans want to revive their model, they should adopt longer views. First of all they should implement plans for the development of poor countries; the elimination of internal poverty; and for extended investments against pollution and for renewable energy sources.

Second, they should reverse the present tendency which polarizes the bigger part of wealth to the highest earning groups and depresses general demand. This can be achieved through progressive taxation;[36] the creation of unemployment benefits; and social services for low-income groups. It is also necessary to eliminate the privileges which are widespread among the upper-middle classes, where unproductive consumption is deeply rooted.

Also the policy against the waste of public money should be redirected. Rather than cutting public services and wages, it should target cutting the privileges of the political class and of public managers, and at the same time should monitor the productivity of public sectors.

Finally we should acknowledge that nowadays, for an economy which is based only on increases in productivity and on strong competition, it is difficult to find ways to reach full employment.[37] One approach is to promote the non-profit sector, by designing services to individuals (care of the disabled, the sick, the aged and children); cultural activities; international cooperation; and the renovation of land and water resources.

Also handicraft and industrial districts should be supported. We should also protect the traditional knowledge and technologies of local markets, allowing them, through patents and registered trademarks, to avoid being swallowed up by multinationals.

Notes

1 See Lippit (2005, pp. 71–84).
2 Kindleberger (1989), fourth lecture (on "Smith's law").
3 See Stiglitz (2003, Ch. 9); Pianta (2001, Ch. 1 and 2).
4 See Pianta (2001, Ch. 5).
5 Romero (2000).
6 See Griffiths and Tachibanaki (2000, Ch. 1, pp. 1–10). On the increase in productivity as a cause of unemployment in Europe, see Moro (1998, pp. 22–24).
7 See Rifkin (2004: Italian edition, pp. xii–xxiv; Ch. 1 to 10).
8 See Fine (2002, Ch. 10).
9 Fine (2002, Ch. 9).
10 Delors Plan (1993).
11 Compare Sylos Labini (1998, pp. 113–114).
12 Compare Rifkin (2004), Italian edition, pp. xxxvii–li, Ch. 17.
13 See Rifkin (2004), Italian edition, pp. xxiv–xxxvii.
14 See Lippit (2005, Ch. 7).
15 For a survey of the criticisms to the welfare state, see Acocella (1999b).

16 See on this Sylos Labini (1999, pp. 273–274).
17 See Knibbe (2010).
18 Compare Sylos Labini (1998, pp. 111–113).
19 See Aglietta (2000).
20 Compare Mackinnon (2001, p. 53).
21 Compare Stiglitz (2003, Ch. 7).
22 Compare Stiglitz (2003, p. 262); Maris (2003, Italian edition, pp. 92, 157). About a similar policy of the World Bank in the first period, see Alacevich (2007).
23 See Knibbe (2010) and, for the USA, Weisbrot (2010).
24 See Roubini and Mihm (2010).
25 On all this, see the effective analysis by Raveaud (2010).
26 See the essays of López Castellano (2007).
27 See Callagher (2010).
28 See for example Dutt (2005).
29 Lewis (1954). On dualism today, see Capasso and Carillo 2009.
30 Compare Guerrieri (2003, pp. 11–12, 15–18).
31 See Salvatici (2003, pp. 131–133). See also Hökman et al. (2003, pp. 32–36).
32 Compare Acocella (1999a), "Introduzione."
33 Compare Acocella (1999a), "Introduzione," pp. 13–14. For a similar analysis about US, see Mandle (2007).
34 Maris (2003, Italian edition, p. 142).
35 See Roubini and Mihm (2010, Italian edition, pp. 352–354).
36 See Watt et al. (2010, pp. 91–101).
37 New Keynesians have been trapped for decades in the futile question, put by neoclassicists, as to whether involuntary unemployment exists or not (see De Vroey 2004). But, as De Vroey himself suggests ("Epilogue"), when an evident fact is incompatible with theoretical models, we should not deny the fact, we should change the type of models.

References

Acocella, N. (ed.) (1999a) *Globalizzazione e stato sociale*, Bologna: Il Mulino.
Acocella, N. (1999b) "Il dibattito sul welfare state," *Globalizzazione e stato sociale*, Bologna: Il Mulino, pp. 169–187.
Aglietta, M. (2000) "La globalización financiera," reprinted in F. López Castellano (ed.) *Desarrollo: Crónica de un desafío permanente*, Granada: Universidad de Granada, pp. 217–234.
Alacevich, M. (2007) *Le origini della Banca Mondiale*, Milan: Bruno Mondadori.
Callagher, K. P. (2010) "Leapfrogging Over Latin America," *Real World Economics Review Blog*, October 4, available at: https://rwer.wordpress.com/?s=Leapfrogging+Over+Latin+America.
Capasso, S. and Carillo, M. R. (2009) "The Legacy of Dualism in New Growth Theory," in N. Salvadori, P. Commendatore and M. Tamberi (eds.) *Geography, Structural Change and Economic Development*, Cheltenham/Northampton, MA: Edward Elgar.
De Vroey, M. (2004) *Involuntary Unemployment: The Elusive Quest for a Theory*, London and New York, NY: Routledge.
Delors Plan (1993) *Crescita, competitività, occupazione. Libro bianco*, Bollettino delle Comunità europee, Brussels and Luxembourg, Supplement 6/93.
Dutt, A. (2005) "International Trade in Early Development Economics," in K. S. Jomo and E. Reinert (eds.) *The Origins of Development Economics*, New Delhi and London: Tulika-Zed, pp. 99–127.

Fine, B. (2002) *The World of Consumption*, second edition, New York, NY and London: Routledge.

Griffiths, R. and Tachibanaki, T. (eds.) (2000) *From Austerity to Affluence*, London: Macmillan and New York, NY: St. Martin's Press.

Guerrieri, P. (2003) "L'Omc [WTO] e le sfide del regime commerciale multilaterale," *Libero scambio e regole multilaterali*, Bologna: Il Mulino, pp. 7–27.

Hökman, B., Hertel, T. and Martin, W. (2003) "I paesi in via di sviluppo di fronte al nuovo Round di negoziati commerciali multilaterali," in P. Guerrieri (ed.) *Libero scambio e regole multilaterali*, Bologna: Il Mulino, pp. 31–55.

Kindleberger, C. P. (1989) *Leggi economiche e storia dell'economia*, Rome and Bari: Laterza, 1990, Italian translation of *Economic Laws and Economic History*, Cambridge: University of Cambridge, 1989.

Knibbe, M. (2010) "Unequal Countries Did Worst—Some Stats on Inequality and Economic Performance," *Real World Economics Review Blog*, October 4, available at: https://rwer.wordpress.com/2010/10/04/unequal-countries-did-worst-%E2%80%93-some-stats-on-inequality-and-economic-performance/.

Lewis, W. A. (1954) "Economic Development with Unlimited Supplies of Labour," in A. N. Agarwala and S. P. Singh (eds.) *The Economics of Underdevelopment*, London: Oxford University Press, 1970.

Lippit, V. (2005) *Capitalism*, Abingdon and New York, NY: Routledge.

López Castellano, F. (ed.) (2007) *Desarrollo: Crónica de un desafío permanente*, Granada: Universidad de Granada.

Mackinnon, N. (2001) "The Limits to Global Markets," in R. Beynon (ed.) *The Routledge Companion to Global Economics*, London and New York, NY: Routledge, pp. 47–54.

Mandle, J. (2007) "Saving Globalization," in M. Forstater, G. Mongiovi and S. Pressman (eds.) *Post-Keynesian Macroeconomics: Essays in Honour of Ingrid Rima*, Abingdon and New York, NY: Routledge, Ch. 13.

Maris, B. (2003) *Antimanual d'économie*, Italian translation, Milan: Marco Troppa, 2005.

Moro, B. (ed.) (1998a) *Sviluppo economico e occupazione*, Milan: Franco Angeli.

Moro, B. (1998b) I caratteri strutturali della disoccupazione italiana, *Sviluppo economico e occupazione*, Milan: Franco Angeli, pp. 9–64.

Pianta, M. (2001) *Globalizzazione dal basso*, Rome: Manifestolibri.

Raveaud, G. (2010) "Manifeste d'économistes atterrés, 01/09/2010" *Real World Economics Review Blog*, September 8, available at: https://rwer.wordpress.com/?s=Manifeste+d%E2%80%99%C3%A9conomistes+atterr%C3%A9s. English translation available at: www.paecon.net/PAEReview/issue54/Manifesto54.pdf.

Rifkin, J. (2004) *The End of Work*, 2nd edition, Italian translation, *La fine del lavoro*, Milan: Mondatori-Repubblica, 2007.

Romero, F. (2000) "The Affluence of Social Democracy in Western Europe (1958–69)," Chapter 8 in R. Griffiths and T. Tachibanaki (eds.) *From Austerity to Affluence*, London: Macmillan and New York, NY: St. Martin's Press.

Roubini, N. and Mihm, S. (2010) *Crisis Economics*, Italian translation, *La crisi non è finita*, Milan: Feltrinelli.

Salvatici, L. (2003) "Le questioni agricole nell'Organizzazione mondiale del commercio," in P. Guerrieri (ed.), *Libero scambio e regole multilaterali*, Bologna: Il Mulino, pp. 121–143.

Stiglitz, J. (2003) *The Roaring Nineties*, Italian translation, *I ruggenti anni Novanta*, Turin: Einaudi, 2004.

Sylos Labini, P. (1998) "Disoccupazione e sviluppo economico," in B. Moro (ed.) *Sviluppo economico e occupazione*, Milan: Franco Angeli, pp. 105–114.

Sylos Labini, P. (1999) "The Employment Issue: Investment, Flexibility and the Competition of Developing Countries," *Banca Nazionale del Lavoro Quarterly Review*, 210(September): 257–280.

Watt, A., Botsch, A. and Carlini, R. (eds.) (2010) *After the Crisis*, Italian translation, *Dopo la crisi*, Rome: Edizioni dell'Asino.

Weisbrot, M. (2010) "Extending the Tax Cuts: The Ninety-Eight Percent Solution," *Real World Economics Review Blog*, October 1.

7 "Eurocrisis"

Origins, the present and perspectives

Paolo Piacentini

1 Introduction

During 2012–2013, speculative attacks on titles of sovereign debt of weaker member countries, endangering the continuation of the common currency area itself, were eventually contained by statements and actions of the European Central Bank, able to convince the market that defaults would not occur at least in a near horizon. However, the institutional and structural flaws of the "eurosystem" are still there, and "eurocrisis," meant as the crisis of the real economies of member countries, facing the effect of fiscal adjustments, appears to get worse.... These notes are meant to recall these original weaknesses and critical developments of the euro area, in a joint consideration of the financial and real aspects of the crisis.

This message on Crisis in Europe, with particular stress on origins and developments of the problems within the euro area, is a main theme of my chapter, which was originally read for seminars held in Japan in winter–spring 2012. Most of the "fundamentals" in the background, and cumulative processes, involved within the "eurocrisis" remain fundamentally robust in the face of contingent developments. In particular, the endogenous weaknesses, and the exogenous shocks, and the description of the possibly perverse effects of imposing a common currency over a set of heterogeneous countries are worth being recalled for their general implications.

2 Eurocrisis—the background

In my previous work on the "eurocrisis," I have always stressed the weaknesses of the political and institutional setting of the Economic and Monetary Union (EMU), and to risks already detectable in earlier periods, of divergent trends for macroeconomic fundamentals of the member countries, endangering the whole construction and governance of Monetary Union, in particular when phases of serious turbulence on the financial markets might occur. Although not wholly convinced, since the origin, about prospects and benefits deriving from the common currency, I could not have however imagined before, say, summer 2011, this dramatic acceleration of the critical events.

This section provides an introductory summary of the fundamental flaws which, in my opinion, were imbedded from the start in the vision and operational rules of the eurosystem, and which have contributed to the current, dangerous, state of things overall.

I will thus refer to three endogenous factors and to two exogenous forces which have acted on the crisis, and whose impact was not adequately perceived at the moment of the setting of the fundamental norms of the EMU's constitution.

Among the endogenous weaknesses of the euro architecture, I would include:

1   poor performance of the member states' economies vis-à-vis the international standards of growth of output and productivity;
2   poor coordination of policies at the Union's central level of governance, coupled to the often loose attitude of individual national governments, in the face of evidence of weaknesses in their trade, or the external and internal debt positions of the public and private sectors of their economy;
3   possibly, the "original sin": that of conceiving an awkward frame of governance and attributions for the policy mix, with a single currency managed by a Central Bank, formally conceived as not responsible for the real macroeconomic performance of the member countries, and wholly dedicated to the single mission of maintaining price stability, coupled to the responsibility for fiscal policies and debt management wholly delegated, instead, to the national governments, whose "orthodox" behavior was to be checked by the key norm of a 3 percent limit for public deficit as a ratio to GDP, as set by the Maastricht Treaty.

Exogenous shocks have impacted upon these already fragile foundations, as these came from the side of:

1   the "globalization" of competition, with the rise of emerging countries and their influence on allocation, or dislocation, of real and financial resources throughout the globe;
2   the disrupting impact of an ever augmenting "financialization" of the global economy, with empowerment given to the "market"—as we euphemistically refer to it, with a single word, to behavior, sentiments and expectations of a financial community—maneuvering resources, whose size is about five times the value of world GDP in stock, and 70 times in terms of the turnover of annual transactions.

The extent of the market turbulence and the role of "innovative finance" (subprime mortgage backed securities, credit default swaps, etc.), which were original triggers for the crisis of 2007–2008, and of which the current "eurocrisis" is possibly one consequential development, could not have been imagined by the founding fathers of the "Maastricht" constitution, who rather took almost for granted a tranquil world in which nominal stability meant, essentially, an inflation-free environment, would have been a sufficient condition for the steady and convergent growth of the member economies.

Things have developed differently, and now the price for myopic or over-optimistic visions and expectations are being mainly borne by the "commoners," outside of a financial elite, who must make out their living out of the employment and income opportunities as offered by the real economy.

3 How bad is the "eurocrisis"?

The debt/GDP ratio of the US had already surpassed the 100 percent mark by 2011, when the federal budget ran a deficit of about 7 percent of GDP; in Japan, the same ratio exceeded 200 percent. At mid-2012, the debt ratio for the whole of the "euro-area" was estimated at around 85 percent, with peaks for Greece (at around 175 percent of GDP even after the recent "haircut") and Italy (120 percent). If "sound" fiscal rules were to be imposed in order to bring down the debt into a "safe" standard (conventionally posited at around 60 percent of the GDP), structural adjustments of public accounts should result in the US or Japan, even more painful than in most European countries. But why, then, the "speculation" targeted since 2010–2011 mainly the instruments of debt denominated in euro? Why even non-speculative traders (e.g., managers of pension or insurance funds dedicated to a safekeeping of conferred savings) were sometimes so eager to get rid of euro-denominated bonds, mainly coming from public debentures of the weaker member countries, but also from issues by the greater banks and institutions of the area (with the only exception given to the purchase of German "Bunds," perceived as the only safe harbor within the continental storm)?

All this started, as we know, from Greece, and the uncovering of malpractices, if not fraud, in the reporting of public accounts and debt management by the Greek government for years. Greece actually accounted for about 4 percent of the total stock of euro-denominated public debt. However this was sufficient to trigger a contagion process, with successive involvement of other peripheral countries of the euro-area: Portugal and Ireland at first. But it was only with the large-scale attack on Italian (and Spanish) debentures, after summer 2011, that the "eurocrisis" entered a potentially catastrophic path. Italy, actually, was the originator of about one fourth of the total amount of public debt titles denominated in euros circulating on the market.

The prospect of a Greek default had already caused enough panic in the financial community, with large falls in the stock values of the banks believed to be most involved. The holding of titles of public debt by banks was a common practice, given also their general acceptance as a collateral for liquidity swaps at the ECB, or for the trading on interbank markets. Italian and Spanish banks traditionally held large stocks of their own national debt mainly for this purpose. Still, before any eventuality of default, the fall in the market values of these holdings has meant cuts for assets of banks, at a moment in which they already had problems in meeting capital reserve requirements.[1] The uncontrolled practice, for "downgrading" by the rating agencies of the public debt of a country, to be generally followed by parallel downgrades of the domestic banks involved, increased market perception of the risks, increasing immediately the difficulties on the front of the availability and costs of liquidity provision.

Also beyond the national banking systems of the countries under attack, the increasing interconnectedness of the banking network over the continent spread risks and fears on the continental scale. The worsening of the situation could be followed, day after day, through the evidence of dramatic increases of the so-called "spread," i.e., the differential of the interest rates on bonds of other Euro-area countries with respect to those paid on the German "Bund." For example, the ten-year-term debentures of Italy, whose spread was only slightly above 100 points at the beginning of 2011, reached a maximum of 575 base-points on November 9 2011.[2] Subsequent events have lowered this spread. However, the increasing fears over the sustainability of Italian debt had, for a time, repercussions also upon France's financial market, since French banks held some €106 billion of Italian debentures, and another €300 billion of other credit toward Italian private counterparts. Eventually this contributed to the downgrading of French debentures from the "AAA" standard.[3]

It can be understood, by now, that a systemic, endogenous mechanism of perverse contagion was put in motion: the flight of foreign investors from bonds of targeted countries being transmitted, through the portfolios of greater banks, to further and further positions, and with the rise in interest rate differentials increasing the difficulties for the roll-over of the debt of countries entering the "black list": Greece, Portugal, Ireland ... and then Italy, Spain. It was even feared that France (and Belgium) might become targets at some point. But then, what would have been left, within the "euro-area," which might have been perceived as "safe" by international speculation? Germany, with a contour of neighboring small countries (Netherlands, Austria), which constituted the deutschmark-centered area of fixed exchanges, in the 1980s?

It is clear at this point that the euro, for as long as it might be kept alive as a medium of exchange and currency unit, had de facto ceased to perform as a truly common currency in an integrated supernational area. Interest rates payable on ten-year debentures ranged in mid-2012 from 1.8 percent in Germany to almost 17 percent in Portugal (not to speak of Greece ...): this should be understood that breakdown of an effective Monetary Union had, in some degree, already occurred. Should not a common currency command near-equal interest rates throughout the area of its circulation? A differential, for the rate of interest, to be kept within the range of 2 percent with respect to the average of the three most "virtuous" countries in the group, was not one of the original key conditions set in Maastricht for joining EMU.

The apparent impotence of the "eurosystem" vis-à-vis these trends on the financial market, over-frightened by expectations of defaults (or partial defaults, as in the case of "trimming" of nominal values of bonds held by banks as in the Greek case) requires a careful reconsideration of the original founding rules governing the European Union and its Central Bank (ECB). Article 103 of the Treaty on the Functioning of the European Union[4] states that: "Community shall not be liable for or assume the commitments of central government, regional, local or other public authorities,…, of any Member State." This norm, commonly known as the "non-bailout clause," prevents the ECB from direct subscription, in the event that tenders (or roll-overs) of debentures of any member state fail to find sufficient demand from the market counterpart, on the "primary" market at issue. As is known, the ECB has massively intervened, in particular after the onset of the Italian debt crisis, on the "secondary" market, in order to check an uncontrolled rise of interest rate spreads. For Greece, Ireland and Portugal, facing virtually no counterpart for their debt roll-over since being "de facto" ousted from the international liquidity market, the duty of keeping them from outright default was taken up by "ad hoc" instruments of the Community, the so-called "European Financial Stabilization Facility" (EFSF) in the first instance, supplemented by conditional loans from the International Monetary Fund (IMF). The original funding for EFSF, at €440 billion, was just sufficient for keeping afloat the above-mentioned countries. There was therefore no capability for intervening in the market in the event of a full escalation of a debt roll-over crisis to larger countries.[5]

Germany, on diverse occasions, spoke of its unwillingness to raise the funding capacity of EFSF, or the endowment of ESM (European Stability Mechanism) due to substitute it in its functions from 2013.[6] Suggestion for forms of a "financial engineering" allowing some "leverage" on original endowments (e.g., EFSF guaranteeing up to 30 percent of the values of new bonds issued by the countries or banks) were advanced, but decisions and hard money were mostly still to come.

If treasuries suffer, what about banks? A liquidity crisis, caused by the increased unwillingness from the demand-side of the market to keep risky positions, is already striking hard on them. European banks collected in 2011 some US$413 billion from the issue of bonds, against repayments for maturity worth $654 billion: a net deficit of $240 billion! The other sources of liquidity are customers' deposits, which appear stagnant if not yet in decline, and some form of "last resort" supply from the ECB. Also on this point, the incompleteness of the constitutive rules for the ECB[7] plays a crucial role: the ECB is not expected to act normally as a lender of last resort.[8] This helped in raising the perception of risk to the potential lender, at a time when European banks, in order to comply with safety standards, were asked to raise additional capital for their "core-tier" requirements for an amount estimated exceeding €100 billion by the end of 2012![9] Treasuries were prevented from further bank rescues by their budget constraints, and banks without public support might have run short of liquidity …; this tie-up of a perverse interdependence between public and private debt represented, and still represents in my opinion, the most dangerous factor of potential triggering for a global, systemic, crisis striking the whole continent. Would, at that point of the story, the countries outside the EMU area be spared? The linkages between financial institutions in the US and in Europe were already sufficient for propagation into an overall crisis of an original shock, i.e., the collapse of the US subprime mortgage securities market, for which the values of the insolvencies involved were much lower than those which would result from the case of the worst scenario occurring, i.e., the event of a "default" of a European state. Not being a specialist in financial market forecasting, I will stop here for the description of the dangerous path on which the euro and the entire institutional framework of European Union have entered. Rather, I will proceed further with some consideration for the "real-side" impact of the evolutions of "eurocrisis."

Let us then consider Greece, which is surely the extreme case, fighting against nightmare conditions, and haunting the imagination of the Portuguese, the Irish, the Italians, the Spaniards, as a possible scenario for an awful future also facing them. The data and evidence for a perverse interaction between successive rounds of budget cuts and a deeper plunge into recession are, in fact, terrible: GDP at market prices, according to the OECD National Accounts database, has fallen by 13.5 percent over the years 2009–2011, and a further by 7 percent for 2012, with recession continuing still in 2013. The unemployment rate has increased from 9 percent in 2009 to 23.6 percent at the end of 2012. Notwithstanding brutal measures of fiscal adjustment—e.g., cuts up to 20 percent of nominal salaries of public sector employees—the debt/GDP ratio could not but increase further, before a recession of this size: it was at 129 percent in 2009, it climbed to 176 percent by the end of 2012, notwithstanding successive operations of "haircuts" and "buy-backs" reducing the value of Greek debenture for private and institutional investors.

The case of Greece is indeed extreme, starting from its origin in the fraudulent reporting of fiscal budgets. But where were the monitoring experts of Eurostat in Luxembourg, when the Center-Right government of Mr. Karamanlis continued for a decade to draft fake budget statements? After the change of government, was the adjustment (i.e., a deficit cut), as promised by the new prime minister in May 2010, worth 11 points of the GDP, deemed really sustainable? In the face of this schedule the Finance Ministers Council of the EU (ECOFIN) promised assistance to Greece worth about €110 billion; of which, only €30 billion were immediately paid-in by the partner countries, with a reluctant Germany delaying effective cash disbursement for further installments on several occasions. In the meanwhile, the macroeconomic and social conditions for the country got worse and worse. After the so-called "Greek Haircut,"[10] banks holding Greek public debt were entitled to preserve only about 35 percent of their nominal values at maturity, against a countervailing issue of new bonds at a lower interest rate "guaranteed" by EU funding. This outcome, which has correctly been called "Almost Default," finished by inflating further the nervousness of the financial brokers, frightened from the prospect that similar events might happen later, and for more consistent stocks of other debt. The conditions and rates required from the market, for the roll-over of the Italian bonds, in fact considerably worsened in the aftermath of this Greek episode. It was also decreed, that the "half-default" was not after all "full" default and thus the holders of Credit Default Swaps (CDSs) should not receive compensation. But what if they did? The counterpart in the emission of CDSs eventually payable were mainly specialized financial funds operating mostly on the other side of the Atlantic: the crisis of the small Greece would have been exported to big USA!

The Greek crisis is an extreme, but perhaps also exemplar, case, which fully evidences the perverse linkages within mismanagement at the national level, the lack of sufficient capability in the monitoring and the regulation at the EU level, the imposition of "shock therapies" for adjustment, which eventually do not appear credible to the financial market, and disastrous results for the real economy. Last but not least, the insufficient, and insufficiently timely, funding for emergency money, mainly because of a German "constipation" when it is about to pay out hard cash, has contributed to the impression of indecision or ineffectiveness of EU-level policy decision.

On December 5, 2011, the Italian government led by Prof. Monti, which had taken over the internationally discredited rule of Mr. Berlusconi, announced a "Save Italy" budget adjustment program, worth €30 billion reduction of deficit through a mix of tax rises (for the greater part) and expenditure cuts. The target was that of reaching a balanced budget by 2013. The change in government was strongly supported by the EU leadership, and in particular from the German–French "diarchy" ("Merkozy" rule) at the time effectively ruling the EU. Italy would have eventually shown enough determination to support its solvability and contribute to the survival of the whole "euro" business.... But Italy, perhaps, was at that time at the starting point of a perverse deflationary adjustment cycle, as Greece stood at the beginning of 2010. "*Fare la fine dei greci*" ("ending up like the Greek") is the current nightmare of the Italians.

Italy certainly has resources, and productive potential, far stronger than Greece. But this might be a problem rather than a "*trump*." "Too Big to Fail" or "Too Big to Save"? An Italian crisis could still be the trigger of a final phase of dissolution of the "euro-area" as it actually stands, striking from the financial side of a sovereign crisis, and the real side of the final social unsustainability of the fiscal adjustments.

Beyond the peculiar national conditions, there still prevails, in my opinion, a fundamental flaw: this is represented by the apparent unawareness, on the part of an orthodox politics following the prescriptions of orthodox finance, of the consequences in terms of the recessionary impact of dogmatic policies targeting only at the public debt. The linkages between the public and the private debts, entailing risks of systemic contagion of episodes of illiquidity, or worse, insolvency, might eventually erode any benefit in the account books which might have been derived from restrictive policies. In the meanwhile, austerity measures will have performed all their Keynesian transmission effects, in terms of contraction of aggregate demand, subsequent fall of incomes and employment, and so forth.

In effect, the "eurocrisis" appears, then and still, bad enough.

4 The original sin: was the euro-area actually not an optimal currency area?

Some may read the actual deployment of the events as an ex post vindication of earlier warnings against the premature launch of a European monetary union, as these were expressed by influential economists, mostly from the US "main-stream" tradition, and often belonging to an older generation still aware of the circumstances and developments of the Great Depression of the 1930s. Was the euro a mistaken project, since its foundation? We recall at this point the terms of an economic debate, lively in the 1980s, precisely when EU leadership was entering the discussion about whether and how to proceed toward monetary union. The fact that the skeptics were mostly US economists encouraged unscientific counterargumentations by euro supporters, who even alluded to hidden interests of US circles in raising doubt upon the sustainability of a European currency extending its coverage upon an area potentially of a larger size than that of the US. Might the euro become concurrent to an established "dollar rule" over a future horizon?

After two decades or so, the arguments that the group of countries entering monetary union did not have, from the beginning, the requisites for constituting an Optimal Currency Area (OCA), appear still well founded.

A monetary union would not be an OCA[11] and, therefore, would not bring beneficial effects for the stability and growth prospect of the involved area, when the participant members are characterized by heterogeneity in their economic structure and potential. In these conditions, should a negative idiosyncratic shock hit a member country, the traditional adjustment paths allowed by exchange rate flexibility will obviously be precluded. To regain competitiveness after the shock, the country inside the monetary union should then engage in a "competitive disinflation" effort, i.e., trying to keep price (and wage) increases below that of partner countries for quite a long period. But this would impact on domestic demand and thus on growth rates, and the adjustment, whenever possible, would have eventually implied higher costs in terms of loss of output potential and increase of unemployment, with respect to a situation in which a domestic currency and room for an independent monetary policy had been maintained.

For the group of countries which eventually joined the euro, two other conditions for a successful operation of an OCA were also seen as deficient: that is, the existence of "federal" institutions endowed with consistent budget resources, capable of acting in a stabilizing role in the face of cyclical events, and a high mobility of factors within the area of the union itself, in particular the mobility of labor over a continental labor market, through which regional unbalances in growth and employment absorption potentials might be partially corrected.

The political leadership in the EU in that period ignored these arguments, sanctioning with the Maastricht Treaty (February 1992) definitive rules and timings for the implementation of EMU at the start of the new millennium. What was the rationale for this determination, even in the face of influential arguments against? I think, essentially, that there was a shared conviction that the establishment of a monetary union would have acted by itself as a force for advancing convergence among participating countries, and for proceeding to further steps toward the integration on fiscal, institutional and political spheres over a whole continental area. The absence of exchange rate risks should favor trade and cross-investment; the common rate of reference interest would have been lower than those internally prevailing before for most countries in the union; the enhanced competition over an enlarged "single market" would have contributed to price transparency and lower inflation; trade unions, sometimes with traditions of militancy and excessive pressure for wage claims, would become more moderate in the face of an awareness of the risks of a competitive displacement in the event of cost increases going out of line with the average standards prevailing elsewhere in the EU.

Disinflation, wage moderation, low interest rates: these conditions appeared in fact to have been realized in the years immediately following the entry into euro. No one could have imagined, at that moment, what sort of macroeconomic and financial environment the world was going to face only few years later.

However, even before, and apart from, the devastating impact of the financial crisis, evidence on the "malfunctioning" of macroeconomic governance, and on the processes of real divergence among the member countries, in the face of an apparent nominal convergence, should have been detectable to the careful observer. The mechanisms eventually leading to divergence rather than convergence were in fact embedded within the fundamentals of the constitution of the monetary union itself. In fact:

1   With a single "reference rate" of monetary interest as set by the common Central Bank, countries with a higher inflation would have enjoyed a lower real interest rate (and vice versa for a country with low inflation because of stagnating economy). This would potentially induce further divergence between the nominal and the real indicators of economic performance.
2   In the second place, the perception of having put aside the balance of payment constraint, as this was binding in the pre-euro era, might have given an excess confidence to countries actually holding unbalanced positions in their current accounts or growing records of external indebtedness.

Both mechanisms may be easily exemplified, with reference to the case of Spain (and of Ireland). An abundant and cheap supply of funds allowed there the financing of an investment boom and an apparently good performance of the economy, in terms of growth rates and reduction of unemployment; only to become aware later that almost all of this performance was only the result of a "housing bubble," triggering dramatic recession immediately upon its collapse at the onset of the financial crisis. Spain had registered, in fact, huge deficits in its current account in the apparently good years of growth: 7.3 percent of GDP in 2005, 8.9 percent in 2006, and 9.99 percent in 2007; no country, with its own currency, and in a context of international capital mobility, could have avoided events leading eventually to currency crisis and devaluation.

For the perverse effect of keeping a common reference rate of nominal interest in front of differential inflation, Ireland can be taken as representative. Ireland experienced inflation rates at around 6 percent over most of the 2000s, meaning negative real interest rates to the borrower. The situation contributed to another case of housing-bubble-led "boom and bust."

But it is not only the weak country, enjoying a "free lunch" of balance of payment deficit, etc., that may initially benefit from a common currency. In fact, if weak countries set aside devaluation risks, the stronger country is freed from "revaluation risks" when faced with consistent and persistent surpluses in its current account.

German performances for exports in recent years have been, in fact, comparable to that of China; the surplus in the German current account reached levels worth 6.5 percent of GDP in 2006 and 7.6 percent in 2007, just opposite to the case of Spain. In the previous regime, Germany would have been forced, sooner or later, to a consistent revaluation for its "D-Mark," with a consequent containment of its trade advantage. This was the experience, by the way, of Japan over recent decades. Being inside the euro-area has permitted Germany to maintain continuing surpluses, which are, in their greater part, the counterpart of deficits of the other partners within an "intra-euro-area" commerce.[12]

The macroeconomic records of Germany have been proposed as a virtuous example for others, combining stability of prices, moderation of wage claims, high performance of productivity and exports, etc. But these were thus widely based on export-led support before a stagnating domestic demand.[13] This model has sometimes been denominated as the "New German Mercantilism": with Germany, apart from a few other smaller countries, being the only nation with a surplus position in the euro-area! This is, in my opinion, further evidence of the real divergence essentially sustained by the mechanics of a monetary union. The structural weakness of member countries, in particular from southern Europe, in front of the challenges of global competition is, certainly, a fundamental, real, factor behind these divergences. It remains however, at least to my comprehension, difficult to understand how these deficiencies in their growth potential might be corrected only through a tighter budgetary discipline being imposed to those countries.

At the federal level, the EU is known for the plethoric inflation of staff and offices at its headquarters in Brussels, and for a high rate of production of norms, recommendations and plans full of "wishful thinking" for the future.[14] However, as for the incidence of expenditures emanating from the federal level, the annual budget in 2011 allocated to all organs of the EU was worth about €142 billion, that is to say 1.1 percent of the combined GDP of the greater community (EU27). There is no parallel, indeed, with the size of US federal budget and expenditure capability.

Immigration flows into the core countries of the EU have been consistent in recent years, but consisted mostly of inflows from outside Europe (North Africa) and, after 1989, from the "transition" countries in eastern Europe, either now included in an enlarged union (e.g., Romania) or still kept apart (e.g., Ukraine and other former Soviet republics). It has also been noticed, in the recent period after the onset of the crisis, an increase of emigration from the marginal areas of southern Europe (e.g., Portugal, southern Italy). Often, this is an emigration of younger persons with a higher education standard and lack of employment opportunities at home. But should this trend be confirmed, is it to be welcomed as a sign of a more integrated continental labor market? Or this might involve losses of human capital potential, further impoverishing the growth prospects of the marginal regions? Andalusia and Ireland were until recently cited as examples of the effectiveness of EU regional policies in increasing "cohesion" and in reducing regional disparities. The crude figures on the recent rise of unemployment there, which have, as at the time of this writing, gone back to levels higher than in the pre-developmental decades, should warn us about the ephemeral nature of many success stories, in the matter of regional development.

At the conclusion of this section, I wish to correct somewhat the impression that, since the conditions for an OCA were not fulfilled, proceeding into a monetary union was the cause of all the misfortunes which occurred thereafter. In social sciences, "counterfactual" experiments are not allowed: had the weaker countries continued in the olden-days circuit of inflation followed by recurrent depreciations, and the stronger countries were constrained in their export drive from appreciation of their currencies, would the real outcomes in terms of growth and employment overall have been better? We are not in a condition to give an unequivocal answer on this point.

The flaw came perhaps not from the fact of the monetary union in itself, but from the incompleteness and rigidity of the political governance on which it has been founded. The weakness of governance and incompleteness of norms were to be fully revealed only when the fundamentals of economic stability were hit by the disastrous impact of financial instability and crisis.

5 Financialization and the "eurocrisis"

"The architects of economic and monetary union had not foreseen the unfolding of the events that led to soaring sovereign spreads in peripheral economies of the Euro-area" is admitted in a recent official document by the EU Commission.[15] It is then clear that at the moment of setting-up working rules, the eventuality of a Global Financial Crisis (GFC), putting at stake the solvability of greater financial institutions and eventually of sovereign states, had not been even conceived as a possible occurrence. Again, there was in this a shortsightedness and over-optimism in expectations on the part of the architects of the euro. The destabilization, by unregulated finance, of the global economy precipitated into emergency the architecture of a construction which had already an inbuilt frailty.

The main factor of incompleteness which is now often stressed, for the EU constitution and the status of its Central Bank, is associated with the fact that this latter, in compliance with Art. 103 of the EU Treaty ("No Bail Out Clause," see above), is in fact prevented from acting as the "lender of last resort." A speculative attack on the sovereign debt of a member state may render new debt issues, or roll-overs of old debt, unfeasible because of that country falling into virtual conditions of illiquidity, given the expectation by the market that the ECB will not provide ultimate support. Actually, the ECB has intervened on the secondary markets, in an attempt to containing the soaring of the interest rate spreads. Respect for the basic rules prevents the ECB from direct intervention on the "primary" market, since this would signify a straightforward "monetization" of the public deficit, the fundamental taboo for the conventional wisdom of orthodox finance. EFSF and its successor, ESM have in fact been set up as facilities for a partial bypass of this norm. Without this instrument, Portugal or Ireland, not to speak of Greece, would have since long defaulted. The delays in the tackling of the Greek crisis in facts encouraged successive targeting of more consistent stocks of sovereign debt, Italian *in primis*. The major counterpart to the issue of bonds are notoriously the domestic (and other euro-area countries') banks, satisfied to keep bonds usable as collateral for liquidity "swaps." This, which was in effect a somewhat indirect way of maintaining debt-financing, has eventually become the triggering factor for the perverse interdependence between the private and the public debt. It is then hardly surprising that banks' ratings are automatically downgraded together with those of their home countries; the values of their reserve assets become thinner for banks, exactly when having to fight to raise further capital to add to their "core-tier" reserve requirements.

This interconnection among financial institutions, in which any default of one particular segment entails the risk of a systemic propagation of illiquidity and eventual insolvency, appears at the core of the GFC originally erupted in the US mortgage markets, and of which the "eurocrisis" might be seen as a possible complication for the worse. A "monetary union," originally conceived in the assumption of a continuing tranquility of a financial environment, can hardly overcome this turn of events.

This is not the occasion for entering definition or qualification, for the notion and impact of the so-called financialization of the global economy. My principal opinion on this point would say, in extreme synthesis, that sizes, unregulated mobility, and targeting at short-term gain, of a "financial" capital have become incompatible with the ordinary instrumentation of control by macroeconomic policy. There is actually no shortage, but perhaps an excess, of loanable funds, i.e., of a "money" capital, chasing for opportunities of placement for the "retention" and the augmentation of their values. There is, if anything, a shortage of debtors in the sense of a counterpart on the market demanding finance for long-term investment projects. An "inducement to debt," on the part of financial intermediaries, even targeting agents with little chances of honoring their debt, has clearly been evidenced from the subprime episode in the USA. The apparent abundance of funds may, further, have induced lax attitudes of some states, in deficit spending and in increasing their stock of debt debentures. The implicit confidence was that abundant market liquidity would in any case have allowed the "roll-over" of debts. Until alarms on sovereign debt defaults, originally triggered by the Greek crisis of end 2009, the market was indeed satisfied with holding these stocks, considered as safer than most privately originated bonds, and easily exchangeable into cash on the secondary market.

But as the "Lehman shock" of September 2008 caused the first wave of global panic in the face of the unexpected event that even one of the oldest and greatest investment banks in the world could go bankrupt, so the Greek crisis has revealed that sovereign European states might go insolvent, as did, e.g., Argentina in 2001. The Greek crisis might have been tackled more effectively, through a timely assurance given to the market, on the part of the "euro-community," that they were prepared to cover all dues. The hesitation on this front, and the evidence of a reluctant attitude of the key country, Germany, in providing ready money, and the inconclusiveness of plans and projects aimed at reinforcing solidarity among the euro-area countries (e.g., the projects for "Eurobonds," jointly issued and partially substituting national debt, which has never taken off),[16] have, step after step, reinforced a market conviction about a structural weakness of the constitution and governance of the common currency. After the "domino effect" investing in the first smaller countries, the attack on Italian (and Spanish) debt revealed that the market had possibly entered a phase of an overall distrust of the euro as an instrument in which to hold "reserves of value." The hypothesis of an ultimate collapse of the monetary union had become, by this point, more than a remote eventuality evoked only in small, discredited, "Euro-sceptic" circles.

However, before our concluding considerations, we must refer to the impact of this situation on the real side of the economy: the enterprises and the workers.

6 Facing a new recession? The consequence of the "eurocrisis" for the real economy

The fundamental rules of operation of national fiscal policies of EU member countries have been governed, thus far, by the so-called "Stability and Growth Pact," which has maintained, with some amendments over time, the original norms as set in Maastricht in 1992, for the limits to public deficit and debt.

The developments of fall 2011 culminated with the dramatic EU Summit of December 9 of that year,[17] which decided for a reinforcement of fiscal coordination among the member states, through an even tighter regulation for public balances, with the prospect of immediate, and automatic, sanctioning of countries going out of line. The announcement of revision, containing a "hard" version of the norm on a balanced budget to be defended in (almost?) every event, has been effectively enacted with the "Fiscal Compact" in March 2012. The norm of a balanced budget is now thus to be inscribed in the constitutional charters of the adhering states.[18]

To an observer, as myself, still convinced about the effective operation of the Keynesian correlations learnt in younger years, a further tightening of the fiscal constraints, going much beyond Maastricht, appears a somewhat frightening prospect. Already within the old rules there was much stress on stability and little room for growth; it is then a case if, since the implementation of the common currency, the actual growth records of "Eurolandia" have been significantly lower than that of other mature countries outside the area, not to speak of the emerging new industrial countries? As is clear from Table 7.1, "Eurolandia" is the only area which actually has recently experienced a "double-dip" recession, with rates of growth for its aggregate GDP falling back into negative values in 2012–2013.

Table 7.1 GDP growth rates, 2008–2013

	2008	2009	2010	2011	2012	2013
Japan	−1	−5.5	4.7	−0.5	1.4	(E) 1.5
UK	−0.8	−5.2	1.7	1.1	0.3	1.7
US	−0.3	−2.8	2.5	1.8	2.8	(E) 1.9
Euro	0.4	−4.4	2	1.6	−0.7	−0.4
OECD total	(E) 0.2	(E) −3.5	(E) 3	(E) 2	(E) 1.5	(E) 1.3

Note
(E) = estimated.

Reinforcing fiscal austerity, appears at this point, like increasing the dose of a medicine which has not proved to be effective. In the meanwhile the patient might enter a terminal condition.

Fiscal solidarity written in these hard terms has been in fact advocated, mainly by Germany, as the necessary precondition for "reassuring the markets" with the aim of pursuing and enforcing solvability of "Euro-debts."

But what is the likely impact on a real economy? With a dip into recession by most countries of the area, may these hard budget constraints be credibly maintained? And eventually, at what cost? No room would be left for the operation of the so-called "automatic stabilizers," when unemployment rates are reaching record levels throughout the continent. The adjustment to the "Golden Rule," starting from current deficits still around 5 percent or 6 percent in 2012 in France, Spain, etc., would force them into a "pro-cyclical" policy deepening the slump. Moreover what if the European banks are compelled at the same time to regain the levels of a "safety standard" of capital requirement?[19] The reserve capital requirements should vary according to the risk-weighted value of assets in stock: but in such a case, should, e.g., holdings of Italian debenture, be calculated at their nominal value at term, or should this be discounted, because of the depreciation on the secondary market, or of expectation over some "haircut" at some term, as learnt from the Greek experience?

Some banks might be unable to raise sufficient capital. The financial market is still shaken by the event of the "near-default" of a Franco-Belgian bank, Dexia, whose operation has been preserved only after state guarantees, provided by French and Belgian treasuries, covering some €90 billion worth of Dexia bonds in circulation. Will similar rescues be compatible with schedules and norms set for balancing public budgets?

Signs of a "credit crunch" pursued by banks fighting to keep themselves within the safety benchmarks, are evident, and are hitting in particular the smaller enterprises of the real economy strongly dependent, in the European context in particular, on bank credit.

Much before the onset of the sovereign debt crisis, I had already stressed the weak prospects of many European economies as far as their real growth is concerned. A perception of risk, about a state defaulting eventually on its debt repayments, might then find itself not only with a bad record in its current budgets. Regaining stability, without growth, is unlikely to be a sufficient condition for eventually exiting from debt crisis. Italy is the benchmark case on this point. Aware of its vulnerability because of the historically high level of its debt/GDP ratio, Italian Treasury (even under Berlusconi) had pursued, for quite a long time, prudential fiscal policies. Italy was in fact in a surplus position for its "primary" balance already in 2010, the only case among greater European countries. Italian banks were said to be relatively safe, because of their small propensity in the past for engaging in operations on derivative markets.

These prudential attitudes may, however, have contributed to a macro-economic performance, which has been less than modest in terms of product and productivity growth, and investment rates, and with a persistently high unemployment and underemployment involving a wider section of its territory (the so-called *Mezzogiorno* in the south). Perception of an intrinsic frailty of the Italian debt position, and the onset of a speculative attack, were then perhaps not induced mainly by the evidence of mismanagement of public accounts, but from the fear of the implication, over the longer run, of a bad growth record, on the capability to meet debt repayment schedules in the future. Would a country experiencing zero, or even negative, growth, be able to service high debt burdens in the coming years? The denominator, not only the numerator, of a debt/GDP ratio is in fact important for market expectation and sentiment.

But at this point it is not an Italian problem only. We ought to carefully reflect on the difficulty of recovering satisfactory rates of growth for the whole of "Eurolandia" given the unpromising trends investing both the supply-side and the demand-side of its economies.

The mainstream approach notoriously gives stress to the supply-side, for the extrapolation of potential growth. On this front, as far as the labor input is concerned, mature European countries would have already experienced a decline in their labor force if not for the compensation from immigration. The "European Employment Strategy," as set by the EU Commission, announced targets for the rise of the average quality of the workforce, and for the lengthening of the active life of older cohorts.[20] However, with persistent stagnation, these targets remain a wishful thinking. A stagnating economy may not absorb increasing inflows of skilled workers, giving rise to phenomena of "over-education" of the workforce with respect to actual requirement in job openings; increasing mandatory retirement ages, or promoting incentives toward longer working lives, may further impact on chances of a quicker inflow into employment of the younger cohorts, or impose additional cost to the firm compelled to "hoard" older workers in a time of weak activity.

What about capital accumulation and investment rates? National accounts normally provide figures for gross investment; in mature economies, it is known that the greater part of this aggregate will be dedicated to capacity substitution, rather than capacity expansion. Actually, in periods of slump, net investments, after subtraction for replacements, might result in negative values.

If we are satisfied with the conventional method of "measuring" technical progress through the residuals of a growth accounting exercise (the estimates of a so-called "total factor productivity"), we might see sluggish records overall in Europe for the last decade, even with notable case of negative rates (a technical regress?).[21] The objectives, set in a Lisbon 2000 agenda, for increasing the R&D to GDP ratios up to 3 percent have, in the meanwhile, failed, and are now reiterated in the Europe 2020 agenda. But austerity budgets are not a factor encouraging higher R&D effort, either by the state or by enterprises. There is a common sentiment that Europe has been an importer and adopter, and never an originator, of the greater innovations arising in the new "digital era."

Let us consider now the demand-side, through an old-fashioned Keynesian forecasting for the prospective growth of the components of an aggregate demand. Private consumption has been sluggish in the whole of the euro-area, including Germany, whose overall dynamism was only propelled by export performance. Can the prospect become better, when fiscal adjustments imply further cuts in welfare provision and a rise in tax burdens, hitting the real disposable income of a "median" European consumer which has not practically increased for ten years?

Global competition and shrinking power of the trade unions have contributed to a weakening of the bargaining power of the working class. The decline of the share of labor in total income is common, in European countries as elsewhere, as evidenced in Figure 7.1.

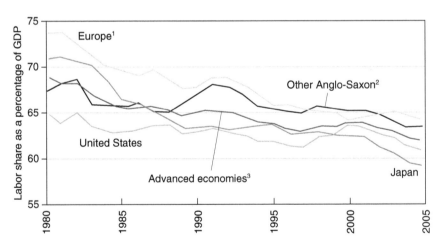

Figure 7.1 The decline in the share of income going to labor in advanced countries (sources IMF, *World Economic Outlook*, 2007).

Notes
1 Europe: all countries as in note 3 below, except the United States and the "Other Anglo-Saxon" and Japan.
2 Other Anglo-Saxon: Australia, Canada, United Kingdom.
3 Advanced economies include Australia, Austria, Belgium, Canada, Denmark, Finland, Germany, Ireland, Italy, Japan, the Netherlands, Norway, Portugal, Spain, Sweden, the United Kingdom, the United States; weighted using series on GDP in US dollars from the WEO database.

A declining share of labor would imply, in the Kaldorian causation, a lower average propensity to consume for the aggregate economy. However, recently, saving rates in most countries have declined. But this may further reflect the increasing difficulty of middle-class households to keep up the standards of living to which they were accustomed.

In a "classical" vision, with lower shares of labor meaning, conversely, a higher share of gross margins left to the firm or distributed as capital income to households, might potential resources for investments increase, compensating the negative impulses to aggregate demand? The experience of the recent past has taught that in mature economies the real investment to income ratio has, in most case, not increased, even with rising shares of profit and rents accruing to the potential investor. While "gross margins" range at about 40 percent of national income in most countries, "I/Y" ratios often fall short of a 20 percent mark.[22] Besides, we should remind ourselves that in some countries most of this investment has gone to housing, rather than to more productive uses, triggering bubbles in the real property market rather than technical progress.

"Luxury" consumption, from the Malthusian intuition, by the wealthier classes, has become by now an important element in sustaining aggregate demand: luxury goods and services, it seems, are those less affected by cyclical events. But not all surplus income is being spent: a greater part will add to a stock of wealth, of a "reserve value," chasing opportunities with further valorization. In hard times, the simple keeping of wealth where its value is safe might become a sufficient target. This brings us to another important implication of "financialization": an increasing inflation of "assets," or titles of wealth, which does not translate into sources for financing of "real" expenditure, investments and enterprise, while they are transacted purely for the purpose of short-term speculative hedge and gain. When a financial panic gains momentum, most of this wealth seeks refuge into some "safe harbor," where nominal values might be preserved, waiting for better days. But are there now, over the global financial scene, enough "safe harbors"? The subprime crisis has shown the frailty of greater banking institutions, on which the "rentier community" had relied for over a century; holding of public debentures was then considered a safer option for portfolios, because it was thought that sovereign states were less likely to default than private operators, and debentures were readily exchangeable, on the secondary market, into cash. But now the contagion of panic hits the sovereign debts of one country after another. The rating agencies have fed these sentiments, through the perverse game of downgrading, or threatening to downgrade, one after another. More and more "hot" money will be chasing for fewer and fewer "stores of values" perceived as safe. (German Bunds? Gold? Swiss banknotes? Is there much else left?)

The response, by national and supernational institutions, entrusted with the governance of monetary and macroeconomic conditions, has addressed this somewhat neurotic behavior of the financial market through attempts to provide "assurances" about the sustainability of the debt instruments issued by states or banks. Unfortunately, these assurances may not, until now, have been wholly convincing in calming market fears.

The insufficiency of policy instruments in the face of the turbulence of the markets is evident. In the case of "Eurolandia," this impression of impotence has been enhanced by the original incompleteness of its founding rules, and, last but not least, by the evidence of a lack of political solidarity among partners. In the meanwhile, the recessive impact of tighter fiscal rules, aimed at reassuring the market, has worked its way throughout the real economy.

7 Concluding notes: what lies ahead?

Will the Euro survive? Will other countries after Greece follow into partial defaults on their sovereign debt? Will this event imply the exiting of individual countries from the euro and reversion to a domestic currency? But how may such a process be pursued, if the treaties state the "irreversibility" of adhesion to the monetary union? What are the costs of resisting, or eventually exiting from, the euro, for a crisis-struck country?

These rhetorical questions haunt the minds of everyone in Europe, these days. I can only see the unpleasant implication of each of those: "staying" at the cost of continuing the perverse cycle of debt/fiscal adjustment/deepening stagnation/ further deficit/further cuts, etc.? This is the scenario of a "Greek syndrome," which is haunting other countries in southern Europe in particular.

What about alternatives? A "partial" defaulting ("haircuts") while formally conserving euro as a common currency, if consensually agreed among the partners, could ease the burden of debt servicing, but would charge losses mainly to "domestic" banks already in difficulty. Should a bank enter serious difficulty in liquidity and capital positions, will the state (or the ECB) intervene in rescue? But then, deficits and debts risk worsening again, with the consequence of further loss of credibility and marginalization of the involved country, and perhaps of the whole eurosystem.

A third scenario should imply, in one way or another, the end of "Eurolandia." Either a weak country will eventually be forced to leave, or it might be encouraged the option of a split between a "northern" euro around Germany, and a "southern euro," appropriately depreciated, linking the weaker countries. This could be preferable to a disorderly sequence of successive collapses, with countries defaulting, returning to their domestic currency and pursuing competitive devaluation.

A unilateral decision, in which a single member country decides to exit the monetary union, is barely mentioned explicitly by politicians in the European states, apart from marginal groups at the extreme right or left of the spectrum (e.g., the National Front of Marine Le Pen in France). There are in fact formal, "sentimental" and practical difficulties in advancing this option. The formal setting of the Lisbon amendment of the EU Treaty, Art. 50, mentions the right of a member to opt out from the European Union altogether, not from the monetary union. Before opting out from the euro-area, a country should be prepared to be ousted from all other European institutions: the single market, free circulation of people and money, regional and agricultural subsidies, etc. The shock and the cost will evidently be high. From the "sentimental" point of view, an expulsion from the eurosystem would mean facing a historical defeat and admitting the failure of some 20 years of efforts and sacrifices, with the loss of face and of the assumed benefits of belonging to a monetary union federating an area covering some of the most developed countries in the world. Disillusion, and frustration, could be comparable to those following defeat at war.

On practical grounds, the change of currency will incur a series of other difficulties: risks of a bank run, the flight of capital and the hoarding of "hard" currency, the disruption of the frame of commercial and contractual agreements, and, eventually, political turmoil and social disorder. Short-run competitiveness may benefit from devaluation, but it is not at all certain that the final effect, with rising inflation and further possible negative evolution, would be better than an "austerity within euro" scenario.

Voices appealing to solidarity, and proposals for innovative technical instrumentation—as for the call for "Eurobonds"—have been left behind, until now, by conservative and prudential attitudes mainly dictated by national interest and electoral calculus. But someone has said that when a ship sinks, not only the third-class, but the first-class passengers will drown. No country, or interest, might eventually gain in the worst scenario.

At the point of drafting this text (spring 2013), the most dramatic manifestation of the "eurocrisis," as mainly experienced during fall–winter 2011–2012, with the precipitation of the titles of sovereign debt of important member countries, pushed into unsustainable levels of costs of refinancing, may seem somewhat to have been contained. The spread on interest rates for the Italian or Spanish debentures are at less than a half of their peaks; even countries at that time surviving on aid seem by now prepared for a "return to market" (e.g., Ireland). The decisive move for this turn has been the declaration of intent, spoken by the governor of the ECB, to be prepared to make an "unlimited" purchase of the sovereign debts of weaker countries on the secondary markets, with a strong statement about the "irreversibility" of the euro. This apparently has pushed the market into less unstable expectations. The latest act in the Greek drama, when in December 2012 a final installment of the EU support plan, worth €34 billion, was eventually paid out upon the condition of further "sacrifices" imposed upon an already exhausted population, has been perceived as proof that stronger partners, Germany *in primis*, desire to keep the Eurozone intact for a while.

Quoting from an authoritative columnist in the *Financial Times*,[23] the eurosystem appears as a "bad marriage (in which) the union may still survive ... because the costs of divorce are so high."

Bad marriages often survive, but what about the final judgment upon the happiness of the partners (and of their offspring in the future)?

Notes

1 Basel II's fundamental rule (so-called "Pillar 1") establishes that minimum requirement for the banks' own capital should reach 8 percent of the total (risk-weighted)

assets value. For details, see Bank of International Settlements (2006). "Basel III," which is being gradually implemented, confirms the requirement with more sophisticated norms concerning evaluation of risks and merits of the credit positions, also for the "derivative" markets.

2 Events (change in government, the enactment of a new austerity package, etc.) have brought down the spread for Italy, remaining mainly in the range 250–350; the uncertainty linked to electoral results of end February 2012 will raise further anxiety on the market, with unavoidable impact on the spread.

3 France's rating was in fact lowered on January 13, 2012 by Standard and Poor at "AA+," followed by similar moves by the other rating agencies.

4 The quotation of the Article is from its original formulation as in Maastricht 1992, and the text was confirmed essentially in the same terms as Art. 125 of the Treaty on the Functioning of the European Union, set in Lisbon, December 2007 and definitively entered in force in 2009 after approval by all national parliaments of the member states.

5 Italy had to "roll-over" about €330 billion worth of titles of public debt in the first half of 2012. Only recently we have learnt that the ECB holds, as at the time of this writing, about 40 percent of the total value of Italian debentures, with evident proof of the effort to sustain, on the secondary market, the demand.

6 The ESM is now in operation for "conditional" aid to member states, with an allocation increased up to €800 billion.

7 For the governing rules of the ECB, the main reference is Art. 282 of the Consolidated Version of the European Treaty, see European Union (2008).

8 In fact, through loans at 1 percent interest rate to banks and other measures of unorthodox "quantitative easing" implemented or announced as possible options in the case of necessity, the ECB seems to have understood these risks and entered practice already followed by the US Federal Reserve in situations of liquidity crisis.

9 The estimate was taken from Alloway (2011).

10 Announced in September 2011, and finally agreed with sufficient adhesion of investors, on March 8, 2012.

11 The seminal reference for definition of "OCA" is Mundell (1961). For a review of the debate centered on the perspectives for the euro, see Eichengreen (1997, Ch. 3 in particular).

12 Intra-EU exports constituted about 64 percent of Germany's total exports in 2007. As a last reference point before the onset of the financial crisis, figures for 2007 are here provided: the Goods Trade Balance was in surplus by US$273 billion for Germany, while France, Spain and UK all run deficits, respectively worth $56 billion, $124 billion and $181 billion.

13 The index for the volume of private consumption in Germany, with 2000 = 100, stood at 109 in 2010, i.e., an yearly average growth rate of less than 1 percent, a part from cyclical oscillations.

14 For the most recent example of wishful thinking on some future Dreamland Europe, we refer to Agenda 2020, which specifies targets to be reached for employment, environmental protection, etc., by the end of the decade. For full text, see EU Commission (2010).

15 EU Commission, Directorate General for Economic and Financial Affairs (2011, p. 12).

16 The issue of Eurobonds, under a "federal" guarantee of all member states, was timidly proposed in the occasion of December 2011 Summit by the official authorities at the level of EU Council and Commission (e.g., by Mr. Barroso), but met, on that as on previous occasions, the opposition of Germany. Germany would indeed pay higher charges on part of its own debt eventually transferred into a Common Debt stock, and risk being the "payer of last resort" in case of insolvency of some other country.... However, the proposal of transfer of all (or part) of national debts into a "federal"

stock is still being invocated by many as the only, and definitive, solution if the euro should continue to exist. For a detailed account on the possible institutional setting up for Eurobond issues, see e.g., Holland (2011).
17 For a concise analysis of the statements and comments in that occasion, see e.g., Peers (2011).
18 The official denomination of the "Fiscal Compact" is "Treaty on Stability, Coordination and Governance of the EMU." More precisely, the norm establishes that a "structural" deficit should not exceed -0.5 percent of GDP; about the correct definition, and statistical calculation, of what is "structural" in a deficit, there is still ambiguity.
19 The ECB's move, on December 20, 2011, of opening credit lines to banks (liquidity/ bonds swaps over one to three year terms) for €500 billion was indicative that an immediate alarm on liquidity market positions and transactions were at that time clearly perceived. Banks immediately have drawn anticipations for €493 billion, practically immediately exhausting the availability of the "quantitative ease" measure.
20 These are included in the Agenda 2020 indicators. For example, the targets for 2020 are set, for 40 percent of the age cohort between 30 to 34 to have completed tertiary education.
21 As from the growth accounting tables elaborated by the Groningen Growth and Development Centre (and available in www.conference-board.org), over the period 2000–2009, Italy registered positive values for an estimated total factor productivity growth only in two years; Spain in none.
22 For example, ratios of gross investment on GDP, in 2008, were at 18.5 percent in Germany, 22.0 percent in France, 21.1 percent in Italy, 16.6 percent in the UK, and 18.0 percent in the USA. The full series is freely downloadable from the World Economic Outlook Databases, by the IMF.
23 Wolf (2013).

References

Alloway, T. (2011) "Europe's Banks Feel Funding Freeze," *Financial Times*, November 27, available at: www.ft.com/cms/s/0/40f27e5c-177f-11e1-b157-00144feabdc0.html# axzz3GnLrV8kh.
Bank of International Settlements (2006) "Basel II: International Convergence of Capital Measurement and Capital Standards. A Revised Framework and Comprehensive Version," Basel: BIS.
Eichengreen, B. (1997) *European Monetary Integration: Theory, Practice and Analysis*, Cambridge, MA: MIT Press.
EU Commission (2010) "Europe 2020: A Strategy for Smart, Sustainable and Inclusive Growth," Brussels, March 3, 2010, COM (2010), 2020 final.
EU Commission, Directorate General for Economic and Financial Affairs (2011) "Public Finances in EMU 2011," *European Economy*, no. 3/2011.
European Union (2008) "Consolidated Version of the Treaty on the Functioning of the European Union," *Official Journal of the European Union*, May 9.
Holland, S. (2011) "A Modest Proposal for Overcoming the Euro Crisis," Levy Economics Institute of Bard College, Policy Note, 2011/3, May, Annandale-on-Hudson: Levy Economics Institute.
Mundell, R. A. (1961) "A Theory of Optimal Currency Areas," *American Economic Review*, 51(4): 509–517.
Peers, S. (2011) "The Euro Area: Comments on the EU Summit Meeting 9 December 2011," available at: www.statewatch.org/analyses/no-162-euro-statement-dec-11.pdf.
Wolf, M. (2013) "Why the Euro Crisis Is Not Yet Over," *Financial Times*, February 19.

8 "We are all Keynesians now"

The paradox of British fiscal policy in the aftermath of the global financial crisis 2007–2009

William Redvers Garside

1 Introduction

When on December 31, 1965 *Time* magazine titled its cover story "The Economy: We Are All Keynesians Now," it was reflecting the widely held belief that Keynes had revolutionized the way the majority of contemporary economists thought about macroeconomics and especially the role of discretionary fiscal policy in sustaining full employment and stable prices. From the 1970s, however, Keynes fell out of fashion as a neoclassical counter-revolution took hold within the USA and the UK in particular, one that stressed the primacy and inherent efficiency of free markets in contrast to meddlesome and distortionary government intervention.

One assumption of the neoclassical model of economic liberalism was that markets were internally self-correcting. They had a natural tendency to clear in any economic downturn via an instantaneous adjustment of wages and prices. Economic agents, moreover, were deemed to possess sufficient information to adjust their economic behavior according to shifting market conditions. Because financial markets could not misprice assets only "light touch" regulation was required. The belief in efficient self-regulating markets underpinned the "Washington Consensus" in favor of free trade, deregulation, privatization, inflation targeting and balanced budgets. Inflation would be controlled by monetary policy and the determination of the level of employment delegated to market forces.[1]

Then Keynes became fashionable again—or so it seemed. The setting was the global financial and economic crisis which struck the industrialized world from 2007–2008. Within a year banking crises and collapses in corporate profits, employment, demand and investment were commonplace within the principal manufacturing and exporting countries of the Western world, ramifications of which were felt even further afield in Asian and Australasian markets. Many feared the outbreak of a second Great Depression. Far from being moribund, Keynes's fundamental insights as to how to avoid such a catastrophe seemed more vital than ever.

For a while it seemed that the lessons of history had been learned. Western governments from 2010 realized that only they could marshal the budgetary

resources on a scale and at a speed needed to prevent global output and employment falling to levels reminiscent of the 1930s.

The immediate background to the developing crisis is well known. Since
2008 the economies of the USA and most of industrialized Europe had been
beset with three distinct problems: a financial crisis which arose initially from a
banking crisis in the United States in 2007 but which rapidly became global,
forcing governments to act to defend their banking systems; a subsequent economic crisis as global financial difficulties eroded liquidity and solvency within
the real economy; and finally a fiscal crisis arising mainly from the remedial policies put in place to deal with a severely weakened banking sector.

It is clear in retrospect that the financial meltdown of 2008 had origins much
deeper than suspect mortgage lending in America. It lay in a decade or more of
extraordinarily cheap money created by vast imbalances in the global economy,
and fed by the huge exchange reserves and current account surpluses of countries such as China (and Japan before it).

With China saving nearly half of its gross national product, abundant capital
inflows, especially to the USA, helped reduce the cost of borrowing. From 2001
global long-term interest rates fell. As Konzelmann and Fovargue-Davies put it:

> Capital account liberalization combined with imbalances in household
> savings rates between Asia and the West contributed to the availability—
> and uptake—of cheap and plentiful debt. In the largely post-industrial
> Anglo-Saxon economies, this money found its way into the consumer
> sector, inflating a property bubble and significantly increasing the ratio of
> mortgage debt to GDP. Consumer leverage also rose; and mortgages were
> made at ever-higher initial loan-to-value ratios, as borrowers and lenders
> assumed that debt burdens would ultimately fall as a result of continued
> house price appreciation.[2]

Banks and institutional investors sought higher and higher returns via the use of
increasingly dubious and risky financial transactions, especially in structured
products geared to real estate. Lending to households ballooned in the USA,
Spain and the UK, often to borrowers who would in earlier years have been
excluded from, or rationed within, the loans market. Subprime loans in particular
offered attractive fee income without the need to raise liabilities to cover the
asset. The asset price bubble in real estate quickly spread to equities.

The global situation down to 2007 mirrored Japan's experience in the 1980s.
Monetary policy was too loose for too long. Central banks failed to monitor adequately the risks of opaque financial instruments and rising home-owner indebtedness. Household debt as a percentage of total disposable income had risen in
the USA from just under 80 percent in 1986 to 100 percent in 2000, and to 140
percent by 2007. In the UK the equivalent figures were 120 percent in 2000 and
175 percent in 2007.

Nor was this happening against the background of robust and stable economic
growth. Prior to the financial crisis Britain had been running a sizeable budget

deficit at the peak of the economic cycle, total expenditure rising from 36 percent of GDP in 1999 to 41 percent by 2005. The UK's economic success story by 2005 had been based:

> on a string of unsustainable factors: soaring private-sector debt, growth in a public sector that employed 40% of the workforce, a bloated banking system, and heavily-pumped up house prices.... With the fortunes of the Labour Party depending on keeping the City happy, no awkward questions were asked about how the City made its huge profits. Macroeconomic policy should have been countercyclical against the credit boom in the private sector, but instead the UK government joined in, with a spending spree that was relentlessly procyclical.... In 2005, when Brown was touting "record economic growth" and an "end to boom and bust," those arguing that the UK should not be running high government deficits in a period of boom and low private-sector savings were simply ignored.[3]

Years of low inflation and economic stability had reduced the perception of risk. Economic purists argued that in a free market financial deregulation would allow capital to flow to its most productive use. Instead financial innovations responded to the low-interest regime and the political pressure to boost spending and home ownership, fueling a credit binge. Banks, which had previously held loans on their books, began to pool and sell mortgage-backed assets in repackaged form, often several times over. This practice of "securitization" had encouraged "arm's-length" transactions, with investors buying bundles of loans linked to unknown customers with whom they had few direct dealings.

When interest rates began to rise and house prices fall in the USA in 2007, the scale of the potential losses arising from lending to those with little hope of repaying in more straitened times—the subprime market—became unnervingly clear. When the securities of subprime mortgage borrowers fell in value banks stopped lending and stock prices plunged. Worrying still was the fact that more than half of the assets backed by subprime loans had been off-loaded essentially as "toxic assets," mainly to European banks.

Then a crisis of liquidity turned into a crisis of solvency. As banks in rich countries became seriously short of capital they began to hoard cash, refusing to lend to each other. This forced down asset prices and consumer spending further. With almost indecent haste, a crisis that had originated in the USA became "a crisis of globalization."[4] A multi-country banking crisis threatened a global economic catastrophe. With banks unable and/or unwilling to lend to each other and with the public fearful of financial insolvency, corporations and small businesses were caught in a downward debt deflation. Lenders stopped lending and those in debt stopped spending, threatening jobs, investment and growth across the global economy. Prior to the crisis consumption in the major industrialized nations had been sustained by house price inflation and rising stock markets. When this was reversed consumption fell and firms' profits declined. Faced with excess inventories, companies cut dividends, capital spending and employment.[5]

2 The call to action

In 2008 few authorities were prepared to allow the market to punish former excesses by permitting banks to fail or to endure protracted decline. With flows of capital between banks and companies severely curtailed and with major exporting countries aghast at the prospect of consumer markets like America denied access to spending power, governments in the USA and in the UK proved ready to print money, to buy toxic assets and to engage in the quasi-nationalization of their banking sectors. Such reactions reflected an important lesson of history—banking crises require prompt and decisive government action using public money either to recapitalize the banking sector or to take over toxic debts.

The UK was cruelly exposed to the developing crisis because of the dominance of finance in its economy. Prior to the crisis of 2008, it had the largest banking sector asset to GDP ratio among the major industrialized nations. In 1970, the value added by banks, real estate and other business services accounted for 15.9 percent of total value added in the UK. By the early 2000s, it had risen to 30.1 percent.[6] In addition, the UK had experienced rapid property price increases during the previous decade and a persistent current account deficit.

The UK had not been immune to risky financial practice. The low interest rate and easy credit environment that had characterized its financial sector before 2007 had encouraged the Northern Rock bank to stretch mortgage lending far beyond its level of deposits. The bank had relied upon short-term wholesale funding to plug the gap (at one point the bank was offering 125 percent mortgages). Once wholesale markets dried up in the aftermath of America's banking crisis Northern Rock was cruelly exposed, unable to roll-over its liabilities. Facing a crisis of solvency it appealed to the Bank of England for emergency assistance in September 2007. On learning this customers panicked, leading to the first run on a British bank in more than 100 years.[7] What worried government officials was that the bank had been undone not by a major withdrawal of deposits by customers but by a run on the bank's liabilities in wholesale funding markets and that similar weaknesses might be exposed elsewhere in the banking system.[8] Initially the Chancellor of the Exchequer announced that the government would offer a 100 percent guarantee on all the bank's deposits. But as house prices continued to fall and depositors continued to withdraw their money the government finally agreed in February 2008 (against the earlier wishes of the prime minister, Gordon Brown) to take Northern Rock into "temporary public ownership."

It was the collapse of Lehman Brothers on September 15, 2008, however, that exposed the Western world to the full implications of the subprime mortgage problem and particularly the threat to banking stability posed by the complex financial products associated with reckless lending. The freeze in money markets which followed on the failure of Lehman Brothers was of particular concern to the UK as almost 70 percent of UK bank funding was at a less than one-year maturity. The asset side of UK banks' balance sheets had been dominated by lending to the housing sector in the run up to the crisis which made the banks especially vulnerable to falling property prices. Vulnerabilities on the liquidity and asset fronts threatened the ability of the banking sector to lend to other sectors of the economy.[9]

The UK was only one of many countries forced to consider emergency policies to bail out banks and other financial institutions. A virtually bankrupt Halifax Bank of Scotland[10] (HBOS), the UK's biggest mortgage lender, was merged with Lloyds TSB in September 2008 at a cost of £12.2 billion. At the end of September the Bradford and Bingley bank collapsed and was taken into public ownership. The Royal Bank of Scotland (RBS) which had joined a consortium to take over ABN Amro in 2007 at an inflated market price almost went bankrupt. It was saved only as part of a £50 billion capital injection into the banking sector and a £200 billion liquidity scheme for buying toxic assets announced on October 8, 2008, which effectively nationalized RBS, HBOS and Lloyds TSB.[11]

Prime Minister Gordon Brown swiftly urged authorities in the USA and the EU to embark upon international coordinated action to recapitalize their banking sectors in the wake of the global financial crisis, either by buying shares in distressed banks or by insuring or buying up "toxic assets" so that banks would have the liquidity required to start lending again on a significant scale. The UK was one of the top three countries with the most costly bailouts over the period 2007–2009 in terms of direct fiscal costs as a percentage of GDP (9 percent), the other two being Iceland (13 percent) and the Netherlands (12.5 percent).[12] In terms of its GDP, the UK had the fourth largest capital injection and the second largest liquidity support among the major industrial countries.[13] Although such preemptive action prevented a systemic failure within the UK banking system (albeit at significant cost to the taxpayer) the reality which few in public office were prepared to voice was that the liberalized market, which was meant to work effectively in the public interest,

> had failed spectacularly. Enormous risks, based upon huge borrowing and debt, had been taken by private market actors, threatening the entire banking system. The taxpayer had been forced to intervene. Profit had been privatized, but risk had been socialized, and eventually nationalized.[14]

We have outlined the scale and urgency of the 2008–2009 financial crisis and the prompt action taken by government principally to indicate its impact upon the level of public debt. It is not our concern here to detail the variety of complex packages developed within the UK to effect bank bailouts and to protect the banking sector as a whole. Our emphasis is upon the related scenario—of when the crisis turned from a lending to a spending crisis causing the economy to stagnate, companies to downsize or close, and workers to be dismissed—prompting the need for a recovery strategy for the "real" as opposed to the narrowly financial economy.

Keynes had warned in the 1930s that the possibilities of financial collapse were always present and that unless governments intervened to offset the reluctance of financial institutions to lend, either because of irrational exuberance or panic, then there was every likelihood that countries would slide into deep and lasting depression. When he advocated deficit spending in the 1930s, however, his goal had been to stimulate demand through public spending to a level where business confidence would be sufficiently restored to encourage the private sector to take up the slack. The lessons of history suggested that in the wake of the banking and financial crises of 2007–2008 a substantial direct injection of public spending would be required to offset the deficiency in output and employment caused by the decline in total lending and spending.

3 Keynes revived? Fiscal responses to the 2007–2008 crisis

After the onset of the crisis in 2007 many countries suffered a severe deterioration in their fiscal position as they put emergency remedial policies in place to safeguard their banking and financial sectors. As Figure 8.1 shows only Australia, Canada, the Netherlands, Spain, Denmark and Sweden were running budget surpluses in 2007. Over the next two years budgetary positions worsened especially in Spain. Both the UK and the USA suffered a worsening of more than 8 percent of GDP.[15]

In the UK it quickly became clear that the government was prepared to abandoned its previous adherence to deficit constraints, notably the "golden rule" under which current budgets were meant to balance over the cycle with an upper limit on public debt of 40 percent of GDP. Alistair Darling, Chancellor of the Exchequer, acknowledged in November 2008 that the "UK ... faces an extraordinary global crisis, which means significantly lower tax revenues, both now and in the medium term. In the current circumstances, to apply the rules in a rigid manner would be perverse and damaging."[16] Some commentators have

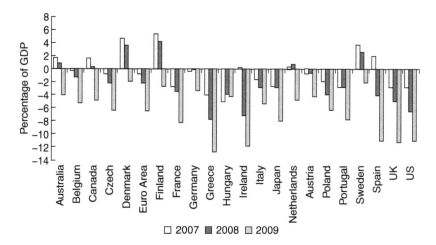

Figure 8.1 Government budget surpluses in the OECD, 2007–2009 (source: Barrell and Holland 2010, p. 123).

rashly interpreted the shift in stance to a long-waited conversion within government to the radical Keynesian agenda: in short that the government was now fundamentally committed to stepping into the breach to prevent any significant worsening of demand and employment which, if left unchecked, could raise the specter of a "return to the 1930s." Both Brown and his chancellor, Alistair Darling, wrote Lee, had "rediscovered the political economy of ... John Maynard Keynes."[17]

The Labour government recognized the need for prompt action to sustain aggregate demand. It introduced a stimulus package in November 2008 which included a temporary cut in the rate of value added tax from 17.5 percent to 15 percent, the bringing forward of £3 billion of capital spending and the injection of an estimated £20 billion of tax breaks and lending to UK businesses and homeowners. To offset the cost, restrictions were placed on personal income tax allowances for those earning over £100,000 from April 2010 and a new higher rate of income tax imposed on earnings in excess of £150,000 effective from April 2011. National Insurance contributions and duties on alcohol, tobacco and fuel were set to rise.[18] As Figure 8.2 shows, a substantial relaxation in the budget deficit had occurred largely as a consequence of emergency assistance to the troubled financial sector.

Nonetheless by March 2009 Mervyn King, Governor of the Bank of England, was questioning whether the UK could afford any further fiscal stimulus. The Bank's preferred strategy was to shift the focus to monetary policy. Interest rates

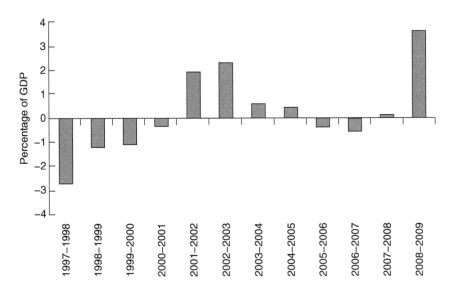

Figure 8.2 Annual change in public sector net borrowing, 1997–2009 (source: Budd 2010, p. 37).

Note
Change is defined as PSNB(% of GDP)$_t$ − PSNB(% of GDP)$_{t-1}$, where PSNB is public sector net borrowing and t is time.

were cut to the historically low level of 0.5 percent (prior to the crisis they had not been reduced to below 2 percent). In addition the central bank injected £75 billion into bank and company balance sheets over three months from March 2009 by buying up government bonds and corporate securities.[19] This quantitative easing was expanded in May 2009 to £125 billion, in August 2009 to £200 billion, in November 2011 to £275 billion, in February 2012 to £325 billion and in July 2012 to £375 billion. Stimulus in other words was to come from the creation of more money in the hope of encouraging greater bank lending. Those of a Keynesian persuasion were concerned less with expanding the supply of money (which may or may not prompt a positive reaction from the banking sector) than with increasing spending out of a deficit financed by bond issues.[20]

Quantitative easing depended for its effect upon financial institutions wanting to lend to households and small firms and upon corporations wanting to invest and raise employment. But as King noted rather limply at the time of the November 2011 cash injection "I can't guarantee that it means that bank lending will rise, but what I do believe is that it won't fall as far as it might otherwise have done."[21] With potential borrowers facing the collapse in the value of their collateral and with households facing overhangs of debt, job losses, falling incomes and wealth there was scant hope that monetary policy alone would be able to raise investment and consumption to the levels needed to invoke a sustained economic recovery.

In any event doubts were already being expressed about how far the government's new fiscal policy amounted to a conversion to Keynesian-style increases in expenditure and transfer payments. More than half of the deterioration in the fiscal balance after 2008 occurred because of expenditures arising out of the financial crisis itself. Such relief had to work through monetary channels to revive the supply of credit and did not directly boost household income or the demand for goods.[22] Discretionary measures taken in the UK in 2008 were judged by the OECD to have amounted to around 1.4 percent of GDP, considerably less than the estimated stimulus of 5.6 percent in the USA and 3 percent in Germany.[23] The UK fiscal stimulus came principally from the revenue side of the budget rather than from spending measures designed to raise aggregate demand.[24]

4 The turn to austerity

Faced with deleveraging in the household and private sector it was essential in the aftermath of the global crisis for the UK to counteract any 1930s-style deflationary spiral. But recourse to greater deficit spending met resistance.

The contrast in the conduct of fiscal policy in the UK from 2010 could not be starker. Forced by the need to recapitalize the ailing banking sector and to deal immediately with the effects of financial constraint on the real economy, the UK authorities, as we noted above, had been quick to join other countries in abandoning cherished rules about self-imposed limits to fiscal profligacy. But shortly thereafter more traditional concerns about the need to rein in public spending and rising debt came to dominate the UK policy agenda. Many observers were struck by the speed with which an earlier Keynesian response to possible economic and financial collapse was replaced with an austerity agenda dominated by cuts in government spending.

Any effort to increase discretionary fiscal spending, preached the Coalition Conservative/Liberal Democrat government elected in May 2010, would merely encourage instability in financial markets, invite adverse reaction by credit rating agencies, and cause a collapse of confidence.[25] In a revival of the "Treasury View" arguments of the 1920s and 1930s, rising sovereign debt was now regarded as wasteful, inflationary in its impact upon interest rates, likely to "crowd out" the private borrowing needed to finance more productive investment, and a sure way of imposing intolerable fiscal burdens on future generations. By contrast, any reduction in public demand would be compensated for by a substantial recovery in private demand nurtured by a more responsible financial and budgetary climate.[26] Fiscal consolidation, in short, was the route to economic and financial recovery.

The alternative view—that is was preferable to await a time when a recovery was underway sufficiently to encourage employment and income to grow together and to boost tax receipts relative to public expenditure so that a reduction in the deficit might be considered to be a responsible economic and political option—was never seriously entertained within official circles. It was as if the policy responses at the time of the crisis had "demonstrated the repressed existence of a kind of bastardised Keynesianism, but then swiftly abandoned once the immediate occasion of their use [had] passed."[27]

The emphasis on fiscal rectitude in the UK was still dominant in the second quarter of 2013 when the country's GDP was already 14 percent below its pre-crisis trend.[28] Even the IMF had argued in 2009 that fiscal spending was likely to be effective during periods of financial crisis when disruptions to the flow of credit were limiting private spending.[29]

The problem for the UK was that it had to face the outturn of the international economic crisis from an already weakened fiscal position. National debt as a percentage of GDP had risen from 26 percent in 1991 to 41 percent by 2005 and to 55 percent by 2010. The UK's rescue of the banks and the increase in social welfare expenditure and reduced taxation that accompanied the recession increased the national debt by an estimated £260 billion between 2007 and 2010.[30] The finance and property sector in the UK furthermore had accounted for half of the increase in tax receipts between 2002–2003 and 2007–2008 which imposed a greater strain on the country's fiscal position that in countries with a smaller financial sector.[31]

In an emergency budget in June 2010 George Osborne, Chancellor of the Exchequer, introduced a series of severe spending cuts equal to a fiscal tightening of 7 percent of GDP over four years beginning in the spring of 2011. Those earning over £18,000 a year would face a cut in tax credits and higher National Insurance contributions. Child benefit was to be frozen for three years and the pay of public employees for two years.[32] The government's October 2010 spending review cut projected outlays by £81 billion with enforced reductions in the costs of central and local government. Total public spending was expected to fall to 40 percent of GDP by 2014.[33]

Table 8.1 Public spending totals (£ millions, current)

	2009–2010 (outturn)	*2017–2018 (projected)*
Current spending	600.9	716.2
Social security benefits	197.1	230.7
Debt interest	30.9	67.1
Net investment	49.5	22.9
Total	669.7	765.5

Source: Office for Budget Responsibility, 2011 and 2012.

Notes
Tax credits are included in social security benefits.
Drawn from: Crafts (2013, p. 271).

The government's overall intention was to reduce cyclically adjusted public sector net borrowing by 8.4 percentage points, from 8.7 percent of GDP in 2009–2010 to 0.3 percent of GDP in 2015–2016. These targets shaped the autumn spending review of October 2010. The discretionary reductions in public expenditure imposed by the Coalition government were intended to be about 60 percent greater by 2014–2015 than had been envisaged by the previous Labour government.[34] As Table 8.1 shows, current UK expenditure was expected to rise by 19 percent between 2009–2010 and 2017–2018 and spending on social security by £33.6 billion. The latter was to be financed, however, largely by a reduction of £26.6 billion in net government investment.[35]

What was especially worrying was that the decision to eliminate the structural budget deficit by 2015–2016. This involved a measure of fiscal tightening much more restrictive than the previous "golden rule" which had allowed government borrowing to cover public investment and to target a current budget balance over the business cycle. Pursuing the goal of a balanced structural budget (that is the budgetary position when the economy is operating at full employment with actual output equal to potential output) ruled out the possibility of any strategic long-term investments in infrastructure, technology and education, for example, but ensured dramatic cuts in public spending.[36] Reviewing the prospect, Sawyer concluded gloomily that:

> The historical experience (at least in the UK) of significant budget deficits indicates that the achievement of a structural balanced budget requires significant changes in savings, investment behaviour and in net export performance. In the (likely) absence of such changes, a balanced budget will not be achieved, and the consequences of public expenditure reduction will be lower economic activity and higher unemployment.[37]

5 Retrenchment: the road to recovery?

The official rhetoric supporting fiscal retrenchment stressed how necessary it was to avoid taking risks with the economy and to limit any damage to confidence.

Even though the fiscal policy mistakes of the 1930s and the dismal record of Japan's tightening of fiscal policy at precisely the wrong time in 1997, which propelled its economy into stagnation, were well known,[38] the Coalition government remained fearful of spooking the markets. It was the job of government seemingly to cut its way out of recession.

The Coalition frequently stressed how fiscal consolidation could actually be expansionary. Increased government spending in its view was unlikely to boost demand since consumers would merely cut back on their expenditures in anticipation of the higher taxes required to fund mounting public debt. Austerity on the other hand would induce more private spending by restoring the confidence of investors and households who would face lower tax liabilities and interest rates because of reduced public spending. This in turn would stimulate market confidence and investment. But there was little empirical evidence to support such a claim. On the contrary, the IMF concluded in 2010 that "A budget cut equal to 1 percent of GDP typically reduces domestic demand by about 1 percent and raises the unemployment rate by 0.3 percentage point."[39]

Although many observers acknowledged the need for the UK to find some form of fiscal accommodation in the medium to long term, it was always doubtful whether the fiscal tightening introduced from 2010 was wise during a period of rising unemployment and falling output. Under less contractionary circumstances a tightening of fiscal policy could in theory be carried out alongside an offsetting relaxation in monetary policy. In more normal times the long-term interest rate determining the borrowing costs of firms for investment would be driven by the expected shift in short-term interest rates over a ten-year time horizon. As monetary policy was loosened, long-term interest rates would be expected to fall thereby stimulating investment and offsetting the effects of fiscal tightening.[40]

Reducing public expenditure during a recession, however, was always fraught with problems. With interest rates at already low levels, it was unlikely that further tightening of fiscal policy would result in an appropriate or timely monetary policy reaction. The speed and magnitude of fiscal tightening in a recession threatens even greater losses in output and employment if it impacts negatively on growth and therefore future tax revenues from which government spending can be financed. With rising unemployment and low job security many UK households and firms found themselves facing severe liquidity problems after 2008. At the time austerity was being imposed with almost ghoulish fervor business confidence and household spending in the UK were in decline. Consumers were prioritizing the deleveraging of debt over spending. Businesses facing stagnant or falling profits were even less inclined to increase investment and employment, thereby exacerbating the economic and fiscal difficulties facing the country. Liquidity constraints, in other words, worked to amplify the effects of contractionary policies on output and employment.[41] Real GDP in the UK shrank by 3.2 percent between the final quarter of 2007 to the second quarter of 2009, employment fell by 455,000 and unemployment increased by 786,000. By the first quarter of 2011 unemployment was 806,000 higher and real GDP almost

1 percent below its final quarter 2007 level.[42] UK real household disposable income fell by about 1.2 percent over 2011.

By mid-2011 there was survey evidence of collapsing confidence in the business and especially construction sectors and of falling sales and profits in the retail sector. This was at a time when the IMF published an analysis of 173 cases of fiscal retrenchment, which showed that they consistently resulted in economic contraction.[43] Austerity ultimately threatened greater unemployment, increased social welfare payments and lower tax revenues as income and output fall in response to reduced spending. The concomitant rise in borrowing costs could only make the burden of debt greater to bear.

It was not as if the UK authorities were driven to fiscal retrenchment because they faced unbearable costs of borrowing or an imminent crisis of confidence. The crisis itself had generated a reduction in global interest rates in the face of high household savings and weak investment. The rates of return on medium length (15-year) index-linked government borrowing in the UK had fallen by December 2009 to around 1 percent, half the level of the previous December (see Figure 8.3). The risks of borrowing were arguably less than the prospect of slowing the economy by cutting spending and raising taxes.[44]

So far as confidence was concerned, there was little evidence at the time austerity packages were being introduced that markets felt the risk of government

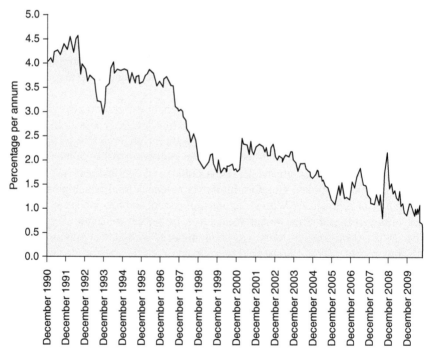

Figure 8.3 Real interest rate on index-linked gilts, 1990–2009 (percentage per annum) (source: Barrell and Kirby 2010, p. 62).

default to be worryingly high.[45] With borrowing relatively cheap and debt default risks low, and with a significant output gap in the UK economy the benefits of fiscal consolidation were open to doubt compared with those that could be enjoyed by delaying spending cuts until after a recovery was underway and the output shortfall reduced.[46]

6 Living with austerity

It would have been more heartening for the UK if the fiscal consolidation embarked upon from 2010 promised greater growth in the medium term. "Just about the worst thing policymakers could do," Farlow commented, "was to emphasize only deficits, have no strategy for dealing with the surpluses generated by the deleveraging process of the private sector, and forget the importance of growth."[47] In the absence of monetary stimulus, a premium was put on supply-side reform. But as Crafts points out, "In terms of its likely impact on the supply side, the trajectory of fiscal consolidation post-2010 does not compare favourably with that of the 1980s, perhaps reflecting tighter political constraints and/or the difference that coalition makes."[48]

The austerity pronouncements as might be expected were particularly silent on spending programs that could ostensibly offset deflation. Infrastructure investment, supply-side tax reforms and improvements in human capital, especially education, were all vital to the growth prospects of the UK but they threatened fiscal probity. Nor was there any serious discussion about how the sustenance of a budget deficit to ward off immediate and medium-term recession might be accommodated. Financial institutions could have been obliged to place some minimum proportion of their asset portfolio into government stock or steps taken to ensure that the central bank would act as lender of last resort to provide money for government outlays.[49]

In retrospect it is tempting to conclude that the marked shift from fiscal support to austerity was no less than political pandering to the financial markets (reflecting the weighty influence of banks and finance within UK political economy) and a reflection of the determination of the Coalition to "transform the 'liberal collectivist' model that characterized the UK during the earlier postwar period into a neoliberal model."[50]

It was inevitable that the large fiscal deficits occasioned by the global financial crisis would lead to widespread concerns about long-term fiscal sustainability and even (correctly as it turned out) possible default within the affected countries. But what caused alarm among some observers in the UK was the speed and depth of the retrenchment that was subsequently imposed and in particular its emphasis upon spending cuts and their potential negative effect on economic growth upon which fiscal health ultimately depended. The Keynesian message—that spending cuts and raised taxation needed the foundation of a strong economy to prevent them becoming self-defeating and the harbinger of greater recession and decline—was lost in clamor for fiscal rectitude. "Printing money to offset cuts in public spending is the flakiest possible route to growth," Skidelsky has commented. "[A]n alternative policy of targeting growth and letting the deficit look after itself would be better for growth and the debt."[51] To Krugman the renewed emphasis on austerity exemplified the pressures piled upon governments (the UK included) by creditor and business lobbies whose real preferences were for "fiscal policy that focuses on deficits rather than on job creation, monetary policy that obsessively fights even the hint of inflation and raises interest rates even in the face of mass unemployment" since that "in effect serves the interests of creditors, of those who lend as opposed to those who borrow and/or work for a living."[52] The irony is that the expenditure reductions imposed during the later years of the crisis were likely in their effects to give rise to even greater budget deficits in the immediate term in order to safeguard prevailing levels of potential output.[53]

Notes

1 Skidelsky (2009, pp. xiii–xiv).
2 Konzelmann and Fovargue-Davies (2011, p. 3).
3 Farlow (2013, p. 24).
4 Skidelsky (2009, p. 168).
5 Skidelsky (2009, p. 14).
6 OECD (2009).
7 Farlow (2013, pp. 95–96).
8 Sentance et al. (2012, p. 109).
9 Ibid.
10 The HBOS banking and insurance company had been formed in 2001 by the merger of Halifax plc and the Bank of Scotland.
11 Kickert (2012, p. 170).
12 Farlow (2013, p. 163).
13 Sentance et al. (2012, p. 115).
14 Lee (2009, p. 25).
15 Barrell and Holland (2010, p. 121).
16 Darling (2008), cited in Hodson and Mabbett (2009, p. 1053).
17 Lee (2009, p. 30).
18 Kickert (2012, pp. 171–172).
19 Skidelsky (2009, p. 21).
20 Farlow (2013, p. 183).
21 Farlow (2013, p. 184).
22 Hodson and Mabbett (2009, p. 1053).
23 OECD (2009).
24 Hodson and Mabbett (2009, pp. 1052–1053).
25 Sawyer (2012, p. 209).
26 See King et al. (2012) and Sawyer (2012, p. 208).
27 Callinicos (2012, p. 75).
28 Wolf (2013).
29 International Monetary Fund (2012).
30 King et al. (2012, p. 11).
31 Farlow (2013, p. 178).
32 Farlow (2013, pp. 243–244).
33 Treasury Committee (2010).
34 Sawyer (2012, p. 207).
35 Crafts (2013, pp. 270–271).
36 Fontana and Sawyer (2011, pp. 49–50).

37 Sawyer (2011, p. 28).
38 I have addressed these issues elsewhere. See Garside (1990 and 2012).
39 International Monetary Fund (2010, p. 113).
40 Holland and Portes (2012, p. 6).
41 Bagaria et al. (2012, pp. 43, 51).
42 King et al. (2012, p. 11).
43 Guajardo et al. (2011) cited in Farlow (2013, p. 247).
44 Barrell and Kirby (2010, pp. 61–62).
45 Barrell and Kirby (2010, p. 63).
46 Barrell (2011, p. 5).
47 Farlow (2013, p. 230).
48 Crafts (2013, p. 270).
49 Sawyer (2012, p. 210).
50 King et al. (2012, p. 201).
51 Skidelsky (2013).
52 Krugman (2012, pp. 206–207).
53 Sawyer (2012, pp. 219–220).

References

Bagaria, N., Holland, D. and Reenen, J. V. (2012) "Fiscal Consolidation During a Depression," *National Institute Economic Review*, 221(1): 42–54.

Barrell, R. (2011) "Fiscal Consolidation and the Slimmer State," *National Institute Economic Review*, 215(1): 4–9.

Barrell, R. and Holland, D. (2010) "Fiscal and Financial Responses to the Economic Downturn," *National Institute Economic Review*, 211(1): 115–126.

Barrell, R. and Kirby, S. (2010) "Fiscal Policy and Government Spending," *National Institute Economic Review*, 214(1): 61–66.

Budd, A. (2010) "Fiscal Policy Under Labour," *National Institute Economic Review*, 212(1): 34–48.

Callinicos, A. (2012) "Commentary: Contradictions of Austerity," *Cambridge Journal of Economics*, 36(1): 65–77.

Crafts, N. (2013) "Returning to Growth: Lessons From History," *Fiscal Studies*, 34(2): 255–282.

Darling, A. (2008) "Maintaining Stability in a Global Economy," The Mais Lecture, Cass Business School, City University, London.

Farlow, A. (2013) *Crash and Beyond: Causes and Consequences of the Global Financial Crisis*, Oxford: Oxford University Press.

Fontana, G. and Sawyer, M. (2011) "Fiscal Austerity. Lessons From Recent Events in the British Isles," *Challenge*, 54(2): 42–60.

Garside, W. R. (1990) *British Unemployment, 1919–1939. A Study in Public Policy*, Cambridge: Cambridge University Press.

Garside, W. R. (2012) *Japan's Great Stagnation. Forging Ahead, Falling Behind*, Cheltenham and Northampton, MA: Edward Elgar Publishing.

Guajardo, J., Leigh, D. and Pescatori, A. (2011) "Expansionary Austerity: New International Evidence," IMF Working Paper 11/158.

Hodson, D. and Mabbett, D. (2009) "UK Economic Policy and the Global Financial Crisis: Paradigm Lost?" *Journal of Common Market Studies*, 47(5): 1041–1061.

Holland, D. and Portes, J. (2012) "Self-Defeating Austerity?" *National Institute Economic Review*, 222(1): 4–10.

International Monetary Fund (2010) *World Economic Outlook (WEO): Recovery, Risk and Rebalancing*, Washington, DC: IMF.

International Monetary Fund (2012) *World Economic Outlook*, Washington, DC: IMF.

Kickert, W. (2012) "How the UK Government Responded to the Fiscal Crisis: An Outsider's View," *Public Money and Management*, 32(3): 169–176.

King, L., Kitson, M., Konzelmann, S. and Wilkinson, F. (2012) "Making the Same Mistake Again—Or Is This Time Different?" *Cambridge Journal of Economics*, 36(1): 1–15.

Konzelmann, S. and Fovargue-Davies, M. (2011) "Anglo-Saxon Capitalism in Crisis? Models of Liberal Capitalism and the Preconditions for Financial Stability," Centre for Business Research, Working Paper No. 422, University of Cambridge.

Krugman, P. (2012) *End This Depression Now!* New York: NY: W. W. Norton.

Lee, S. (2009) "The Rock of Stability? The Political Economy of the Brown Government," *Policy Studies*, 30(1): 17–32.

OECD (2009) *Fiscal Packages Across OECD Countries*, Paris: OECD.

Sawyer, M. (2011) "UK Fiscal Policy After the Global Financial Crisis," *Contributions to Political Economy*, 30(1): 13–29.

Sawyer, M. (2012) "The Tragedy of UK Fiscal Policy in the Aftermath of the Financial Crisis," *Cambridge Journal of Economics*, 36(1): 205–221.

Sentance, A., Taylor, M. and Wieladek, T. (2012) "How the UK Economy Weathered the Financial Storm," *Journal of International Money and Finance*, 31(1): 102–123.

Skidelsky, R. (2009) *Keynes: The Return of the Master*, London: Allen Lane.

Skidelsky, R. (2013) "Labour Should Hammer Home One Simple Message on the Economy," *The Guardian*, August 13.

Treasury Committee (2010) *Spending Review 2010*, HC 544–1, London: The Stationery Office.

Wolf, M. (2013) "We Still Live In Lehman's Shadow," *Financial Times*, September 18.

9 Beyond de-globalization in Japan

Yutaka Harada

1 Introduction

With the collapse of the Berlin Wall in 1989, East European countries joined the world market. China had already joined at the end of 1970s. Despite these trends, Japan failed to enter the age of globalization.

Globalization, here, means the free movement of people, goods and money across national boundaries. Their movement to and from Japan did not expand with the end of the Cold War, compared to earlier periods. In short, Japan was "de-globalized" in relative terms, and Japanese attitudes toward globalization became more negative. This is the theme of Section 2 of this chapter.

The Section 3 shows that Japan's exports, investments, and cross-border movement of people declined in relative terms, and explains the factors behind this trend.

The Section 4 discusses how Japan should move forward in Asia and the rest of the world in the light of the changes caused by globalization.

The final section offers my conclusions. I will emphasize that Japan's de-globalization is strengthened by deflationary monetary policy and bad employment situations caused by the policy since the 1990s. Negative Japanese attitudes to globalization will be weakened with the improvement of the employment situation caused by a bold monetary expansion under Prime Minister Abe administration from the end of 2012.

2 Japanese attitudes toward globalization

In a poll among 25 countries conducted by the World Economic Forum in 2011, Japan had the most antagonistic attitude toward globalization. While 19 countries were favorable to globalization, Japan was opposed, along with France, Spain, Russia and Argentina. To a question on how globalization would change rights, working conditions and salary, only 16 percent of Japanese answered that they would improve as a result of globalization, while 67 percent said they would become worse. The 16 percent favorable response was the lowest among the 25 countries, while the 67 percent unfavorable response was the second highest after Argentina, which was going through an international financial crisis at that time.[1]

Additionally, recent discussions in Japan on TPP (Trans-Pacific Partnership), which is a US-led FTA (free trade agreement) among 12 countries in the Asia-Pacific area, show Japan's feelings of xenophobia. A book antagonistic to TPP written by a young official in the Ministry of Economy, Trade, and Industry has sold more than 150,000 copies, according to the publisher.[2] A search for Japanese books about TPP on the Amazon site in Japan results in 400 hits. Among them, 84 include the term "TPP" in the title or subtitle, and among these 84 books, 58 are opposed to TPP, 11 can be considered neutral, and only 15 support TPP.[3]

Japan's interest in globalization has certainly increased since the 1980s. Of the articles carried by the national daily *Asahi Shimbun*, there were only 63 that included the term "globalization" in the 1980s; this increased to 2,887 articles in the 1990s, to 7,653 articles in the first decade of the 2000s, and 2,491 articles in 2011 and 2012.[4] There were 2,491 articles in just two years, so it would be safe to conclude that Japanese interest in globalization has strengthened in recent years. It is difficult to judge whether people have become pro or con, however, since I cannot find a survey of Japanese attitudes toward globalization spanning several decades. I suspect, though, that people have become more opposed as Japan's economy stagnated. Japan's long slump had a significant impact on the Japanese negative attitude to globalization.

While I have been unable to find a survey that exactly addresses this problem, there is one poll of newly hired personnel that shows new workers answering "No" when asked whether they want to work abroad rising from 28.7 percent in 2004 to 36.2 percent in 2007 to 49.0 percent in 2010 and to 58 percent in 2013.[5]

In contrast to the attitudes of the Japanese public, Japan is actually a front-runner in terms of globalization. In Thomas Friedman's *The Lexus and the Olive Tree*, Lexus—the high-end brand of Toyota Motor Company—is seen as a symbol of globalization, while the olive tree is a symbol of local culture, land, and people.[6] Japanese society is highly globalized, yet at the same time, people are antagonistic to globalization.

This may appear to be a contradiction, but for people in small Japanese towns, antagonistic feelings are reasonable. Until the early 1990s, globalization meant that the companies that had hired them moved their operations abroad, and in the 2000s, globalization meant that the companies that had hired them might lose out in global competition, leaving only low-paid jobs or no jobs in Japan.[7]

In the end of the 1980s, a lot of Japanese blue-collar workers went to Asia to train local workers, which meant a promotion for them. The training of local workers by Japanese workers is depicted by Nakazawa.[8]

Until the early 1990s, the Japanese felt that Japan and jobs for the Japanese were expanding in the world. Now, however, the Japanese feel that the country is shrinking. This feeling is correct. Japan's world shares of exports, investments and managers in many fields have continued to decline since the 1990s until now. I will explain the changes by using data in the next section. I also point out that wrong monetary policy accelerates the trends.

3 Japan's declining share of the world economy

I believe that the antagonistic feeling toward globalization is associated with Japan's "de-globalization." The Japanese feel that domestic companies cannot compete with foreign companies, leading to reductions in wages and, ultimately, the loss of employment. It is not important whether this is a fact or not; what is more important is that the Japanese think this way.

The effect of globalization on the Japanese economy seems to be important not only for the economy as a whole but also for income distribution. It is, however, difficult to find a study demonstrating that income distribution has become worse in Japan because of globalization.[9] A simplified view of globalization assumes that it causes declines in prices of manufactured goods, forcing down wages of blue-color workers while leaving wages of white-color workers intact. This should mean that income distribution becomes uneven, but we cannot find studies to support such a simple assumption. Takashi Yamamoto's painstaking work did not find any evidence that international trade increased inequality in the Japanese manufacturing industry.[10]

If prices of imported goods decline because of globalization, people's real income increases. They can now actually enjoy lower prices for clothing, electric appliances, cellular phones and other items caused by global competition.

There are many studies[11] in Japan showing that Japan's income distribution has become unbalanced, but the main reason observed is aging. Income distribution becomes unequal in higher age groups. As the share of older people increased in Japan, overall income distribution became unequal, although income distribution within age groups tended to become more equal. The studies on Japanese income distribution rarely refer to globalization.

3.1 Globalization and inequality in other countries

In other countries as well, the effect of globalization on income distribution is not clear. According to Milanovic, some studies assert that globalization has little effect on income inequality, but other studies show that globalization expands income inequality in low-income countries.[12]

Contrastingly, an IMF report shows that trade (exports) has the effect of decreasing income inequality, while foreign direct investment expands income inequality.[13] The combined effects of these two trends produce a slight expansion of inequality. At the same time, the report shows that progress of technology is the most important factor in determining income inequality. The effect of globalization on income inequality is different in developed and developing countries. In developed countries, the effect of globalization on equality was large but that of technology was small, while in developing countries, that of technology was overwhelmingly large. Additionally, the study found that in developed countries, imports from developing countries decreased inequality, and in developing countries exports of agricultural products decreased inequality. This supports my former argument for Japan.

3.2 Shrinking Japan

Figure 9.1 shows trends in the GDPs (converted to current dollar terms using ordinary exchange rates) of major countries and areas. The GDP data has been partly adjusted for inflation. The GDP of countries with high inflation has a tendency to decrease as the exchange rate decreases.

The figure clearly shows that US GDP steadily grew, China and developing Asia (practically speaking, Asia excluding Japan[14]) rapidly expanded, while Japan's GDP did not grow after 1995. The figure also shows Germany and South Korea for reference. It is difficult to see the trends of these countries in the figure because of the fluctuations, but Germany and South Korea annually increased by an average of 3.6 percent and 6.8 percent from 1990 to 2012, respectively, while Japan increased by 3.0 percent.

3.3 PPP is a better indicator

The exchange rate reflects productivity in trade-related sectors, but does not reflect that of domestic sectors, and the GDP of domestic sectors is underestimated in less-developed countries. Additionally, exchange rates abruptly fluctuate without significant reasons. Thus, exchange-rate-converted GDP is not necessarily a good indicator of economic prosperity of a country. Actually, Japan's stagnation started in 1990, but Japanese GDP increased through 1995 because of the yen's appreciation.

Figure 9.2 shows GDP on a current purchasing-power-parity basis of the same countries. PPP GDP here is expressed in current dollars, and it reflects inflation.

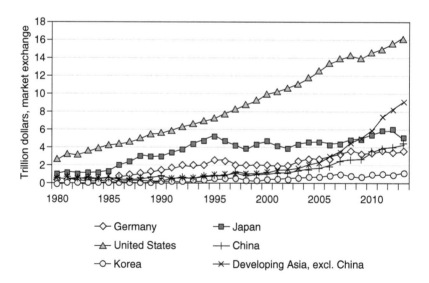

Figure 9.1 Trends of GDP (exchange rate) of major countries and areas (source: International Monetary Fund, World Economic Outlook Database, April 2013).

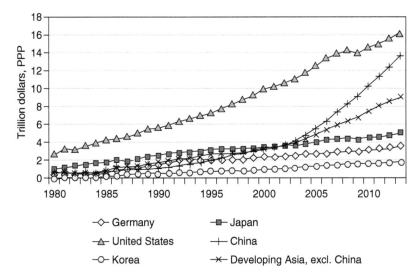

Figure 9.2 Trends of GDP (purchasing power parity) of major countries and areas (source: International Monetary Fund, World Economic Outlook Database, April 2013).

The fluctuations of growth rates here are milder, and the GDPs of less-developed countries are larger. The US GDP steadily grew, as in Figure 9.1, but the pace of growth of China and developing Asia appears to eclipse that of the US.

In the figure, it is difficult to see the growth trends of Germany, South Korea and Japan, but Germany and South Korea annually increased by an average of 3.7 percent and 7.4 percent from 1990 to 2012, respectively, while Japan increased by 3.1 percent.

Korea's growth rate is much higher than that of Japan, but Germany's is higher only by 0.6 points (3.7 percent–3.1 percent). This difference might not seem important, but 0.6 points becomes 14 points in 22 years. This means that Japan's GDP would be larger by 14 percent now if Japan's growth rate, too, was 3.7 percent.[15]

The per capita GDP of South Korea was much smaller than Japan's in 1990, so it would be natural that Korea's growth rate would be higher than Japan's, according to the convergence theory or catching-up theory.

Both the convergence theory and catching-up effect suggest that low-income countries can grow faster than high-income countries because the low-income country can learn from the advanced products, technologies and institutions of high-income countries.[16] It is easier to imitate rather than to create from scratch.

In 2012, the per capita PPP GDP of South Korea was $32,272, and Japan's was $36,266. Since Korea's is smaller than Japan's only by 11 percent, Korea may exceed Japan in several years' time. This suggests that Japan's growth rate has been too low.

3.4 Japan's decline in the share of trade

If we look at trade, Japan's stagnation becomes clearer. Figure 9.3 shows the indexes of export volume (1980 = 100) for China, developing Asia, the US, Germany, South Korea and Japan. It shows that exports by China, developing Asia, and South Korea rapidly increased by 27.27-fold, 10.92-fold and 11.08-fold, respectively, from 1990 to 2012, but those by the US, Germany and Japan were flat.

The differences between the US, Germany and Japan are not readily visible in the figure, so I excluded China, developing Asia and South Korea and the result is Figure 9.4, which shows that the export volumes of the three countries did not change significantly until 1990, at which point Japan's growth was slightly higher. After 1990, Japan's exports slowed. German and US exports increased by 3.30 and 3.06 times, respectively, from 1990 to 2012, while Japan's increased by only 2.32 times over the same period.

Why did this happen? The yen's appreciation was clearly a major factor behind the stagnant exports. The ¥$ and won/$ exchange rates are shown in Figures 9.3 and 9.4. In these figures, a rise in the line means a depreciation, as exchange rates are expressed per dollar in Japanese and Korean currencies. An abrupt yen appreciation in the middle of the 1980s, in the early 1990s, and after the Lehman shock in 2008 dampened Japan's exports, as shown in Figure 9.3.

The effect of the yen's appreciation becomes clearer when Japan and Korea are compared. When the yen appreciated in the middle of the 1980s, the won depreciated. The won was stable when the yen appreciated in the first half of the

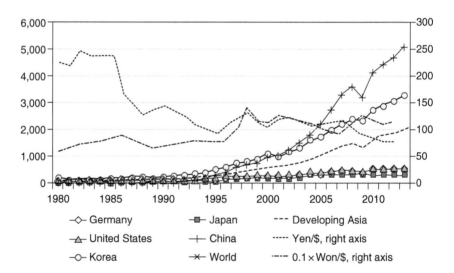

Figure 9.3 Trends of exports volumes of major countries and areas (source: International Monetary Fund, World Economic Outlook Database, April 2013).

Note
Exports volume is volume of exports of goods and services.

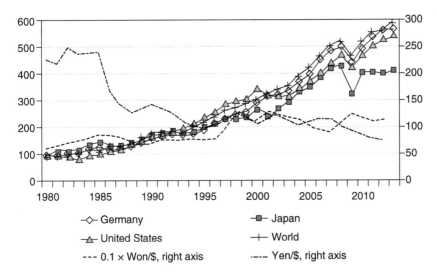

Figure 9.4 Trends of exports volumes of major countries and areas excluding China and Developing Asia (source: International Monetary Fund, World Economic Outlook Database, April 2013).

Note
Exports volume is volume of exports of goods and services.

1990s. And the yen appreciated after Lehman shock, while the won depreciated. In the three cases of the yen's appreciations, Japanese exports always stagnated.

In the case of Korea, the effects of the won's depreciation on exports had not been clear, but after the Lehman shock, it became clear that the won's depreciation helped Korean exports recover smoothly, as suggested in Figure 9.3.

As a result, Japan's share of trade in the world, and especially compared to developing Asia, declined. Japan is a neighbor to developing Asia and is in the best geographical position to incorporate the region's economic dynamism. If Japan could expand exports by incorporated developing Asia's dynamism, Japan's growth rate would not have been lower than that of Germany; it probably would have been closer to that of South Korea.

Jorgenson and Nomura[17] have shown that Japan's real effective exchange rate exceeded Japan's PPP exchange rate by 78 percent. And Okada and Hamada[18] have pointed out that the excessively high exchange rate caused a decrease not only in domestic production among export-oriented manufacturers but also in domestic investment, which instead was channeled into foreign direct investment.

Japan's yen appreciation has been caused by Japan's deflationary monetary policy, which has badly affected the Japanese economy, as I have mentioned in the past. While developing Asia has aggressively learned from Japan and other advanced countries, Japan's establishment tried to preserve its vested interests by manipulating the Japanese system dominated by regulations, complicated subsidies and human networks, admittedly decreasing the efficiency of the Japanese economy. It is difficult to deny that the malfunctioning monetary policy had an extremely negative impact on the Japanese economy, especially when we see the recovery of Japanese economy under the expansionary monetary policy of Bank of Japan Governor Haruhiko Kuroda, who was appointed by Prime Minister Shinzo Abe.[19]

3.5 Japan's ratio of exports to GDP did not increase

Figure 9.5 shows the ratios of exports to GDP of major countries. The ratio of South Korea increased from 28.0 percent in 1990 to 56.2 percent in 2011, that of China increased from 16.1 percent to 31.4 percent, and that of Germany increased from 24.8 percent in 1990 to 51.6 percent in 2012, reflecting rapid export growth. That of Japan, however, increased from 10.3 percent 1990 to 15.1 percent in 2011, and that of the US also only increased from 9.6 percent to 14.0 percent.

In these countries, exports and imports increased practically at the same speed although I did not show the data in the Figure. Higher ratios of exports to GDP do not mean that GDP increased through an expansion of net exports (exports less imports).

Japan's imports increased more than its exports, but this was a reflection of increases in mineral fuel prices and liquid natural gas imports following the Fukushima Daiichi nuclear power plant accident.

Usually, export industries have relatively high productivity among industries in a country. This is what is taught in the comparative advantage in trade theory.

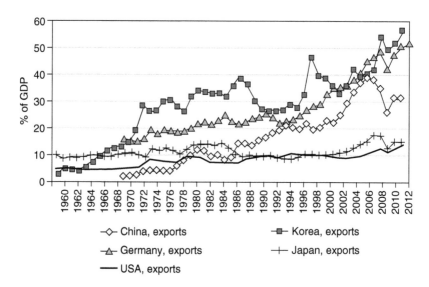

Figure 9.5 Shares of exports and imports of major countries, 1960–2012 (source: World Bank, World Development Indicators).

When shares of exports and imports to GDP of a country increase, the country replaces inefficient industries with efficient ones, as a result of which the average productivity of the country increases. South Korea, Germany and China enjoyed such merits, but Japan and the US did not do so sufficiently.

Additionally, China's ratio declined after the Lehman shock, caused by a slump in the US and Europe after 2008 and also by an expansion of inefficient public expenditures to stimulate the economy. The same thing happened in Japan at a lower level. The ratio of Japan's exports to GDP increased before the Lehman shock but declined after that because of world economic stagnation, the yen's appreciation, and an expansion of inefficient public investment.

The last item, especially, caused the yen's value to rise, and offset the effect of an expansionary fiscal policy.[20] The same mechanism was at work in China, with the exchange rates of Japan and China appreciating after the Lehman shock.

3.6 Japan's net capital outflows declined

Japan's exports stagnated, which also meant that Japan's investment abroad stagnated, since net exports are net capital outflow.

Net exports equal net capital outflow. This means that Japan's net investment abroad declined. Japan has thus been relatively de-globalized since 1990. As shown in Figure 9.6, Japan's net capital outflows did not decline from the 1980s to early 2000s but declined thereafter.[21] By contrast, those of Germany and

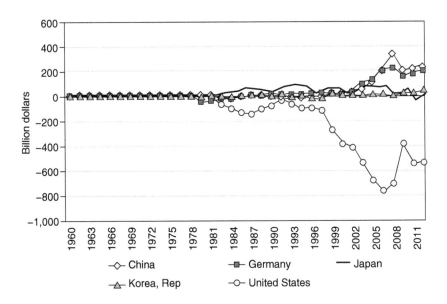

Figure 9.6 Net capital outflows of major countries, 1960–2011 (source: World Bank, WEI).

Note
Net capital outflow=net exports, net exports are shown.

China increased from the early 2000s. Their capital outflows have exceeded $200 billion and are around $300 billion.

Net capital outflow is negative in the US, which means that the US accepted foreign investment, but at the same time this allows the US to invest abroad. This is partly because the US is the key currency country. I will examine this in the next section on direct investment.

3.7 Japan's foreign direct investment declined

Figure 9.7 shows foreign direct investment. In this figure, only China shows a net inflow, and other countries show a net outflow. The figure clearly shows that the US has actively made direct investments. The US has invested $150 billion a year on average since 2007 as at the time of this writing. The US can borrow money and invest it abroad. China now receives approximately $250 billion of foreign direct investment a year.

Japan's foreign direct investment had two booms; one toward the end of the 1980s, and the second from 2007 to at least the time of this writing. Both booms were induced by the yen's appreciation, but the effect has been different. The first boom occurred in the period of a domestic investment boom (Japan was in the midst of a bubble economy), and employment expanded, with unemployment decreasing to nearly 2 percent. The Japanese people did not worry about their jobs.

The second boom, however, occurred after Japan experienced a long stagnant economy, shrinking employment and deteriorating labor conditions, which must have caused antagonistic attitudes toward globalization.

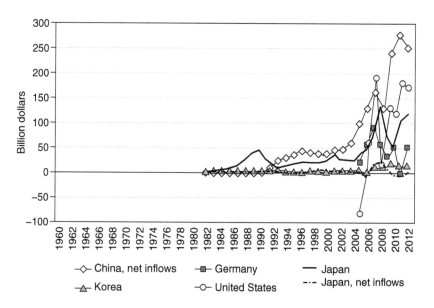

Figure 9.7 Foreign direct investment of major countries, 1960–2012 (sources: World Bank World Development Indicators; JETRO, Direct Investment Statistics).

In the second boom, Japanese automakers continued to invest, but after 2007 up to the time of writing, the food, pharmaceutical, mining, retail and finance industries have played more important roles. In 2008, the finance industry invested $52 billion, which was 40 percent of Japan's total direct investment of $130 billion,[22] but it lost tens of billions of dollars. The industry believed that US financial institutions were undervalued after the Lehman shock, but they were still overvalued.[23]Additionally, food and pharmaceutical companies lost a lot of money in their investments.[24]

3.8 International labor migration and Japan

Japan has been experiencing "two lost decades." But it has still enjoyed high living standards and high wages compared to other Asian countries. Asian workers have thus been moving into Japan. While Japan did not welcome a massive inflow of unskilled labor, Japan is now cautiously trying to attract skilled labor but has been unsuccessful so far. The number of foreign workers in Japan is still limited.

The ratio of foreign to domestic workers in Japan is only 1.1 percent, while the shares in Germany and South Korea are 9.4 percent and 2.1 percent, respectively.[25] Foreign labor in Japan, however, increased from 486,000 in 2010 to 718,000 in 2013, according to the Ministry of Health, Labor and Welfare.[26]

There appear to be many foreign workers in Japan illegally, but the real situation is not clear. The Ministry of Health, Labor and Welfare and the Immigration Bureau of Ministry of Justice have estimated the size of the illegal foreign labor pool from the number of illegal over-stayers, but they do not have the exact figure.

The number of illegal over stayers is declining, falling from 170,839 in 2007 to just 62,009 in 2012.[27] The number of foreigners working legally in Japan was 686,000 in 2012. So, the number of foreign workers would be only 748,000 (62,009 + 686,000) even if all the over-stayers are assumed to be illegal foreign workers.

3.9 Foreign students in Japan and Japanese students abroad

Japan is still considered a country of opportunity and opulence for foreign students. Foreign students in Japan increased even during the "lost decades," even though Japanese students going abroad, including the US, decreased as shown in Figure 9.8.

The data regarding Japanese student abroad and in the US is strange in that there were more Japanese students in the US than the total number abroad from the latter half of the 1980s to the early 1990s. The trends for both figures are roughly the same, though, with Japanese students abroad and in the US declining in recent years. The share of Japanese students at US universities has significantly declined. The share was 10 percent in 1995 but declined to 2.6 percent in 2009, while Chinese and Korean shares increased to 25.4 percent and to 9.5 percent, respectively.[28]

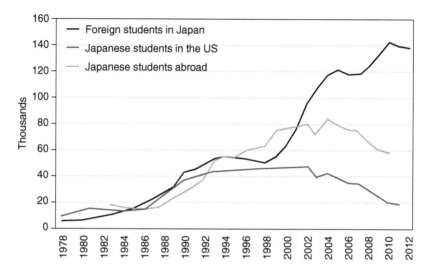

Figure 9.8 Japanese students in the US and foreign students in Japan (sources: Student Support and Exchange Division, Ministry of Education, Culture, Sports, Science and Technology until 2003, and Japan Student Services Organization after 2004; Institute of International Education, "International Student Totals by Place of Origin, 2010/11–2011/12"; Open Doors Report on International Educational Exchange, 2012, www.iie.org/opendoors).

The number of foreign students in Japan failed to grow significantly in the 1990s, but it began rising again in the first decade of the 2000s, and now 140,000 foreign students are in Japan, as shown in Figure 9.8. The Japanese system has several advantages for foreign students, although the Japanese language is a barrier to many. Tuition at Japanese universities is low compared to US universities; some universities have earned high marks in world university rankings,[29] and foreign students in Japan are allowed to work for 28 hours a week,[30] which is an advantage for students from poor families.

Japanese students in the US increased during the bubble years in the second half of the 1980s, remained steady in the 1990s, and began to decline after 2000.

This trend might be quite reasonable considering the situation faced by the younger generation in Japan. Japan's domestic market is relatively large, with a GDP that is still the third largest in the world after China (when converted into dollars). There are many regulations and complicated subsidy systems in the Japanese economy, and human networks are key to doing business successfully. This means that the domestic elite has a grip on power. Politicians, bureaucrats, business leaders, journalists and scholars are domestically oriented. They think that they can make a profit by manipulating the system, and studying abroad is of no use in understanding the domestic systems.

During the bubble years, Japan's large companies and financial institutions sent their young personnel to US universities, making such companies attractive employers for bright university graduates in Japan. In the Japanese system, it was difficult for companies to differentiate the bright students from common ones in the early stages of entrance to the company, but they nonetheless sent some young personnel to US universities. Many workers quit the company after earning their MBAs, so this practice of financing workers' education abroad declined. This was essentially a subsidy for young workers, encouraging them to go abroad, but the subsidy gradually disappeared as profits of Japanese companies began to shrink. The number of Japanese students going abroad might be at the appropriate level right now if one weighs the merits of staying in Japan or going abroad.

4 The impact of globalization

Japanese companies have seen their global share decline in almost every economic field because other countries have caught up to Japan and also because Japan has been unable to properly respond to change. Japan has been de-globalized, and xenophobic attitudes have prevailed. What can and should Japan do in the light of the changes that have swept across in Asia and the world?

4.1 Terms of trade and living standards

The decline of Japan's competitiveness was partly caused by the yen's abrupt appreciation, as I mentioned above. The development of other countries is not necessarily bad for the Japanese economy. If other countries manufacture the same goods as Japan, and Japan's terms of trade declines, then this would reduce living standards in Japan. There has been no significant decline, though, in Japan's terms of trade.

Many Japanese economists argue that the effect of the exchange rate is not important in the long run and that Japanese wages will converge on the lowest wages in developing countries. They then argue that this is the result of the factor price equalization theorem, but they never show any empirical studies.[31] If so, Japan's terms of trade must have declined sharply, but this did not happen.

Figure 9.9 shows Japan's terms of trade and the mineral fuel price index (2005 = 100). The terms of trade declined sharply when mineral fuel prices increased, but if the effects of mineral fuel price are excluded, Japan's terms of trade remained quite stable. From 1990 to 2012, Japan's terms of trade increased from 81.6 in 1990 to 88.2 in 2012.

If another country succeeded in manufacturing goods similar to those that Japan produced, what can Japan do? First, the impact is not large. It should appear in the terms of trade, but change of the terms of trade is small if it excludes the effect of energy price increase. Second, the proper response would not be to shut those products out. This would do nothing to prevent the country from exporting to other markets. Restricting the imports of certain goods would simply mean having to pay for more expensive goods. This is clear in the case of agriculture. Because of import restrictions on agricultural goods, Japanese food prices have increased, thereby reducing Japan's standard of living.

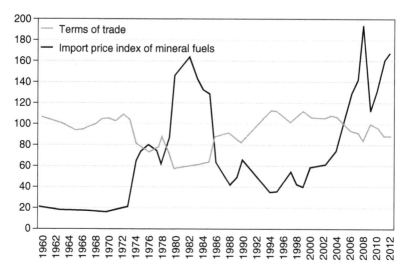

Figure 9.9 Terms of trade, 1960–2012 (source: Ministry of Finance).

Protecting employment is certainly important. But there would be no need to restrict imports if there were full employment, and this is something that can be achieved through monetary policy. Japan's unemployment rate declined to 3.6 percent in March 2014 with the expansionary monetary policy being encouraged by the Abe administration.

4.2 What can Japan do?

Japan has lost some of its competitiveness. The magnitude is exaggerated, as the change in the terms of trade is very small if it excludes the effect of energy price increases, as I already explained. Per capita income, however, has stagnated compared to the countries of developing Asia since the 1990s, and its share of exports in the global market has declined. Japan's prices of exports have fallen, and Japanese companies have had to fight with foreign competitors. The Japanese may thus be inclined to think that globalization is something bad, but it is not possible to close off a country to protect against competition and maintain the same living standards.

Japan took a national seclusion policy in 1639 as a response to the spread of Catholic Christianity. The Tokugawa shogunal government disliked anything that could cause internal conflict after the struggle for national unification and a protracted period of civil war. The shogunal leaders considered Catholicism in the same light as the Jodo Shinshu Buddhists, who held considerable sway in the Muromachi and Warring States periods. The Tokugawa government successfully subjugated the Jodo Shinshu Buddhists but could not do the same for the Catholics, so it oppressed them and finally secluded the country to prohibit the inflow of Catholicism. As a result, Japan remained untouched by new movements in Europe and the US, such as the Industrial Revolution and imperialism, and it did not increase production and technology, which served as the basis for the strength of a country.

A seclusion policy cannot be an answer to a loss of competitiveness. When Japan's export prices decline, what can be done? The answer is not to close Japan's doors, because this would not help boost exports. When Japan's imports increase, should the country protect its domestic industries by raising tariffs? This is not the solution, because it would increase domestic prices and reduce people's real income. Japan's real income has been reduced because of a protective agricultural policy.

A fear of globalization comes from fear of unemployment, but employment can be created monetary expansion. This chapter explains that decline of competitiveness in export industry is induced by rapid yen appreciation and deflationary monetary policy. Japan's recent monetary expansion by "Abenomics" (Prime Minister Abe's economic policy) since December 2012 proves that monetary expansion can create jobs. Unemployment rate decreased from 4.3 percent in December 2012 to 3.6 percent in April 2014. Labor shortage occurs in some low-wage industries. I suppose that monetary expansion has power to change people's negative recognition to globalization to some extent.

4.3 Lessons from the US experience

When the competitiveness of domestic and export industries in a country declines, what can and should we do? "Not to protect domestic industries and let workers move to other industries" is the right answer. The terms of trade decline when the competitiveness of export industries declines, and real income decreases. The effect might be serious to some industries, but the decline was small for the whole country. The terms of trade did not change if the effect of energy prices is excluded.[32] If a country subsidizes its export industry to boost its competitiveness (actually, such subsidies would be in violation of World Trade Organization rules), it would need to raise taxes. If a country protects domestic industry, the higher cost of products and a rise in taxes would lower the real income of the country, but workers would not have to move to another industry. If the country does nothing, workers in uncompetitive industries would have to move to other industries, where wages may be lower.[33]

This adjustment occurred in the 1970s in the US in response to Japan's challenge. The US basically adopted a "Not to protect domestic industries and let workers move to other industries" policy in the 1970s and the 1980s. Real wages in the US declined because of loss of competitiveness in manufacturing sector, but employment, especially among women, increased. Relatively low-wage jobs increased, and many more women started to work. The US long-term real GDP growth rate has been very stable. The growth rate in the 1960–1970 was 4.3 percent, after which the growth rates in 1970–1980, 1980–1990 and 1990–2000 were 3.2 percent, 3.3 percent and 3.5 percent respectively; it has been 1.8 percent in 2000–2013. Productivity growth of the US declined, but employment expanded, and the growth rate of real income did not decrease. The expansion of employment and growth of GDP were supported by women's participation in the labor market.[34]

5 Conclusions

In this paper I focused on the facts and data elucidating Japan's de-globalization and discussed their meanings, from which I can draw the following conclusions.

First, I explained that the Japanese are inclined to become xenophobic and antagonistic to globalization. This cannot be proven completely, but I feel I did succeed in suggesting that this tendency began to appear in the 1990s, after Japan experienced a long period of economic stagnation.

Second, I illustrated how the Japanese economy shrank compared to other Asian countries, especially China and South Korea. Japan's per capita PPP GDP stagnated, and South Korea was fast approaching Japan's level.

Third, Japan lost its share of exports in developing Asia, and I explained that this was caused by the yen's rapid appreciation. This is clear when compared with South Korea, although I do not deny that Japan has many structural problems as well.

Fourth, Japan's foreign investment declined in the 1990s; after the Lehman shock, Japan's direct investment soared, but a substantial share was made by Japanese banks and security companies that acquired troubled financial institutions in the US and Europe, but in hindsight, these institutions were bought at inflated prices.

Fifth, people did not migrate to Japan because Japan does not allow unskilled laborers to enter Japan and because Japan's policy of inviting skilled foreign labor is too timid. Foreign students in Japan, however, continued to increase even after the Japanese economy stagnated. Japanese students in the US decreased, but there is a reason for this.

Sixth, factor equalization theory exaggerates the problems of globalization, and Japan's terms of trade did not significantly decrease. There is no study to support that Japan's inequality was strengthened by globalization.

Seventh, I have made clear that "Not to protect domestic industries and let workers move to other industries" is the right policy to minimize the decline of living standard when Japan's terms of trade deteriorate because of global competition, although the deterioration is exaggerated.

Eighth, an expansionary monetary policy can expand employment, and labor shortage can give confidences to people to challenge the globalization. At least, in Japan the labor shortage situation started in 2014.

Acknowledgment

I am grateful for helpful comments from the other authors of this book, especially from the editor, Professor Toshiaki Hirai, and from Professor Asahi

Noguchi, Professor Hideo Ohashi and Professor Yuko Adachi. Remaining errors
are my own.

Notes

1 "Gurobaruka, Nihonjin ni kyohikan (Globalization: Rejection of Globalization among
  Japanese)," *The Asahi Newspaper*, February 3, 2012. See also Cabinet Office, Japanese Government (2004 Chapter 3 Section 2.3).
2 The book is Nakano (2011).
3 I retrieved the URL on July 28, 2013. Among the 15 books in favor, one is my book,
  Harada and Tokyo Zaidan (Tokyo Foundation), *TPP de sarani tsuyokunaru Nihon*
  (*Japan Will Be Strengthened by TPP*), Tokyo: PHP Kenkyujo, 2013. I judged the attitudes of books to TPP based on introductions of books by publishers on the site.
4 The results are gotten by retrieving articles of Asahi Newspaper in Kikuzo Visual
  (Asahi Newspaper Online Article Database).
5 The SANO Institute of Management, "Shinnyuu Shain no Grobaruka Ishiki Chousa
  (Polls of New entrant personnel on Globalization) July 2013," available at: www.
  sanno.ac.jp/research/global2013.html.
6 Friedman, revised and updated edition (2012).
7 Of course, antagonistic feelings to globalization come from various fields, such as
  industries that lose competitiveness (this is partly included in the explanation in this
  chapter); industries with vested interests like agriculture and food security; or feelings
  that inflow of any foreign cultures destroys good Japanese cultures and customs. I will
  only discuss feelings that based on clear facts.
8 Nakazawa (2011) pp. 121–122.
9 This idea comes from Heckscher model. It argues that free trade has tendency to
  equalize returns to production factors (factor price equalization theorem). See
  Krugman et al. (2012, pp. 91–104), for example. The HOS model is composed of
  labor and capital, but it can be extended to three factors—unskilled labor, skilled
  labor and capital. In the three-factor model, the wages of unskilled labor in a high-
  income country tend to decline to level of wages in a low-income country according
  to the model.
10 Yamamoto (2004).
11 The most comprehensive study is Otake (2005).
12 Milanovic (2005).
13 International Monetary Fund (2007).
14 Developing Asia defined by IMF World Economic Outlook Data Base April 2013 is
   composed of 27 Asian countries excluding Hong Kong, Japan, Korea, Singapore and
   Taiwan. The Database April 2014 uses the grouping of Emerging and Developing
   Asia, which includes 29 Asian countries excluding the same five countries.
15 Growth rate of PPP GDP per economically active population (15–64 years old) of
   Germany is 3.7 percent from 1990 to 2010, and that of Japan is 3.4 percent (economically active population is based on the World Bank Data Bank). Germany's growth
   rate is higher than Japan's even if we compare growth rates of PPP GDP per economically active population.
16 See Weil (2013, pp. 87–88) and Easterly and Levine (1997), for example.
17 Jorgenson and Nomura (2007).
18 Okada and Hamada (2009).
19 Japan's mistaken monetary policy is explained in Harada (2012, pp. 223–239).
20 This is derived from Mundell–Fleming model (see Mankiw 2013, Ch. 13, for
   example).
21 The declining trend does not depend on dollar terms. The ratio of net capital outflow
   to GDP also declines from 1–2 percent in the 1990s to zero or negative after 2010.

22 JETRO, "Direct Investment Statistics, Japan's Direct Investment Abroad by Sector" (Balance of Payment Base, Net, Flow) www.jetro.go.jp/world/japan/stats/fdi/.

23 Nomura Securities bought the European and Asian business of Lehman Brothers that went bankrupt in September 2008, but they failed in making a profit from the business ("Riiman Baishu no Shippai (Failure of Lehman Acquisition)," *J-CAST News*, January 25, 2014).

24 Daiichi Sankyo (pharmaceutical company) lost ¥300–400 billion by acquisition of Ranbaxy (Indian Pharmaceutical Company) (Toyokeizai Online, "Daiichi Sankyo ga Mondai no Indo Kogaisha wo Jisshitsu Baikyaku (Daiichi Sankyo practically sold the problematic subsidiary company)," April 9, 2014). Kirin Bier spent ¥2 trillion for acquisitions in these years, but it cannot make a profit ("Gosan Tsuduki no Sukinkari-oru Baishu (Miscalculation continues in acquisition of Schincariol (Brazilian Bier Brewery),)" Diamond Online, November 11, 2011). See also, "Abunai Kigyo Baishu (Risky M&A)," *The Toyo Keizai*, June 7, 2014.

25 The Japan Institute for Labor Policy and Training, Data Book Kokusai Roudou Hikaku (International Comparisons of Labor), 2014. Table 2-16, available at: www.jil.go.jp/kokunai/statistics/databook/2014/ch2.htm.

26 Ministry Health, Labor and Welfare, "Gaikokujin Koyou no Todokede Joukyou (Survey on Foreign Labor)," available at: www.mhlw.go.jp/stf/seisakunitsuite/ bunya/koyou_roudou/koyou/gaikokujin/gaikokujin-koyou/06.html.

27 Immigration Bureau, Ministry of Justice, Honpo ni okeru Fuho Zairyusha Suu ni tsuite (On the number of illegal over stayers in Japan), January 1, 2013, available at: www.moj.go.jp/nyuukokukanri/kouhou/nyuukokukanri04_00031.html.

28 Institute of International Education, "International Student Totals by Place of Origin, 2010/11–2011/12." Open Doors Report on International Educational Exchange, 2012, available at: www.iie.org/opendoors.

29 There are many rankings of universities, but The Times Higher Education—Thomson Reuters (THE-TR) in the UK, and Academic Ranking of World Universities (ARWU) conducted by Shanghai Jiao Tong Universities show that several Japanese universities are in the top 100.

30 Tokyo Bureau of Labor, Ministry Health, Labor and Welfare, HP Frequent Questions, http://tokyo-roudoukyoku.jsite.mhlw.go.jp/yokuaru_goshitsumon/gaikokujinkoyou/Q4.html.

31 Saito (2000) and Noguchi (2002). About factor price equalization theorem, see note 9.

32 Harada et al. (2003) Figure 6.6.

33 The relationship between decline of terms of trade and real income is formally explained in Harada et al. (2003).

34 Gender Equality Bureau, Cabinet Office, Japanese Government (2012, Figure 8).

References

(Articles in newspaper and online journals are excluded.)

Cabinet Office, Japanese Government (2004) *Keizai Zaisei Hakusho* (*Survey on Economy and Public Finance*), Tokyo: National Printing Bureau.

Easterly, William and Levine, Ross (1997) "Africa's Growth Tragedy: Politics and Ethnic Divisions," *Quarterly Journal of Economics*, 112(4): 1203–1250.

Friedman, Thomas L. (2012) *The Lexus and the Olive Tree*, revised and updated edition, New York, NY: Picador.

Gender Equality Bureau, Cabinet Office, Japanese Government (2012) "Danjo Kyodo Sankaku Kaigi, Kihon Mondai Eikyo Chosa Senmon Chosakai Hokokusho (Report of Council on Gender Equality, Expert Committee on Basic Problem and Effect

Research,)" February, Tokyo: Government of Japan, available at: www.gender.go.jp/kaigi/senmon/kihon/kihon_eikyou/pdf/spinv_frep_1-2.pdf.

Harada, Yutaka (2012) "Policy Issues Regarding the Japanese Economy: The Great Recession, Inequality, Budget Deficit and the Aging Population," *Japanese Journal of Political Science*, 3(2): 223–253.

Harada, Yutaka and Tokyo Zaidan (Tokyo Foundation) (2013) *TPP de sarani tsuyokunaru Nihon* (*Japan Will Be Strengthened by TPP*), Tokyo: PHP Kenkyujo.

Harada, Yutaka, Kuzumi, Masayuki and Iijima, Ryuusuke (2003) "Amerika wa ikani Nihon no Chosen ni Taio shitaka (How Did the US Respond to Japan's Challenge?)," Chapter 6 in Motoshige Ito (ed.) *Nicchu Kankei no Keizai Bunseki* (*Economic Analysis of Japan and China Relations*), Tokyo: Toyo Keizai Shinposha.

International Monetary Fund (2007) *World Economic Outlook 2007*, October, Washington, DC: IMF.

Jorgenson, Dale W. and Nomura, Koji (2007) "The Industry Origin of US–Japan Product Gap," *Economic Systems Research*, 19(3): 315–341.

Krugman, Paul, Obstfeld, Maurice and Melitz, Marc J. (2012) *International Economics*, ninth edition, Boston, MA: Pearson/Addison-Wesley.

Mankiw, N. Gregory (2013) *Macroeconomics*, eighth edition, New York, NY: Worth Publishers and Palgrave Macmillan.

Milanovic, B. (2005) "Can We Discern the Effect of Globalization on Income Distribution? Evidence from Household Surveys," *The World Bank Economic Review*, 19(1): 21–44.

Nakano, Takeshi (2011) *TPP Boukoku Ron* (TPP Invites the Ruin of Our Country), Tokyo: Shueisha.

Nakazawa, Takao (2011) "8 Chusho Kigyo no Kaigai Shinshutsu to sono Tokucho (Extension Abroad and Their Characteristics of Small Industries)," in Takahiro Fujimoto and Takao Nakazawa (eds.) *Gurobaruka to Nihon no monozukuri* (*Globalization and Japan's monozukuri*), Tokyo: Hoso Daigaku Kyoiku Shinkokai.

Noguchi, Yukio (2002), "Defure eno Taio wo megutte (On Response to Deflation)," *ESP*, January.

Okada, Yasushi and Hamada, Koichi (2009) "Jisshitsu Kawase Reto to Ushinawareta 10 Nen (Real Exchange Rate and the Lost Decade)," *Seisaku Bunseki*, 4(1/2), March.

Otake, Fumio (2005) *Nihon no Fubyodo* (*Inequality in Japan*), Tokyo: Nihon Keizai Shinbunsha.

Saito, Seiichiro (2000) "Bukka Geraku (Price Decline)," *Ekonomisuto*, December 19.

Weil, David N. (2013) *Economic Growth*, third edition, Harlow: Pearson.

Yamamoto, Takashi (2004) "Impact of International Trade on Wage Inequality in Japanese Manufacturing Industries," PhD dissertation, University of Hawaii.

10 Trade friction with no foundation

A review of US–Japanese economic relations in the 1980s and the 1990s

Asahi Noguchi

1 Introduction

The purpose of this study is to present evidence that, contrary to conventional wisdom, public opinion can critically influence economic policy in a negative manner. Democracy is generally defined as a form of government in which all member citizens have an equal right in the decisions that affect their lives. One of its consequences is that a dominant notion held by the public becomes the most decisive factor in public decision-making process. Although democracy is assumed to be the best means of governance and to have no rivals, its defects have been well known since it was first adopted. If the political masses are no wiser than the political elites, as is the usual scenario, political performance in a democracy would likely be unfavorable compared with that of an elitist auto-cracy. History has shown the veracity of this supposition by presenting us with cases in which policy decisions made in the name of the public have had disas-trous consequences.

It is a matter of course that a democracy maintains some mechanism to prevent itself from degenerating into a "mobocracy." Democracy is usually assumed to involve a process of making decisions after considering all options. With such preconditions, an optimistic believer in democracy would expect that a wise opinion would eventually prevail in the course of a public argument. Democratic societies typically provide platforms on which to engage in many levels of public expression and argument, from grassroots political meetings to national assemblies. As the majority of the public obtains information and expert views regarding an issue for which a political decision must be made from a variety of print (magazine and newspaper) and electronic (television, radio and Internet) outlets, the mass media usually plays an important role in the course of reaching a public consensus. If the democratic process worked ideally, a wise opinion expressed by a reliable expert would persuade the public to promote transformation of the opinion into an actual policy in the name of the public will.

The problem with this picture is that it is overly idealistic regarding most situ-ations and only holds true if the public is sufficiently wise to choose the best opinion among those expressed publicly. Unfortunately, society often faces various problems that are too subtle or complex for lay people to fully comprehend.

Although it is expected that experts would provide appropriate and reliable information to the general public, they have failed or been unable to do so in many cases. Moreover, experts often disagree among themselves, leading them to present contradictory opinions that may lead to confusion within the public sphere. As in all professions, not all experts are always reliable, and it is not feasible to expect the public to be able to decide which are reliable and which are not.

This chapter presents a case study in economic policymaking that illustrates how a prevalent and deep-rooted public idea based on a misguided belief can influence economic policymaking in a clearly detrimental manner. This case study, in which experts who could have disabused the public of their misguided belief either could not or failed to do so, also illustrates a scenario in which the democratic process does not function in the intended, idealistic manner. Specifically, this chapter examines the trade friction that existed between the US and Japan during the 1980s and the 1990s and the associated economic policies that contributed to this friction. Although the nature of trade between the US and Japan had been the source of economic and political dispute between both countries for many years, the emergence of trade friction during the 1980s and the 1990s was undoubtedly its most serious manifestation. The characteristics of the trade friction during these decades were relatively different to those in previous decades. It was only during these decades that macroeconomic variables, such as the current-account surplus and deficit, as well as the trade volumes of specific industries, became a focus of the dispute. When a tremendous amount of negotiation aimed at "correcting the current-account imbalance" failed to yield any concrete agreement, the US government went so far as to threaten Japan with trade sanctions, posing the risk of creating a trade war between the US and Japan.

When this epoch in economic policymaking is examined, it becomes apparent that such friction was neither necessary nor inevitable, reflected in the fact that the US–Japan trade dispute ceased at the exact moment in the last half of the 1990s that the US government stopped criticizing Japan's current-account surplus. This fact also reveals that the friction was not truly the result of contradictory interests between the US and Japan but merely of misguided public opinion in the US. In this sense, the friction had no real foundation. The misguided public opinion that drove aggressive US trade policies toward Japan was the belief that Japan's current-account surplus was harmful to the US economy and should thus be reduced. Despite its widespread acceptance, this opinion had no basis in reality. When the warnings of many economists in both the US and Japan regarding the fallacy of this dominant notion failed to attract much public attention, it continued to prevail within the public sphere, and ultimately influenced economic policy to the detriment of both the US and Japan.

Fortunately, the trade friction between the US and Japan has not been reproduced during the 2000s. That does not mean, however, a similar kind of dispute will not be provoked between the both countries in the future. Broadly speaking, trade friction is quite commonplace in this globalizing world. Globalization mostly promotes economic growth of engaging countries, but gives rise to various kinds of discontent as its outcome. These two consequences are exactly the light and the shade of globalization. This study reveals that some of the discontents appearing in the process of globalization are actually illusion rather than reality.

This chapter is organized as follows. Section 2 briefly summarizes a general framework for economic policymaking first proposed by Hamada and Noguchi (2005) that focuses on the role of ideas in the process of economic policymaking. Section 3 describes the development of the US–Japan trade friction until the mid-1990s, and Section 4 presents the related arguments on the subject that were presented by two different groups of US experts: the revisionists and the economists. Section 5 concludes the discussion by considering the lessons that have been learned from this epoch in economic policymaking.

2 The primary determinant in economic policymaking: interests or ideas?

The choice of an economic policy typically reflects the influence of various economic interests within a society. A policy may affect different strata of society differently, as can be observed in the case of trade liberalization. While a policy of trade liberalization may be harmful to some stakeholders, such as import competitive producers, it may be beneficial to the society as a whole. As a result, the choice of a policy largely depends on the amount of political power exerted by social groups that are attempting to further their different economic interests.

Another significant factor in the choice of a policy is the influence of a deep-rooted and widespread idea held by the public. In some situations, such an idea can pose a greater challenge to the realization of a good policy than can a vested interest. Politicians, journalists, policy officials and voters are likely to oppose a policy that contradicts their preconceived ideas, even if experts agree with the policy almost unanimously. In such a case, realization of the policy is highly unlikely, regardless of the policy's social desirability.

Much of the literature in political science, public economics and sociology has focused on examining the influence of economic interests, ideas and ideology on policymaking from various viewpoints. These analyses can be roughly categorized into two standpoints, that is economism and idealism. Economism holds that the realization of policies is primarily based on economic interests, and that ideas and ideology are merely derivations of these interests. Marxian materialism, which posits that high-level social structures, such as ideology, are exclusively determined by lower structures, such as economic interests, is one of the most conspicuous examples of this view. The rational choice theory, which now occupies the mainstream of political science and upon which the traditional political science and sociological literature rests, can be categorized as a form of economism, even though its analytical framework differs radically from that of Marxian materialism. On the other hand, idealism holds that ideas and ideology are based on motives that are not necessarily reducible to economic interests, while not denying the importance of economic interests.

Traditional literature of political science and sociology often rests on this viewpoint.

Examining the viewpoints of major economists concerned with economic policymaking allows for the identification of the two contrasting emphases on economic interests or ideas. The most famous statement regarding these different emphases was made by Keynes in the last chapter of *The General Theory of Employment, Interest and Money* (1936), in which he maintains that ideas are generally far more important than interests.

> The ideas of economists and political philosophers, both when they are right and when they are wrong, are more powerful than is commonly understood. Indeed the world is ruled by little else. Practical men, who believe themselves to be quite exempt from any intellectual influences, are usually the slaves of some defunct economist. Madmen in authority, who hear voices in the air, are distilling their frenzy from some academic scribbler of a few years back. I am sure that the power of vested interests is vastly exaggerated compared with the gradual encroachment of ideas.
>
> (Keynes 1978 [1936], p. 383)

On the other hand, Stigler and Becker, representatives of the "Chicago school" of economists, pointed out in their investigations the decisive role played by economic interests in individuals' political behavior (Stigler 1971; Becker 1983). Their finding led them to conclude that the political as well as the economic actions of individuals are dominated by self-interest, especially when political actions have economic consequences. On the basis of their investigation of economic policymaking, they further concluded that the interests of pressure groups are reflected through their influence on political parties and that their influence is generally the most decisive in politics.

As do most economists, Stigler assumed that as a *homo economicus*, an individual would act as a rational agent in the political sphere. Similarly, political agents such as politicians, bureaucrats, policy officials, pressure groups and voters would act according to cost–benefit considerations in the political marketplace, just as economic agents such as consumers and producers act according to the principles of utility maximization and profit maximization in the competitive market. In addition, Stigler extended the concept of a competitive market by positing that scientific discoveries, inventions and academic contributions are the products of competition among scientists, engineers and intellectuals motivated by economic incentives in the intellectual marketplace.

The "Virginia School" of economists, represented by Buchanan and Tullock (Buchanan and Tullock 1962), similarly emphasized the primal role of economic interests in politics. Along with the Chicago School economists, they developed a research strategy, later referred to as "public choice theory," that has had an extensive impact on political science research and led to the development of "rational choice political theory." The basic premise of the rational choice theory is that the political as well as the economic decisions made by individuals are

realizations of their utility-maximization behaviors. This standpoint is analytic-
ally quite useful. The theory can explain every political phenomenon by resting
on the robust premise that individuals always make decisions that increase their
satisfaction. The robustness of this premise is undeniable as individuals undoubtedly choose what is desirable for them. Thus, this theory can serve as the
premise for logical human behavior.

Before the emergence of rational choice theory, one of the most familiar
approaches in the field of political science was social typology by which social
phenomena were categorized into several types, or *Idealtypus* in Weberian terminology, according to some useful criterion. A primary drawback of using this
methodology is that it usually results in a tautology rather than an explanation.
For example, using this typology could result in a statement such as "Japan's
politics is bureaucratic because Japan is a bureaucratic country," which simply
repeats the terminology and provides no explanation of why Japan's politics is
bureaucratic. In contrast, the rational choice theory can explain using definitive
reasoning why a political phenomenon, categorized as bureaucratic, could be
observed in Japan.[1] In this sense, the superiority of using the rational choice
theory as an analytical tool is apparent.

Although accepting the fundamental utility of rational choice theory, Hamada
and Noguchi (2005) pointed out its basic defect. They explained that although
the rational choice theory is exclusively concerned with the economic interests
of individuals, it does not consider how individuals recognize their economic
interests. The rational choice theory's assumption that individuals make political
decisions to improve their situation is relatively acceptable in itself. However, it
should be noted that their decisions are always based on their judgment, which
may be correct or incorrect, that certain choices will produce beneficial results
for them. These judgments heavily depend on individuals' perceptions regarding
the realization of their interests; that is, on a cognitive model in which individuals can recognize whether their economic interests will be satisfied or
harmed by a decision. In this sense, every individual decision, whether economic
or political, is based on a certain idea or a concept by which a specific interest is
judged. These judgments lead to an intended result when the idea or the concept
behind them is well grounded in a scientific sense. However, when individuals
judge their interests merely according to a preconceived idea that has no basis in
the reality, which they are likely to do in certain situations, their decisions are
likely to have unintended and negative results. In either case, the economic interests that motivate individuals' decisions are relatively subjective in nature, being
neither obvious nor objective.

This comprehension of economic interests necessitates the reconsideration of
the "interests versus ideas" schema that currently dominates the thinking of
many social scientists, including economists and political scientists. As discussed above, because every individual economic and political decision is based
on the results of the individual's use of a cognitive model that identifies the most
beneficial choice, the decision reflects no contradiction between the individual's
interests and ideas. If a case arises in which either interests or ideas appear far

more crucial than the other in policymaking, it is either that the policy consequences of the decision are evident or that they are not evident. It is thus this "evidentness" of a policy consequence that determines the true nature of conflicts in policymaking.

Generally speaking, there are substantial differences between experts and non-experts regarding their levels of information and knowledge, regardless of the subject; otherwise, experts would not be regarded as such in society. As far as economic policymaking is concerned, however, these cognitive differences in the society would do no harm if the possible consequences of a certain policy are sufficiently evident even to lay people such that they can readily infer how the policy would deliver its benefits and costs to each member of the society. In such a case, these cognitive differences would be unlikely to give rise to a conflict in policy decisions, even if differences among economic interests could be a source of the conflict. Economic policies whose possible consequences are relatively evident in this sense usually include trade policies, government regulations and public investments.

Individuals often base their conception of a trade policy on a common cognitive model that assumes that trade liberalization would lower the prices of imported goods, thus harming importers of goods within competitive industries while benefiting general consumers by decreasing the prices of these goods. This inference is relatively legitimate even from an academic point of view. It is sufficiently consistent with mainstream trade theories, including the Ricardian trade model and the Heckscher–Ohlin–Samuelson model, which continue to be taught in university economics classes throughout the world.[2] Similarly, individuals also often base their conception of public investment on a common cognitive model that assumes that public investment provides pecuniary benefits to local builders and non-pecuniary benefits to local economies as a whole while imposing burdens on taxpayers.

Although the above examples indicate that there exist cognitive models in which the policy consequences appear relatively evident, there may be other cases in which the policy consequences are not readily evident. When the consequences of a policy are not readily apparent, the cognitive models used to judge it tend to be more diverse. In some cases, they may be so diverse that no common cognitive ground can be achieved within a society, or their diversity may give rise to serious conflict among alternative cognitive models that contradict one another. For example, it is difficult to establish a definite cognitive model to make decisions regarding macroeconomic policy, such as decisions regarding monetary or currency policy. Such difficulty is due to the fact that macroeconomic policy is more abstract than the policies discussed previously because it initially appears unrelated to the everyday life of individuals, and drawing logical and scientific inferences of the policy consequences regarding decisions in this area requires a certain degree of expertise and discipline. Possession of such expertise and discipline is, however, confined to a limited number of experts who comprise a minority of society.

Moreover, the experts themselves may use different cognitive models when making decisions in a certain area. Such cases create the possibility that a less reliable model prevails among the public because of its frequent exposure in the mass media, which naturally places more importance on a model's appeal to the public than its reliability. The worst-case scenario is one in which the public is misled by unreliable notions regarding the issue in focus. As will be shown in the following sections, it is exactly this scenario that occurred in the 1980s–1990s in regard to the trade relationship between the US and Japan.

3 Development of the US–Japan trade friction to the mid-1990s

The history of the US–Japan trade friction after World War II began in the 1950s. The first notable sign of friction appeared in 1955, when the US government's lowering of import duties on textile goods led to an influx of them from Japan into the US. From that time on, the US textile industry was under severe competitive pressure from Japanese textile imports, symbolized by the "one-dollar blouse." The US textile industry then began to urge the US government to take some measures to restrict the importation of textile goods from Japan. Although the US government was moved by this demand to protect the US textile industry, it was hesitant to take overt action to restrict the importation for fear of being criticized as protectionist. Therefore, instead of directly restricting imports, the US government asked the Japanese government to take measures to restrict exports to the US. Being too weak to resist US demands at that time, the Japanese government complied, albeit unwillingly. In 1957, the agreement on the textile trade was established between both governments prescribing that Japan would voluntarily restrict the export of textile goods to the US for the following five years. It was only the beginning of voluntary export restraints (VERs) that were to be utilized later as a customary measure to protect US industries suffering from the import of Japanese goods.

Between the 1950s and the 1980s, the Japanese economy was one of the fastest growing in the world, much like the Chinese economy has been since the 1980s. The Japanese economy not only grew rapidly but also changed drastically. In the 1960s, the leading industries in Japan shifted from labor-intensive industries such as textiles, to capital-intensive industries, such as steel and shipbuilding. In the 1970s, this leading position was gradually occupied by technology-intensive industries, such as machinery and automobiles, until it was replaced by even more technology-intensive industries, such as electronics and semiconductors, in the 1980s. This shift in the leading industries in Japan from labor-intensive to capital-intensive and then to technology-intensive reflected a shifting comparative advantage in the Japanese economy. As described in a textbook on international trade theory, a comparative advantage for one country regarding a certain category of goods always leads to a comparative disadvantage for another country such that the country that enjoys the advantage exports the goods and the country that suffers from the disadvantage imports them. Therefore, a shifting comparative advantage for certain goods in Japan would lead to a comparative disadvantage for those goods in the US such that Japan would export the goods and the US would import them.

This phenomenon can be clearly observed in the trade relations between the US and Japan during the 1980s and 1990s. The goods that the US imported from Japan changed successively from textiles to steel, then from steel to machinery, then from machinery to automobiles, then from automobiles to semiconductor components, and so on in accordance with the comparative advantage currently enjoyed by Japan. Every shift led to a similar conflict. While Japan's export of steel to the US was the major source of conflict in the 1960s, its export of color televisions was the major source of conflict in the early 1970s, that of automobiles in the early 1980s, and that of semiconductor components in the mid-1980s. In all these cases, the conflict was of virtually the same nature. The US industry under competitive pressure from the import of Japanese goods complained about "unfair" competition from Japan and lobbied the US government to take action to ease the situation. Consequently, the US government compelled the Japanese government to take measures to restrict exports and accept a bilateral agreement prescribing Japan's obligation regarding VERs.

Among all these conflicts, the two most significant, both economically and politically, were those regarding the automobile and semiconductor industries. Until the 1970s, the condition of the US automobile industry and that of its major players—General Motors, Ford, and Chrysler, the so-called "Big Three"—was believed to represent the US economy itself. This conception changed drastically in the 1980s because of the oil crisis in the late 1970s. The worldwide hike in oil prices promoted the export of Japanese automobiles to the US by making small and fuel-efficient Japanese cars more attractive to US consumers. When car imports from Japan seriously threatened the Big Three at the beginning of the 1980s, they were obliged to downsize their operations and lay off workers. As the rate of unemployment in Detroit, Michigan, known as "Motor Town" for its status as a center of automobile production, continued on an upward trajectory, anti-Japanese feeling spread throughout the US. Reacting to this situation, both governments engaged in the customary bilateral negotiations, which resulted in a 1981 agreement that Japan would voluntarily restrain its car exports to the US, as was expected.

The subsequent conflict regarding the semiconductor industry was another situation that was later repeatedly referred to as a case study in trade friction. Until the mid-1980s, US semiconductor producers had enjoyed a dominant position in the market. Then Japanese semiconductor producers began to expand the exports of semiconductor goods to the US, making the position of the US makers quite fragile. This swift invasion of Japanese semiconductor goods to the US semiconductor market shocked both the US business community and the public. At that time, the semiconductor industry was believed to be the "highest" of all high-tech industries. The fact that US semiconductor producers were losing market share to Japanese producers was, therefore, considered a sign that the US was losing its competitive edge to Japan. The measure taken to address this conflict, therefore, differed from those taken in previous cases. There was a strong opposition inside the US business community regarding the customary measure of forcing Japan to restrict its exports of semiconductor products, as the US computer industry at that time was completely dependent on semiconductor components made in Japan, which were superior to those made in the US with respect to both price and quality. In light of this situation, the US government asked the Japanese government to accept a novel measure termed a voluntary import expansion (VIE) that required Japan to increase its imports of semiconductor goods produced in the US to a prescribed target level. When the US–Japan Semiconductor Agreement was signed in 1986, it was assumed that it contained an unofficial clause stating that Japan would increase its import of semiconductor goods up to 20 percent of the domestic market.

The primary factor behind the US–Japan conflict, as well as the motivation for the measures taken to settle it, was the desire of US industries to avoid the costs of adjusting and restructuring their operations to the greatest extent possible. In the literature on public choice theory, the pursuance of activities that seek to manipulate the economic or political environment in order to increase one's benefits or decrease one's costs is referred to as *rent seeking*. The VERs and VIEs that the US government imposed on Japan were the result of rent-seeking activities carried out by US industries facing competitive pressure from Japanese exports. As the main motivation of US industries was the pursuance of their economic interests, the rational choice theory is the most appropriate framework to apply to their situation.

During the 1980s, the nature of the US–Japan conflict gradually changed. Although the trade conflict regarding specific industries continued, a new element entered the picture. From the beginning of the 1980s, the external imbalances of both countries, the current-account deficit in the US and the current-account surplus in Japan, had been increasing (Figure 10.1). These external

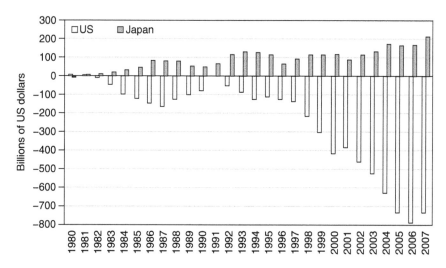

Figure 10.1 The current account in the US and Japan, 1980–2007 (source: International Financial Statistics, IMF).

imbalances are basically macroeconomic phenomena arising from macro-economic factors, most importantly the state of domestic saving and domestic investment in each country. For the majority of the US citizens, these external imbalances were merely additional evidence that the US economy was losing its competitive edge to Japan, encouraging the voices in the media criticizing Japan's "unfair" trade practices to become more strident as the years passed.

By the end of the 1980s, the perception that Japan was primarily responsible for the current-account deficit in the US had virtually become a common-sense notion among the US public. Influenced by the growing public antipathy toward Japan, in 1988, the US Congress passed the Omnibus Trade and Competitiveness Act, which amended Section 301 of the Trade Act of 1974. Soon referred to as "Super 301," this amendment authorized a measure intended to resolve US bilateral trade deficits, which were considered as consequences of trade barriers to US exports in foreign countries. As Super 301 granted the US government the power to force foreign countries to eliminate unfair trade practices under the threat of unilateral retaliation, it became quite apparent that Super 301 was targeted at Japan.

Although the attitude of the US Congress had become increasingly adversar-ial toward Japan, the Reagan and Bush Republican Administrations attempted to confine their trade policies to traditional approaches to the greatest extent pos-sible while calling for more openness. The Structural Impediments Initiatives (SII) held during 1989 and 1990 between the Bush and Japanese administrations at the time were barely within this category. It was only when the Clinton Demo-cratic administration gained control of the White House in 1993 that a decisive change occurred in the US trade policy approach toward Japan. The approach taken by the Clinton administration to cope with Japan was quite different from that of previous administrations in its adoption of the "objective criteria" in assessing whether Japan had actually eliminated unfair trade practices. The idea behind this approach was that the US should force Japan to take concrete meas-ures to reduce its trade surplus with the US and assess its progress in doing so not qualitatively but rather quantitatively. One measure that the Clinton adminis-tration proposed to accomplish this objective was the implementation of a VIE, a measure introduced in the US–Japan Semiconductor Agreement of 1986. The Clinton administration also urged Japan to accept VIEs for other important industries such as the automobile industry. By such measures, the US govern-ment was overtly acknowledging the necessity of managed trade and abandoning the traditional principle of free trade.

With this strategy in mind, in February 1994 President Clinton held a top-level meeting with Morihiro Hosokawa, the then Prime Minister of Japan, in which Clinton ardently insisted that Japan should accept the use of objective cri-teria in assessing its progress toward reducing its current-account surplus. Hoso-kawa ultimately rejected Clinton's proposal. In spring of 1995, further negotiations were held between Ryutaro Hashimoto, the then Minister of Inter-national Trade and Industry of Japan, and Mickey Kantor, the then US Trade Representative. At that time, the issue in dispute was whether Japan would accept the use of objective criteria regarding car imports from the US. To force the Japanese government to accept the use of such criteria, Kantor threatened Hashimoto that the US would sanction Japan by imposing a 100 percent tariff on luxury cars imported from Japan if Japan refused to accept the criteria. Although initially a settlement appeared unlikely and US sanctions against Japan seemed unavoidable, both governments suddenly announced on June 28, 1995 that an agreement had been reached. Although nothing appeared to have been agreed to in fact, a trade war had been avoided.

4 Revisionists or economists? Understanding the US–Japan current-account imbalance

As the increasing trade imbalance between the US and Japan during the 1980s and the 1990s intensified the US public's criticism of Japan's "unfair" trade practices, the US government felt ever greater pressure to compel Japan to reduce its current-account surplus. The rigid stance of the Clinton administration was manifested in its repeated insistence that Japan should accept the objective criterion for reducing its trade surplus. The subsequent course of events clearly demonstrates that public opinion, whether informed or misguided, often plays a crucial role in policymaking.

Among the various factors that influence public opinion, the extent of the public's access to various media sources is one of the most important, with the manner in which the public interprets the information presented by the media being just as important as the information itself. As interpreting the information in an appropriate manner often demands a great deal of expertise and discipline, depending on the issue, societies call on the services of various experts entrusted to interpret the information in their area of expertise. When these experts present their interpretations to the public through mass media, including magazines, newspapers and television programs, as is their customary manner of disseminating information, they influence the development of public opinion.

In the case of trade friction between the US and Japan in the 1980s–1990s, the most vital information influencing US public opinion was a figure that showed an increasing current-account imbalance between the US and Japan. Within the US mass media of the 1980s and the 1990s, experts on the so-called "Japan problem" greatly influenced public opinion by utilizing this figure as an index of "trade unfairness" between the two countries. In the opening of its August 7, 1989 cover story titled "Rethinking Japan" (Neff 1989), *Business Week*, a prominent weekly news magazine, expressed the general understanding of the issue within US journalists at that time:

> After years of haggling, the U.S. still runs a $52 billion annual trade deficit with Japan, and Japanese society remains closed in crucial ways. As a result, a radical shift in U.S. thinking about Japan is under way. This revisionist view holds that Japan is really different—and that conventional free-trade policies won't work. Once, such views would have been dismissed as "Japan-bashing." But now they have an intellectual base.

As explained here, these experts, mostly not so much economists as journalist, insisted that because the Japanese economy was fundamentally different from the market economy, at least according to their understanding of it, the US should take more drastic measures and go beyond conventional policies toward Japan to address its unfair trade practices. These experts came to be called revisionists because they called for a revision of the formerly dominant notion that Japan would gradually change its practices in accordance with US interests.

In the same issue, *Business Week* also introduced the major works and backgrounds of four of the most influential revisionist writers, Clyde Prestowitz, Karel van Wolferen, Chalmers Johnson and James Fallows (Neff and Magnusson 1989). Although their views varied in respects, they contained three core ideas: that conventional free trade policies had been so generous to Japan that they had damaged US interests, as manifested by the trade deficit; that Japan's increasing trade surplus was a result of its unfair trade practices; and that the US should take definite measures to correct the US–Japan trade imbalance. The results of an opinion poll jointly conducted by Business Week and Harris (*Business Week* 1989) reflected the influence of these experts on public opinion, as revealed in a summary of the findings:

> Americans are worried about the U.S. trade deficit—and they know whom they blame. Fully 69% of the public think the trade imbalance with Japan is a serious issue. Although many believe that the quality and price of American exports to Japan are at fault, still more—68%—think Japan is imposing unfair barriers to U.S. products. That's up from 54% the last time we asked that question, in March, 1985. How to remedy the situation? Protectionism and trade sanctions, Americans say by a wide margin. They favor targets for American exports to Japan and tariffs and quotas on Japanese products in the U.S.

This summary indicates that the revisionist perception had been quite prevalent among the public since at least the end of the 1980s.

Revisionist ideas were influential among not only lay people but also politicians and policymakers. In the midst of the Kantor–Hashimoto negotiations regarding Japan's acceptance of objective criteria for the importation of automobiles from the US, *The Wall Street Journal* described the strong connection between revisionist ideas and recent US policy initiatives (Hamilton 1995):

> Washington's trade showdown with Tokyo will do more than determine whether Japan swallows more U.S. car parts. It will put to the test some influential ideas about how America should deal with its great economic rival. This trade fight is becoming a trial for controversial "revisionist" views that hold that the U.S. can't count on traditional market forces to rein in Tokyo's huge trade surplus. The revisionists argue that Japan's economy differs fundamentally from that of other nations. Washington, they say, must force Japan to open its markets and adopt less-adversarial trade practices.

Despite the conspicuous influence of revisionist ideas on public opinion and actual policy, particularly between the late 1980s and the mid-1990s, the ideas of renowned economists that completely contradicted the revisionist view had entered the public sphere and become more strident as revisionist thinking became more and more prevalent. However, these economists' views did not gain wide acceptance because of their inability to present their views in a manner that the public could understand or in a manner that was appealing to a general audience. Their views were expressed most plainly in an "Open Letter to President Clinton and Prime Minister Hosokawa" (Bhagwati et al. 1993), which was publicly released by a group of prominent economists concerned with the outcome of the upcoming Clinton–Hosokawa summit meeting on US–Japan trade policies. Jagdish Bhagwati, the organizer of the group, later revealed that "the letter carried as many signatures as could be gathered in less than a week" (Bhagwati 1999, p. xxvi). The signatories to the list, who numbered over a hundred, included leading economists specializing in international economics and the Japanese economy, such as Paul Krugman, Robert Baldwin, Alan Deardorff, Anne Krueger, Ronald Findlay, Robert Stern, David Weinstein, Gary Saxonhouse and Hugh Patrick, as well as the five Nobel laureates James Tobin, Lawrence Klein, Paul Samuelson, Robert Solow and Franco Modigliani. As demonstrated in the following passage, the writers clearly disagreed with the Clinton Administration's position that trade policies should be based on the use of objective criteria, as well as the public conception that Japan was purposefully engaging in unfair trade practices to the detriment of the US economy:

Managed Trade Is Wrong
The US demands for managed trade with Japan are misguided, and we urge that Prime Minister Hosokawa continue resolutely to "say no" to them and, better still, that President Clinton abandon them. The principal factor underlying such demands for managed trade has been the crude and simplistic view that Japan is importing too few manufactures owing to "structural barriers" which make Japan "special." Hence only the imposition on it of import commitments, known as "voluntary import expansion" (VIE), will get Japan to increase its imports commensurate with its reduction of conventional trade barriers. But the imposition of quantitative targets, as in the case of semiconductors and now sought in other sectors, would be a retrograde step.

No to Surplus Reduction Targets
Prime Minister Hosokawa also needs to reject the US administration's demands for a target on the reduction of Japan's external current-account surplus. Targets here are inappropriate: not only do they focus on the wrong end of the stick, they also pose a great danger of inflicting damage in matters of trade and global savings. Perhaps most important, Prime Minister Hosokawa and President Clinton must not encourage, by focusing on the surplus reduction targets, the notion that Japan's trade surplus is self-evidently wicked and harmful to the rest of the world. The surplus reflects an excess

of Japanese savings over its domestic investment and can be harnessed to help finance the many urgent needs for capital today—in Russia, in India, in the Middle East and elsewhere. It is myopic for the US to create the impression that Japan's surplus is harmful when its own past profligacy and current budgetary deficit have crippled its ability to finance its own needs, much less those of the rest of the world.

(Bhagwati et al. 1993)

It is not easy to ascertain the extent to which the views of these economists influenced US public opinion. However, on June 9, 1995, *The Wall Street Journal* reported,

So far, the threats to impose $5.9 billion of sanctions on Japanese luxury cars on June 28 unless the Japanese bow to U.S. demands have been resoundingly popular domestically. By a margin of 72% to 19%, the public approves of President Clinton's sanctions plan.

(Davis 1995)

As this article was published about six months after the Bhagwati "Open Letter" had been published, it may be reasonably inferred that the letter had exerted virtually no influence.

Although the economists' views might not have had any influence on the general public, they must have had some impact on the Clinton Administration. As Bhagwati later revealed (Bhagwati 1999, p. xxvi), the administration's reaction was not one of respect or even disregard but of overt embarrassment:

The Clinton administration's response to our letter was one of fury, with the rapid-response and disinformation machines going into fast forward. While I myself had an exchange of letters on the substance of Japan's trade with a prominent economist within the administration, no effort was made to bring in the eminent trade economists who had signed the letter to discuss the issues with Ambassador Mickey Kantor or his advisers, even though most of the signatories were Democrats. Instead, some of the Nobel laureates who had signed were hassled. And their natural embarrassments were played up in a congressional hearing, where Senator Max Baucus of Montana dutifully asked about the letter and the Noble laureates, and Roger Altman, then deputy secretary of the Treasury, translated those embarrassments into self-serving and misleading assertions that the Nobel laureates had had second thoughts! Wonders will never cease.

5 Barriers to the prevalence of good ideas: lessons learned from the US–Japan conflict

Comparison of the views of the major economists and the revisionists reveals contradictory notions regarding the meaning of current-account surplus and current-account deficit. The economists did not attempt to prove or disprove whether "structural barriers" actually existed within the Japanese economy but rather that such barriers, if they truly existed, could not be the cause of the vast current-account imbalance between the two countries. On the other hand, the revisionists, as well as the majority of the US public, undoubtedly accepted that this imbalance was the most apparent evidence of the existence of "structural barriers" within the Japanese economy. In this sense, the revisionists and the economists were viewing the same information but interpreting it in a very different manner.

To understand why the economists were positing that "structural barriers" had no effect on the current-account imbalance but rather that "the surplus reflects an excess of Japanese savings over its domestic investment," basic knowledge regarding the balance of international payments is needed. In the following simple formula

$$(S-I)+(T-G) =X-M,$$

S denotes private saving, I private investment, T government income, G government expenditures, X the value of exports, and M the value of imports. According to the formula, any current-account imbalance $(X-M)$ is a reflection of a surplus or a deficit in the savings of an economy as a whole, which can be deduced by adding the saving–investment balance of the private sector $(S-I)$ and that of the public sector $(T-G)$. On the basis of this formula, the economists concluded that the primary reason why the US current-account deficit had been increasing since the beginning of the 1980s was a decreasing private saving–investment surplus, an increasing public deficit, or both. The economists were well aware that the macroeconomic policies of the Reagan Administration in the first half of the 1980s, especially those policies regarding decreasing taxes and increasing military expenditures, had led to a vast government deficit, which in turn had led to a corresponding current-account deficit in the US economy.

The cause of the coexistence of the public and current-account deficits—referred to as the "twin deficits" by the economists—in the US economy since the 1980s can be readily identified from the formula. The economists could, therefore, assert with confidence that any measure to correct the current-account imbalance would be in vain unless it altered the savings–investment balance. Thus, the economists maintained that the implementation of VIEs for Japan would not only harm trade practices but also fail to correct the current-account imbalance. Above all, they believed that equilibrating the current account of any country would be needed only in the long run. Japan's current-account surplus was not harming the US economy, they argued, but rather helping it, as the existence of a surplus meant that Japan could make its savings available to other countries, including the US, in greater need of foreign capital.

Examination of the economists' arguments clearly indicates that they believed that the conflict between the US and Japan was simply the product of a misunderstanding regarding the true significance of the current-account imbalance, and that this misunderstanding had led to the implementation of policies that the public assumed to be benefiting the US economy but were not truly doing so. There is no doubt that the public approved of these policies because they believed that they furthered their interests, even though this belief had no basis in reality. Therefore, it can be concluded that the trade friction between the US and Japan in the 1980s–1990s regarding the current-account imbalance had no real substance in the sense that there was no real conflict between the economic interests of both the countries.

This episode in economic policymaking provides many lessons for future policymaking. Above all, it demonstrates that a prevalent idea among the public can play a crucial role in policymaking, and if this idea is unsound, it can lead to unnecessary conflicts. Moreover, if an unsound idea becomes sufficiently widespread and accepted, it can prevent the acceptance of a more sound idea proposed by reliable experts, limiting the ability of these experts to address a conflict. The only good that could come from such a case would be in retrospect: that is, in the lessons that it could provide for future policymaking, as did this episode in economic policymaking, to prevent its recurrence in the future.

Notes

1 Ramseyer and Rosenbluth's (1993) was a successful application of the rational choice approach to the political economic process in Japan.
2 One of the most basic theoretical results obtained from both the Ricardian model and the Heckscher–Ohlin–Samuelson model is that any country engaged in trade is always better off after engaging in trade than before engaging in trade from the standpoint of the country as a whole. Although these models usually disregard the costs that importing competitive industries would pay after engaging in trade by assuming that the adjustment costs are zero, these costs are implicitly existent in these models because the importing competitive and comparatively disadvantaged industries would inevitably contract after engaging in trade.

References

Becker, Gary S. (1983) "A Theory of Competition Among Pressure Groups for Political Influence," *The Quarterly Journal of Economics*, 98(3): 371–400.

Bhagwati, Jagdish (1999) *A Stream of Windows: Unsettling Reflections on Trade, Immigration, and Democracy*, Cambridge, MA: MIT Press.

Bhagwati, Jagdish, Krugman, Paul, Baldwin, Robert, Collins, Susan, et al. (1993) "Open Letter to President Clinton and Prime Minister Hosokawa," transcribed in "The 5th Column: 'Reject Managed Trade'," *Far Eastern Economic Review*, November 4, 1993: 26.

Buchanan, James M. and Tullock, Gordon (1962) *The Calculus of Consent*, Ann Arbor, MI: University of Michigan Press.

Business Week (1989) "What Americans Think of Japan Inc.," *Business Week*, August 7: 19.

Davis, Bob (1995) "U.S.'s Quick-Hit Strategy May Backfire in Long Run," *The Wall Street Journal*, June 9: A9.

Hamada, Koichi and Noguchi, Asahi (2005) "The Role of Preconceived Ideas in Macro-economic Policy: Japan's Experiences in the Two Deflationary Periods," *International Economics and Economic Policy*, 2(2/3): 101–126.

Hamilton, David P. (1995) "U.S. 'Revisionists' on Japan Get Their Way," *The Wall Street Journal*, June 8: A8.

Keynes, John Maynard (1978 [1936]) *The Collected Writings of John Maynard Keynes: Vol. 7, The General Theory of Employment, Interest and Money*, London: Macmillan.

Neff, Robert (1989) "Rethinking Japan," *Business Week*, August 7: 12–20.

Neff, Robert and Magnusson, Paul (1989) "Rewriting the Book on How to Deal with Japan," *Business Week*, August 7: 17.

Ramseyer, Mark J. and Rosenbluth, Frances (1993) *Japan's Political Marketplace*, Cambridge, MA: Harvard University Press.

Stigler, George J. (1971) "The Theory of Economic Regulation," *Bell Journal of Economics*, 2(1): 3–21.

Part III
Emerging nations—BRICs

11 Globalization, policy autonomy and economic development

The case of Brazil

Fernando J. Cardim de Carvalho[1]

1 Introduction

A well-established fact described by the literature on economic development is the importance of balance-of-payments constraints on economic growth. Developing economies depend on the foreign provision of certain classes of goods, such as capital goods and some types of raw materials, to increase their growth rates. Even import-substitution strategies cannot entirely overcome these constraints. In fact, import-substitution processes tend to make the balance-of-payments constraints even more binding, given that, when imports are stripped down to essential goods, it may be impossible to produce or to invest without them.

Facing the need to pay for essential imports, developing countries may either promote exports or get into foreign debt. When industrialization got up to speed in Latin America, after World War II, promoting exports did not seem to be very promising. It was widely believed that the kind of goods those countries could export consisted mostly of unprocessed or little processed raw materials which would fetch declining prices in world markets, thereby increasing continuously the effort required to finance imports. This view prevailed in the region for decades. It would only effectively change when the experience of Asian economies showed there were ways to increase exports that were compatible with sustained industrial development. In the Brazilian case, it was only in the early 1970s that increasing exports became a priority for policymakers and even then not for long.

The second possibility of paying for essential imports was getting into debt. This was the choice or, better, the default option of most, if not all, Latin American countries in the twentieth century, including Brazil. Financial cycles in developed economies periodically made access to financial resources in international markets very easy. Of course, times of easy access were always followed by "sudden stops" of capital inflows which caused balance-of-payments crises serious enough to wipe out, in many cases, the gains of the preceding expansion. Orthodox economists expected that foreign direct investment would flow to these economies attracted by their supposedly higher marginal productivity of capital. They were never sufficient, however, to finance current account deficits. "Growing with support from foreign savings" always meant accumulation of foreign debt with all of its perverse consequences for sustained development.

Import substitution was the most common development strategy adopted by Latin American countries after World War II, including Brazil. Besides its promise of inward-looking economic development, import substitution was also a powerful *political* notion, feeding on nationalist feelings of domestic businessmen, middle classes, workers and, frequently, important sections of the armed forces, always an essential political actor in the region. For many of these groups, import substitution was above all a strategy to break a country's dependence of more advanced economies.

Import substitution strategies usually entailed an active, even if indirect, role for the state in directing the economic process, but frequently also a direct participation through the creation of state-owned enterprises. Import controls were used to guarantee that scarce foreign exchange was used mainly to pay for essential imports. Capital controls were designed to prevent capital flight since periods of excess capital inflows into the region were rare.

The oil crises of the 1970s and the secondary shocks they induced put an end to the import-substitution experience in Latin America. The sudden and steep rise in imports could only be accommodated by a similar increase in foreign debt. The effort to do so led to the foreign debt crisis of the early 1980s. The three largest Latin American economies, Argentina, Brazil and Mexico, were severely hit by the sudden closure of financial markets to the region. Negotiations between banks and indebted countries, intermediated by the IMF, lasted almost a decade and resulted in the forced acceptance of liberalizing reforms by the crisis countries.[2] From the late 1980s onwards, the Brazilian economy grew increasingly integrated into the world economy. For all practical purposes, the globalization of the Brazilian economy started in those years.

To say that globalization began in the 1980s obviously does not mean that external economic relations were not important for the Brazilian economy before that time. I am proposing here to take globalization to mean not the mere engagement in commercial or even financial transactions with foreign partners, but the taking steps to increase the degree of integration between domestic and foreign markets. In other words, globalization is a process where the barriers that insulate in some degree the domestic economy from developments taking place in the rest of the world are progressively dismantled so that domestic and international markets are increasingly unified. In this sense, for example, trade may be intense even though two economies keep their markets separated, with their own different prices, practices, rules, etc. Globalization, in contrast, is the process in which markets are increasingly unified, with prices (and, in the case of financial markets, interest rates) converging to a common level (converted at the appropriate exchange rate and taking into consideration objective factors such as transportation costs).

In what follows, the distinction between internationalization and globalization will inform the interpretation of the Brazilian experience after World War II. A central proposition of this chapter is that while Brazil pursued an import-substitution strategy of development, it sought to increase its economy's internationalization but took active steps to prevent its globalization. To demonstrate the relevance of the distinction, in Section 2 we will outline the process through which the Brazilian economy developed in the period after World War II until the mid-1990s. The choice of 1994 as a watershed in Brazilian economic development is explained by the success of the price stabilization plan that allowed high inflation to be vanquished after more than 25 years of failed attempts, and is the subject of Section 3. The relevance of price stabilization for the present discussion is that integrating the domestic economy into international goods and assets markets became a central pillar of the fight against inflation which gave it wide public support. Section 4 is dedicated to integration in financial markets. Section 5 explores implications of globalization for economic policy autonomy in the Brazilian case. Section 6 concludes the chapter.

2 The Brazilian economy and the world economy

2.1 Import substitution, or internationalization without globalization

Brazil became independent of Portugal in 1822. In the period between 1500, when the Portuguese arrived on the western shores of South America, and 1822, Brazil was mainly a commercial enterprise focused on natural-resource-based exports. First it was sugar, produced on a large scale from sugarcane. Later were gold, rubber and coffee, among other agricultural or mineral products. Independence in fact did not change the picture. The newly independent Brazilian economy boomed with coffee exports from the second half of the nineteenth century to the 1930s, when the Great Depression in the more advanced economies stimulated the creation of the domestic industries that would plant the seed of the import-substitution process implemented after World War II.[3]

Import substitution actually began as a spontaneous process in which local entrepreneurs endeavored to attend the domestic demand for consumer goods that used to be satisfied by imports. Of course, only technologically simple goods could be actually produced by indigenous firms. The country remained dependent on imports both for more sophisticated consumer goods and for capital and many intermediate goods. The depression was followed by World War II, so that the disruption of international trade lines lasted long enough to allow many firms to consolidate, creating an embryonic local manufacturing sector. In the early 1940s, protecting and extending the incipient manufacturing sector gradually became a conscious policy priority. Brazil was led in those years by a civilian dictator, Getúlio Vargas, who negotiated with President Franklin Roosevelt the construction of a steel plant in Rio de Janeiro State in exchange for the country's participation in the war against the Axis. When the war was over, Brazil was a very different country than it was before the depression. After a brief liberal interregnum, Vargas, who had been deposed in 1945, was again elected president, and was succeeded later by Juscelino Kubitschek.

Both leaders presided over a decade characterized by the implementation of active industrial policies to favor the rapid growth of manufacture. Vargas created state companies that rapidly became leading actors in the development process, such as the oil company, Petrobras (with a monopoly of production, refining and distribution of oil), and the National Economic Development Bank, BNDE (later renamed National Economic and Social Development Bank, BNDES), to supply long-term finance to private and public investment. Kubitschek, in contrast, relied mostly on foreign private investors who were invited to build productive plants in the country to supply its growing internal market.[4]

President Kubitschek took a large step in the direction of *internationalizing* the Brazilian economy but, in two important senses he did *not* move the economy toward *globalization*. The economy was internationalized in the obvious sense that the share of foreign-owned firms' output in the value of total output increased in the period. The most visible face of industrialization in the second half of the 1950s was in fact the construction of a domestic (although foreign owned) car industry in Brazil. However, opening the domestic market to foreign producers was concomitant with the adoption of stringent import-control measures that made it practically impossible to import cars into the country. Whoever wanted to sell cars, trucks or buses in Brazil had to produce them locally. At the same time, of course, whoever decided to initiate local production could be satisfied that domestic markets were highly protected against competitors producing cars in other countries. Internationalization became thus an *alternative* to globalization. Far from unifying markets, as is expected, at least theoretically, from a globalization or an integration process, internationalization actually allowed local producers to be insulated from competitors located in other countries.

The second sense in which the Kubitschek experience distanced Brazil from international integration was that foreign firms were welcome as long as they accepted playing a leading but not exclusive role in the development of the manufacturing sector. Again, the car industry is the best example of this principle: foreign producers were allowed to assemble the vehicles in the country (and benefit from the tightly protected domestic market) but the production of parts was reserved to domestic private producers, except when they involved more advanced technology (as it was the case of the production of engines), which the foreign producers could import from their other productive facilities abroad.[5]

Kubitschek's policies allowed the Brazilian economy to grow and to be transformed very quickly in the 1950s. Heavy public investments were in fact added to private investments in the period, through large public-works projects such as the construction of the new capital, Brasília, very far from the more populous cities of the Brazilian coast. Once the large wave of investments was completed, it was followed, as it was perhaps inevitable, by a loss of dynamism in the early 1960s. Inflation was also accelerating, creating important social tensions in the period, to which a political crisis was added. The tension accumulated until it led to a military coup in 1964, which created a military regime that would last until 1985.

The military rulers did not follow a consistent path. A peculiarity of the authoritarian regime installed in 1964 was that it was ruled by the Armed Forces (in fact, the Army) as a *corporation*, instead of by an individual dictator, as in the case of Argentina, Chile, etc., in the same period. During the period there were "elections," in which the candidate anointed by the High Command would be "elected" president by Congress (which was kept open but was depurated of unreliable members). As a result, every few years, a new group of military commanders would take over the presidency and pursue the policies they judged adequate. Thus, after a few years of economic liberalism, right after the coup, a strongly interventionist group took power willing to pursue even more rapid industrialization than before by using all the discretionary policy instruments they had at their disposal. The goals were similar to those of President Kubitschek, to promote fast growth, but now not only of manufacturing but also of agricultural and export industries.

The swan song of import substitution in Brazil came just after the first oil shock in 1973. The sudden doubling of the price of imported oil put the Brazilian economy at a crossroads. Facing a heavy bill in foreign exchange, the country could opt for decelerating growth to reduce imports, keeping the economy "cold" until either the price of oil fell or exports grew enough to allow footing the oil bill. The alternative was to begin a new effort at import substitution, creating industries that would not only allow domestically produced goods to substitute imported goods but also open the possibility of exporting those same items. An ambitious development plan was unveiled in 1974 to create those industries, which implied, however, sharply increasing foreign indebtedness in the short to middle term.[6] In the 1970s, developing economies could only borrow from banks at variable interest rates (usually indexed to the Libor). It was clearly a Ponzi scheme: Brazil was going to borrow short to invest long, speculating that loans would be repeatedly rolled over in increasing volumes (because of the capitalization of interest payments) and at interest rates compatible with the expected returns in foreign currency from those investments which would ultimately allow the liquidation all the liabilities created to fund them.

Most of planned investments were at least partially implemented, but the Ponzi scheme could not resist the unexpectedly sharp increase in Libor induced by Paul Volcker's anti-inflationary policies in the late 1970s and early 1980s. As a result, Brazil (together with Argentina and Mexico) went bankrupt in 1982, initiating a protracted process of debt renegotiation that would mean the end of import-substitution policies and of controlled internationalization to allow globalization to set in in its stead.

2.2 *Liberalization and globalization*

As is well known, the steep rise in oil prices resulting from the two oil shocks of the 1970s generated larger revenues for oil exporters than they could possibly use for consumption or investment purposes. A large share of those revenues was thus kept as deposits in international banks, which transformed them into loans to countries with balance-of-payments deficits. The excess supply of liquidity pushed interest rates down, attracting opportunity borrowers especially among oil importers in difficulty. Latin American countries, such as Argentina, Brazil and Mexico, borrowed mostly from US banks with which they had a long-term relationship. When they became insolvent in 1982, a potential bank crisis in the US was the other side of the coin of the foreign debt crisis in Latin America.

In this context it was not surprising that the US government should step into the negotiations conducted between a committee of large banks and representatives of government of the crisis countries to overcome their insolvency. Negotiations were long and hard, with borrowers demanding a "haircut" on the value of their debt and banks resisting these demands, insisting instead, with the support of the US government, that those countries had to proceed to institutional reforms that would open their economies to foreign interests and raise the probability that they would repay their foreign liabilities. As the negotiations went on, the IMF was put in charge of overseeing the reforms and stabilization policies that borrowers had been forced to accept. Meanwhile, many proposals were advanced to deal with the problem of debt itself, but it was only with the Brady Plan, in 1989, that a definitive solution was found. The Brady Plan imposed a "haircut" in the value of the debt, as demanded by borrowing countries, and implemented an ingenious securitization scheme in which developing countries accumulated debt was replaced by negotiable bonds secured by US Treasury bonds. As a quid pro quo, borrowing countries would reform, liberalize and seek to stabilize their economies.

Brazil was the last country in the region to settle its debts in the context of the Brady Plan in 1994. Liberalizing reforms, however, had already been going on since the second half of the 1980s.

Trade barriers, capital controls and discrimination of foreign direct investment were all falling by the end of the 1980s. Non-tariff trade barriers were being removed as a result of negotiations in the context of the Uruguay Round. In 1999 the Brazilian government also accepted the obligations of Article VIII of the IMF, establishing current-account convertibility. As a result, administrative controls of imports, that had been in use for decades, were eliminated. "Undesirable" imports could now only be prevented by the imposition of tariffs, within limits set by the same global trade negotiations, and to the extent that the tariff system was in fact efficacious to prevent them.

Capital controls, on the other hand, were dismantled gradually, in a process that began in earnest in 1988 and still proceeds. Brazilian law regulating foreign currency transactions had relied since the 1930s on the principle that only financial resources that had been internalized had a right to return. This meant that nobody has a legal *right* to send money abroad unless one could show that there had been a previous inflow of the same value (plus the income it might generate). Brazilian residents could only send money abroad when authorized by the proper authorities (or by smuggling, of course, running the risks of criminal prosecution).

Capital inflows, on the other hand, also faced a number of restrictions. Financial investment by non-residents in Brazilian domestic capital markets was not allowed. Only foreign direct investment and borrowing by firms and state entities were accepted.

Capital controls began to be dismantled in 1988 when capital inflows to buy shares negotiated in the stock exchanges, through dedicated investment funds, were allowed. The government justified this initiative with the need to increase the liquidity of the markets for company shares to reduce their cost of capital and, hopefully, to facilitate their investments. Stock exchanges turnover and liquidity benefited in fact from the opening to foreign investments. The downside of the initiative, however, was the increased dependence of stock prices on foreign capital movements. Stock prices have ever since reflected events taking place in other countries (that lead foreign investors to come and go) rather than Brazilian economic "fundamentals." The latest information available, for October 2014, shows that slightly over 27 percent of all stock sales and purchases on the São Paulo Stock Exchange, by far the largest in the country, were made by foreign investors.[7]

In the early 1990s, capital outflows, by Brazilian residents, began to be liberalized until it reached almost complete freedom in the early 2000s. The need to obtain authorization was replaced by mere information requirements surrounding remittances abroad. Even the information requirements were enforced only above thresholds that were continuously increased in value. The principle that capital controls were needed to ensure systemic stability was substituted by the alternative principle that capital controls should only be applied in the cases in which there was some evidence of criminal behavior in the origin of the transaction (such as in the case of money laundering by drug dealers, for instance).[8]

Dismantling non-tariff trade barriers and capital controls put Brazil on the path to international financial integration. Now, in contrast to the period between the end of World War II and the 1980s, the goal was not only to intensify the country's relations with foreign economies *on its own terms* but to actually become a piece of a larger economic system, a cog in the machine of the world economy. A conscious attempt to remove the remaining barriers to international integration survived even the substitution of the center-right government of Fernando H. Cardoso by the center-left government of Luiz Inácio Lula da Silva. Only the deepening of the international crisis in the early 2010s would partially (and perhaps temporarily) stop this trend. In fact, by the early 2010s, globalization had come to be seen as a crucial element of the macroeconomic environment that had allowed long-lasting high inflation to be vanquished in 1994.

It should perhaps not be too surprising that integration advanced much faster in financial markets than in the goods markets. In the next two sections, recent trends toward globalization will be discussed separately, first with respect to the goods markets, and afterwards in relation to assets markets. Later, in the concluding section, both threads will be reunited to allow some discussion of perspectives for the near future.

3 Trade liberalization, the *Real* Plan, exchange rate overvaluation and international integration

The Brazilian economy stagnated in the two decades after the oil shocks. Inflation accelerated and became dysfunctional after 1979, even in the presence of mechanisms such as the widespread indexation of contracts that had been designed to neutralize its impact on the real economy. The acceleration of inflation bankrupted the state, strangling its capacity to invest and renew economic infrastructure facilities, such as roads, highways, ports, hydroelectric plants, etc. Moreover, the uncertainty surrounding the future of a high-inflation economy was big enough to suffocate any private animal spirits that may have existed. The purchasing power of wages was unpredictable even in the short term, making it impossible for households to make any sort of plan and narrowing dramatically the market for durable consumption goods. Given the circumstances, stagnation was not the worst problem most people feared, the persistence of high inflation was.

In 1990, a new president, the first elected in free elections after the military regime was ended, began his term adopting a shock plan against inflation, which took his name, the Collor Plan. The plan did not work and after a relatively short pause, prices began to rise even more rapidly than before. At the same time in which President Collor's economists were trying to salvage their price stabilization plan, they also implemented a package of trade liberalization measures designed to increase domestic competition and, hopefully, improving productivity and the quality of domestically produced goods. Many administrative controls were abolished and tariffs were sharply reduced in relation to their previous peaks.

Those measures did not have the expected positive effect on local production. In fact, given the environment of deep uncertainty fed by the failure of the Collor Plan—to which one should add the mismanagement of the economy by the federal government and the impact of a political crisis created by accusations of corruption in government made by one of the president's brothers and former associate—the Brazilian economy, after a fall in 1990, returned to its state of stagnation. The corruption charges leveled against the president led to his resignation in 1992. The vice-president, Itamar Franco, completed his term. In his short time in office, President Franco was able, however, to implement in 1994 a complex stabilization plan, known as *Real* Plan (named after the new currency that was introduced as part of the package of policies), that finally allowed inflation to be brought under control. One of the pillars of the stabilization strategy was in fact trade liberalization, so that the measures adopted under President Collor not only were maintained, they were actually extended and deepened.

From 1986 to 1994, many attempts at breaking the spine of the inflation process had been attempted. All resorted to the imposition of (expected to be temporary) price freezes. The plans consisted also of measures to change monetary and fiscal policies, reform the state and so on, but most of them ended up relying almost solely on price controls, which tended to lose their effectiveness very quickly. In fact, political support for price controls was usually widespread, making it diffi-cult for democratically elected governments to eliminate them and use demand management policies instead. The result of this dilemma was that controls tended to be eliminated only when they had completely lost their efficacy, demoralizing the very notion of stabilization plan.

The *Real* Plan did not rely on price controls. In fact, markets were kept free to price goods as sellers wanted and buyers allowed. Instead of price controls, the plan relied on the competitive pressure of imports on local producers, made pos-sible by the previous trade liberalization initiatives. In fact, the pressure was made greater by the overvaluation of the domestic currency that followed its cre-ation, in July 1994. Domestic interest rates were kept very high causing a deluge of capital inflows to increase the value of the *Real* with respect to the US dollar (it went from R$1 = US$1, in July 1994, to R$0.80 to US$1 three months later). A trade surplus in July 1994 rapidly transformed itself into a deficit by Novem-ber, but heavy capital inflows were more than enough to cover the current-account deficit.[9]

It was not realized at the time, even by economists working on the stabiliza-tion plan, that the reliance on imports cheapened by liberalization *and* exchange rate over-appreciation was to become a sort of original sin that would resist all later attempts at penitence made by successive federal administrations. Cheap imports not only became the mainstay of low inflation rates but the exchange rate channel became the main transmission channel of monetary policy to this day, even if its efficacy varied from time to time.

For the purposes of the present discussion, the importance of this factor is that *globalization became an intrinsic and central element of price stability policies in Brazil.* Domestic markets were no longer to be insulated from competitive pressures coming from the international economy. On the contrary, it was expected that domestic prices would converge to world prices (at least for trada-bles; prices of non-tradables have always been a much more difficult problem do deal with). Ideally, if complete globalization was reached, not only should Bra-zilian prices diverge from world prices no more than necessary to cover trans-portation and other similar "structural" costs, but, *which was far more important,* they could not grow faster than world prices. Globalization should become a potent anti-inflation weapon.

In the 1990s, in accordance with this strategy, there was ample denationaliza-tion of the Brazilian economy, particularly of its manufacturing sector. Protec-tive measures had been removed too suddenly to allow domestic producers to adapt to competitive pressures from abroad. Financial costs, which had always been a problem for local producers, were raised further by the high-interest-rate policy adopted by the federal government to attract capital inflows and to subdue domestic aggregate demand. Exchange rate overvaluation was the mercy shot delivered against local producers that made them incapable of competing both abroad and domestically with foreign competitors. Foreign direct investment was freely welcomed into the country, a large share of which consisted only of pur-chases of local businesses, including some state-owned companies in process of

Table 11.1 Share of exports and imports in the value of domestic manufacture (%)

	2010	2011	2012 (1stQ)
Exports	14.6	15.0	15.2
Imports	19.1	20.7	21.1

Source: www.cni.org.br/portal/data/files/00/FF808081374D209601375C94BF156CE0/Coeficientes%20de%20Abertura%20Comercial%20n%C2%BA%2001%20-%20Jan-Mar%202012%20-%20V2.pdf.

privatization. Arrangements to preserve room for local businesses were considered outmoded and inefficient, purely rent-seeking initiatives. During President Fernando H. Cardoso's two terms in office and Lula da Silva's first term the notion prevailed that this development was unavoidable or even rather good, and that the role of the state should be confined to ensuring macroeconomic stability to allow the private sector to bloom.

International integration in the goods market, however, has been limited by two factors. First, the size of the country's internal market allied to its geographical area still allows a large room to local producers to occupy. Of course, this is not a permanent feature, the space for local manufacturers diminishes continuously, but it still leaves them with some breathing room, while they wait for more favorable policies from the government. Data in Table 11.1 shows that export and import coefficients for the manufacturing sector are still relatively low but they also show that domestic producers' loss of local markets to foreign firms is still growing.

The second factor limiting globalization is the large sector of non-tradables which is, by definition, beyond the reach of global suppliers. Even here, however, equilibria are unstable. Sectors that used to be considered non-tradables, such as superior education, are nowadays a "normal" business and international groups have been actively acquiring local private universities. Other sectors, such as health care, are undergoing the same process of increasing foreign presence. Only suppliers of personal services of a more primitive kind, like housemaids and car mechanics can in fact breathe safe in such an environment.

4 Liberalization of the capital account and globalization of the assets markets

The trend toward financial integration initiated in 1988 has been sustained more consistently and successfully than in the case of goods markets. Measures were taken to liberalize all classes of capital inflows as well as outflows. In fact, integration was favored even by policies that, in theory, had nothing to do with financial flows, such as the suspension of the legal obligation of exports to convert their foreign revenues into domestic currency. As a result, domestic financial assets markets became highly integrated into international markets, opening the way to a convergence of domestic asset prices (and interest rates) toward world market levels.[10]

This last statement may sound paradoxical, since the Brazilian economy is widely known for its high interest rates, frequently mentioned in the financial press as the country where the highest interest rates in the world are paid, which is actually true. Two features of Brazilian financial markets are the main culprit. First, convergence means that local asset prices tend to a common level, *considering their idiosyncratic risks.* Financial and other relevant risks on average are still perceived as being higher in Brazil than in the world markets. Second, the influence of the state on the formation of domestic interest rates is still very high. The maturity of the term structure of interest rates is limited to short and middle terms and public debt securities dominate local securities markets. Under these conditions, high interest rates paid by the government set a high floor for all other market rates, regardless of the risk investors actually perceive. Government action cannot prevent the operation of market forces in financially open economies. But it can induce disequilibria that can actually last for a long time. In the case of Brazil, the imbalance caused by the government maintaining higher domestic interest rates than could be justified by idiosyncratic risk factors was the accumulation of reserves and sustained exchange rate appreciation (which had some perverse feedback effects on the productive sectors, as described in the preceding section).

It is always very difficult to measure exchange rate overvaluation. Any measure is sensitive to starting points and to the choice of price indices that would describe the evolution of real exchange rates. The uncertainties related to this calculation are reflected in the large number of estimates of the extent to which the *Real* super-appreciation in the years after high inflation was instrumental in vanquishing. Nevertheless, even if the calculations differ, there is no important disagreement around the phenomenon itself. Moreover, its impact on the real economy, particularly in the loss of competitiveness of local manufacturing in international *and* in domestic markets, is also undeniable. Table 11.2 shows the clear deterioration of the balance-of-payments position of the Brazilian economy since 2010.

Finally, the data of reserve accumulation also suggests excess inflows absorbed by the government and, thus, higher interest rates than would be set by private transactors alone: the volume of reserves increased from US$289 billion in December 2010 to US$369 billion in September 2013.[11]

One interesting aspect of the Brazilian experience is the survival, practically the sole case in Latin America among the largest economies in this respect, of

Table 11.2 Balance of payments – Brazil (US$ billion)

	January–August 2012	*2012*	*January–August 2013*
Current account	(−)32	(−)54	(−)58
Trade balance	13	19	(−)4
Capital account	54	70	63

Source: www.bcb.gov.br/?INDECO (downloaded October 18, 2013).

legal restrictions on the operation of foreign banks. In fact, although banks which are already operating in domestic markets enjoy the same rights of domestic banks (public and private), foreign banks that wish to begin operations in Brazil have to obtain a specific authorization to do so, issued by the president of Brazil. This does not necessarily reflect a view that foreign banks may be deleterious to the economy. It is rather a problem of legal inertia. The role and structure of the financial system is considered in Brazil a constitutional matter. When the 1988 constitution was written, right after the end of the military regime, it was decided that this matter should be left to later consideration, prioritizing the changes in the political regime. While one waited for the new rules, the existing financial structure was "frozen," including the set of foreign banks that had been admitted into the country before the new Constitution. An escape valve was created, giving the president of Brazil the power to allow, on an individual basis, a foreign bank to operate in the country "if necessary," and some banks actually benefited from this possibility. The case remains, however, that the entry of new foreign banks is strictly regulated. To this day the Brazilian system is still dominated by large public and private domestic institutions. As a result, among the five largest banks in the country in 2012 (by value of assets), two are state-owned (Banco do Brasil and Caixa Econômica Federal), two are private but domestically owned (Itaú-Unibanco and Bradesco) and only one is foreign (Santander), in the fifth place.

Existing restrictions on the entry of foreign banks, however, did not prevent the march toward financial globalization. In fact, if one splits the existing financial structure into two sectors, the first providing retail services to customers, and the other wholesale and investment banking, one quickly realizes that it is in the second sector where the trend toward globalization is the strongest. Customers in this sector are not prevented from doing business by geographical limitations on the access to international institutions. It really does not matter much where the customers are or where the financial intermediaries are or where investors are. In the retail segment, in contrast, customers rely heavily on reputation and the possibility of establishing long-term relationships with banks and, in this case, foreign banks were no match for domestic banks in Brazil.

5 Globalization and economic policy

The jury is still out on the gains a developing country can obtain from globalization. In the case of Brazil, results are in fact ambiguous. On the one hand, as already explained, integration in the international economy, especially in the goods markets, was instrumental in vanquishing inflation, the importance of which cannot be underestimated. On the other hand, it has increased the exposure of the Brazilian economy to the volatility of the international economy, which cost the country a lot, especially in the 1990s and 2000s. Although one should avoid simplistic arguments, the economy has stagnated for most of the period when integration was increased. Some argue that stagnation was due to too much exposure, others advance the argument that stagnation resulted from the timidity with which integration was pursued. Undeniably growth has been disappointing since the 1980s but it is not clear the extent to which globalization as such has contributed to this performance. This has been the subject of a heated local debate and seems still far from reaching any conclusion.

If the gains of globalization are still being evaluated, the picture is clearer with respect to its impact on policymaking. It is well known that liberalized capital accounts are not compatible with fixed exchange rate regimes if monetary authorities want to preserve their autonomy to set monetary policy (the so-called *impossible trinity*). But in the real world the incompatibility is not restricted to fixed exchange rates. The volatility of international capital flows is also incompatible with *floating* exchange rates. What changes from one regime to the other is the variable that has to assimilate the impacts of capital flows volatility. Under fixed exchange rates, domestic interest rates become more volatile. Under floating exchange rates, it is exchange rates themselves that will bear the brunt of capital flows volatility. Trying to manage exchange rates in order to distribute the impact of capital movement volatility among exchange and interest rates, besides being a difficult task in the absence of capital controls, tends to create other imbalances such as excess loss or accumulation of foreign reserves.[12]

After the *Real* Plan, Brazil experimented with a pegged exchange rate regime in the period 1995–1999, switching to a floating regime after the balance-of-payments crisis of 1999. More recently, monetary authorities implemented a "dirty float" strategy. In the period between 1995 and 1999, domestic interest rates were set with the direct intent to attract capital inflows in the volume necessary to sustain the policy of using imports to combat inflation. The authorities achieved their goal—inflation was in fact contained and dramatically reduced in the period, but at the cost of accumulating external debts that came to haunt the economy after the Asian crises of 1997 and the Russian crisis of 1998. By December 1998 capital flight intensified in Brazil leading to the balance-of-payments crisis of January 1999. The floating exchange rate regime created some limited room for monetary authorities to set interest rates. In fact, not only did capital movements remain a strategic variable to sustain macroeconomic stability but adherence to an inflation-targeting monetary regime in 1999 created new balance-of-payments constraints on the freedom to set domestic interest rates. Under inflation targeting, given the importance of the exchange rate to the behavior of domestic prices (direct and indirect, through its impact on expectations), a devaluation forces domestic prices upwards compelling the central bank to raise interest rates anyway. The explanation for the rise changes, not the substance of the policy.

These limits to monetary policy autonomy are well-known to apply practically everywhere. Perhaps less well stressed is the fact that autonomy to set economic policies *in general* is reduced by globalization, not just monetary policy autonomy.

Of course, this should not be surprising. Integration means that the national economy becomes part of a larger whole and can thus no longer behave as an entirely independent unit. The possibility of moving financial resources into and out of the country creates the possibility of "voting with their feet" for wealth holders. The possibility is obviously asymmetric: transaction costs involved in receiving or remitting money tend to be relatively high in value but they do not increase significantly with the size of the transaction favoring, therefore, larger operations. Also, every large financial institution tries to establish stable client relationships with richer clients and keeping open financial lines of communication with other countries is an important instrument to do it. Within such a context, policymakers are permanently constrained in their ability to fulfill progressive reform pledges no matter how clearly voters state their wishes in elections. Two examples from the recent Brazilian experience stand out in this particular. In 1998, when President Fernando H. Cardoso was seeking re-election he pledged to re-orient his government's policies toward growth and distribution, alleging that, after the victory against inflation, he was well qualified to lead a "social-democratic" turn in Brazilian politics. Markets reacted very badly to this kind of rhetoric which was very quickly shelved. It is difficult, however, in this episode, to isolate balance-of-payments changes that may have strengthened the pressure on Cardoso since the country was already beginning to experience the effects of the Russian crisis and the burden of its own accumulated imbalances.

The second episode was much more obvious. In 2002, Lula da Silva was running again to succeed Cardoso as president of Brazil, as he had been trying to since the 1989 elections. This time, however, he was poised to win. A few months before the actual vote, the financial markets realized that Cardoso's candidate did not stand a fighting chance of beating Lula da Silva. A double financial crisis erupted when financial institutions began to dump their portfolios of public debt securities maturing after the date Lula da Silva was expected to be inaugurated and capital flight intensified. Market pressures on the interest rates of public debt and on exchange rates were heavy forcing Lula da Silva to issue an "open letter to the Brazilian people," but addressed in fact to financial markets, in which he pledged not to change Cardoso's macroeconomic policies in his eventual term in office. Markets calmed down, Lula da Silva was elected, and fulfilled his part of the deal strictly, at least during his first term in office.

6 Conclusion

For most of the twentieth century, the Brazilian economy grew and developed relying on an import-substitution strategy. The conditions in which this strategy was conceived and implemented, after an initial period in which development had been largely spontaneous, more or less determined how the domestic economy would relate to the international economy. Import substitution, as pursued in Brazil, meant an effort at rapid industrialization led by the state where, even though autarchy was not a goal, internationalization could be accepted, in the sense that foreign direct investment was welcome in many stages of the process, but globalization was not. Foreign business could take part in the development process but preserving strategic policy autonomy was among its most highly valued features.

In contrast, the conditions in which the import-substitution strategy exhausted its possibilities, in the late 1970s, also more or less determined the new pattern of relationship between the Brazilian and the international economy. Liberalizing reforms were imposed under duress, as conditionalities demanded in exchange for the help to renegotiate a foreign debt that had gotten out of hand.

As a result, Brazil was increasingly integrated into the international economy, allowing its economy to become more and more globalized, which means that domestic markets work more and more as parts of a larger unit instead of an autonomous unit, as was the goal during the import-substitution times. The chapter explains the reasons why the process was stronger in the financial assets markets than in the goods markets, but globalization is a trend, not yet a final result, and Brazil is clearly following the path to an ever-deeper integration with the world economy.

The international crisis initiated in the United States in 2007 reduced the speed of globalization. The disorganization of the international economy weakened the pressures on emerging markets to find their "places" in a crystalized international structure. Local governments found new room to develop some autonomy in policymaking. As the situation normalizes, in some sense, however, the space for autonomous developments clearly narrows. This is especially problematic for countries like Brazil, where liberalizing reforms have already advanced so much. Politically, it is much harder to roll back liberalization, after many interest groups have already been formed around the markets that were open, than to keep existing restrictions. The violent and persistent criticism met in the press and in financial markets by very timid attempts to partially restore some controls on capital inflows to avoid currency overvaluation, as excess liquidity was created in the United States and Europe in recent years, vividly exemplifies the difficulty of reining in these markets again.

Notes

1 Emeritus Professor of Economics, Institute of Economics, Federal University of Rio de Janeiro. Financial support from the National Research Council of Brazil (CNPq) is gratefully acknowledged.
2 A similar pattern of behavior is currently being observed in the "rescue packages" negotiated by the so-called troika (the European Commission, the European Central Bank and the International Monetary Fund) with the crisis countries in the periphery of the Eurozone.
3 There is a vast literature on the process of import substitution in Latin America, and in Brazil in particular. Classic references to the Brazilian experience include Furtado (1984), Baer (2013), Tavares (1964) and Fishlow (1972).
4 Again, the classic discussion of the changes which were necessary to give the state instruments to promote rapid industrialization is presented in Lessa (1964).
5 A description and evaluation of this process is found at EED (2004).
6 By far, the best description and evaluation of the import-substitution policies adopted in the period is unfortunately only available in Portuguese, in Castro and Souza (1985).
7 See http://bmfbovespa.com.br/renda-variavel/BuscarParticipacao Investimento.aspx? Idioma=pt-br, downloaded October 29, 2014.
8 Most of the initiatives related to the liberalization of the capital account were taken by the central bank, in a move that many see as illegitimate, since the bank could not overrule a principle established in federal law. Moreover, the central bank authorities

simply neglected all the literature pointing out the macroeconomic and systemic risks created by the free movement of capital in and out of the country. For a discussion of these risks, see Cardim de Carvalho (2002–2003).

9 There was a balance-of-payments crisis in the early months of 1995, the contagion of the Mexican crisis, that forced the government to adopt a few emergency measures to stop capital flight, mainly through a steep increase in interest rates. When the situation normalized, after the US government built a rescue package for Mexico, capital inflows also normalized allowing the continuance of the policy relying on increasing foreign indebtedness.

10 The process of liberalization of the capital account is critically reviewed in detail in Cardim de Carvalho and Souza (2008 and 2014).

11 Source: www.bcb.gov.br/pec/sdds/port/templ1p.shtm, downloaded in October 18, 2013. Few Brazilian economists have been so vocal in alerting against the macroeconomic risks of maintaining an overvalued currency as Bresser-Pereira. See, for instance, Bresser-Pereira (2009).

12 A very informative discussion of the role of capital controls in the international monetary system created in Bretton Woods is offered by Eichengreen (2008).

References

Baer, W. (2013) *The Brazilian Economy: Growth and Development*, Boulder, CO: Lynne Rienner Publishers.

Bresser-Pereira, L. C. (2009) "A tendência à sobreapreciação da taxa de câmbio," Escola de Economia de São Paulo, *Discussion Papers*, 183.

Cardim de Carvalho, F. (2002–2003) "Strengthening the Defenses of the Brazilian Economy Against External Vulnerability," *International Journal of Political Economy*, 32(4): 35–48.

Cardim de Carvalho, F. and Souza, F. E. P. (2010) "Financial Regulation and Macroeconomic Stability in Brazil in the Aftermath of the Russian Crisis," January, available at: www.itf.org.ar/pdf/documentos/65-2010.pdf.

Cardim de Carvalho, F. and Souza, F. E. P. (2014) "Lessons of the 2008 Crisis," in Luiz Carlos Bresser-Pereira, Jan Kregel and Leonardo Burlamaqui (eds.) *Financial Stability and Growth: Perspectives on Financial Regulation and New Developmentalism*, Abingdon: Routledge.

Castro, A. B. and Souza, F. E. P. (1985) *A Economia Brasileira em Marcha Forçada*, Rio de Janeiro: Paz e Terra.

Eichengreen, B. (2008) *Globalizing Capital: A History of the International Monetary System*, 2nd edition, Princeton, NJ: Princeton University Press.

EED (Evangelischer Entwicklungsdienst) (2004) *Foreign Direct Investment: High Risk, Low Reward for Development*, October, Bonn: EED.

Fishlow, A. (1972) "Origins and Consequences of Import Substitution in Brazil," in L. E. di Marco (ed.) *International Economics and Development: Essays in Honor of Raul Prebisch*, New York, NY: Academic Press.

Furtado, C. (1984) *The Economic Growth of Brazil: A Survey from Colonial to Modern Times*, New York, NY: Praeger.

Lessa, C. (1964) "15 Años de Política Económica," *Boletín Económico de América Latina*, November, Santiago de Chile: CEPAL.

Tavares, M. C. (1964) "Auge y declinación del proceso de sustitución de importaciones em Brasil," *Boletín Económico de América Latina*, March, Santiago de Chile: CEPAL.

12 The Indian economy under economic reforms

Responses from society and the state[1]

Sunanda Sen

1 Introduction

This chapter deals with the integral role of markets in the context of the economic policies pursued by the developing countries, with mainstream theory and the principles used in formulating such policies. Reliance, in particular, is placed on the experience of India as a developing country which has implemented largely market-oriented economic reforms.

Section 2 below deals with the conceptual debates on markets in economic theory and policy which in Section 3 is followed by the central theme of the chapter dealing with state, society and markets in India. Section 3 includes analysis of the early years of industrialization in India which has been followed by steady advances of the market. Next it deals with deregulated finance and labor market reforms, the two major planks in India's reform process. The section ends with an analysis of the failed performance of economic reforms, public protests, and remedial responses by the state in India. The concluding section brings back the conceptual issue of the "Double Movement" of Polanyi which has a lot of relevance in an analysis of state–society relations, especially with the advent of the market in center stage as happened in India.

2 Markets in economic theory and policy

Markets today remain integral to the politics and economics of mainstream neoliberal doctrines. Policy prescriptions, ultimately deriving from the dominant official positions, often share an uncritical acceptance of such positions, thus attaching a great deal of importance to the expansive path of the market. A free market as viewed in neoliberal economic doctrines is supposed to provide opportunities for an economy to maximize output, while providing the best possible returns to capital along with the best available wages for labor.

Viewed from an alternative perspective shared by Marxist circles, the market as an institution can be seen as necessary to promote the expansion of capitalist production processes. Thus capitalism is made possible by the free market, which enables production to be based on wage labor, commodity production, exchange, and capital accumulation, in turn made possible only under wage labor and commodity production.[2] From this angle, market advances are treated as the necessary prerequisite for a capitalist expansionary process. They ensure transformations for competitive capitalism through the compulsion, on the part of capital, to improve productivity, and in the process to extract surplus (labor) value by employing labor working on low wages (equivalent to necessary labor) for survival.

Among the Marxian economists, debate on the historic and institutional specificities of capitalism refers to the role of the markets as an adjunct to capitalism. For the school led by Immanuel Wallerstein and Gunder Frank, the markets remain central in bringing about a world system integrated by trade and exchange—a process that has been underway since the sixteenth century. The process, according to them, also heralded the advent of capitalism.[3] Opposing this position, Maurice Dobb argues that trade and the markets, while necessary, are not sufficient to warrant a path of capitalist expansion. As pointed out, there can be trade even under serfdom, while limiting the accumulation and expansionary process of capitalism. It is held that in the absence of wage labor and commodity production for exchange, it is not possible to have an expanded reproduction which makes for capitalism by using surpluses from wage labor.[4]

However, those positions, while relevant in the context of the accumulation process under advanced capitalism, are not directly relevant for the developing countries, where production and exchange continue to depend on several non-market relations. As the mainstream economists hold, the markets here are distorted, and are responsible for the backwardness of these economies, so that liberalizing and opening up the markets should be a logical cure-all for low growth and underdevelopment.[5]

In our view, to understand the dynamics of capitalist accumulation, one needs to go beyond the standard tools of economics. It is pointed out, in the classic work by Karl Polanyi,[6] that in all societies a set of protective as well as countervailing forces can be found which regenerate and sustain the "mutually supportive relations" in society. As the sphere of the market is enlarged with capitalist expansion, it tends to subordinate and destroy the social fabric with standardized capitalist values embedded in the culture of the global market. This is done by violating the basic human nature as well as such requirements of indigenous people as are fundamental and intertwined with family, community and social relations. In terms of this position, unlimited expansion of the capitalist system along with the market, while generating fast output and accumulation growth, are responsible for causing "dispossession, displacement and human degradation."[7]

Markets (with their adjunct, capitalism), in this alternate view, are sustainable only when they can be "embedded" in society. To some extent this can be achieved with attempts on the part of institutions, including the state, to act in a manner which conforms to the preferences of society. It is usually done by regulating and stabilizing the market economy to achieve some degree of political legitimization. However, in most cases such attempts may well meet with a failure.

Markets, as described above, have sprouted in a large number of countries today, including the transitional economies. For the majority of these countries, and in particular for the developing countries, the expanding market most often remains "dis-embedded" from society. The process often generates reactions from civil society in the country, in the form of social and political protest movements. These reactions, while impairing the pace of the market orientation of society, also help the market itself and the state by bringing up to the surface its limits in terms of what the members of society are ready to accept. Described by Polanyi as a "double movement,"[8] it is a process that is expected only in a functioning democracy.

There remain, however, considerable discrepancies between what is sought after in terms of the social and political movements within a country and what is achievable. The mediating role provided by the state here assumes a great degree of significance in these liberal market economies, where the state is subject to an "existentialist contradiction" between unfettered competition and expansion of capitalism, on the one hand, and the political necessity of sustaining a minimal façade of a mutually supportive and self-reinforcing society on the other.

Rejecting this position, the neoliberal mainstream lobby continues to treat the market as the sole arbiter, using the narrow "economism" of supply and demand. It thus ignores the role of the social institutions which shape civil society, the social and political movements in such societies, and the responses which these social and political movements are capable of eliciting from the state, the community and other voluntary groups.

3 Markets, the state and society in India

The problems which arise with steady expansion of the market are amply evidenced in the rapid transformations of the economy and society which the developing countries are currently going through with globalization. As mentioned above, there has been a similar process in India, which has moved from partial planning and industrialization over the first two or three decades after the country's independence in 1947 to full-scale economic reforms in the direction of liberalization since 1991.

As was to be expected, the response shown within the country, beset by persisting stagnation, unemployment and poverty, consisted of protests and resistance movements on the part of the social and political groups in different parts of the country. The sequence also included policy responses from the state, largely in the form of corrective measures to address the protests and discontent within the country. Both the protests and the policy responses on the part of the state have assumed a greater degree of significance over time, especially with the growing poverty and widening disparity in the Indian economy. It is worth mentioning here that despite the temporary boom the economy experienced, especially during the second half of the first decade of the twenty-first century when GDP was growing on average at nearly 9 percent per year, the living conditions of the majority in the lower income brackets failed to show much improvement.

Conceptually, the popular uprisings as well as the state-led recompenses, however small, can be related to what is described as the Polanyisque "double movement" under capitalist expansion.[9] We can observe the three elements of the "double movement" in India: (1) the state policies (intervention/liberalization) and their impact on the state of the economy and society; (2) the movements originating from civil society and the political groups; and (3) the response of the state in the form of remedial measures.

To bring the above processes into perspective, we will consider the country's progress to a full-fledged market economy, from the early years of planning and industrialization during the 1950s to the economic reforms which started formally in 1991. We will draw attention to the changes which transformed the economy from the early pattern of developmental state to its current shape, placing the market center-stage.

In the following pages we will consider how the "double movement" developed in the context of India, dwelling on the interlinks and the reciprocity between the state and society, relating it in particular to the current phase of globalization, capitalist expansion and marketization.

3.1 Early years of industrialization followed by steady advances of the market

Policymakers in independent India led by the ruling Congress Party followed a path of industrialization which was couched in terms of a closed economy model. Following the example of Soviet industrialization, the policies relied on an import-substituting strategy for industrialization with heavy industries, a large public sector, licensing and controls over trade and industry as well as external payments, and an emphasis on development in science and technology. The initial growth spurts experienced during the first decade or so after independence were followed by economic stagnation in the mid-Sixties. This, along with external pressures, especially from the World Bank and the United States, brought the country up against a steep currency depreciation as well as cuts in capital expenditure, cuts in private investment and a general increase in prices. Intermittent agrarian crises, industrial stagnation and rising food prices, which intensified labor unrest and mass movements at an unprecedented level during the period from the late Sixties to the end of the Seventies, forced the state to come forward with some remedial actions. Alongside the resentment and protests voiced by the opposition political parties as well as the general public, armed resistance movements were demanding land reform in the countryside of Eastern India (Naxalbari). The state responded with a ten-point regulation program which included nationalization of the banks and insurance sector, state trading, controls over monopolistic practices, public distribution of grain and some land redistribution measures. The latter two in particular aimed to address the increasing poverty as well as the armed uprising in the countryside. To deal with the balance-of-payments crisis, exchange control in the external sector was consolidated by the Foreign Exchange Regulation Act (FERA) in 1973 for the prevention of foreign exchange leakage and money laundering. A brief spell of non-Congress-led government followed in the period from 1977 to 1979, continuing with a populist pro-poor agenda which aimed to help small industry, encouraging decentralized administration and implementing food subsidy and employment schemes.

These trends were soon to be reversed as the Congress Party came back to power in the early 1980s with an explicit agenda to introduce a rightward shift in official policies, duly endorsed by the IMF in its conditional loan package to India in 1981. Strict limits were imposed on fiscal deficits as a proportion of the GDP and in the space of a few years several deregulatory measures were introduced in the areas of trade, technology and finance, especially between 1984 and 1989, when Rajiv Gandhi took over as prime minister. Policy measures were brought in to address the growing socioeconomic problems in the economy, with a limited employment program and some measures to improve health, education and the status of women. The set of policies toward further liberalization and deregulation continued with the successive regimes which came to power in the following years, including the National Front between 1989 and 1991. What is noteworthy is that each of these parties and the governments led by them were bent on following a market-oriented neoliberal policy.

3.2 Formal launch of economic reforms: 1991

Economic reform to address the external economic crisis faced by India was the main point on the agenda of the Congress Party which came to power in 1991. The government saw it as a necessity because of the worsening economic situation, with depleted official reserves, large deficits in the balance of payments, and sharp decline in growth rates in almost all the sectors of the economy. In similar crises the Indian state would come forward with some measures of welfarist or developmental policies, but this time economic reform was considered the sole panacea and cure-all to combat the economic crisis. The shift in policy was to dismantle the prevailing controls and regulations in the economy: on trade, technology, finance and even labor. Looking back, the year 1991 can be taken as a watershed in India's official position on economic policies, bent on a series of measures designed to deregulate the economy.

As it turned out, by the mid-1990s there was implicit consensus across India's political parties on the need to forge ahead with the reform process as an irreversible path or the TINA (There Is No Alternative). Deviations from it, at the level of state governments, even represented by left-wing parties, were not seen. As the reader will recall, underlying the policies on economic reform was the neoliberal doctrine of growth through efficiency in free markets, which by this time had already acquired wide acceptance in the official circles of India.

3.2.1 Liberalized trade and technology

As for trade liberalization, the opening up came with the scrapping of quantitative licensing and sharp reduction in duties on imports, both of which were in compliance with the WTO norms. Naturally, the country's import-intensity rose, from 14 percent to 32 percent of GDP between 2000 and 2012.[10] It is worth pointing out that rising imports as a proportion of output, while providing inputs to investment as well as consumption in terms of the new import-intensive technology, also dampen, at least in the short run, the demand for domestic output by an equivalent amount. Displacing import-substituting industries with import-intensive ones can thus be a cause of what we have labeled elsewhere as an "import-led GDP compression."[11] While new products catered to the demand of the upper income groups on the domestic market, the upgraded technology deployed in those also required less labor and more capital and skill per unit of output.

The process of import liberalization had several implications for the Indian economy: one, for example, on the entry of subsidized agricultural products from advanced economies, which made it difficult for local produce to compete in the domestic market. Again, new technology imports, especially of FDI-led production, made it difficult for large sectors of the Indian industry to compete on an equal footing.

Liberalization of the economy has also been instrumental in importing technology, largely capital intensive. In India the advances in indigenous R&D for science and technology over the earlier decades was a fallout of the national patent regime in the country, in which patent rights in India (and also in other developing countries) could only be granted to process technology, and for in-house innovations by local producers. The pattern changed as the use of technology was freed from all restrictions, following the norms set by the WTO initiative for Trade Related Intellectual Property Rights (TRIPs). It may be mentioned here that in terms of neoliberal arguments, technology is viewed as a free public good when the markets are free, and is thus accessible to all countries and for all individuals—a position in accord with the proposition that "the world is flat."[12]

Facilities for open access to technology have also encouraged the inflow of foreign capital to India. With a concerted move on the part of the government to entice FDI inflow over the last few years, FDI shot up from $4.0 billion in 2000–2001 to $46.5 billion by 2011–2012, followed by a marginal drop to $36.8 billion in 2012–2013.[13] Relaxation of the prevailing controls on flow of external finance as well as fiscal incentives along with the ongoing labor market reforms provided further appetite for foreign capital, which was perfectly ready to enter and make use of the expanding domestic market in India. While the inflow of FDI to India does not compare with the spectacular flow to China, which is more than ten times as much, it still stands out as a major achievement among the Emerging Economies.[14]

3.2.2 Deregulated finance

Reforms in India also encompassed several aspects in the realm of *finance*. Official policies on financial reforms included steps to curtail fiscal deficits, use of monetarist measures to target inflation, banking reforms (advocated by the Bank of International Settlement—BIS) to attain financial stability (while failing to provide credit to small and medium industries, or indeed to the poor), and finally, liberalization of external transactions.

Among the above measures, fiscal discipline, initiated in the early 1980s, has gathered momentum. Following the IMF-World Bank recommendation of a stabilization package, a ceiling on fiscal deficit was instituted in India in terms of the Fiscal Reforms and Budget Management Act (FRBMA) of 2003. Successive cuts in the fiscal deficit of the central government as proportion to GDP followed, reducing it from 6.0 percent in 2008–2009 to 4.6 percent by 2011–2012. The cut in the primary deficit[15] (the gap between [defense expenditure, capital expenditure and subsidies] and [tax and non-tax revenue]) was even sharper, dropping from 2.6 percent to 1.6 percent over the same period. With expenditure on defense as a proportion of GDP remaining steady between 1.1 percent to 1.4 percent between 2008–2009 and 2011–2012, the axe came down on major subsidies (for food, fertilizers and petroleum) and capital expenditure. The share of major subsidies actually fell from 2.2 percent (2008–2009) and 2.1 percent (2010–2011) to 1.5 percent (2011–2012) of GDP. As for capital expenditure, which had stood at 2.4 percent (2007–2008) of GDP, it reached a low of 1.8 percent (2011–2012). The gap between the fiscal deficit and the primary deficit has recently been increasing, with interest payments at 3 percent or above of the GDP.[16]

The FRBMA-led fiscal discipline made it obligatory on the part of the government to borrow from the market in order to meet the excess of its expenditure over revenue and other non-debt receipts. This entailed sales of government securities to banks and non-banks, instead of direct acceptance by the central bank (Reserve Bank of India—RBI) which had so far been the practice. This marketized purchase of government securities turned out to be a risk-free option. The buyers included both corporations and banks. The latter's purchase conformed to the capital adequacy norms of the BIS (Basel), which required risk-cover on bank loans. But the measure simultaneously reduced the liquidity which financial institutions could advance to SMEs and the poor for productive activities.[17]

The reform also deregulated the interest structure for banks. Today interest rates on both deposits and advances can be fixed according to what they consider as profitable in the capital market. Norms for priority sector lending, which has continued at 40 percent of net credit by the public sector banks since their nationalization in 1979, have now been diluted. Thus no targets are set for credit advanced to the small sector units, which receive only around 13 percent, and to the weaker section (only 5.4 percent) of the total bank credit flow.[18] These changes openly flout the social norms of the traditional credit policy.

The steady process of capital account opening in India has, since 2003, allowed Foreign Institutional Investors (FIIs) free entry in the country's stock markets, creating ample opportunities for speculation and arbitrage. The recent inflow of portfolio capital has by far exceeded that of the FDIs, creating an atmosphere of speculation-led finance in the economy. Data available from the RBI indicates that the FDI inflow was $34.29 billion for 2012–2013, corresponding to less than one fifth of the gross portfolio inflow during the year ($173.76 billion).

It is worth mentioning here that in contrast with what could be achieved in real terms with FDI (initial public offerings—IPOs) in the primary stock market, short-term portfolio investment catering to the secondary stock markets is incapable of generating fresh investment demand, at least in the first round. Rather, it would create opportunities for speculation, generating uncertainty and volatility in the stock markets while pushing up the returns on financial assets, vis-à-vis both their earnings (the price/earnings ratios) and those on industrial securities. Investment by 3,041 public limited companies in industrial securities, as reported by the RBI, actually fell from 42.1 percent on average during 2002–2003 and 2003–2004 to 7.8 percent on average between 2009–2010 and 2010–2011. The rest naturally goes in the direction of financial securities.[19]

Financial liberalization has thus opened up new opportunities for speculation, which in effect is diverting a considerable part of the investible surpluses away from the industrial sector. Inclinations on the part of corporations and banks to invest in high-yield financial assets had an added impetus with the employees' stock option (ESOP) system, through which the senior employees were paid in part with company stocks. This encouraged the company managers to invest more in financial assets, not only to improve their corporations' balance sheets but also to enhance their personal wealth. ESOPs in the IT companies, as in the US, have been used as a device to attract and retain the skilled employees.

With a steady pace of deregulation in the financial market, speculation in derivatives is taking on a major role. FII-led investment, a large part of which was made in the derivatives market, increased many times more than the transactions in the primary market for IPOs (which create equivalent physical assets). Derivatives in India are used for trading in markets for stocks, currency, real estate and even commodities. According to the latest estimates for 2012–2013, derivative trading in equities, currency and interest rate swaps came to Rs664.97 trillion[20] which is almost 30 times the value of cash trade in the stock markets at Rs23.83 crores[21] during the year. One can also compare the secondary transactions to the rather paltry sum of transactions in the primary market[22] at Rs2.81 trillion, of which the IPOs played an even smaller part (Rs0.06 trillion).[23] Much of the zeal in derivatives trading can be accounted for with the uncertainty in these markets, often generated by volatilities and changing expectations in the international markets. As pointed out earlier, short-term investment such as that in derivatives does not contribute to real output, which is the case with investment via IPOs and other primary market transactions.

It is a fairly straightforward matter to draw the conclusion that the financial reforms in India have neither been for growth in terms of physical assets nor for a fair distribution of the credit flow such as to be not only equitable but also productive. The country has, rather, provided opportunities for speculation in financial assets on such a scale as never witnessed before. Speculation has been considerably facilitated by communication technology, with investors having the facilities to manage their portfolios at the click of a button!

Financial liberalization, with uncontrolled flow of short-term finance from overseas, and to some extent the rising levels of FDI inflow, have done damage to the autonomy of monetary policy on the part of the authorities. As pointed out in the literature, an open capital account (which in India is nearly complete but for resident outflow) and a managed exchange rate leave little leeway for autonomy in monetary policy. Pressures to manage the exchange rate within an acceptable band, which ensures external competitiveness for tradables while sustaining net flow of foreign investment from abroad, often give a dual signal to policymakers. Thus an appreciated local currency, while continuing to attract foreign investors, may prove a disaster for local exporters. This makes it obligatory for the central bank to mediate the market and tone down the currency appreciation by purchasing foreign currency. However, additions to official exchange reserves, which amount to high-powered money, can, in the absence of sterilizing actions by the monetary authorities, push up the supply of money. It thus becomes one more responsibility for the central bank to control the money supply, by raising the domestic rate of interest and/or, as the RBI had been doing, by selling bonds to the public as well as raising the CRAR ratios. Monetary policy in such cases is no longer determined by the domestic requirements and thus ceases to be autonomous. This reflects the trilemma faced by developing countries like India with open capital markets, managed exchange rates and autonomy in monetary policy.[24]

3.2.3 Labor market reforms

Economic liberalization in India has severely impacted the status of labor in the economy. We may mention, in this respect, the official sanction and formalization of casualization in terms of the state-sponsored National Commission of Labor (NCL1992).[25] This was a part of what is described as "systematic arrangement" which, under globalization, was supposed to conform to "competitive capitalism" by introducing "cost-cutting" (evidently achieved with casualization) and the "maximum intensity of labor usage." With casualization and large-scale migration of labor, the contractors have played an important role as intermediaries, profiting from the labor recruitment system. The Report by the NCL had nothing to offer in terms of recommendations on the above labor recruitment practice. Nor did it have any suggestions for the sector employing unorganized labor, which comprises the majority of the workforce in India. Unorganized labor, employed between the formal and informal sectors of industry, constituted around 91 percent of the workforce in 2009–2010.[26] All that was officially recommended by the NCL for this vast pool of unorganized workers was to provide some measure of social security, which was passed in the Indian Parliament in 2008.

It is worth mentioning here that the call for flexible labor in the market, as embodied in the official policies following upon the NCL recommendations, was based on the claim that labor in the process of flexibilization can be not only more productive but can also restore to the workers the much-needed freedom (option) over her/his own freedom in managing her/his own "time." This approach, originating from the methodological individualism that provides the theoretical basis to achieve complete laissez-faire, has been used in mainstream economics to justify unemployment in advanced countries with notions such as the NAIRU (non-accelerating inflation rate of unemployment).[27]

On the whole, labor in India has been subject to a dual process of expropriation—stagnant growth in the major sectors of the economy (which include industry and agriculture, both growing at less than 2 percent during 2012–2013[28]) and the oppressive labor legislation, especially in that by allowing the recruitment of casual labor it guarantees scant benefit on a permanent basis. Official policies designed, as we have seen, to provide for flexibilization of labor were intended to give foreign investors incentives to invest in India by introducing guaranteed labor market flexibility within the country. Incidentally, the scrapping of labor laws in favor of labor market flexibility in India, opening up to "hire and fire" policies, was relevant not only for the FDI-controlled units but also in the EPZ (export processing zone) units in different parts of the country, which had from the outset enjoyed the privilege of operating without following the laws of the land. Also, the move for large-scale privatization of industries, which was often used by the government to raise resources in the name of gaining efficiency, also raised the pressures in favor of labor flexibility. Thus the use of casual labor in larger proportions has also been common in units owned by local capital.[29]

Pressures to dismantle the existing labor laws, even in the organized sector where labor was relatively protected, were often induced by an interest in boosting the FDI inflow as well as the calls for cost-cutting by industry, both local and foreign controlled, in order to retain global competitiveness thanks to cuts in the wage bill. The official position in the country was explicit in the NCL Report, which openly recommended the use of contract labor in view of the uncertain demand from global markets.

3.3 Failed performance of economic reforms, public protests, and remedial responses by the state

Unemployment, poverty, malnutrition, food shortages, food prices rising under speculation, agrarian distress with farmer suicides, widening economic disparities within the country and aspiration gaps prepared the ground for protests which in recent years have spread far and wide in the country. The contrast between the high-speed performance in the prosperous pockets of the economy and abject poverty/acute distress for the rest has contributed to an atmosphere of growing discontent and anger, on a scale which had no precedent. Despite the high or even moderately high growth rates in the Indian economy, especially in the period from 2003–2004 to 2010–2011 when the average growth in GDP was at 8.51 percent, employment growth as reported by official sources was only 1.9 percent on average in the period from 1999–2000 to 2009–2010. While the low level of employment in organized industry absorbed very few in the workforce, even those who were employed were mostly on a temporary basis. Those workers could not avail themselves of benefits like pensions, medical support, paid leave, etc. to complement their wages. Moreover, the wages of these workers were usually set at levels far below the respective labor productivity—a fact which can be explained by the weakened bargaining power of labor in the prevailing scenario. As for the unorganized sector, which has little to do with the prevailing labor laws, it provides nearly 90 percent of the working population in the country. Occupations in the unorganized sector are often referred to in terms of the "self-employed"—providing resources and finance as well as labor on their own. It is natural for labor in such activities to be paid meager sums, either in formal terms as wages or as imputed value of their contribution, often within families. It is thus hardly surprising that the majority of these people live a life close to subsistence.

In contrast with the slow growth and stagnation in the rest of the economy, India's service sector has witnessed a remarkable upsurge, mainly on the strength of the IT sector. It continued to grow at around 11 percent, even after the 2008–2009 crisis, and was contributing to more than one half of the annual GDP growth. However, in the services confined largely to IT, which included the skill-intensive Business Processing Organizations (BPOs), not much could be expected in terms of jobs. As for finance, which also saw a take-off with steady liberalization of the sector, jobs were mostly open to the skilled, while providing profits to those who were in the financial business. The free flow of finance, especially led by FII, was responsible for the marked volatility in markets for stocks, currencies and even commodities. Accumulation of exchange reserves, while generating a sense of complacency in terms of financial stability, has not provided the much-needed autonomy for the monetary authorities, as discussed earlier.

The structural shift in the economy, from brick-and-mortar industries and agriculture to the prosperous services sector, while contributing to GDP growth, proved a failure in terms of employment. Thus we observe a scenario of "jobless growth," with employment in organized industry and services growing at around 1 percent per annum. The pattern even prevails in the high-growth industries with annual average output growth at 20 percent and above, which have employment growth falling far behind, for the rise in labor productivity was made possible by raising capital-intensity per unit of labor. In the absence of offsetting factors such as expansion in the scale of production, employment growth in these industries failed to keep pace with output growth.

It thus remained for agriculture and the informal sector in industry and services to fill in the vacuum in the jobless market for labor, and to support at least 75 percent or more of India's working population who live in the countryside. But the slow or even negative growth of agricultural output in recent years, along with the use of new technology for crops, have made even agriculture less dependent on labor, especially in North India. It is equally unlikely that the services will accommodate the unemployed, both skilled and unskilled, on the scale needed at the moment.

It come as no surprise that poverty seems to have intensified over recent years. In a recent calculation based on a nutritional measure of poverty which considers an adult calorie intake below 2,400 calories per day as the benchmark for poverty,[30] the proportion of people in poverty seems to have risen, from 57 percent of the rural population in 1973–1974 to 73 percent by 2009–2010. The pattern was no less acute for people in the urban areas, where the proportion is found to rise from 58.5 percent to 75.5 percent over the same period. The study challenges the much lower poverty estimates offered by India's Planning Commission, which claims that proportions at 33.8 percent in rural and 20.9 percent in urban areas for 2009–2010.[31] There is, however, ample evidence to confirm the spread of poverty, with one third of the population living on $1 to $2 per day and with their well-being as indicated by the ranking of India in the Global Human Development Index as low as 123 in recent times.

4 Conclusion: the "double movement" of Polanyi

We now dwell on the theme developed earlier in this paper on the "double movement" under capitalism. With economic reforms failing to bring in positive gains for the population in terms of economic conditions and persisting poverty for the masses, resistance and protests movements have become widespread and recurrent. Frequently voiced by civil society, protest is also expressed by the opposition political parties, questioning the policies of the party in power. Repressions by the state machinery along with situations of abject poverty have in some cases changed the forms of protest, with extremist groups turning militant. As protest takes serious turns in form as well as content, the state usually responds with measures to provide some relief, at least in the short run. Thus to continue with a minimal façade of democracy—the minimum mandatory for an elected government—the Polanyisque "double movement" lingers on under capitalism, continuing despite innate apathy on the part of the authority in power, which at best introduces some palliatives.

Recent measures introduced by the Indian state include some legislation in favor of what is perceived as "inclusive development." They include the right to work at a minimum wage in rural areas for at least 100 days in terms of the National Rural Employment Guarantee Act (NREGA) and the Food Security Bill, which offers five kilograms of cereals per month at subsidized rates for two thirds of the population. It is expected to reach out to 1.2 billion people, at a cost of approximately $19.5 billion to the exchequer.[32] As claimed by the exchequer, "The proposed legislation marks a paradigm shift in addressing the problem of food security—from the current welfare approach to a right-based approach."[33] Besides the right to employment and food, there are other "right-based" provisions which include the rights to information (RTI), education, and social security for unorganized workers. Legislation or actions running parallel include the schemes for farm loan waivers, the drive against hoarding to combat an increase in food prices, and related measures. A similar if belated awakening is also visible in the private sector, which is ready today to take on a minimal corporate social responsibility.

While none of these measures are expected to halt the steady advances of the market or address poverty at root level, as well as slow growth in the country, the moves continue to remain little more than symbolic gestures, albeit helping to restore some minimal balance between growth, equity and development. Their effectiveness, in addressing poverty and unemployment along with the other malaises in Indian polity and society, can only be tested over time, with possible continuation of the "double movement" as at present.

Notes

1 Part of this chapter was used in a series of lectures I delivered at the Università del Salento in September 2011. The draft was later included in an e-book by Cosimo Perrotta and Claudia Sunna (eds.), *Globalisation and Economic Crisis*, University of Salento, 2013. Updated statistics as well as new facts and concepts have been used to prepare the present version.
2 Dobb (1946).
3 Sweezy (1950) and Wallerstein (1974).
4 Dobb (1946). See also Khan (2005).
5 See Sen (2007).
6 Polanyi (1944).
7 Levitt (2005, p. 171).
8 Polanyi (1944). See also Levitt (2005).
9 Polanyi (1944).
10 See World Bank "Imports of Goods and Services (% of GDP)," available at: http://data.worldbank.org/indicator/NE.IMP.GNFS.ZS.
11 See Sen (1992).
12 Friedman (2007).
13 See "Fact Sheet on Foreign Direct Investment (FDI) From April, 2000 to July, 2013," available at: http://dipp.nic.in/English/Publications/FDI_Statistics/2013/ india_FDI_July2013.pdf.
14 However, there are some anomalies between the FDI definitions as used in China and India. An attempt was made in 2002 to correct these anomalies by changing the FDI definition in India as per IMF norms to include reinvested earning and inter-corporate borrowings. As a result the gap between FDI inflow in India and China has slightly narrowed down since then. However, some gaps still exist in accounting practices: for example, imports of capital goods used in Foreign Enterprises are treated as FDI in China which is not the case in India.
15 Primary deficit equals the fiscal deficit less interest payments.
16 Government of India (2012–2013, p. A59).
17 We can take here a closer look at the strict credit-risk norms introduced by the BIS. Focusing earlier on Capital Adequacy Ratios (CAR) and, more recently, on a Credit Risk Adjusted Ratio (CRAR), the norms, while helping to improve the quality of bank portfolio by cutting back the Non-Performing Assets (NPAs) in bank portfolios, also created hurdles for the poor as well as persons running small and medium industry, both being subject to financial exclusion. We observe a sharp decline in the flow of credit to the poor and the SMEs, whose share of credit from Public Sector Banks and private banks has fallen sharply in recent years. See Sen and Ghosh (2005); see also Sen and Gottschalk (2010).
18 Government of India (2012–2013, p. 108).
19 Reserve Bank of India Bulletin, relevant years.

20 Reserve Bank of India (2013, Appendix Tables).
21 Government of India (2012–2013, p. 122).
22 Government of India (2012–2013, p. 120).
23 Government of India (2006–2007).
24 See Sen (2012).
25 Government of India (2002). See also Sen and Dasgupta (2009, pp. 188–205).
26 Kannan (2012).
27 See Sen and Dasgupta (2009, pp. 1–22).
28 Government of India (2012–2013, p. 3).
29 For an account of labor insecurity under labor flexibility, see Sen and Dasgupta (2009, pp. 158–174).
30 Patnaik (2013).
31 Patnaik (2013, p. 46).
32 Pain (2013).
33 Government of India (2013).

References

Dobb, M. (1946) *Studies in Development of Capitalism*, London: Routledge.
Friedman, T. L. (2007) *The World is Flat*, New York, NY: Picador Trade Paperback.
Government of India (2002) *Report of the National Commission on Labor*, New Delhi: Government of India.
Government of India (2006–2007) *Economic Survey*, New Delhi: Government of India.
Government of India (2012–2013) *Economic Survey*, New Delhi: Government of India.
Government of India (2013) *Lok Sabha (Parliament) National Food Security Bill 2011, 27th Report*, New Delhi: Lok Sabha Secretariat.
Kannan, K. P. (2012) "How Inclusive is India's Growth?" *Indian Journal of Labor Economics*, 55(1): 31–35.
Khan, M. H. (2005) "The Capitalist Transformation," in Jomo K. S. and E. S. Reinert (eds.) *The Origins of Development Economics*, London: Zed Books, pp. 69–80.
Levitt, K. (2005) "Karl Polanyi as a Development Economist," in Jomo, K. S. (ed.) *Pioneers of Development Economics*, London: Zed Books, pp. 165–180.
Pain, P. (2013) "India's New Food Security Bill Makes Right to Food a Law," September 28, *truthout.org*, available at: http://truth-out.org/news/item/19106-indias-new-food-security-bill-makes-right-to-food-a-law.
Patnaik U. (2013) "Poverty Trends in India 2004–05 to 2009–10," *Economic and Political Weekly*, October 5, 48(40): 43–58.
Polanyi, K. (1944) *The Great Transformation: The Political and Economic Origins of Our Time*, Boston, MA: Beacon Press.
Reserve Bank of India (2013) *Annual Report 2012–13*, Mumbai: Reserve Bank of India.
Reserve Bank of India Bulletin, relevant years, available at: www.rbi.org.in/scripts/ BS_ViewBulletin.aspx.
Sen, S. (1992) "Import Liberalisation as a Tool of Economic Policy Since Mid-Eighties," *Economic and Political Weekly*, 27(12): 585–594.
Sen, S. (2000) *Trade and Dependence: Essays on the Indian Economy*, Delhi: Sage.
Sen, S. (2007) *Globalisation and Development*, New Delhi: National Book Trust of India.
Sen, S. (2012) "Managing Global Financial Flows at Cost of National Autonomy: China and India" in H. Herr, T. Niechoj, C. Thomasberger, A. Truger and T. van Treek (eds.) *From Crisis to Growth: The Challenge of Debt and Imbalances*, Marburg: Metropolis-Verlag.

Sen, S. and Dasgupta, B. (2009) *Unfreedom and Waged Work: Labor in India's Manufacturing Industry*, Delhi: Sage.

Sen, S. and Ghosh, S. K. (2005) "Basel Norms, Indian Banking Sector and Credit to SMEs and the Poor," *Economic and Political Weekly*, March 19, 40(12): 1167–1178.

Sen, S. and Gottschalk, R. (2010) "Basel Norms in India and Brazil," in R. Gottschalk (ed.) *Basel II and Developing Countries*, Basingstoke: Palgrave Macmillan.

Sweezy, P. (1950) "The Transition from Feudalism to Capitalism," *Science & Society*, 14(2): 134–157.

Wallerstein, I. (1974) *The Modern World System*, Atlanta, GA: Academic Press.

13 A mixed effect of globalization on China's economic growth

Hideo Ohashi

1 Introduction

China is currently the largest exporter and foreign exchange holder in the world. In 2010, it surpassed Japan in GDP to become the second largest economy in the world after the United States. Since the reform and opening-up policy was implemented at the end of 1970s, China has sustained the highest economic growth in the world and successfully transformed itself from an agrarian to an industrial society and from a command to market economy.

There is no longer any doubt that China has considerably benefited from globalization, which has accelerated its economic growth and reform. China's income per capita dramatically increased 30-fold in the past three decades of the reform era. At present, however, China is faced with a variety of distortions and discrepancies left from such rapid economic growth including growing inequality, increasing the socially vulnerable, intensifying social unrest, worsening of the environment and flourishing corruption.

This chapter illustrates a mixed effect of globalization on China's economic growth and considers a new direction in its development strategy. Section 2 reviews the process of China's globalization in the past 35 years of the reform and opening-up policy. Sections 3 and 4 highlight China's disparities at home and abroad: income inequality and global imbalances. Section 5 discusses China's efforts in its development strategy to shift from an investment/foreign demand-driven and resources/energy-intensive growth to a more balanced, consumption/domestic demand-led and resources/energy-conserving model. Section 6 concludes.

2 Reform and opening-up policy under globalization[1]

2.1 Foreign direct investment (FDI)

Before launching the reform and opening-up policy at the end of 1970s, China as a large economy was historically a self-sufficient and inward-oriented country. The People's Republic of China (PRC) was founded with these legacies in October 1949, and as a socialist country took a cautious stance to participating in the international division of labor dominated by advanced capitalist countries. One year later, China joined the Korean War in October 1950. As a result, the United Nations imposed an economic embargo upon China, and thus it was practically impossible for China to get into the international economic system. In the 1960s, after China was confronted with the Soviet Union, from which it had received invaluable economic assistance in the previous decade, it suffered a heavy burden of loan repayments to the former alliance partner. These historical experiences led China toward isolation from the outside world and adoption of *zili gengshen* (self-reliance) policy. Implementing the reform and opening-up policy, therefore, must be an unprecedentedly drastic policy change since the founding of the PRC.

In the early 1980s, China's reform and opening-up policy started with establishing four special economic zones in Guangdong (Shenzhen, Zhuhai and Shantou) and Fujian (Xiamen) to attract FDI. These zones served as an entry point for the acceptance of foreign capital and technology, a base for export processing, and an experimental site for capitalist economic management. Foreign business could enjoy preferential tax treatment while both the central and local governments invested in infrastructure in these zones. In addition to attracting FDI, the Chinese government also sought financing from foreign governments and international financial institutions in the form of official development assistance (ODA) and other loans.

In 1984, 14 cities such as Dalian, Tianjin, Shanghai, Guangzhou and other major coastal cities were opened to foreign capital. In the second half of the 1980s, Changjiang or Yangtze River (Shanghai, Jiangsu and Zhejiang), Zhujiang or Pearl River (Guangdong), Minnan (Fujian) Deltas, and Liaodong and Shandong Peninsulas were for the entire region opened to foreign business. In 1992, the upper and middle areas along the Yangtze River, border cities and major inland cities followed suit. China thus reached the final phase of "all-round and multidimensional opening-up" by opening up the whole country to FDI from abroad.

China has been successful in attracting foreign capital, and is currently the second largest host country of FDI in the world, absorbing over $100 billion annually since 2010. The FDI accounted for more than 15 percent of total investment in fixed assets in the mid-1990s, and since then has directly contributed to increases in industrial production, employment, tax revenue and foreign trade in China. In general, FDI takes the form of transfer of managerial resources which include knowledge, production technology, management know-how, marketing experience, human skill, intellectual property, market status, information-gathering ability, and research and development (R&D) capacity. FDI has extensively raised the productivity of Chinese industries through the spill-over effects on them.

Getting into the twenty-first century, Chinese firms began to invest abroad on a massive scale in response to the government policy of *zouchuqu* (going-out) in search for new market opportunities, natural resources and strategic assets including key technologies, international brands and sales outlets. In 2013, a total of 95 Chinese companies were listed in the *Fortune Global 500*, ranking second after the United States (*Renmin Ribao*, July 9, 2013). Being typically seen in three major oil companies,[2] these Chinese firms have grown into global companies, raising huge amounts of money by listing on the Hong Kong, New York, and London stock markets, and aggressively entering the global markets. Thus FDI both inward and outward has remarkably strengthened the competitive global position of Chinese industries, and led to an unprecedented economic growth in China

2.2 Foreign trade

From 1978 to 2012, China's foreign trade increased amazingly by 187-fold. China has also been the world largest exporter and the second largest importer since 2009, while it was ranked in the twenty-ninth in world trade in 1978. China accounted for 11.2 percent and 9.8 percent of the world's exports and imports respectively in 2012.

In the transitional period to the economic opening to the outside world in the early 1980s, a number of Chinese political and academic leaders pointed out the benefits from foreign trade, particularly export, as follows. Foreign trade activities create demands in themselves. Export is regarded as an important source of foreign exchange, which enables China to import capital and intermediate goods essential to economic growth and to get easy access to the advanced technologies embodied in them. Having a wide range of spill-over and demonstration effects, foreign trade leads to productivity gain, technological progress and capital accumulation in Chinese industries at a developing stage.

In fact, China has significantly benefited from foreign trade. With the opening-up to the outside world, a number of competitive foreign products entered the domestic market in China, while Chinese firms involved in export were faced with their competitors in the global market. Foreign trade exposed them to severe competition at home as well as abroad. Competitive pressure engaged Chinese firms in developing new products, innovating technology and upgrading industrial structure for survival. Imported capital and intermediate goods with advanced technologies also raised productivity and reduced production costs.

Expanding production let the economies of scale work properly, and increasingly raised productivity in Chinese industries. With an increase in export production, China gained a sizable amount of foreign exchange, which enabled it to import more consumer as well as capital and intermediate goods. Needless to say, some Chinese firms were forced to exit the market as a result of losing against the competition. Resource reallocation and productivity have been remarkably improved through such tough competition.

In addition, income growth accompanied by an expansion of production diversified Chinese consumers' behavior to a great extent, and stimulated them to import a variety of foreign products. Foreign trade has accelerated economic growth in China by upgrading not only the production but also the consumption structure.

2.3 FDI–trade nexus

In the postwar period, East Asia economies got on the track of high economic growth, heavily depending on their exports to the United States. By the 1980s, the newly industrializing economies (NIEs) achieved rapid economic development by engaging in the following triangular trade—importing capital and intermediate goods from Japan, assembling and processing them into final goods, and exporting them to the United States. In the second half of the 1980s, the NIEs were faced with surges in factor prices in a deteriorating investment environment, and finally moved their production plants to China for their export production to the US market. In the 1990s, Japanese and US manufacturers also established large-scale production bases mainly for the purpose of importing a variety of products manufactured at their plants in China.

In the reform era, an FDI–trade nexus has emerged whereby FDI accelerates economic growth in China and enlarges exports, which in turn attracts another influx of FDI. This virtuous cycle between FDI and trade has been boosting economic growth since the early 1990s and resulted in China becoming the "factory of the world" (Ohashi 2005b).

The dynamic FDI–trade nexus built up multilayered export production network, increased intra-regional trade, and placed China at the center of the international division of labor in East Asia. A new triangular trade has been shaped as follows. Export industries of neighboring economies in East Asia export intermediate goods to their production plants in China, where imported intermediate goods are assembled and processed with abundant labor into final goods, which are ultimately exported to the huge market in the United States. From the 1990s to the mid-2000s, as China expanded exports to the United States, it inevitably increased imports of parts and materials from its neighbors. As a result, China has a large trade surplus with the United States and Europe, while it has a significant trade deficit with its neighbors.

According to Mori and Sasaki (2007) using the "Asian International Input-Output Tables," the production inducement effect of China has been expanding in the Asia-Pacific region in the first half of the 2000s. Regional interdependence has further deepened by an increase in intra-regional trade of intermediate goods, and China as a "factory of the world" has played the most important role in creating regional intermediate demands. As of the mid-2000s, however, East Asian economies were still heavily dependent on the outside-regional final demands of the United States.

As a result of sustained economic growth and rising income in China, there is a new indication that China has recently become a main source of regional final demands. Through a decade of the 2000s, processing-trade imports have dropped little by little while general-trade imports have gradually increased in China's foreign trade. Paying attention to a distinct decline in intermediate goods ratio to the total imports, Park and Shin (2010) indicates that China's trade deficits with Korea and Taiwan was mostly composed of parts and components in 1996, but final goods occupied a larger part in 2007. It might well be able to conclude that

China has become a main source of regional final demands in East Asia. Faced with the international financial crisis in the late 2000s, China has changed shape to the "market of the world."

2.4 Market transition

China's "socialist market economy" set as a development model by the Chinese Communist Party (CCP) in 1992 is not totally different from the economic systems in advanced capitalist countries. In China's economic system, however, the government has a tendency to intervene in the market more recurrently and extensively than those of advanced capitalist countries. At the same time, Chinese firms including the state-owned enterprises (SOEs), foreign invested enterprises (FIEs) and private firms are competing against one another in this system more aggressively than those of advanced capitalist countries.

Market transition is most clearly reflected in the structure of industrial production by ownership. According to the *China Statistical Yearbook 2012*, the state-owned and state-holding enterprises accounted for 26.2 percent of gross industrial output value in 2011. The share has dropped consistently from 49.6 percent in 1998. FIEs' share, once rising to more than 30 percent, declined to 25.9 percent in 2011. The share of "other companies" substantially representing private companies has risen from 25.6 percent to 47.9 percent in the same period (National Bureau of Statistics of China 2012, pp. 508, 518, 538). These changes have been caused at first by the opening-up policy to encourage FIEs, then by the reform policy to promote private business and privatization of SOEs.

In pursuing the opening-up policy, both FIEs and international transactions have remarkably increased in number. Quantitative expansion has resulted in qualitative changes in China's economy. Foreign companies brought global standards into China in such areas as corporate governance, accounting, technology and other business customs. Chinese firms have effectively tried to adapt themselves to the existing international economic regimes of trade, investment, services, finance, intellectual property, energy and communication. The opening-up policy has boosted market transition in China by globalizing the firms and industries.

In this context, China's accession to the World Trade Organization (WTO) in 2001 symbolized the integration of China into the global economy. From the viewpoint of globalization, as China increasingly set up its presence in the global economy, it was regarded as an indispensable member of the WTO regime. China's current positive commitments to the free trade agreement (FTA) undoubtedly show that it is fully conscious of invaluable benefits from foreign trade. Trade liberalization has so much in common with market-oriented reforms. In other words, the opening-up policy has effectively encouraged market-oriented reforms in China.

3 Rising domestic disparity

3.1 Rising Inequality

In the reform era, China's rapid and sustained economic growth raised the level of household income and improved the living standard of the poor. The poverty rate fell from more than 65 percent to less than 10 percent as some 500 million people were lifted out of poverty (World Bank and Development Research Center of the State Council 2012, p. 4). However, the fruits of economic growth were not proportionately shared among the people, and there was no mechanism to ensure more equitable distribution of wealth in China.

As a result, inequality has climbed steadily as reflected by the Gini coefficient throughout the reform period (Figure 13.1). In the early 1980s, the agriculture and rural reforms raised the income of peasant households and as a whole reduced the inequality to some extent. After the mid-1980s, when the primary focus of the reform and opening-up policy was placed on the industry and urban sectors, the regional disparity widened rapidly mainly because of massive inflows of foreign capital to these sectors. In the late 1990s, the reform of SOEs caused large-scale unemployment and a number of successful entrepreneurs

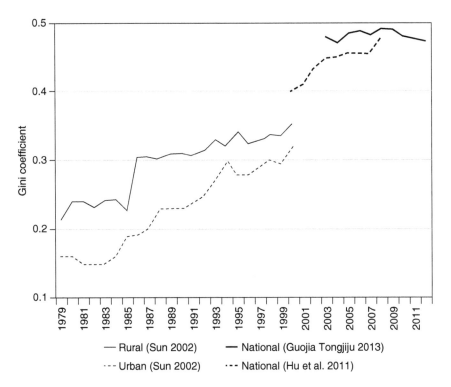

Figure 13.1 Rising inequality in China (Gini Coefficient) (sources: Sun 2002, p. 389; Hu et al. 2011, p. 1433; Guojia Tongjiju 2013).

emerged at the same time. Rising income inequality led to expanding disparity between the "winners" and the "losers" in the competitive market-oriented reform.

At present, China is a high income inequality country by the standard of East Asia,[3] although there are a number of developing countries with higher income inequality than China in the world. According to the State Bureau of Statistics (Guojia Tongjiju 2013), China's Gini coefficient once rose to 0.491 in 2008, and then showing a slight decline, as if it were following the Kuznets curve—the inverse U-shaped pattern of inequality.[4] Nowadays, the wages of migrant workers are rising noticeably and the economic growth rates of inland areas are much higher than those of prosperous coastal cities. However, the social survey conducted by Beijing University in 2012 reported that the disparities across the whole population were mirrored by large divides between the richest and the poorest, indicating that there was a desperate income gap of 234-fold between the richest and the poorest 5 percent households (*Nanfang Chengshibao*, July 18, 2013).

Needless to say, it is impossible to attribute rising inequality only to the reform and opening-up policy. Current inequality is an extension of the following experiences in China. First, initial disparities have existed since the early times of the Chinese Empire. As a physically big country, China has had large urban–rural and coastal–inland disparities. Large disparities in income and living standards have therefore existed between coastal cities and inland rural villages.

Second, the socialist management system under the planned economy reinforced disparities in the pre-reform era. The *hukou* (residence register) system, for example, confined most of the rural population in people's communes and prevented their migration to urban areas with high productive industrial sectors. Fiscal transfers to poverty areas did not work effectively under the decentralized and inflexible administration system.

Finally, after launching the opening-up policy, urban residents in coastal cities have become major beneficiaries of foreign trade and FDI. In the reform era, the reform and opening-up policy have certainly raised household income and living standards as a whole, but at the same time it has led to rising disparities in China.

3.2 Disparity in the outward oriented development

The reform and opening-up policy are based on the theory of *xianfu* (earlier enrichment) proposed by China's paramount leader, Deng Xiaoping, in the reform era. He rejected the false egalitarianism in the name of equality under the socialist system and motivated people to get rich. The theory of earlier enrichment allowed some people and areas under the right conditions to get rich sooner, also suggesting that the early wealthy should help the poor and step by step the whole society would realize the ultimate goal of common wealth (Deng 1983, p. 142). At the early stage of implementing the reform and opening-up policy, the first part of Deng's words was disproportionately emphasized, and the second part to offer hands to the poor was temporarily overlooked. Gaps and disparities were widely accepted by the Chinese people who began to seek wealth.

Following Deng's theory of earlier enrichment, in January 1988, then-CCP General Secretary Zhao Zhiyang proposed the Development Strategy of the Coastal Region (*Renmin Ribao*, January 23, 1988). He emphasized opening up the whole coastal region with better infrastructure and human resources, to seize the historical opportunity of international industrial adjustments triggered by appreciation of Japanese and NIEs currencies, and to promote the processing trade of labor-intensive industries utilizing rich labor resources in coastal region.

Zhao's proposal was based on the theory of *guoji jingji daxunhuan* (great circulation of international economies) published by Wang Jian, an economist of the economic institute of the State Planning Commission. He gave top priority to export industries and infrastructure development in the coastal region in the first phase, then to the labor-intensive industries in inland areas in the second phase. In so doing, China would finally promote capital/technology-intensive industries with foreign exchange gained by export (*Jingji Ribao*, January 5, 1988).

Despite having much consideration for inland areas, the Development Strategy of the Coastal Region drew harsh criticism as being conducive to regional disparity of coastal–inland areas. Then, Zhao made little mention of the strategy under criticism, but regardless of policy preferences, production factors were inherently directed to and concentrated in the coastal region with better conditions for economic development.

The Development Strategy of the Coastal Region was premised on the dual economy comprising the underproductive traditional sector with surplus labor and the profit-seeking modern sector with advanced technology. In other words, Zhao proposed to borrow the development experiences of the NIEs, which had successfully caught up with the front-runners of advanced economies in a shorter period of time by promoting production and export in labor-intensive industries under the condition of "unlimited supplies of labor" (Lewis 1954).

China's political leaders were fully aware of economic success achieved by the NIEs, with which they had cultural affinity.[5] In addition to the economic success of the NIEs, China's economic development strategy had been deeply affected by the policy recommendations of the World Bank. Since China joined the IMF/World Bank system in 1980, the World Bank had proposed a number of critical reforms to China. Particularly, the Development Strategy of the Coastal Region seemed to have absorbed the concept of outward-oriented development and appeared in the *World Development Report*, 1987 edition, featuring the relationship between industrialization and trade (World Bank 1987). The *Report* clearly presented that the outward-oriented economies were better than the inward-oriented economies in their economic performance. Coupled with the neoclassical resurgence in economic theory, the outward-oriented strategy inevitably accompanies liberalization and deregulation under a small government, which are closely related to globalization of the world economy.

The *Report* explicitly indicated a significant correlation between economic performance and outward-oriented strategy, although it is not easy to demonstrate the causal relationship between them. Obviously, the main idea of the *Report* stimulated Zhao to propose the new development strategy because it also emphasized the concept of *waixiangxing fazhan* (outward-oriented development).

3.3 Rising inequality in incomplete reforms

In the mid-2000s, the CCP leadership represented by Hu Jintao and Wen Jiabao set a new goal for building a *hexie shehui* (harmonious society) to curb disparities, corruption and environmental degradation, in other words, to redress distortions and discrepancies caused by the reform and opening-up policy.

Inequalities triggered by the opening-up policy are exacerbated by incomplete reforms. China's economic reform at the early stage was usually characterized as incrementalism in comparison with the "big bang" reform in Russia. Incrementalism means a gradual approach to an economic reform to use the existing framework, to ensure stability and to avoid collisions with vested interests. Incremental reform does not deal with redistribution of assets themselves, but focuses on the increment part of assets. It could be effectively implemented in the form of a dual-track system composing of both planned and market economies. In a dual-track system of this kind, it is really difficult to reform the core sectors of a planned economy such as the SOEs and state-owned banks. At the same time, a dual-track system inevitably accompanies rent-seeking activities primarily between planned and market economies.

By the turn of the century, a dual-track system was already dispersed in an accelerated market-oriented reform for the preparations for accession to the WTO. But there is not yet any definite and transparent rule for asset ownership, which currently contributes to rising inequalities in China. Housing for example is estimated to account for almost a half of household wealth (Ohashi 2005a, p. 175). In a huge real estate boom in major cities, a disparity in urban–rural housing wealth is significantly higher than the urban–rural income gap.

Inequalities are also reflected by the disparities in opportunities. It is true that China successfully expanded the coverage for social services and a safety net after the SOEs reform accompanying sizable unemployment in the late 1990s. But the opportunities for enhancing human capital, living a healthy life and having trustworthy social security measures depend on where a person lives and what kind of resident registration he or she has—rural or urban, coastal or inland, and migrant or local resident in urban areas. Particularly, the residence registration system prevents migrant households from having good education, health care and housing in urban areas. Despite China's recent efforts to expand coverage for social services and social security, there is unbridgeable gap in status between migrant and local residents. China is still at the stage of facilitating access to opportunities and promoting greater equality.

It is quite natural that the fruits of economic growth should be distributed to certain people and localities endowed with production factors such as capital, technology and entrepreneurship. Human capital equipped with higher education and technology should get greater access to the fruits. The beneficiaries from the reforms have been recurrently produced in China, while a number of "losers" in the reforms have also emerged in the past decade. Moreover, China's economy is still in a transition to a market economy. Being far from a perfectly competitive market, it is prone to market failure. At the same time, it is occasionally trapped in the "government failure," which has a tendency to intensify disparities in China.

4 Growing global imbalances

4.1 Global imbalances and China

The rise of China's economy has provided a wealth of opportunities not only to China but to the world economy as a whole. At the same time, from the viewpoint of global imbalances, China as the world's largest exporter and foreign exchange holder frequently receives harsh criticism from current account deficit countries, especially the United States. China has given top priority to economic growth without properly considering investment efficiency, resources and environmental constraints, and the limit of "extensive growth" heavily depending on capital investment. Excessively export-dependent and FDI-led growth is also held so much in doubt.

Since the 1980s, a primary focus of global imbalances has been placed on the huge current account surplus of Japan. By the early years of the twenty-first century, China's current account surplus soared and amounted to more than $420 billion in 2008. In general, the following arguments have been made as to the causes of current global imbalances.

First, savings shortages and overspending in the United States are repeatedly indicated. Increased military spending for anti-terrorism and recurrent tax cuts considerably increased the budget deficit. In the real estate boom, financial engineering enabled general households to expand consumption to the maximum on a basis of future income. As a result, US household consumption expenditure exceeded its disposable income, and household savings were turned negative in 2006. According to then-Premier Wen Jiabao, the global economy fell into a serious imbalance because an economy (implying the United States) maintained excessive consumption depending on the "twin deficits" and huge debts (*Financial Times*, February 1, 2009).

Second, excessive issuance of US dollars is also criticized. After then-President Nixon cancelled the direct convertibility of the US dollar to gold in 1971,[6] there is no consensus on international key currency. The US unilateral attitude for seeking seigniorage profit has significantly erased international confidence in the US dollar. Immediately before the G20 London Summit in April 2009, Governor Zhou Xiaochuan of the People's Bank of China highlighted the following contradiction. A particular currency of a specific country is widely accepted as an international reserve currency, while the country is individually pursuing its own national interests. Proposing to create a reserve currency beyond the framework of the sovereign state, Zhou put forward an idea to expand the function of the special drawing rights (SDR) at the International Monetary Fund (IMF) (*Xinhuanet*, March 24, 2009). Zhou's proposal was obviously a sharp criticism of the US monetary policy.

Third, a saving glut all over the world also leads to much debate. According to then-Chairman Bernanke of the Federal Reserve Bank (Fed), current account surpluses of oil exporters rose as oil revenues surged. Major industrial countries had both strong reasons to save to help support future retirees and increasingly limited investment opportunities at home because workforces were shrinking. And the countries that had escaped the worst effects of the crisis but remained concerned about future crises also built up reserves (Bernanke 2005). As stated by former Treasury Secretary Paulson, several years prior to the international financial crisis, high savings in oil-producing countries and China became a downward pressure on interest rates, which led to a credit bubble on a global scale and to a collapse in the end (*Financial Times*, January 2, 2009). From the viewpoint of the United States, China's excess savings flowed into the US financial and capital markets on a massive scale for abundant investment opportunities, which resulted in the current global imbalances.

Finally, not a few US lawmakers try to attribute China's current account surplus to its mercantilist and developmentalist policies including export promotion, import substitution, undervalued exchange rate, financial repression and industrial policy. These measures artificially enhance the competitiveness of Chinese products in the US market, while China prevents US products from getting into its domestic market (USCC 2012).

4.2 China's responses to global imbalances

China's abundant foreign exchange reserves and huge current account surplus are usually regarded as symbols of trade friction between China and the rest of the world. In addition, faced with the excessive liquidity they cause, China is under pressure to undertake cautious macroeconomic management. In this context, China launched the following policy measures to curb exports and expand imports in the mid-2000s. Obviously, these measures were taken in view of the negative effects of macroeconomic imbalances on China's domestic economy.

China embarked on restructuring of export industries. Among others, *lianggao yizhi* (high energy and resource consuming, high polluting, and primary resources) products/industries were tightly targeted for adjustment of production. The target was later expanded to low value-added, low-tech and labor-intensive products/industries and the "symbolic items" of trade friction.

China also took the border control measures to discourage exports and spur imports. First, export-related value-added tax (VAT) rebate was gradually reduced. An export-tax rebate system was originally launched as an incentive for promoting exports in 1994. But a rebate cut was introduced in 1999 to curb the trade surplus, and by the middle of 2007 it was applied to most of customs clearance items in China.

Second, the processing trade was adjusted to curb exports and to upgrade its industrial structure. In the mid-2000s, the FIEs accounted for 80 percent of the processing trade, comprising most of the trade surplus in China. It is often indicated that the FIEs gained a large amount of profits in the processing trade through transfer pricing while Chinese firms received only a small sum of processing fees.[7] Moreover, the processing trade mainly dealt with low value-added, low-tech and labor-intensive products. Chinese firms were basically dependent on imports in high-tech industries (Zhongguo Renmin Yinhang Huobi Zhengce Fenxi Xiaozu 2006, pp. 29–30). The processing trade's banned list of 804 items was announced in November 2006 and its restriction list of 1,853 items in August 2007.

Third, export duties were introduced. The main objects of taxation are resource products whose export capacities were very limited by a surge in domestic demands. As for the "symbolic items" of trade friction such as steel products, China took extensive export controls that combined a couple of the measures mentioned above. At first, in April 2007, the government abolished the export VAT rebate system for 83 items. Then, in May 2007, it introduced the export license system for some steel products. Finally, in June 2007, export tax was applied to 142 items including energy-consuming steel products and rare metals.

Correspondingly, the Foreign Investment Industrial Guidance List was revised in November 2007, which showed a similar selective stance toward export industries. First, China tightly restricted FDI in energy-consuming and polluting industries, low-tech products and real estate. Second, it promoted not only high-tech, energy-conserving and environment-friendly industries but also tertiary industries including finance, logistics and services in the coastal region. Third, it encouraged labor-intensive export industries in inland areas.

At the same time, China has deeply committed to the expansion of imports by dispatching purchase missions to the United States and European countries, and by improving access to China's domestic market.

4.3 China's exchange rate adjustment

Since the trade friction between the United States and Japan intensified in the 1980s, the United States has repeatedly requested Japan to appreciate the Japanese yen as the main means to redress the current-account imbalance. As seen in the cases of the "Nixon shock" in 1971 and the Plaza Accord in 1985, however, the exchange rate adjustments did not contribute significantly to reducing the US current-account deficit. Unless the saving–investment balance is effectively corrected, it is impossible to improve the current-account imbalance. Former Chairman Greenspan of the Fed explicitly pointed out that the revaluation of the Chinese currency (*renminbi* or RMB) had little impact on the US imports from China, and the US imports of textiles, light manufactures, assembled computers, toys and similar products would in part shift from China as the final assembler to other emerging-market economies in Asia and in Latin America (Greenspan 2005).

China has taken an extremely cautious stance toward capital liberalization. In the global economy today, financial transactions are far larger in value than the deals of the real economy. Developing countries are substantially at risk of capital liberalization because their financial sectors are not institutionally matured enough to withstand instability caused by huge capital movements. Under the "impossible trinity,"[8] China has maintained the pegged exchange rate to the US dollar and secured independent monetary policy by limiting capital flows. After China's accession to the WTO, however, as capital flows dramatically increase, China is in a transition to a more flexible exchange rate regime in order to maintain independent monetary policy. So far as China adheres to the pegged exchange rate to the US dollar, there is no alternative for China but to follow the US monetary policy.

In July 2005, China embarked on the RMB reform, which consisted of devaluing the RMB by 2 percent against the US dollar and adopting a managed floating system. Since the RMB reform was launched, except for the period of international financial crisis approximately between summer 2008 and spring 2010, the RMB has constantly risen against the US dollar. In other words, China accepted the appreciation of RMB. But this is not because China responded to foreign pressures caused by trade friction, but because it gave priority to controlling inflation and maintaining an independent monetary policy. As a result, the US dollar continued to fall against other major currencies and the RMB has been substantially appreciated since the RMB reform was launched.

Contrary to expectations, however, China actually increased exports to the United States during the period of rising RMB. In this regard, there are a variety of explanations; for example, Chinese export firms reduced their profit margins to avoid the impact of RMB appreciation. But it is almost impossible to find any evidence that positively supports such an explanation. According to Goldstein and Lardy (2009, p. 23), the RMB was appreciated by 9 percent against the US dollar from June 2005 to August 2007, but there were no changes in the import prices of Chinese products in the United States in the same period. It is therefore not the export prices in terms of a real effective exchange rate but the productivity difference between tradable and non-tradable goods that raised the competitiveness of Chinese products in the global market. Productivity gains of China's export industries successfully absorbed the negative impacts of the RMB appreciation.

What has enhanced the productivity of export industries in China? Obviously, the FDI, technology transfer and organizational innovation played very important roles in the rapid industrialization in China. In addition to those, being located at a hub of the regional export production network, China has become the "factory of the world." In this context, China is deeply involved in the export production network in East Asia, which has brought productivity gains to its export industries (Ohashi 2006).

First, the product architecture revolution has made positive contributions to rapid industrialization in China, where the FIEs specialize in manufacturing and exporting modular products.[9] A preference for modular products has enabled China to swiftly catch up with advanced economies in some industries.

Second, the fragmentation of integrated manufacturing processes into smaller production blocks has increased FDI and the intra-industry trade in East Asia. Since modular products have well-standardized interfaces, they can be manufactured in the most suitable places for each manufacturing process. In addition, innovation in telecommunications and logistics has dramatically reduced the service-link costs between production blocks. A number of manufacturers tend to place China in the center of the export production network in East Asia.

Third, the agglomeration of industries attracts FDI in China. Manufacturers tend to cluster together in order to reduce their production and business costs. They can gain a number of advantages from quick procurement and delivery of parts and components at industrial clusters, which enable them to share technology and information, to reduce transaction costs and to enhance their political voice.

5 New direction in China's economic development

5.1 China's saving–investment balance

The series of policy measures described above reflects China's efforts to ease trade friction, but it is impossible for these "border controls" to reduce a current-account surplus. Indeed these measures could temporarily contribute to a reduction in trade surplus, but they are likely to lead to depreciation of the RMB exchange rate. As a result, the "border controls" would encourage export in the long run. So long as the saving–investment balance is firmly maintained, both export control and import promotion measures would not be able to change the trade balance at all.

In fact, China's rising disparities should be considered from a basic viewpoint of the saving–investment balance. China has excessively accumulated savings since the mid-1990s. The other side of the coin is that China has maintained a sizable current-account surplus at the same time (Figure 13.2). In the past, there were certainly some economies with excess savings primarily due to investment slumps. But China's investment and saving rates have respectively continued to rise since the turn of the century, and the saving rate in particular has been at a high level of more than a half of GDP since the mid-2000s.

Having a considerable influence on household consumption, excess savings are prone to producing rising disparities in China. China's household final consumption expenditure fell to a low level of 35.7 percent of GDP in 2012, almost half the level of household final consumption expenditure in the United States. Since the low-income households tend to spend a higher share of their income than the high-income households, it is really important to correct income disparities.

A long-awaited reform plan of income distribution was released by the State Council in February 2013 (Guowuyuan 2013). The new 35-point reform plan is

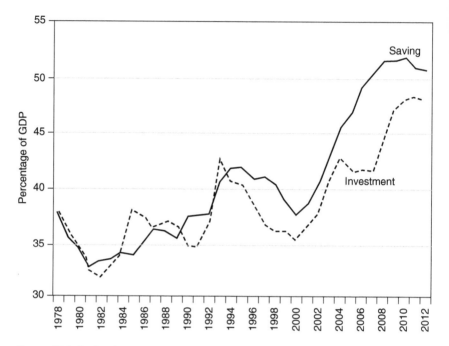

Figure 13.2 Saving-investment balance in China (as per cent of GDP) (source: National Bureau of Statistics of China 2013, p. 62).

aimed at doubling personal income by 2020, raising the minimum wage, loosening controls on lending and deposit rates, and increasing spending on education and affordable housing. The plan also encourages the SOEs to spend more of their profits on reducing inequality, and gives the steps for a further interest rate reform to give a better return to depositors.

In this context, the government is vigorously engaged in rebalancing the economy, and shifting it away from heavy reliance on investment and exports to increased consumption in order to ensure stable economic growth.

5.2 Rebalancing the Chinese economy

In order to redress domestic disparities and global imbalances, it is necessary for China to eliminate excess savings effectively. According to the "life cycle hypothesis" in the analysis of household savings on a basis of the age structure of the population, an increasing dependency ratio of children and the elderly to the working population aged between 15 and 64 years simply means an declining saving ratio, and vice versa (Horioka and Wan 2006).

In the case of China, on the one hand, coupled with a decreasing birth rate triggered by adopting the one-child policy in the late 1970s, the child dependency ratio has drastically fallen to its lowest level. On the other hand, China is about to enter the era of an aging society and the old-age dependency ratio is still moderate at the current stage. Considering customary factors, China's excess savings at present entirely reflect a relatively low level of total dependency ratio in households (Figure 13.3).

China's savings are also influenced by the following factors. First, China needs to maintain a certain level of saving to investing in poverty. Second, the RMB appreciation should be an important policy measure to increase purchasing power and to spur consumption. Third, from the viewpoint of encouraging consumption, it is critically important to reinforce the safety net, which was shredded in the process of enterprise reform in the late 1990s. In addition to slowing the growth of disposable income of households, increasing precautionary savings caused by insufficient social security has raised the saving rate and led to a consumption slump in China. Both education and housing, for which Chinese enterprises were responsible during the pre-reform period, have become heavy burdens for households under the beneficiaries-pay principle in the reform period. Both of them currently serve as the main driving forces to encourage precautionary savings.

Moreover, China's redistribution policy is also fraught with serious problems. Fiscal revenue has been increasing as a whole due to sustained strong growth, but public expenditure for social services and security currently shows a downward trend. As a result, fiscal resources are transferred in an opposite direction from households to the government.

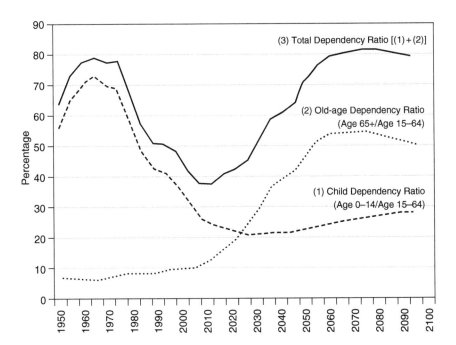

Figure 13.3 Child and old-age dependency ratios to working population in China (source: UN 2011).

5.3 *Reducing corporate savings*

It is a great challenge for the time being that China should efficiently reallocate excess savings of the corporate sector to the household sector to spur private consumption. China's corporate sector has been recently produced good performance as a whole for the following reasons.

First, Chinese companies in general have enjoyed low input costs. Fuel, power and water prices have been maintained at a lower level for a long time. Land acquisition costs also have been far below the market prices. Forcible expropriation and incomplete compensation have frequently caused social unrest and riots in rural areas. Moreover, Chinese firms have been indifferent to environmental protection costs.

Second, Chinese firms, large-sized SOEs in particular, have fully benefited from low capital costs. Most of them are usually able to get easy access to bank loans under the financial repression. Since Chinese banks held huge amounts of non-performing loans in the late 1990s, they have favored large companies as being safe and secure borrowers. Immediately after the international financial crisis triggered by a collapse of Lehman Brothers in fall 2008, China launched economy-boosting measures costing RMB4 trillion to ensure 8 percent growth. The SOEs turned out to be the biggest beneficiaries from these policy measures, which further strengthened the tendency of SOE dominance in China's economy or *guojin mintui* (advancement of state-owned sector and retreat of private sector). Meanwhile, China's small and medium-sized enterprises (SMEs) cannot usually get any bank loans, and most of them have no choice but to rely on self-financing. In this way, the SMEs also accumulate excess savings. China's corporate sector as a whole has excess savings, structurally.

Third, Chinese firms have made the best use of low-cost labor. After a number of manufacturers suffered from a labor shortage in the Pearl River Delta in 2004, they finally changed their wage policies and began to raise minimum wages. The Labor Contract Law was enforced in 2008 in order to provide workers with a sufficient degree of protection. Wages have since then continued to rise, and a number of labor disputes have been repeatedly reported in the Chinese media. Until the mid-2000s, Chinese firms distributed a smaller portion of their profits to workers under the conditions of "unlimited supplies of labor." The labor share or compensation of employees in GDP fell from 52.8 percent to 39.7 percent between 1997 and 2007, while corporations' operating surplus rose from 20.4 percent to 31.3 percent in the same period.

China is still at the critical stage of promoting further economic reform including correction of factor prices, adjustment in income distribution and strengthening corporate governance. Financial reform is particularly vital to accelerating market transition to consumption/domestic demand-led growth and to rectifying domestic disparities and global imbalances.

6 Conclusion

In the long term, it would be difficult to reverse the trend of globalization in the world economy. In the short term, however, the process of globalization is temporarily at a standstill due to the prolonged economic stagnation after the international financial crisis. First, the resonance of business cycles among major economies has considerably faded out. Second, the international capital flows have fallen sharply. Finally, the regional free trade agreement (FTA) has become a main framework of the international trade regime while the multilateral trade negotiations at the WTO have been sluggish.

In the quest for consumption/domestic demand-led growth, China's economy is gradually deviating from the past high-growth path. Considering a drop in the potential economic growth rate mainly due to demographic change, it is almost impossible to foresee China's double-digit economic growth in the near future. In 2012, China's working population decreased for the first time. Surplus labor forces are almost eliminated in the coastal areas because new job opportunities are massively created in the inland labor markets under the strategy of China's Western Development. Even if China's economy goes through a phase of recovery, the growth rate will not return to the high levels seen before.

Since Premier Li Keqiang took office in March 2013, he has taken a different policy path from that of his predecessor. His economic policy framework was summarized as "Likonomics" consisting of three pillars—no stimulus, deleveraging and structural reform. There seems to be a consensus that China should tolerate slower growth and focus on structural reform (Huang 2013).

Faced with increasing opposition from the vested interests in the 1990s, then-Premier Zhu Rongji pushed through structural reform using external pressure over China's accession to the WTO as the main driving force for structural adjustment. Globalization certainly caused China's widening disparities and deteriorating imbalances, but it could continue to function as an external pressure to promote structural reform.

Notes

1 As for the general picture of China's earlier reform and opening-up policy, see Ohashi (2003 and 2005a).
2 They are China Petrochemical Corporation (Sinopec), China National Petroleum Corporation (CNPC), and China National Offshore Oil Corporation (CNOOC).
3 Economic development in East Asia is often characterized as growth with equality.
4 Kuznets (1955) documented that as countries developed, income inequality first increased, peaked and then decreased using both cross-country and time-series data.
5 In particular, Deng Xiaoping is noted for a deep appreciation of Singaporean experiences, stating "the social order is good in Singapore. They have a strict management system. We have to learn from their experiences" (Deng 1993, pp. 378–379).
6 It is called the "Nixon shock" in Japan.
7 In the case of cost structure in manufacturing iPhone, for example, what belongs to China is only 3.6 percent of the shipping price (Rassweiler 2009).
8 In macroeconomic management, there must be a trade-off of choosing two, not all, of the three policy choices: monetary independence, exchange rate stability and financial

openness. This is called the "impossible trinity" or the "trilemma" in international finance.

9 Since the interface is essentially standardized, parts and components of modular products can be widely outsourced in the open market with lower prices and easily assembled by unskilled workers.

References

Bernanke, B. S. (2005) "The Global Saving Glut and the U.S. Current Account Deficit," Federal Reserve Board, March 10, available at: www.federalreserve.gov/ boarddocs/speeches/2005/200503102/default.htm.

Deng, X. (1983) *Deng Xiaoping Wenxuan* (*Selected Works of Deng Xiaoping*), Beijing: Renmin Chubanshe (People's Publishing House).

Deng, X. (1993) *Deng Xiaoping Wenxuan* (*Selected Works of Deng Xiaoping*), Volume 3, Beijing: Renmin Chubanshe (People's Publishing House).

Goldstein, M. and Lardy, N. R. (2009) "China's Exchange Rate Policy: An Overview of Some Key Issues," in Morris Goldstein and Nicholas R. Lardy (eds.) *Debating China's Exchange Rate Policy*, Washington, DC: Peterson Institute of International Economics.

Greenspan, A. (2005) "Testimony of Chairman Alan Greenspan," Committee on Finance, US Senate, June 23, available at: www.federalreserve.gov/boarddocs/testimony/2005/20050623/default.htm.

Guojia Tongjiju (State Bureau of Statistics) (2013) "Ma Jiantang Jiu 2012 Nian Guomin Jingji Yunxing Qingkuan Da Jizhe Wen (Ma Jiantang Had a Press Conference on the Current Conditions of National Economy)," January 18, available at: www.stats.gov.cn/tjgz/tjdt/201301/t20130118_17719.html.

Guowuyuan (State Council) (2013) "Guanyu Shenhua Shouru Fenpei Zhidu Gaige de Ruogan Yijian (Several Opinions on Deepening the Reform of the Income Distribution System)," February 3, available at: www.gov.cn/zwgk/2013-02/05/content_2327531.htm.

Horioka, C. Y. and Wan, J. (2006) "The Determinants of Household Saving in China: A Dynamic Panel Analysis of Provincial Data," *NBER Working Paper*, No. 12723.

Hu, Z., Liu, Z. and Gong, Z. (2011) "Zhongguo Zongti Shouru Jinixishu de Guji (Estimates of China's Overall Income Gini Coefficient): 1985–2008," *Jingjixue Jikan* (*China Economic Quarterly*), 10(4): 1423–1436.

Huang, Y. (2013) "'Likonomics' Policies in China," *East Asia Forum*, July 7, available at: www.eastasiaforum.org/2013/07/07/likonomics-policies-in-china.

Kuznets, S. (1955) "Economic Growth and Income Inequality," *American Economic Review*, 45(1): 1–28.

Lewis, W. A. (1954) "Economic Development with Unlimited Supplies of Labour," *The Manchester School*, 22(2): 139–191.

Mori, T. and Sasaki, H. (2007) "Interdependence of Production and Income in Asia-Pacific Economies: An International Input-Output Approach," *Bank of Japan Working Paper Series*, No. 07-E-26.

National Bureau of Statistics of China (2012) *China Statistical Yearbook 2012*, Beijing: China Statistics Press.

National Bureau of Statistics of China (2013) *China Statistical Yearbook 2013*, Beijing: China Statistics Press.

Ohashi, H. (2003) *Sirizu Gendai Chugoku Keizai 5: Keizai no Kokusaika* (*Series Contemporary Chinese Economy 5: Internationalization of Economy*), Nagoya: University of Nagoya Press.

Ohashi, H. (2005a) *Gendai Chugoku Keizairon* (*Contemporary Chinese Economy*), Tokyo: Iwanami Shoten.

Ohashi, H. (2005b) "China's Regional Trade and Investment Profile," in David Shambaugh (ed.) *Power Shift: China and Asia's New Dynamics*, Berkeley/Los Angeles, CA: University of California Press, pp. 71–95.

Ohashi, H. (2006) "The Response of Japanese Business to the Rise of China: Competitiveness of Manufacturing Industries," in Glenn D. Hook and Harukiyo Hasegawa (eds.) *Japanese Responses to Globalization*, Basingstoke: Palgrave Macmillan.

Park, D. and Shin, K. (2010) "Can Trade with the People's Republic of China Be an Engine of Growth for Developing Asia?" *Asian Development Review*, 27(1): 160–181.

Rassweiler, A. (2009) "iPhone 3G S Carries $178.96 BOM and Manufacturing Cost, iSuppli Teardown Reveals," iSuppli press release, June 24, available at: www.bloomberg.com/apps/news?pid=newsarchive&sid=aSK_Yy2kPY7I.

Sun, X. (2002) *Zongliang Pingheng, Shouru Fenpei yu Hongguan Tiaokong* (*Total Balance, Income Distribution and Macro Control*), Beijing: Zhongguo Jihua Chubanshe (China Planning Press).

UN (2011) "World Population Prospects: The 2010 Revision" Population Division, Department of Economic and Social Affairs, United Nations, available at: http://esa.un.org/wpp/Documentation/WPP%202010%20publications.htm.

USCC (2012) *2012 Report to Congress*, August 13, Washington, DC: U.S.-China Economic and Security Review Commission, available at: http://origin.www.uscc.gov/sites/default/files/annual_reports/2012-Report-to-Congress.pdf.

World Bank (1987) *World Development Report 1987: Industrialization and Foreign Trade*, Washington, DC: World Bank.

World Bank and Development Research Center of the State Council (2012) *China 2030: Building a Modern, Harmonious, and Creative Society*, Washington, DC: World Bank.

Zhongguo Renmin Yinhang Huobi Zhengce Fenxi Xiaozu (Small Group of Monetary Policy Analysis, People's Bank of China) (2006) *Huobi Zhengce Zhixing Baogao: 2006 nian Disan Jidu* (*China Monetary Policy Report Quarter Three, 2006*), November 14, available at: www.pbc.gov.cn/history_file/files/att_11623_1.pdf.

14 Dynamics of state–business relations and the evolution of capitalism in Russia in an age of globalization

Yuko Adachi

1 Introduction

What kind of capitalism is being developed in Russia? This question, much posed when the reform proceeded with the collapse of the Soviet Union, remains relevant more than decade on. As the "variety of capitalism" approach suggests, there are various types in place in the developed economies. Contrary to some predictions, the process of globalization has not resulted in a convergence of capitalism.

Outside the developed economies, types of emergent capitalism are discussed in the contexts of the economics of transition among the economies of Central and Eastern Europe, and the rise of the BRIC (Brazil, Russia, India, China) countries, both groupings that include Russia. Russia has been faced with simultaneous adjustment to the changing internal and external environments. Following the disintegration of the Soviet economic system, Russia's systemic transformation from communism to capitalism took place in a setting of increasing globalization. Furthermore, as Russia's economy grew, it sought to establish a position in the global economy as a member of the BRIC emerging markets.

Against this backdrop, this chapter traces the development of "capitalism Russia style" since the collapse of the Soviet economic system. The chapter reveals some features that characterize Russia's emerging and evolving system. It puts particular focus on the development of the corporate sector and the emergence of business entrepreneurs as key factors in the nurturing of a market economy. In analyzing the dynamics of state–business relations, we argue that a better understanding of a complex mix of change and continuity in the business–state interactions helps to explain the contour of "capitalism with Russian characteristics."

2 Rise of business groups and entrepreneurs

Following the disintegration of the Soviet Union in 1991, the Russian government launched a major liberal market reform. The policy was based on liberalization, privatization and macroeconomic stabilization. Market reforms during the 1990s, particularly privatization, led to the formation of large business groupings in Russia. Big business became a major actor in the political economy of Russia; in fact, one of the most distinctive features of the emergent Russian corporate system was the rise of business groups led by business entrepreneurs.

In 1997, when the initial waves of privatization were over (see below for a discussion of privatization), there were some ten large business groups—which became known as the "Big Ten" (Pappe 2000, pp. 206–210), as shown in Table 14.1. According to another major study, in 2002 the ten largest business groups—all private, none state-owned—accounted for 38.7 percent of industrial output, 21 percent of capital investment, more than 31 percent of exports and 22 percent of profit tax payment (Dynkin and Sokolov 2001; Dynkin 2004).[1] According to a survey of 64 medium and large enterprises, eight groups—(1) Menatep (Yukos), (2) Interros, (3) Millhouse (Sibneft)/Russian Aluminum, (4) Sistema, (5) Alfa Group, (6) Lukoil, (7) Surgutneftegaz and (8) AvtoVaz—controlled roughly 86 percent of the revenues of privatized companies (Boone and Rodionov 2001). Many core enterprises were transferred to private owners as a result of the loans-for-shares privatization program.

Groups generally were formed around an industrial enterprise in one of the natural resources sectors such as hydrocarbon or metals. At the initial stage of formation in the 1990s, most industrial groups included a commercial bank which acted as the particular group's own credit organization. A study by Dynkin and Sokolov (2001) shows that they acted as accounting centers, providing channels for transferring resources abroad, accumulating the group's financial resources, and acting as depositaries for securities and as share registers. In addition, the groups included trading, insurance, investment, leasing and transportation companies, medical recreational organizations, construction companies, etc.

Establishment of a group allowed these businesses to achieve reduced transaction costs, compensate for lack of a functioning banking system, obtain some sort of protection of their assets, and cushion against the adverse effects of the economic transformation. In the 1990s in particular, in the absence of the market institutions observed in the developed economies, Russian businesses learned to operate using their own devices in the form of a business group structure that compensated for institutional constraints (Perotti and Gelfer 2001).

Russia's leading businesses are mainly in the oil and gas, and metals sectors. The companies in these sectors continue to occupy the top rankings in the leading business journal *Ekspert*'s listing of largest companies by sales (see Table 14.2 for rankings in 2003 and 2013).[2] The natural resources sectors, such as energy and metals, have been the drivers of Russia's economic recovery since Russia's financial crisis of 1998, following a period of continuous transformational recession in the 1990s. According to the OECD (2004), the natural resources sectors contributed more than a third of Russian GDP growth in the period 2001–2004. The fuel, non-ferrous metals and forestry sectors accounted for nearly 70 percent of the growth in industrial production in 2001–2004, with the oil sector contributing roughly 45 percent (OECD 2004).

The list of the major business groups a decade later, as shown in Table 14.3, indicates that, of those that were established and became major ones in the

Table 14.1 The ten big groups in 1997

Group	Core financial institutions	Core business	Group's key figures
Lukoil	Imperial (Bank), Lukoil-Garant (Insurance), Lukoil-reserve-invest	Lukoil (Oil), Arkhangelskteologobycha (Extraction)	Vagit Alekperov
Menatep	Menatep Bank, Menatep SPb (Bank)	Yukos (Oil), VSNK (Oil and Gas), Omsk tire, Moscow tire, Apatit, Vosklesensk, Volga pipe, Nitron, Volgotanker (Transport)	Mikhail Khodorkovsky
Interros-Onexim	Onexim Bank, MFK Bank, Balt-Onexim Bank, Alba, Renaissance Capital, Eastern Investment, Swift, Interros-soglasie, Renaissance insurance, Interros dostoinstvo	Norilsk Nickel (Metals), Sidanko (Oil), Rusia Petroleum, NLMK (Metal), Perm Motors (Auto), Servernaia Verf, Severo-Zapadnoe Parakhodtsvo (Shipbuilding)	Vladimir Potanin, Mikhail Prokhorov
Inkom	Inkom Bank	Babaevsky (food), Rotfront (food), SAMEKO (metal)	Vladimir Vinogradov
Berezovsky-Smolensky	SBS Agro, Agroprom Bank, Edinyi Bank, KOPF Bank,	Signeft (Oil), Aeroflot	Boris Berezovsky, Aleksander Smolensky
Alfa	Alfa Bank, Alfa Capital	TNK (Oil), Alfa cement	Mikhail Fridman, Viktor Vekselberg
Most	Most Bank, Spasskie vorota (insurance)	Most Development, Media-Most	Vladimir Gusinsky
Sistema	Moscow Bank of Reconstruction and Development, Lider (insurance)	Mikron, Kvant, MTS	Vladimir Evtushenkov
Rossiiskii Kredit	Rossiiskii Kredit	Lebedinsky GOK, Mikhailovsky GOK, Achinsk alumina, KRAZ	Vladimir Malkin
Gazprom	Gazprom Bank	Gazprom	Viktor Chernomyrdin

Source: Pappe (2000).

Table 14.2 Russia, company ranking, 2003 and 2013: *Ekspert* 400: rating of major Russian companies by product sales

2003				2013			
Rank	Company	Industry	Sales in 2002 (RUB million)	Rank	Company	Industry	Sales in 2012 (RUB million)
1	Gazprom	Oil and gas	613,754.0	1	Gazprom	Oil and gas	4,764,411
2	RAO UES	Electric power engineering	503,409.0	2	Lukoil	Oil and gas	3,615,692
3	Lukoil	Oil and gas	484,480.6	3	Rosneft	Oil and gas	2,098,000
4	Yukos	Oil and gas	356,657.3	4	Russian Railways	Transport	1,540,323
5	Surgutneftegaz	Oil and gas	200,945.0	5	Sberbank	Banking	1,346,500
6	TNK	Oil and gas	190,524.5	6	TNK-BP	Oil and gas	1,241,000
7	Sibneft	Oil and gas	149,797.0	7	Sistema	Multi-branch holdings	1,064,200
8	Rusal	Metals	124,106.4	8	Surgutneftegaz	Oil and gas	849,575
9	AvtoVaz	Machine building	119,432.0	9	Transneft	Transport	732,375
10	Tatneft	Oil and gas	108,689.5	10	MRSK (Rossiiskie seti)	Electric power engineering	621,633

Source: www.expert.ru.

Table 14.3 Major groups in 2008

Group	Core business	Main components include	Group's key figures
Gazprom	Gazprom (gas)	Gazprom (gas), Novatek (gas), Nortgaz (gas), Gazpromneft (formerly Sibnert) (oil), Sibneftgaz, Slavneft, Mosenergo (power generation)	Aleksei Miller
Lukoil	Lukoil (oil)	Lukoil, Lukoil-Neftekhim (petrochemical), Polief (petrochemical), TGK8 (power generation)	Vagid Alekperov
Tatneft	Tatneft (oil)	Tatneft (oil), Tatneftgeogizika, Zenit (finance)	Shafagat Takhautdinov
MDM Group	Various	SUEK (coal), TGK12 (Kuzbassenergo), Evrokhim, MDM Bank	A. Melnichenko, S. Popov/V. Rashevsky
Severstal	Severstal (steel)	Severstal (steel), Silovye mashiny, Sveza etc.	Aleksei Mordashov
NLMK	NLMK (steel)	NLMK (steel), Universal Cargo Logistics, Northwestern Shipping Company, Volga Shipping Company, Zenit bank	Vladimir Lisin
Metalloinvest	Metalloinvest (steel)	Metalloinvest (Lebedinsky and Mikhailovsky GOKs), Norilsk Nickel, Uralmash, Megafon, Kommersant, 7TV (media)	A. Usmanov
Evraz-Milhouse	Evraz (steel)	Evraz (steel), Yuzhkuzbasugol (coal), Zapsib power plant	A. Abramov, R. Abramovich
Interros	Norilsk Nickel (nickel)	Norilsk Nickel, Polyuszoloto, Rusiapetroleum, Profmedia, Rosbank etc.	V. Potanin
Oneksim group	UC Rusal (aluminium)	TGK4, UC Rusal, InterGeo, Polyuszoloto, MFK Bank, Soglasie (insurance) etc.	M. Prokhorov
UGMK	UGMK (steel)	UGMK, Kuzbassrazrezugol, Uralskoe zoloto, Transmash holding	Iskander Makhmudov
Basel	UC Rusal (aluminium)	UC Rusal, Norilsk Nickel, Kranoyarsk GES, Irkutskenergo, Russneft, GAZ (automobile), Continental management (Pulp and Paper), Bazelcement, Rospechat (publishing)	Oleg Deripaska
Renova	Various	TNK-BP, UC Rusal, Electric power companies like Irukutskenergo, TGK5,6,7,9 etc.), Slantsy (oil)	Viktor Vekserberg
Alfa Group	TNK-BP (oil)	TNK-BP (oil), Slavneft (oil), Vimpelcom (telecom), Megafon (telecom), Golden Telecom (telecom), X5 (retail), Evroset (retail), Alfa Bank (bank)	Mikhail Fridman
Sistema	MTS, Comstar (telecom)	MTS (telecom), Skylink (telecom), Comstar (telecom), Svyazinvest (telecom), Bashneft (oil), MBRD (bank)	Vladimir Evtushenkov
Rostekhnologii	Rosobroneksport	Rosobroneksport (arms trade), VSMPO-Avisma (titanium), AvtoVaz (automobile), Russian Helicopter, Kamaz (automobile), Khimprom (chemical), Russpetsstal (steel) etc.	Sergei Chemezov

Source: Pappe and Galukhina (2009, pp. 239–286).

1990s, most are still active today (Pappe and Galukhina 2009). However, there are some differences, mainly the demise of Menatep (Yukos) group and the emergence of the State Corporation Rostekhnologii (Rostec). As will be discussed later, this reflects the growing involvement of the state in the economy.

3 The rise of business elites

3.1 "Oligarchs" in new Russia

In the 1990s, the process of transformation to a market economy gave rise to a new generation of business elites who facilitated the creation of the business groups discussed above. Kryshtanovskaya and White (2005, p. 295) define business elites as "the top echelon of entrepreneurs, who thanks to their financial and economic resources have a significant influence on the taking of decisions of national importance."[3] Throughout the years of the Yeltsin and Putin administrations, these large enterprises and the business elites, and their formal and informal ties with the state, influenced the course of Russia's political economy.

The individuals controlling the big business groups became known colloquially as "oligarchs," and they largely correspond to the Russians named in the lists of billionaires compiled by magazines such as *Forbes*. The Russian version of *Forbes* was first published in 2004 (Table 14.4 shows the 2004 and the 2013 rankings). Russian businessmen first entered the *Forbes* list in 1997. Boris Berezovsky was first among the Russians, followed by Mikhail Khodorkovsky and Vagit Alekperov.[4]

During the Yeltsin era, Berezovsky boasted that seven oligarchs controlled about half of the Russian economy in 1996. Of those seven, two (Vladimir Potanin and Mikhail Fridman) are still active in the business world. Those three tycoons who had confrontations with Yeltsin's successor, Putin, either fled Russia (Berezovsky and Vladimir Gusinsky), or were imprisoned (Khodorkovsky).[5] The remaining two failed to survive the 1998 Russian financial crisis.

In the 1990s, the privatization program known as loans-for-shares enhanced the position of politically well-connected entrepreneurs—the oligarchs. The loans-for-shares program was criticized widely as a series of rigged auctions that allowed the shares in some of Russia's most valuable enterprises to be transferred at a fraction of their potential market value to a small select circle of buyers. The program, which was implemented in 1995–1997, represented a second phase in Russia's privatization policy. In the first phase of the privatization policies under Yeltsin, rapid and large-scale privatization of state-owned enterprises took place starting in 1992, through the exploitation of privatization checks or vouchers. The government distributed these privatization checks to all Russian citizens with the idea of achieving a wide range of private owners.

Loans-for-shares reflected a shift in the government's priority from rapid privatization to a more selective approach based on selling off some of its valuable enterprises mostly in the oil and metals sectors. The government offered its shares in these enterprises in exchange for bank loans, through a series of

Table 14.4 Forbes Russia list, 2004 and 2013

2004					2013				
Rank	Name	Net worth (million US$)	Source	Age	Rank	Name	Net worth (million US$)	Source	Age
1	Mikhail Khodorkovsky	15,200	Oil (Yukos)	43	1	Alisher Usmanov	17,000	Steel, Telecom, Stocks (Metalloinvest, Mail.ru, Megafon etc.)	59
2	Roman Abramovich	12,500	Oil (Sibneft)	37	2	Mikhail Fridman	16,500	Banking, Retail, Telecom, (Alfa Group, X5, Vimpelcom)	48
3	Viktor Vekselberg	5,900	Oil, Metals (Renova TNK-BP)	47	3	Leonid Mikhelson	15,400	Gas, Petrochemicals (Novatek, Sibur)	57
4	Mikhail Prokhorov	5,400	Nonferrous metals (Norilsk Nickel-Interros)	36	4	Viktor Vekselberg	15,100	Metals, Energy, Telecom (Renova group)	56
5	Vladimir Potanin	5,400	Nonferrous metals (Norilsk Nickel-Interros)	43	5	Vagit Alekperov	14,800	Oil (Lukoil)	62
6	Mikhail Fridman	5,200	Oil, banking, telecom (Alfa Group)	39	6	Andrei Melnichenko	14,400	Investments	41
7	Vladimir Lisin	4,800	Steel (NLMK)	47	7	Vladimir Potanin	14,300	Nonferrous metals (Norilsk Nickel-Interros)	52
8	Oleg Deripaska	4,500	Aliminum Rusal–Basel)	36	8	Vladimir Lisin	14,100	Steel (NLMK)	56
9	Aleksei Mordashov	4,500	Steel (Severstal)	38	9	Gennadi Timchenko	14,100	Trading	60
10	Vagit Alekperov	3,900	Oil (Lukoil)	53	10	Mikhail Prokhorov	13,000	Investments (Onexim Group)	47

auctions. First, the investors, primarily banks established by Yeltsin-era oligarchs, offered loans to the government. In exchange, the government allowed the
banks to manage their company shares, which served as collateral for the loans.
The rights to manage the state's shares were auctioned off in 1995. In the second
stage, the government could either recover these shares by repaying the loans, or
sell off the shares being used as collateral. In 1997, the government divested
itself of these shares, which enabled the first-round auction winners to continue
owning and managing them. Companies such as Yukos, Surgutneftegaz, Lukoil,
Norilsk Nickel, Sidanko and Sibneft were privatized through this policy action.
These companies became the core of the leading business groups.[6]

The idea of loans-for-shares originated with Potanin (see Table 14.4), who suggested it to the government, and Anatolii Chubais, first deputy prime minister, who
declared his determination implement the idea using any means (Chubais 1999,
p. 184). With the forthcoming presidential election in 1996, and the threat posed
by the Communist leader, who was gaining popularity, both business and the government were keen to see Yeltsin re-elected, to keep the market reform process
going, and to prevent the renationalization of wealth. Thus, the exchange of property for political and financial support ahead of the presidential election in 1996
was considered one of the main motivations of the loans-for-shares scheme (Freeland 2000). Although the government's need to raise money for the budget was
also a rationale for the scheme, the revenue raised from it was not substantial
(Allan 2002). Overall, the result of the loans-for-shares was: the formation of
strong ties between the banking sector and industry; the emergence of domestic
strategic owners with longer-term interest in their companies; and the securing of a
political alliance between the government and business (Pappe 2000).

3.2 Privileged access to business opportunities ...

In Russia, entrepreneurial success has depended crucially on opportunity,
approval and the right to engage in lucrative business, which were afforded by
strong ties to the regime. These ties were an important factor in business creation
in the early stages of transition to a market economy and continued to be so
during the late Gorbachev period and the Yeltsin era, and also under Putin.

Kryshtanovskaya (1996, 2005) describes the origins and backgrounds of the
business elites using the concept of "authorized class" (*upolnomochennyi klass*).
Toward the end of Soviet period, in an economy where the exchange of political
power for property was taking place, this was often achieved by a state body del-
egating permission to conduct business activity to its authorized representatives.
Kryshtanovskaya (1996) argues that "authorization" or approval to engage in the
kind of commercial activity that brings in super profits became a special privilege—a kind of a license to be rich—in the 1990s in Russia.

The initial development of Russian big business, which was controlled by the
oligarchs, owed much to their being "authorized" or allowed to get rich. For
example, by the mid-1990s, these oligarchs had accumulated wealth as the heads
of "authorized banks" with exclusive privileges to handle the finances of various

government agencies. The loans-for-shares privatization program, which saw the state's handing over of the most profitable enterprises to a select few who were politically well connected, can also be considered an "authorization" process.

3.3 ... and abilities

Although access was crucial, it was not enough; the ability and skill to make use of the given business opportunity was also essential. As a result of privatization, those with privileged access acquired some of the potentially valuable, former state-owned enterprises. However, enterprises privatized in the 1990s as part of the privatization program were not immediately functional business units able to operate in a market economy. They needed to be reorganized to turn them into "real" firms. This applied to the core industrial firms in the business groups discussed above, including Yukos, Norilsk Nickel, etc. The tasks of making Soviet-type enterprises into functional and coherent business units were formidable. Thus, those who emerged as successful business leaders were the ones who not only were able to accumulate assets following privatization, as new owners, but also were able to regroup these assets into a firm that could operate in a market-oriented environment. Further, following consolidation, those business leaders' task was to make their business units grow as global players (Adachi 2010).

As the consolidation of privatized entities into coherent business firms proceeded, their transformation into global scale businesses progressed. Over time, companies became less concerned with problems specific to post-Soviet Russia, such as tidying up the disintegrated organizational structure brought about by the collapse of the Soviet economic system and privatization. They faced new, more market-focused challenges as they became more integrated in the international market, and as the scope of their activities expanded globally. With these developments, the determinants of firm-level competitiveness took on a market-oriented character, including outdoing rivals over sales, and achieving greater market share, profitability, productivity, market capitalization, etc. (Adachi 2006b).

In addition to these factors, and particularly for those firms operating in Russia's natural-resources sectors, it was important to be able to reduce vulnerability to political risks, such as ad hoc state interventions, and to cooperate and work effectively with the government. The dismemberment of Yukos Oil Company discussed below had implications for the ability and competitiveness of large private firms working in the so-called "strategic sectors" of the Russian economy, such as resources sectors.

4 State advances in the resources sectors

4.1 "Yukos affair"

Putin's rise to the presidency in 2000 saw a consolidation of state power and increased state grip on the economy's strategic sectors, especially hydrocarbons.[7]

A series of actions was designed to re-establish or expand state control in Russia's energy sector. The most prominent and important was the "Yukos affair"—a campaign against Yukos, Russia's one time largest and the most profitable oil producer, which involved demands for back taxes and revocation of licenses, the arrests of its CEO Khodorkovsky and his business associate Platon Lebedev, and eventually dismemberment of the company.

In 2003, the Russian authorities initiated a criminal investigation into Yukos's top executives. In October of that year, Khodorkovsky was arrested on charges including fraud, embezzlement and tax evasion. In 2004, Yukos was presented with a demand for unpaid back taxes.[8] In December 2004 Yuganskneftegaz, Yukos's main and most attractive production subsidiary, which accounted for about 60 percent of Yukos's production, was sold at auction. The buyer was a previously unknown, mysterious company called Baikal Finance Group. Eventually, Rosneft, a state-owned oil company, announced its purchase of Baikal Finance Group, and the head of the Rosneft subsidiary was appointed as the new head of Yuganskneftegaz.

The "Yukos affair" was considered as a politically motivated attack on Khodorkovsky and Yukos by the Kremlin. Khodorkovsky, regarded as the most successful of the oligarchs, was targeted because of his political ambitions which included support for non-pro-presidential parties, and Yukos's commercial interests which completely differed from the state's interests as defined by the Kremlin.[9] Yukos's plan to build private pipelines put pressure on state-controlled companies such as the pipeline monopoly Transneft. Moreover, following the merger between Yukos and Sibneft to create the world's fourth largest oil producer in 2003, it was widely believed that Yukos Oil's owners were planning to sell a large stake in Yukos to a Western oil major.[10] When a question was raised in an interview in October 2003 about this possible transaction, Putin said: "As regards purchasing part of the Yukos company, … we are talking about a possible major deal here, and I think it would be the right thing to do to have preliminary consultations with the Russian government on this matter."[11]

Although the president considered that foreign technology and expertise were much needed to develop Russia's oil and gas industry, the Kremlin considered oil and gas the country's strategic sectors and considered also that the oil companies' major plans should be aligned with state objectives. As Putin made efforts to consolidate state power and to strengthen Russia's economy, big business was expected to contribute to this project by fulfilling the role expected of it by the state. However, Yukos's owners were not cooperative. Olcott (2003, p. 3) describes it thus: "While Vladimir Putin recognizes the importance of market forces and the need to protect private property, he believes that both must be managed to insure that neither takes precedence over the interests of the state."

The Yukos affair coincided with the company's dramatic transformation from an enterprise associated with corporate governance abuses, to one of Russia's most respected companies with a strong commitment to good corporate governance and transparency. Yukos has been a company notorious for its non-transparent business practices and violation of the rights of minority shareholders during the 1990s (Adachi 2006a). However, when the core owners centralized and consolidated corporate control to establish a functioning vertically integrated entity, the company made a turn in policy and achieved a highest level of corporate transparency among the Russian companies.

This increase in corporate transparency took place as firms decreased dependence on the state. According to Stulz (2005, p. 1614), "The ability of the state to favour some firms and expropriate others can make a lack of transparency more advantageous for the firms that are favoured by the state than those that are not." In other words, from the point of view of the state, transparent businesses are much harder to control than those that maintain close ties with the state. Too much independence from the state was not to be tolerated in the Russian oil sector, which, unlike the case in most other oil-producing countries around the world, had fallen into private hands after privatization.

The demise of Yukos was accompanied by the rise of the state-owned Rosneft. This has become the largest oil company in Russia and is successful globally. It is in ninety-ninth position in the 2013 *Fortune 500* ranking, and is growing and expanding its operations worldwide.[12]

The Yukos affair was followed by Gazprom's acquisition of oil company Sibneft, controlled by another oligarch, Roman Abramovich. Gazprom obtained around 70 percent of Sibneft, and Gazpromneft was established. Other Gazprom-related developments included Gazprom's acquisition of majority interests in the previously 100 percent foreign-controlled Sakhalin-2 project, then the world's biggest privately funded energy development. It involved freezing the environmental permits held by a Shell-led consortium (Sakhalin Energy) to develop Sakhalin-2, and the incident was viewed as evidence of the rise of resource nationalism because it worked to limit the level of foreign participation.

4.2 Limiting foreign participation in strategic areas

Limiting foreign access, which, by implication, facilitates access by state-controlled Russian companies to strategic sectors of the economy, has become an important issue under the Putin regime. The debate over the adoption of two related rules that regulate business–state relations should be highlighted here. These are the so-called strategic investment law and the amendments to the subsoil law.[13]

One of the last pieces of legislation Putin signed as president in 2008 was Russia's new law on investment in strategic sectors, which placed restrictions on foreign investment in strategic enterprises by specifying those sectors of the Russian economy regarded as "strategic." The law on strategic investment—which defined 42 types of activities in such areas as defense, natural resources, aviation, aerospace and nuclear industries as strategic—aimed to clarify the rules for foreign investment in Russia's strategic industries. The strategic sectors law was adopted in 2008 after being designated as a legislative priority for government in 2005 (Gati 2008; Pomeranz 2010; Adachi 2009).

According to the new rules, foreign companies required permission from a government commission when seeking to acquire more than 50 percent of the voting shares in a Russian company in one of the 42 strategic areas. Foreign state-owned companies faced even stricter rules. Permission was required to acquire more than 25 percent of voting shares in most companies. In activities related to the development of strategic mineral deposits, foreign companies investing in Russian companies developing "strategic fields" required permission for stakes of 10 percent, and for foreign state-owned companies the limit was 5 percent. So the foreign state-owned companies operating in strategic fields faced very tight constraints.[14]

The strategic law accompanied the adoption of amendments to the subsoil law, which established the criteria for a "strategic field" (described in the legislation as a subsoil plot of federal significance). Fields were classed as "strategic" if their reserves exceeded the limit set by the state, and participation in auctions or tenders for the development of these strategic fields is allowed only to companies that are majority (more than 50 percent) owned by Russian investors. Initially, specific reserve limits were established (oil fields—150 million tons; gas fields—one trillion cubic meters), but the definition of strategic fields was later broadened at the expense of foreign participation—a sign of the government's growing assertiveness over the management of subsoil resources. The reserve limits for oil and gas fields were reduced (oil to 50–100 million tons; gas to only above 750 billion cubic meters) as a result in part to lobbying by Gazprom (Adachi 2009).

In practice, the law allows for preferential treatment for state-owned oil and gas companies—namely Gazprom and Rosneft. The Russian government preferred that the state enterprises, rather than foreign or privately owned firms, should develop its strategic fields. At the same time, the state-owned companies seemed to have the power to influence the law-making process resulting in a bidirectional dynamic. In addition, private Russian companies were accepting of the preferential treatment allowed to the state-controlled companies. Vagit Alekperov, head of Lukoil, commented when the company ceded majority control of a planned project to the state-owned Gazprom, "Gazprom is our big brother. The big brother must have 51 percent."[15] Thus, there has been an "understanding" of the rules of the game, with the government preferring state ownership over private ownership in the oil and gas sector.

The fact that state-owned Rosneft and Gazprom were favored by the subsoil-use legislation is in line with the administration's intent to create "national champions" in strategic sectors. In his academic writing, entitled "Mineral Natural Resources in the Strategy for Development of the Russian Economy," published in 1999, Putin had outlined the role of mineral resources as basis for Russia's economic development.[16] He also emphasized the importance of state support in facilitating economic growth by establishing large conglomerates which can be globally competitive. As Putin (1999) put it, "the creation, with full support from the state, of large financial-industrial groups-corporations … that will be able to compete with Western transnational corporations," and will allow government more easily to pursue the state's interests (Putin 1999; Balzer 2006). As shown here and also below, the president means what he says, i.e., as he became president he has been putting his ideas into action.

The strategic law came into force in 2008, and under Medvedev's presidency, the prime minister has acted as chair of the government commission responsible for granting permissions related to foreign investors' access to strategic sectors. Following implementation of the law, the commission headed by Putin met regularly and considered applications submitted by foreign investors to acquire shares in Russian companies in the strategic sectors.[17]

5 State involvement in the economy

As a result of market reforms and privatization, the private sector came to represent a major part of Russian economy. According to the EBRD (European Bank for Reconstruction and Development), the private sector represented 5 percent of GDP in 1991, and 70 percent in 1999. The EBRD shows that the share remained at 70 percent until 2004 before falling by 5 percent in 2005. Then the share stayed at 65 percent from 2005 to 2010 (See Table 14.5).[18]

There is a range of data indicating that state involvement in the economy has become more visible with the coming to power of Putin. For example, according to a report by BNP Paribas, Russia's state-owned sector has grown since the early 2000s and now accounts for half of the economy (Tseplyaeva and Eltsov 2012). In the oil sector, the state controlled 10 percent of oil production in 1998–1999; in 2013 it controlled between 40 percent and 45 percent. State ownership in the transport sector is 73 percent, and in the banking sector is 49 percent (see Table 14.6). In 2006, according to estimates by the Institute of Economy in Transition (Gaidar Institute), the size of the state-owned sector was 38 percent of Russian GDP. The Ministry of Economic Development estimates that the share reached 40–45 percent in 2008. Then global economic crisis of 2008 only accelerated the process, with the state-owned sector growing to 50 percent in 2009 (Tseplyaeva and Eltsov 2012).

The OECD (2009, 2011) reports that the degree of state control in the Russian economy is extensive due to the extent of state ownership and state control over economic activity. The OECD's Product Market Regulation (PMR) indicators assess the extent to which the regulatory environment is conducive to competition

Table 14.5 Private sector share of GDP

	1991	1992	1993	1994	1995	1996	1997	1998	1999
%	5	25	40	50	55	60	70	70	70

	2000	2001	2002	2003	2004	2005	2006	2007	2008
%	70	70	70	70	70	65	65	65	65

Source: EBRD, *Transition Reports* various issues.

Table 14.6 State ownership by sectors, 2011

Sectors	Percentage
Transport	73
Banking	49
Oil and gas	45
Utility	35
Machinery	15
Telecom	14
Metallurgy	1

Source: Tseplyaeva and Eltsov (2012).

in goods and services markets, and show that the extent of state involvement in the economy is higher in Russia than in any other OECD member country (see Table 14.7).

Also, the government has been increasing the level of state ownership among the largest Russian companies listed on the stock exchange. According to Troika Dialog, the share of market capitalization of the Russian equity market controlled by the state rose from 24 percent in 2004 to 40 percent in 2007 (OECD 2009). In 2012, BNP Paribas reported that the share of state-owned companies in the top 50 Russian listed companies (by market capitalization) exceeded 50 percent. Among the top 50, total market capitalization of private companies was 11,047 billion rubles compared to Gazprom, Rosneft, Sberbank, and other state-owned companies at 3,696 billion, 2,261 billion, 2,079 billion, and 4,031 billion rubles, respectively (Tseplyaeva and Eltsov 2012).

Using other data, Radygin and Entov (2008, p. 25) explain the extent of state control of the economy: the *Ekspert* 400 data mentioned above shows that in 2004 the state controlled 81 out of 400 large companies (with total sales of US$145 billion), and in 2006 the figures were 102 companies and US$238 billion. In 2004, 34.7 percent of the consolidated revenues of 400 companies was

Table 14.7 The extent of state control[1]

	Russia	OECD average	OECD emerging markets[2]	Euro area[3]	United States
State control	4.39	2.03	2.54	2.19	1.10
Public ownership	4.28	2.91	3.46	3.08	1.30
Involvement in business operations	4.50	1.15	1.61	1.30	0.90

Source: OECD (2009).

Notes
1 Index scale of 0–6, 6 being the most extensive control.
2 OECD emerging markets: Czech Republic, Korea, Mexico, Poland, Turkey.
3 Euro area: Austria, Belgium, Finland, France, Germany, Italy, Luxembourg, Netherlands, Portugal, Spain.

under the control of the state; in 2007 this figure was nearly 40 percent. There has also been increasing monopolization of the economy: according to the anti-monopoly agency and the Russian Federal Statistics Service (Rosstat), in 2003, 20 percent of Russia's GDP was attributable to 52 companies compared to 11 companies in 2006 (Radygin and Entov 2008).

One of the symptoms of increased involvement of the state has been that blurring of a line between politics and economics, the state and business. For example, Tseplyaeva and Eltsov (2012) argue that the line between the state-owned sector and the federal budget is becoming blurred as state-controlled companies invest heavily in ambitious state projects even when they are not directly related to the company's core business. For example, they show that Gazprom was the second biggest investor after the federal government, in the 2014 Sochi Olympic Winter Games, and of its 100 billion-ruble investment, only 31.5 billion rubles can be considered related to the company's core business, the Druzhba-Sochi gas pipeline (Tseplyaeva and Eltsov 2012, p. 2).

6 Creation of "state corporations"

The Russian state's involvement in the economy was enhanced by the creation of a number of entities called *Gosudarstvennaya korporatsiia*, or "state corporations." The first state corporation was created in 1999. The 1999 amendment to the 1996 Federal Law "on Non-commercial Organizations (FZ-N7)" introduced a provision for the state corporation existing as a non-commercial organization. The second state corporation was set up in 2003, with six more established in 2007 shortly before the end of Putin's first term. State corporations, particularly those created in 2007, were set up to act in a public policy capacity in key sectors, with first priority given to pursuing an economic modernization strategy. They act as instruments enabling investment of public funds in the domestic economy and restructuring of state enterprises.

As mentioned above, the legal status, a state corporation is that of a non-commercial organization. It is neither a joint stock company nor a state unitary enterprise—the usual or more familiar types of corporate entity in Russia.[19] However, a state corporation is in fact composed of various subsidiaries including state-owned joint stock companies, which do operate as commercial organizations.[20]

Besides the federal law on non-commercial organizations which contains the state corporation as a distinct legal form, a separate federal law is formulated to set up each state corporation. For example, state corporation Rosatom is established based on the 2007 Federal Law "on State corporation for atomic energy 'Rosatom'" (FZ-N171), and Rostekhnologii (Rostec)—on the 2007 Federal Law "on State corporation 'Rostekhnologii'" (FZ-N270). Each state corporation is being founded on the basis of contributions of state funds or property. In the period May to November 2007, some US$20 billion was transferred to the six newly established state corporations as their charter capital (Sakwa 2011). State assets transferred from government to a state corporation belong to the state corporation. Given this arrangement, there have been criticisms that these asset transfers represent a covert form of privatization of state property (Sakwa 2011; Volkov 2008).

Moreover, the special legal status of the state corporation exempts it from some of the obligations of competitions law and bankruptcy law, and puts it beyond the control of the Audit Chamber (Sprenger 2008). State corporations are obliged to publish annual reports on the use of their assets, but are not obliged to hold shareholder meetings as part of their governance (Sprenger 2008).

The six newly established state corporations are Vneshekonombank (Development Bank), Rosnano, Rostekhnologii (Rostec), Rosatom, Olimpstroi, and the Housing and Utilities Reform Fund.

Vneshekonombank (VEB—Bank for Development and Foreign Economic Affairs) was established as the national development bank, with the aim of modernizing and diversifying the Russian economy and improving its competitiveness. The main responsibilities of VEB are to provide support for industrial and infrastructure projects of strategic importance to the Russian economy. When the global economic crisis affected Russia, VEB, backed by government and the central bank, played a key role as emergency lender to stabilize Russia's financial market in 2008–2009.[21]

Rostekhnologii, recently renamed Rostec, was set up to facilitate development, production and export of hi-tech industrial products. It is a reflection of the state's effort to consolidate state assets in the industry and defense sectors. Its core enterprise is Rosoboroneksport, an exclusive state intermediary for arms and other military equipment. Rostec's holdings include Oboronprom, an aerospace holding company involved in the production of aircraft including helicopters, AvtoVaz, Russia's largest automaker, VSMPO-Avisma, the world's largest producer of titanium, and Kalashnikov, which makes assault rifles.[22] The head of Rostec at the time of writing is Sergei Chemezov, who is believed to be close to Putin. According to some reports, Chemezov has long wanted to establish Rostec and lobbied for its creation since 2005 (Cooper 2010).

Rosatom integrates more than 250 enterprises and scientific institutions, including all Russia's civil nuclear companies, nuclear weapons facilities and research organizations. Atomenergoprom, is a wholly state-owned holding company which includes the Russian civil nuclear industry. It is headed by Sergei Kirienko, at the time of this writing.[23]

Olimpstroi is a state corporation established to implement a state program to build the infrastructure for 2014 Sochi Olympic Winter Games, and further development of the area.[24]

The Housing and Utilities Reform Fund is intended to help renovate old living spaces, and water and sewerage pipelines.[25]

Rosnano aims to build a competitive nanotechnology industry in Russia based on innovation by Russian scientists and transfer of technologies from abroad. It was reorganized as a joint stock company in 2012.[26]

There was a discussion about creating state corporation for road construction. Avtodor was established in 2009, but was created as a state company (State

Company Russian Highways) instead of a state corporation. State company (*Gosudarstvennaya kompaniia*) is yet another newly created type of entity with the status of a non-commercial organization like a state corporation. Only the name is different. Perhaps this reflects criticism of the creation of state corporations at the time. The first and so far the only (at the time of this writing) state company was created on the very date when the amendment was made to the Federal Law on Non-commercial Organizations of 1996 to have a provision for state company.

Thus, each state corporation differs. In each case, their creation was ad hoc, and they do not constitute a homogeneous category. Nevertheless, these six state corporations can be grouped into three categories: First are those that function as investment funds—VEB and Rosnano; second are project operators such as Olimpstroi; third is industrial conglomerates which includes Rostec and Rosatom (Savitskii et al. 2011).

The principle underlying their creation would seem to be that if there is a problem that needs to be addressed then a new state structure, managed by a trusted individual, should be established to deal with it.[27] For example, Chemezov is considered a trusted manager by President Putin, as is Kirienko of Rosatom. In addition, for the authorities, or more concretely, for the president, the state corporation was seen as a way to reduce bureaucratic costs, which enabled quicker decision-making and implementation of priority projects.[28]

However, in terms of their ownership, governance mechanism and accountability, there are questions and concerns.[29] Dmitrii Medvedev, Russia's president from 2008 to 2012, is critical of state corporations for their ineffectiveness and lack of transparency. He ordered that they should be reorganized as joint stock companies, or a time limit set for their existence, or that they should be disbanded.[30]

Nonetheless, despite criticisms of state corporations, the rationale for their establishment was provided in Putin's contribution to the business daily *Vedomosti*, published in January 2012, under the banner: "We Need a New Economy." It was one of a series of articles published in major Russian newspapers laying out his policy platform in the wake of his second term (second round) as president. He claimed that Russia's industrial policy priorities dictated the decision to create state corporations and other state-owned holding companies and that there was a need to consolidate state assets that were "officially government-owned but managed disjointedly, and which had often lost all links with their respective research and design centers" (Putin 2012). The state's lead was deemed imperative to integrate key assets in order to enhance competitiveness in the global market. Putin (2012) claimed that "The strategies of the large industrial holding companies were aimed at creating internationally competitive corporations, with high market capitalization and stable or expanding niches on the global market." There is some resonance with the idea expressed in his academic writing mentioned above.

In addition to state corporations in a strict sense of the term, there are a number of state-owned, vertically integrated conglomerates, most notably United

Aircraft Building Corporation (OAK), and United Shipbuilding Corporation (OSK). These two entities were created by presidential decrees as wholly state-owned joint stock companies based on the consolidation of state assets. In his platform article, Putin specifically named OAK and OSK, in addition to Rostec and Rosatom, as priority state-controlled structures.

7 State–business interactions from Yeltsin to Putin

In the Yeltsin era, the growing power of private big business was evident. Business engaged in efforts to forge close ties with state structures, and to be represented on government and legislative bodies that supported particular business interests (Yakovlev 2003). State institutions became too closely involved with business, and vice versa. Thus it was argued that the state had fallen prey to "state capture," allowing special interest groups, such as powerful businesses, to shape the regulations to their own advantage (Hellman et al. 2000).

Despite the element of "state capture," the pattern of state-business interaction nevertheless was more top-down, in a sense that the protection afforded by the state enabled the rise and growth of big businesses (Rutland 2001). The Yeltsin administration "authorized" the rise and expansion of big business run by oligarchs who, in return, provided the administration with the resources for maintaining power (Volkov 2003). In this context, an alleged unwritten pact made between Putin and Russia's big businesses in 2000—reassurance that their property rights would be respected in exchange for their remaining outside of politics—implies the top-down character inherent in Russia's business-state relations.[31]

A state-business interrelationship that developed in the post-Soviet period was the system built on informal exchanges and unwritten agreements. The difference between the Yeltsin and Putin periods is the increased degree of state dominance: As Hanson and Teague (2005, p. 674) point out, greater dominance by the state over business was possible because Putin, on coming to power, was able to establish central control over the machinery of the state, and Russia's economic recovery since 1998 has strengthened the public finances. At the same time, it should also be mentioned that in the wake of the Yukos affair, companies started to pay more taxes: The gap in the legislation on domestic offshoring, enabling pervasive tax evasion, was closed after the arrest of Khodorkovsky. Thus the state authorities' assertiveness over the oil companies enabled better extraction of taxes from them (Appel 2008; Goldsworthy and Zakharova 2010).

With Putin's coming to power in 2000, the personal influence of the Yeltsin-era oligarchs diminished. However, according to research conducted by Kryshtanovskaya, the role of the business elites in society has continued to grow, and the proportion of business representatives in key decision-making positions in the top administration, the Duma, and government ministries, has increased. In 2003, 20 percent of government ministers were from the world of big business (Kryshtanovskaya and Khtorianskii 2003; Kryshtanovskaya and White 2005).

As the wave of oligarch visibility ebbed, a new group of business elites emerged. These include many of the so-called *siloviki*—individuals with military, security services and law enforcement backgrounds. Major companies that were formerly controlled by Yeltsin's oligarchs, were passed to the *siloviki*. Igor Sechin, considered to be a close associate of Putin, runs Rosneft, which became the leading oil company after the takeover of Yukos. Berezovsky and Abramovich were the former owners of AvtoVaz and Aeroflot. AvtoVaz became included under the umbrella of the state corporation Rostec, controlled by Chemezov, with a security services background. Viktor Ivanov, another veteran ally from the *siloviki*, who served as Deputy Head of the Presidential Staff under Putin, was made chairman of Aeroflot. While the 1990s were a golden age for Yeltsin's oligarchs, the post-Yeltsin years were dominated by Putin's comrades. Treisman (2007, p. 142) calls these *siloviki*-oligarchs the "silovarchs" and says that, "with silovarchs now controlling the commanding heights of the Russian economy, the security forces' takeover of corporate boardrooms is coming to define Putin's regime."[32] There is an observation that the "informal board of directors" has been formed around Putin to manage state-owned companies in the strategic sectors (Kupchinsky 2006). Although this does not have to mean that the "informal board of directors" is not able to manage the company well, it does enhance the insider-dominated image of Russian state-owned companies. And this tendency does not help to improve the overall investment climate, which Russia has long attempted to achieve, in order to be better integrated into the globalized economy.

8 Conclusion

What is the defining feature of state-business relations in the context of development of Russia-style capitalism almost two decades after transformation began? When Yeltsin was in power, capitalism Russian-style was depicted as oligarchic capitalism: the state had been captured by the powerful business tycoons with political clout. Under Putin's state capitalist model, a vision was encouraged of a system with enhanced state power: the business has been captured by the stronger state. However, as this chapter demonstrates, the situation is more nuanced. For example, those first oligarchs of the Yeltsin era were less powerful than they were portrayed. Their power and influence, ultimately, were "authorized" and approved by the state. Also, while enhanced state power has attracted much attention under Putin, the state is not sufficiently strong as to be able to be independent of business and other interests. What is important here, is that there has been continuous systemic dependence: big business has always depended on the state for its development in Russia, and the authorities have always needed the resources of big business in order to maintain power.

Thus, as Russia progressed toward the foundations of a capitalist system in the post-Soviet period, a conflation between business and state resulted. There was a blurring of the boundaries between the two, and their interpenetration and interrelations were continuously dynamic, with a swinging pendulum of power and influence between them. When becoming president, Putin, in a meeting with the oligarchs said that: "It is sometimes very difficult to understand where the state ends and the business starts, and where business ends and the state begins."[33] Putin set out to change the nature of the relationship between business and state—so that the state could keep an "equidistance" from business. As it turned out, in practice, some businesses are more equally distanced than others, and the alleged tacit pact between Putin and big businesses mentioned above appears more an exchange of property rights protection for businesses being socially responsible and politically cooperative.

This chapter has shown that the state's visibility in the economy has increased under Putin, and we can identify some underlying principles for the increasing state involvement. As has been demonstrated, state participation is encouraged especially in the strategic sectors of the economy, and preference is given to state-controlled companies over private domestic and foreign companies. Moreover, the creation of national conglomerates is expected to act as industrial and public policy tools, and big businesses in general are supposed to cooperate in pursuing state interests.

The basic idea is that the state has a developmental role to play in guiding Russia's capitalist development in a highly globalized world. According to Putin (2012):

> The successful experience of economic modernization in countries like Korea and China shows that a push in the right direction from the government is necessary, and that the outcome from such a push outweighs the risk of making a mistake.

What we can observe from the foregoing discussion is that it is Putin's "push" that is currently shaping capitalism with Russian characteristics.

Although the state could play a constructive role, the risks associated with "push" or state guidance could also be considerable. Its involvement in the economy has generally been ad hoc in character in Russia, rather than a result of a clear well-thought-out strategy related to the types and extent of the activities needed. In addition, political motives and profit motives may conflict, resulting in loss of efficiency. Finally, an opportunity for collusion between state and business could breed rent-seeking and corruption. Thus, excessive state intervention in the economy could have a damaging impact on the entrepreneurialism and activities of Russian business groups, which have been important drivers of Russia's economic development in the post-Soviet period.

Notes

1 These ten are: Lukoil, Menatep-Yukos, Interros, Bazel/Millhouse Capital, Severstal, Alfa-Renova, Surgutneftegaz, Sistema, AvtoVaz and MDM group.
2 In relation to the role of big businesses in the Russian economy, experts estimated in

2004 that private business groups in Russia were responsible for some 20–22 percent of Russia's GDP. Klepach and Yakovlev (2004) highlight that data from a World Bank study suggesting that Russian big business contributed between 9.5 and 17 percent of Russia's GDP, underestimates the actual contribution of big companies. These authors estimate that were state-owned companies (Gazprom, RAO UES, Transneft) to be included, the contribution of big business to GDP would increase to 27–28 percent. See also Guriev and Rachinsky (2005).

3 See also Kryshtanovskaya (2005, pp. 292–294), Kryshtanovskaya and White (1996).
4 www.forbes.ru, accessed September 20, 2013.
5 Khodorkovsky was released from prison in 2013 and now resides outside of Russia.
6 There are many studies which deal with the rise of oligarchs of the Yeltsin period and loans-for-shares. See for example, Freeland (2000), Goldman (2003) and Hoffman (2002).
7 E.g., Hanson (2009), Rutland (2008) and Tompson (2007).
8 By the end of 2004, these claims totaled US$25 billion. *Financial Times*, November 29, 2004.
9 For the analysis of Yukos affair, see in particular Hanson (2005a), Tompson (2005) and Sakwa (2009).
10 *Ekspert*, October 13, 2003.
11 www.mid.ru/Bl.nsf/arh/5101C9EDDCDA246243256DB90040776A?OpenDocument, accessed October 31, 2014.
12 http://money.cnn.com/magazines/fortune/global500/2013/full_list/, accessed September 30, 2013.
13 The law is entitled the Law "On the procedure for making foreign investments in commercial entities that have strategic importance for the national defense and security of the Russian Federation," Federal Law No. 57-FZ of April 29, 2008, available at http://document.kremlin.ru/doc.asp?ID=045671, accessed July 30, 2008; and the amendment to the subsoil law was introduced by the Law "On the introduction of amendments to certain provisions of legislative acts of the Russian Federation in connection with the adoption of the Federal Law 'On the procedure for making foreign investments in commercial entities that have strategic importance for the national defense and security of the Russian Federation'" Federal Law No. 58-FZ of April 29, 2008, available at http://document.kremlin.ru/doc.asp?ID=045672, accessed July 30, 2008.
14 There has been an amendment to the law, easing restrictive threshold for foreign companies. See Bank of Finland (2012).
15 "Lukoil Sees Gazprom Leading New Projects," *St. Petersburg Times*, November 21, 2006.
16 The article by Putin (1999), published in an annual edition of St. Petersburg Mining Institute, where he had received his *kandidat* degree in 1997, is translated in Balzer (2006). See also Balzer (2005).
17 http://ria.ru/economy/20120502/639194361.html, accessed September 2, 2013. It has become apparent that these investments often are not really "foreign" but are what are known as "round-trip investments" of Russian capital via offshore havens such as Cyprus.
18 EBRD, *Transition Reports*, various issues, available at: www.ebrd.com/pages/research/publications/flagships/transition/archive.shtml.
19 And it is not singled out in the type of juridical person recognized by the Civil Code.
20 For State Corporations, see Sakwa (2011), Volkov (2008), Butler (2008) and Avdasheva and Simachev (2009).
21 www.veb.ru, accessed September 3, 2013.
22 www.rostec.ru, accessed September 3, 2013.
23 www.rosatom.ru, accessed September 3, 2013.
24 www.sc-os.ru, accessed September 3, 2013.

25 www.fondgkh.ru, accessed September 3, 2013.
26 www.rusnano.com, accessed September 3, 2013.
27 Pappe and Galukhina (2009); also remarks by Pappe in Shokhina (2007).
28 By creating new specialized entities, the authorities are in a way denying the effectiveness of existing state institutions (Shokhina 2007). At the same time, it can also be pointed out that informal and personified governance under the Putin regime (so-called *ruchnoe upravlenie*, or manual governance) is being formerly institutionalized, as it were, with the set-up of state corporations.
29 "Medvedev Demands Plan to Revamp State Corporations," *The Moscow Times*, November 16, 2009, www.themoscowtimes.com/sitemap/free/2009/11/article/medvedev-demands-plan-to-revamp-state-corporations/389486.html; Maria Antonova, "Medvedev Orders Probe of State Corporations," August 10, 2009, www.themoscowtimes.com/print/article/medvedev-orders-probe-of-state-corporations/380370.html.
30 Currently, Olimpstroi and Housing and Utilities Reform hand have limited time-span. For Olimpstroi, see Orttung (2013).
31 For the discussion on the relations between Putin and oligarchs, see also Tompson (2005b) and Sakwa (2008).
32 *Kommersant*, September 13, 2006. As another example, in 2006 the son of Nikolai Patryshev, Director of the Federal Securities Service, was appointed an adviser to the Chairman of the Board of Rosneft.
33 www.vesti7.ru/news?id=3352, accessed September 5, 2013.

References

Adachi, Y. (2006a) "Corporate Control, Governance Practices and the State: The Case of Russia's Yukos Oil Company," in T. Mickiewicz (ed.) *Corporate Governance and Finance in Poland and Russia*, Basingstoke: Palgrave.

Adachi, Y. (2006b) "The Development of Russian Firms: Organisational Cohesion and Competitiveness in the Energy and Metals Sector," paper presented at BASEES Annual Conference, April 1–3.

Adachi, Y. (2006c) "The Ambiguous Effects of Russian Corporate Governance Abuses of the 1990," *Post-Soviet Affairs*, 22(1): 65–89.

Adachi, Y. (2009) "Subsoil Law Reform in Russia under the Putin Administration," *Europe-Asia-Studies*, 61(8): 1393–1414

Adachi, Y. (2010) *Building Big Business in Russia: The Impact of Informal Corporate Governance Practices*, Abingdon and New York, NY: Routledge.

Allan, D. (2002) "Banks and the Loans-for-Shares Auctions," in D. Lane (ed.) *Russian Banking: Evolution, Problems and Prospects*, Cheltenham: Edward Elgar, pp. 137–159.

Appel, H. (2008) "Is it Putin or Is it Oil? Explaining Russia's Fiscal Recovery," *Post-Soviet Affairs*, 24(4): 301–323.

Avdasheva, S. and Simachev, I. (2009) "Gosudarstvennye korporatsii: mozhno li otsenit' korporativnoe upravlenie?" *Voprosy ekonomiki*, 6: 97–110.

Balzer, H. (2005) "The Putin Thesis and Russian Energy Policy," *Post-Soviet Affairs*, 21(3): 210–225.

Balzer, H. (2006) "Vladimir Putin's Academic Writings and Russian Natural Resource Policy," *Problem of Post-Communism*, 53(1): 48–54.

Bank of Finland (2012) "Foreign Strategic Investment Law Continues to Evolve (Russia)," *BOFIT Weekly*, January 13, 2012, available at: www.suomenpankki.fi/bofit_en/seuranta/seuranta-aineisto/pages/vw201202_1.aspx.

Boone, P. and Rodionov, D. (2001) "Rent Seeking in Russia and the CIS," paper prepared for the EBRD Tenth Anniversary Conference.

Butler, W. (2008) "Treaty Capacity and the Russian State Corporation," *American Journal of International Law*, 102(2): 310–315.

Chubais, A. (1999) "Kak dushili privatizatsiiu," in A. Chubais (ed.) *Privatizatsiia po-rossiiskii*, Moscow: Vagrius.

Cooper, J. (2010) "Security Economy," in M. Gaelleoti (ed.) *The Politics of Security in Modern Russia*, New York, NY: Ashgate.

Dynkin, A. (2004) "Krupnyi biznes: nashe nasledie," *Vedomosti*, January 20.

Dynkin, A. and Sokolov, A. (2001) *Integrirovannye biznes-gruppy—proryv k modernizatsii strany*, Moscow: Tsentr issledovanii i statistiki nauki.

Freeland, C. (2000) *Sale of the Century*, London: Little, Brown and Company.

Gati, T. (2008) "Russia's New Law on Foreign Investment in Strategic Sectors and the Role of State Corporations in the Russian Economy," Akin Gump Strauss Hauer & Feld LLP.

Goldman, M. (2003) *Piratisation of Russia*, London: Routledge.

Goldsworthy, B. and Zakharova, D. (2010) "Evaluation of the Oil Fiscal Regime in Russia and Proposals for Reform," *IMF Working Paper*, No. 10/33, February.

Guriev, S. and Rachinsky, A. (2005) "The Role of Oligarchs in Russian Capitalism," *Journal of Economic Perspectives*, 19(1): 131–150.

Hanson, P. (2005) "Observations on the Costs of the Yukos Affair to Russia," *Eurasian Geography and Economics*, 46(7): 481–494.

Hanson, P. (2009) "The Resistible Rise of State Control in the Russian Oil Industry," *Eurasian Geography and Economics*, 50(1): 14–27.

Hanson, P. and Teague, E. (2005) "Big Business and the State in Russia," *Europe-Asia Studies*, 57(5): 657–680.

Hellman, J., Jones, G. and Kaufman, D. (2000) "Seize the State, Seize the Day: State Capture, Corruption and Influence in Transition," *World Bank Policy Research Working Paper* No. 2444.

Hoffman, D. (2002) *The Oligarchs*, Oxford: Public Affairs.

Klepach, A. and Yakovlev, A. (2004) "V zaschitu sil'nykh," *Ekspert*, April 26.

Kryshtanovskaya, O. (1996) "Finansovaya oligarkhia Rossii," *Izvestiya*, January 10.

Kryshtanovskaya, O. (2005) *Anatomiya rossiiskoi elity*, Moscow: Zakharov.

Kryshtanovskaya, O. and Khtorianskii, F. (2003) "Biznes-elita Rossii: genesis, sotsial'nyi sostav, rolevye funktsii," in Z. Golenkova (ed.) *Sotsial'aya stratifikatsiia rossiiskogo obshchestva*, Moscow: Letnii sad, pp. 25–252.

Kryshtanovskaya, O. and White, S. (1996) "From Soviet *Nomenklatura* to Russian Elite," *Europe-Asia Studies*, 48(5): 711–733.

Kryshtanovskaya, O. and White, S. (2005) "The Rise of the Russian Business Elite," *Communist and Post-Communist Studies*, 38: 293–307.

Kupchinsky, R. (2006) "Russia: Putin's Former Colleagues Make Up Today's Energy 'Team'," RFE/RL February 15, available at: www.rferl.org/content/article/1065792.html.

OECD (2004) *Economic Surveys: Russian Federation*, Paris: OECD.

OECD (2009) *Economic Surveys: Russian Federation*, Paris: OECD.

OECD (2011) *Economic Surveys: Russian Federation*, Paris: OECD.

Olcott, M. B. (2003) "Vladimir Putin and The Geopolitics of Oil," The James A. Baker III Institute for Public Policy of Rice University, October.

Orttung, R. (2013) "Sochi 2014: The Political Economy of Russia's Mega Project," PONARS Eurasia Policy Memo, September.

Pappe, I. (2000) *"Oligarkhi": Ekonomicheskaya khronika 1992–2000*, Moscow: HSE.

Pappe, I. and Galukhina, I. (2009) *Rossiiskii krupnyi biznes*, Moscow: HSE.

Perotti, E. and Gelfer, S. (2001) "Red Barons or Robber Barons? Governance and Investment in Russian Financial-Industrial Groups," *European Economic Review*, 45(9): 1601–1617.

Pomeranz, W. E. (2010) "Russian Protectionism and Strategic Sectors Law," *American University International Law Review*, 25(2): 213–224.

Putin, V. (1999) "Mineral'no-syryevye resursy v strategii razviitia Rossiiskoi ekonomiki (Mineral Natural Resources in the Strategy for Development of the Russian Economy)," *Zapiski gornogo instituta*, 144: 3–9, translated in H. Balzer (2006) "Vladimir Putin's Academic Writings and Russian Natural Resource Policy," *Problem of Post-Communism*, 53(1): 49–54.

Putin, V. (2012) "O nashikh ekonomicheskikh zadachakh," *Vedomosti*, January 30.

Radygin, A. and Entov, R. (2008) "V poiskakh institutsional'nykh kharakteristik ekonomicheskogo rosta," *Voprosy ekonomiki*, 8: 4–27.

Rutland, P. (2001) "Introduction: Business and the State in Russia," in P. Rutland (ed.) *Business and the State in Contemporary Russia*, Boulder, CO: Westview Press.

Rutland, P. (2008) "Putin's Economic Record: Is the Oil Boom Sustainable?" *Europe-Asia Studies*, 60(6): 1051–1072.

Sakwa, R. (2008) "Putin and Oligarchs," *New Political Economy*, 13(2): 185–191.

Sakwa, R. (2009) *Quality of Freedom: Khodorkovsky, Putin and the Yukos Affair*, Oxford: Oxford University Press.

Sakwa, R. (2011) *The Crisis of Russian Democracy: The Dual State, Fractionalization, and the Medvedev Succession*, Cambridge: Cambridge University Press.

Savitskii, K., Markin, K. and Mogrydhva, V. (2011) "Gosudarstvennye korporatsii kak element modernizatsii rossiiskoi ekonomiki," *Proekt: Vklad institutov razvitiya v realizatsiyu strategicheskikh prioritetov Rossiiskoi Federatsii*.

Shokhina, E. (2007) "Vlast' ne doveryaet gosudarstvu?" *Ekspert*, no. 45, December 3.

Sprenger, C. (2008) "The Role of State-Owned Enterprises in the Russian Economy," paper for OECD Corporate Governance Roundtable, October.

Stulz, R. (2005) "The Limits of Financial Globalization," *Journal of Finance*, 60(4): 1595–1638.

Tompson, W. (2005a) "Putting Yukos in Perspective," *Post-Soviet Affairs*, 21(2): 159–181.

Tompson, W. (2005b) "Putin and the 'Oligarchs': A Two-Sided Commitment Problem," in A. Pravda (ed.) *Leading Russia: Putin in Perspective*, Oxford: Oxford University Press.

Tompson, W. (2007) "Back to the Future? Thoughts on the Political Economy of Expanding State Ownership in Russia, Political Implications of Russia's Resource-Based Economy," available at: http://eprints.bbk.ac.uk/509/.

Treisman, D. (2007) "Putin's *Silovarchs*," *Orbis*, 51: 141–153.

Tseplyaeva, J. and Eltsov, Y. (2012) "Russia: The Land of the Bountiful Giants," BNP Paribas, October 22.

Volkov, V. (2003) "The Yukos Affair: Terminating the Implicit Contract," PONARS Policy Memo 307.

Volkov, V. (2008) "Russia's New 'State Corporations': Locomotives of Modernization or Covert Privatization Schemes?" PONARS Eurasia Policy Memo 25.

Yakovlev, A. (2003) "Interaction of Interest Groups and Their Impact on Economic Reform in Contemporary Russia," Working Paper of the Research Centre for Eastern European Studies, Bremen, 51.

Index

Page numbers in *italics* denote tables, those in **bold** denote figures.

accounting 5–6
Adachi, Yuko 254–77
advertising 120
agriculture 118, 123, 229
Aldrich–Vreeland Emergency Currency
    Act 91
Arenas, Roberto 81
Argentina 51, 165
Asahi Shimbun 166
Asian financial crisis 1997 30–1, 50
Asian International Input-Output Tables
    237
austerity 19, 20–1; United Kingdom (UK)
    156–8, 161–2
autotelism 33

Bagehot, Walter 95, 100
bailouts 19, 20, 21, 35, 93–4, **99**, 100, 153;
    deal-making and special purpose
    vehicles 95–6; eurocrisis 132
balance of payments constraints 203
Bank of England 155–6
banks: "too big to fail" doctrine 22, 36, 98,
    109; Bradford and Bingley bank 154;
    capital requirements 141; community
    development banks (CDBs) 111; deposit
    insurance 109–10; and the eurocrisis
    130–1; Halifax Bank of Scotland
    (HBOS) 154; investment banks 28, 41,
    106–7, 108, 109, 111, 214; legal
    restrictions on foreign banks 214;
    liquidity and solvency 109, 110, 132,
    151; megabanks 20, 35, 36, 38–9, 40,
    110–11; Minsky's views on 106–12;
    Northern Rock crisis 152; reserves
    101–3, 107, 139; Royal Bank of
    Scotland (RBS) 154; Shadow Banking

System (SBS) 13, 21–2, 30, 33, 34, 39,
    105; underwriting 28, 108, 110; *see also*
    Federal Reserve Bank (FRB)
Becker, Gary S. 187
Berezovsky, Boris 259
Bernanke, B. S. 93, 101, 244
Bhagwati, Jagdish 79, 196, 197
Born, Brooksley 29
Bourdieu, P. 52
Bradford and Bingley bank 154
Brady Plan 1989 208
Brazil 203–18; balance of payments
    position *213*; Brady Plan 1989 208;
    capital account liberalization and
    globalization of the assets markets
    212–14, 217–18n8; capital controls
    208–9; car industry 206; Collor Plan
    210; denationalization of the economy
    211–12; economic growth 17; floating
    exchange rates 215; foreign debt crisis
    of the 1980s 204; foreign direct
    investment (FDI) 11; globalization
    204–5; globalization and economic
    policy 214–16; import substitution 204,
    205–7, 216; inflation 210; interest rates
    213; internationalization of the
    economy as an alternative to
    globalization 206–7; legal restrictions
    on foreign banks 214; liberalization
    and globalization 207–9; military
    regime 207; non-tradables sector 212;
    oil shock 1973 207; paying for
    essential imports 203–4; Ponzi scheme
    207; price controls 210–11; price
    stability 211; *Real* Plan 211; share of
    exports and imports in the value of
    domestic manufacture 212, *212*; trade

liberalization 210, 211; *see also* BRICs (Brazil, Russia, India and China)
Bretton Woods regime 13, 46, 47–8; Bretton Woods II (BWII) world 56–7; scarce-currency clause 79
BRICs (Brazil, Russia, India and China) 16–18; GDP *18*; presence in the world economy 17–18; significance of financial liberalization 33–4
Britain *see* United Kingdom
Brown, Gordon 153, 155
bubble phenomenon 6–7
Buchanan, James M. 187–8
Business Week 194–5

Cairncross, A. 52
capital 4; capital account liberalization 212–14, 217–18n8; capital accumulation and investment rates 142–3; capital development 108–10, 111–12; capital liberalization and China 246; capital requirements 141; capital transactions 11; controls 208–9; flows 49–50, 57, 75, 76; net capital outflows 173–4, **173**
capitalism: accounting 5–6; authoritarian capitalism 124; bubble phenomenon 6–7; corruption and injustice 7–8; debt contract 6; disparity problem 8–9; dynamics 4; essentials of the capitalistic system 4–6; finance capitalism 104, 105; and globalization 3–26; managerial welfare-state capitalism 104; market price 5; and markets 4, 219–20; money manager capitalism 104, 105, 111; uncertainties and ambiguities 5–6
Carabelli, Anna M. 46–70
Cardim de Carvalho, Fernando J. 203–18
Cardoso, Fernando H. 17, 215
Cedrini, Mario A. 46–70
Chang, H.-J. 52
Chemezov, Sergei 269, 270
Chicago school of economists 187
China 234–53; capital liberalization 246; capitalistic system 14, 15–16; child and old-age dependency ratios to working population 248–9, **249**; current account surpluses 243, 244; Development Strategy of the Coastal Region 241; disparities in opportunities 242; disparity in the outward oriented development 240–2; domestic disparity 239–43; economic growth 234; exchange rate adjustment 245–7; export-promotion (XP) strategy 79; FDI-trade

nexus 237–8; foreign direct investment (FDI) 234–6, 247; Foreign Investment Industrial Guidance List 245; foreign reserves and inflation control 78–9; foreign trade 236; GDP 168, **168**, 169, **169**; and global imbalances 243–5; *guoji jingji daxunhuan* (great circulation of international authorities) theory 241; income inequality 239–40, **239**; incrementalism 242; inequality in incomplete reforms 242–3; Labor Contract Law 250; market transition 238; measures to discourage exports 244–5; net capital outflows **173**, 174; new directions in economic development 247–50; processing trade 245; production of cheap goods 122–3; rebalancing the economy 248–9; reducing corporate savings 250; reform and opening-up policy 234–8; *renminbi* (RMB) reform 245, 246; saving–investment balance 247–8, **248**; state default on debt repayments 250; state-owned enterprises (SOEs) 238, 239–40, 242, 248, 250; *xianfu* (earlier enrichment) theory 240; *see also* BRICs (Brazil, Russia, India and China)
China Statistical Yearbook 2012 238
classical dichotomy 6, 7
Cold War 14
collateralized debt obligation (CDO) 107
Colombia 80–4, 84–5n4
commercial globalization 122–3
Commodity Futures Modernization (CFM) Act 2000 29
community development banks (CDBs) 111
commutative justice 8
comparative advantage 71–86; Colombia example 80–4, 84–5n4; comparative advantage in trade theory 172–3; global growth 77; global imbalances and distortions to comparative advantage 78–80; Japan 190–1; ladder of comparative advantage 73–7; productivity and market size 71–2; Singaporean example 77–8; Wicksell effect 73
Consumer Financial Protection Bureau (CFPB) 34, 36, 37, 38
Consumer Financial Protection Safety and Soundness Improvement Act 37–8
consumption 116–17, 151; unproductive consumption 118–19

Cordray, Richard 37, 38
corruption 7–8, 22–3
Crafts, N. 161
credit default swap (CDS) 107, 133
crisis response 89–114; accounting for the
    FRB response to the 2007 crisis 96–8,
    97, *98*; background to FRB's response
    to 2007 crisis 89–90, 91–4; balance
    sheet recession 102–3; cumulative
    facility totals *99*; deal-making and
    special purpose vehicles 95–6;
    disaggregated FR assets **102**; facility
    percentage of bailout total **99**; FRB's
    lack of transparency 90, 92–3;
    incentives following the rescue, 2007
    crisis 98, 100; liquidity and solvency 95;
    Minskian view on financial system
    reform and crisis response 104–12;
    Minsky's stages approach 104–5;
    Minsky's views on money and banking
    106–12; nature of the global financial
    crisis 2007 and the FRB's response
    95–104; policy implications of the
    FRB's response to the 2007 crisis 100;
    quantitative easing policy 91, 96, 100–4;
    similarities between the FRB and the
    Treasury 93–4
Cruz, M. 57
currency: China's exchange rate
    adjustment 245–7; exchange rate
    overvaluation 213; exchange rates
    79–80, 168; floating exchange rates 215;
    optimal currency areas (OCA) 134–8;
    scarce-currency clause (Bretton Woods)
    79
Currie, Lauchlin 72, 80, 81–2, 83

Darling, Alistair 154, 155
Davidson, P. 54, 57
deal-making 95–6
debt: collateralized debt obligation (CDO)
    107; debt contract 6; debt deflations
    112–13, 151; debt ratios 130, 133, 150;
    household debt 111–12, 151; state
    default on debt repayments 141–2
deflation 6, 19, 54; debt deflation 112–13,
    151
demand management 82
democracy 184–5
Deng, Xiaoping 15, 16, 240–1
deposit insurance 109–10
derivatives 226
Dexia (bank) 141
Dimand, R. W. 48

diminishing returns theory 73–4, 75, 76
disparity problem 8–9
Dobb, Maurice 220
Dodd–Frank Act 21, 35–40, 100
Dooley, M. P. 56–7
Dynkin, A. 255

Echeverry, Juan Carlos 80–4
Economic and Monetary Union (EMU)
    128, 129
Economic Consequences of the Peace, The
    (Keynes) 49
economic policymaking 186–90
economics 10
economism 186
Economist, The 46
Economy, The: We Are All Keynesians
    Now (article) 149
Eltsov, Y. 267
emergency lending authority 40
employment 10, 81, 124, 137–8, 142;
    decline of income share going to labor
    143–4, **143**; women 179, 180
Enron 29
Entov, R. 266–7
environmental policies 117
European Bank for Reconstruction and
    Development (EBRD) 266
European Central Bank (ECB) 121, 128,
    131–2, 138–9
European Employment Strategy 142
European Financial Stabilization Facility
    (EFSF) 132, 139
European Stability Mechanism (ESM)
    132, 139
European Union (EU) 19–20, 21, 41–2;
    agriculture policy 118; background to
    the eurocrisis 128–30; capital
    accumulation and investment rates
    142–3; commercial globalization 122–3;
    consequences of the eurocrisis for the
    real economy *141*, **143**; consequences of
    the eurocrisis for the real economy
    140–5; debt ratio 130; economic crisis
    and globalization 115–27; euro area as
    an optimal currency area (OCA) 134–8;
    and financial globalization 121–2;
    financialization and the eurocrisis
    138–40; fiscal crisis, real meaning of
    119; future of the euro 145–6; GDP
    growth rates 140, *141*; Greek crisis
    133–4, 139–40; immigration/emigration
    137–8; market glut and repetitive goods
    120–1; nature of the eurocrisis 130–4;

opting out 145–6; public sector productivity 118; Stability and Growth Pact (SGP) 140; unproductive consumption 118–19; welfare state and development prospects 116–17, 123
experts 184–5, 189, 194, 195
exports: export-promotion (XP) strategies 79; ratio of exports to GDP 172–3, **172**; trends 170–2, **170**, **171**; voluntary export restraints (VER) 190, 191

Fallows, James 195
Fantacci, L. 61
Farlow, A. 161
Federal Deposit Insurance Corporation Improvement Act (FDICIA) 1991 95
Federal Reserve Bank (FRB) 34, 35, 38–9, 95–104, 110; response to global financial crisis (GFC) 2007 89–90, 91–4; *see also* crisis response
Felkerson, J. A. 97, 98
financial globalization 3–4, 12, 13; action on financial instability in the EU 41–2; action on financial instability in the UK 41; Asian financial crisis 1997 30–1; bailout and early recovery of the megabanks 35; BRICs (Brazil, Russia, India and China) 18; distorted capitalistic system 42; Dodd–Frank Act 35–40; economic significance of financial liberalization 32–3; and the European Union 121–2; financial regulation reform, need for 42–3; Financial Regulatory Reform Act 34–42; freedom and markets as concepts that need rethinking 42–3; geopolitical significance of financial liberalization 32; and the instability of the world economy 27–45; instability of the world financial system 29–32; leadership usurpation by US–UK financial capital 13–14; Obama's financial regulatory reform proposals 34; promulgators for the GLB Act 29; separation of commercial banking from investment banking 28; Shadow Banking System (SBS), rise of 30; significance of financial liberalization for the BRICs 33–4; subprime loan crisis 31–2; unfairness, growing perception of in the US 35; US financial liberalization - Glass–Steagall Act (GS) and Gramm–Leach–Bliley (GLB) Act 27–9
financial instability hypothesis (FIH) 104

financial liberalization 10, 22, 32–4; economic significance 32–3; geopolitical significance 32; India 227
Financial Regulatory Reform Act 34–42
Financial Services (Banking Reform) Act 2013 41
Financial Times 146
FIRE (finance, insurance, real estate) sector 112
firms 4; risky speculative deals 30; uncertainties 5
Fischer, Stanley 11
flexible labor 227–8
Folkerts-Landau, D. 56–7
Food Security Bill (India) 230
Forbes 260
forced saving 8
foreign direct investment (FDI): China 234–6, 237–8, 247; India 11, 225–6, 231n14; Japan 11, 174–5, **174**, 180; United States (US) 174, **174**
Fortune Global 500 236, 264
Fovargue-Davies, M. 150
Frank, Gunder 220
Friedman, Milton 9–10, 13
Friedman, Thomas 166

Garber, P. 56–7
Garside, William Redvers 149–64
Gazprom 264, 265, 268
GDP 6, *18*, 150, **169**; China 168, **168**, 169, **169**; Germany 137, 168, **168**, 169, **169**; Greece 133; growth rates 140, *141*; Korea 168, **168**, 169, **169**; purchasing power parity (PPP) 168–9, **169**; ratio of exports to GDP 172–3, **172**; Spain 136; trends 168, **168**; United Kingdom (UK) 159–60; United States (US) 168, **168**, 169, **169**, 179–80
general equilibrium theory 10
General Theory of Employment, Interest and Money (Keynes) 53, 54, 56, 187
Germany 19, 132; current account surpluses 137; GDP 168, **168**; net capital outflows 173–4, **173**
Glass–Steagall (GS) Act 10, 11, 27–8, 32, 34, 106, 108
global financial crisis (GFC) 2007 119, 139, 149–50; accounting for the FRB response 96–8, **97**, *98*; *99*; government budget surpluses 154, **154**; UK government action 152–4; *see also* crisis response
Global Human Development Index 230

globalization: Brazil 204–5, 206–7; and capitalism 3–26; collapse of the Soviet Union 11–12; commercial globalization 122–3; and comparative advantage 71–86; economic policy and globalization in Brazil 214–16; favorable factors xviii–xix, 9–12; financial globalization 3–4, 12, 18, 27–45, 121–2; financial liberalization 10, 22; gated globalization 46–8, 62–3; "global imbalances" world 56–8; impact on Japan 177–80; and income inequality 167; Japanese attitudes to globalization 165–6; Keynes and today's globalization 58–62; and Keynes's sounder political economy ideal 46–70; leadership usurpation by US–UK financial capital 13–14; Lehman shock and the present 20–2; liberalization and globalization in Brazil 207–9; liberalization of capital transaction 11; market system globalization 3–4, 12; Market System I—end of the Cold War and convergence to the capitalistic system 14–16; Market System II—rise of the emerging countries 16–18, *18*; market system integration—euro system and EU 19–20; nature of 115–16; and neoliberalism 9–10; New Industrial Revolution 11; types of globalization 12–20
gold standard 48–9, 53, 56, 60
Goldstein, M. 246
Gorbachev, Mikhail 12
Gore, C. 51
Gramm–Leach–Bliley (GLB) Act 28, 29, 34
Gramm, Phil 29
Great Depression 20, 27, 49, 52, 104, 105
Greece 130, 132; debt ratio 133; financial crisis 133–4, 139–40; GDP 133
Greenspan, Alan 28, 29, 245–6

haircuts 97, 133, 141, 145, 208
Halifax Bank of Scotland (HBOS) 154
Hamada, Koichi 171, 188
Hanson, P. 271
Harada, Yutaka 165–83
Hayek, Friedrich 9–10, 13
Heckscher, Eli 74
Heckscher–Ohlin–Samuelson trade model 189, 199n2
hedge funds 30–1, 33, 42
Helleiner, Eric 46, 60
Hilferding, Rudolf 104

Hirai, Toshiaki 3–26, 27–45
Hirschmann, A. O. 61
Housing and Utilities Reform Fund (Russia) 269
housing finance 81–4

idealism 186–7
imports: import-substituting industrialization (ISI) strategies 79; import substitution 204, 205–7, 216; India 224–5; paying for essential imports 203–4
Increasing Returns and Economic Progress (Young) 72, 81–2
increasing returns theory 75, 77
incrementalism 242
Independent Commission on Banking 41
India 219–33, 225–6; agriculture 229; deregulated finance 224–7; derivatives 226; "double movement" 221–2, 230–1; economic growth 17; economic reforms 1991 223; employees stock option (ESOP) system 226; employment issues 229–30; financial liberalization 227; fiscal deficit 225; Food Security Bill 230; foreign direct investment (FDI) 11, 225–6, 231n14; Foreign Institutional Investors (FII) 225–6; industrialization and market advances 222–3; initial public offerings (IPOs) 226; interest rates 225; labor market reforms 227–8; liberalized trade and technology 224–5; markets in economic theory and policy 219–21; markets, the state and society 221–30; National Rural Employment Guarantee Act (NREGA) 230; poverty 230; production of cheap goods 122–3; public protests at economic reform failures 228, 230; sales of government securities to banks 225; unorganized labor sector 229; *see also* BRICs (Brazil, Russia, India and China)
Indian Currency and Finance (Keynes) 52, 58
individualism 56
inflation 6; Brazil 210; Colombia 82–3; dangers of failure to control 80; foreign reserves and inflation control 78–9
injustice 7–8, 22–3
innovation 75–6
innovative finance 129–30
interests versus ideas schema 188–9
International Clearing Union (ICU) 53, 54–5, 59, 60, 61

International Monetary Fund (IMF) 11, 50, 51, 60, 79, 122, 132, 159, 244
investment 108, 112, 120, 121–2; capital accumulation and investment rates 142–3; conflict between investment in internationally traded goods and housing investment 83; employees stock option (ESOP) system 226; foreign institutional investors (FII) 225–6; investment banks 28, 41, 106–7, 108, 111, 214; investment to income ratio 144; public investment 189; *see also* foreign direct investment (FDI)
Ireland 132, 136, 138
IT industry 11
Italy 130, 131, 134; debt/GDP ratio 142

James, H. 47
Japan **176**; attitudes to globalization 165–6; attitudes to Trans-Pacific Partnership (TPP) 166; Catholicism 178–9; current account surpluses 243; decline in the share of trade 170–2, **170**, **171**; declining share of the world economy 167–77; deflationary monetary policy 171–2; foreign direct investment (FDI) 11, 174–5, **174**, 180; GDP 168, **168**, 169, **169**; globalization and income inequality in other countries 167; impact of globalization 177–80; income distribution 167; and international labor migration 175; IT industry 11; "Lost Two Decades" 13–14; monetary expansion 179; net capital outflows 173–4, **173**; ratio of exports to GDP 172–3, **172**; significance of financial liberalization 33; students 175–7; terms of trade and living standards 177–8, **178**; and the US experience 179–80; *see also* US-Japanese economic relations 1980s and 1990s
Johnson, Chalmers 195
Johnson, Harry G. 83
Jorgenson, Dale W. 171

Keynes, John Maynard 6, 10, 20, 46–70, 108, 112, 117, 119, 149; American gift to Britain proposal 54–6; and Bretton Woods 47–8; defense of policy space 52–6; on deficit spending 153–4; dilemma of the international system 49; *Economic Consequences of the Peace* 49; *General Theory of Employment, Interest and Money* 53, 54, 56, 187;

"global imbalances" world 56–8; *Indian Currency and Finance* 52, 58; and international economics 51; protectionism 60; "Schachtian" experiment 53–4; sounder political economy between all nations ideal 48; and today's globalization 58–62; *Tract on Monetary Reform* 53; *Treatise on Money* 49, 52, 53; *Treatise on Probability* 52; vitality of Keynes's reasoning in times of gated globalization 62–3
Keys to the Future (Echeverry) 80–4
Khodorkovsky, Mikhail 259, 263
Kindleberger, C. P. 115
King, Mervyn 155–6
Kirschner, J. 60
kleptocracy 32
Konzelmann, S. 150
Korea, GDP 168, **168**
Kregel, J. A. 49, 58, 59
Krugman, P. 162
Kryshtanovskaya, O. 259, 261, 271–2
Kurz, Heinz 73

Lardy, N. R. 246
layering 107
Lehman shock 20–2, 30, 32, 139, 152–3
Levy Institute 112
Lewis, W. Arthur 122
Lexus and the Olive Tree (Friedman) 166
Lincoln provision 36
liquidity 40, 95, 109, 110, 132, 151
Long Term Capital Management (LTCM) 31
luxury goods 144

Maastricht Treaty 134, 140
Malthus, Thomas Robert 116, 144
markets 4; capital market liberalization 49–50; derivatives 42; in economic theory and policy 219–21; gluts 116, 120–1; market judgement 122; market non-existence and opaqueness 42; market system globalization 3–4, 12; market system integration—euro system and EU 19–20; markets, the state and society in India 221–30; need for rethinking 42–3; open markets 71–2; productivity and market size 71–2; self-corrective nature of 149; social embedding 220–1; unification 115; usurpation of profits 8
Marshall Plan 56

Marxian materialism 186
McKinley, Terry 78
migration 77, 80, 116, 137–8, 175, 227
"Mineral Natural Resources in the Strategy for Development of the Russian Economy" (Putin) 265–6
Minsky, Hyman 89, 90, 104–12; stages approach 104–5; views on money and banking 106–12
monetarism 10
money market mutual funds (MMMF) 107
moral hazard 33, 96, 104
Mori, T. 237
mortgages 20, 31–2, 36, 82, 107, 150, 151, 152–3; mortgage-backed securities 94, 96, 100–1, 103–4, 129–30

National Rural Employment Guarantee Act (NREGA) 230
nationalism 20
neo-colonialism 117
neoliberalism 9–10, 32, 42, 52, 119; collapse of 20, 22; effect on investments 121–2; effects on Europe 123–4
New Deal 104, 105
new growth theory 75
New Industrial Revolution 11
new trade theory 75
Newton, S. 59–60
Noguchi, Asahi 184–200, 188
Nomura, Koji 171
Northern Rock 152
NYFed (New York Reserve Bank) 92

Obama, Barack 20–1, 34
Ohashi, Hideo 234–53
Ohlin, Bertil 73, 74, 189, 199n2
Okada, Yasushi 171
Olcott, M. B. 263
Olimpstroi 269, 270
Omnibus Trade and Competitiveness Act 1988 193
"Open Letter to President Clinton and Prime Minister Hosokawa" 196–7
optimal currency areas (OCA) 134–8
Organisation for Economic Cooperation and Development (OECD) 266–7

Pareto optimum 5, 8
Park, D. 237
pension funds 111
Perrotta, Cosimo 115–27
Piacentini, Paolo 128–48

PI[I]G[S] (Portugal, Ireland, [Italy] Greece and [Spain]) 19
Plan of the Four Strategies 80, 81
Plaza Accord 1985 13
Polanyi, Karl 220, 221
Ponzi schemes 207
Portugal 74, 132
poverty 79, 117, 221, 222, 228, 230, 239, 249
Prestowitz, Clyde 195
prices: controls 210–11; market price 5; oil prices 12, 13; stability 211
Primary Dealer Credit Facility 97–8, **97**, **99**, *99*
profits 112; usurpation 8
protectionism 60
public choice theory 187, 192
public opinion 184–5, 185–6; US–Japanese economic relations 1980s and 1990s 194–7
public sector 118, 124
purchasing power parity (PPP) 168–9, **169**
Putin, Vladimir 15, 17–18, 263, 264, 265–6, 270, 271, 271–2, 273

quantitative easing policy 91, 96, 100–4, 155–6

Radygin, A. 266–7
rational choice theory 186, 187–8
rationality 5
Reagan, Ronald 10, 13
renewable energy 117
rent seeking 192
rent theory 73–4
repetitive goods 120–1
"Rethinking Japan" (article) 194–5
Ricardian trade model 189, 199n2
Ricardo, David 73–4
risk retention responsibility provision 40
Rodrik, Dani 47, 51, 59, 63
Romer, Paul 75
Rosas, Luis Eduardo 81
Rosatom 269, 270
Rosnano 269
Rosneft 263, 264, 265
Rostekhnologii (Rostec) 269, 270
Royal Bank of Scotland (RBS) 154
Rubin, Robert 11, 29
Russia: access to business opportunities and abilities 261–2; business elites 259–61, *260*, 271–2; business groups and entrepreneurs 254–9, *256*, *257*, *258*; capitalistic system 14–15;

creation of "state corporations" 268–71; hedge funds 31; limiting foreign participation in strategic areas 264–6; loans-for-shares program 259, 261; private sector share of GDP 266, *266*; privatization 259, 261; *siloviki* 272; state advances in the resources sectors 262–6; state–business interactions from Yeltsin to Putin 271–2; state–business relations dynamics and the evolution of capitalism 254–77; "state capture" 271; state involvement in the economy 266–8, *266*, *267*; subsoil law 265; "Yukos affair" 262–4; *see also* BRICs (Brazil, Russia, India and China)

Sandilands, Roger J. 71–86, 73
Sasaki, H. 237
Sawyer, M. 158
Say's Law 6, 10
"Schachtian" experiment 53–4
Schumpeter, Josef 106
securitization 8, 108, 151, 208
self-sustaining growth 72
Sen, Sunanda 219–33
Shadow Banking System (SBS) 13, 21–2, 30, 33, 34, 39, 105
Shin, K. 237
shock therapy 14, 15, 31
Silva, Lula da 216
Singapore 77–8
Singer, Hans W. 59, 61
Skidelsky, R. 60, 61, 161–2
Smith, Adam 71–2, 81–2, 108, 112
social typology 188
Sokolov, A. 255
Solow, Robert 75, 76
solvency 95, 109, 110, 151
Soviet Union 11–12, 14–16, 18
Spain 136
special investment vehicles (SIVs) 30
special purpose vehicles 95–6
specialization 74, 76, 82
Stability and Growth Pact 140
Stigler, George J. 187
Stiglitz, J. E. 50, 51
stock markets 8, 226
street names 28
stress tests 38–9
Structural Impediments Initiatives (SII) 193
students 175–7, **176**
Stulz, R. 264

subprime loans 30, 31–2, 36, 43, 79, 108, 144, 150, 151
Summers, Lawrence 11, 29
Super 301 193
supervisory assessment fees 40
Swan, Trevor 75

Tarullo, Daniel 38–9
TBTF (Too Big To Fail) idea 36
Teague, E. 271
terms of trade 177–8, **178**
Thailand 30–1
Thatcher, Margaret 10, 13
Time magazine 149
"too big to fail" (TBTF) doctrine 22, 36, 98, 109
Toronto G20 21
toxic assets 151, 152, 154
Tract on Monetary Reform (Keynes) 53
Trade and Development Report 1981–2011 (UNCTAD) 62–3
trade barriers 208
trade liberalization 210, 211, 224–5
Trade Related Intellectual Property Rights (TRIPR) 225
trade unions 118, 135, 143
Trans-Pacific Partnership (TPP) 166
Treatise on Money (Keynes) 49, 52, 53
Treatise on Probability (Keynes) 52
Treaty on the Functioning of the European Union 131–2, 138
Treisman, D. 272
Tseplyaeva, J. 267
Tullock, Gordon 187–8

UNCTAD 62–3
underwriting 28, 108, 110
United Aircraft Building Corporation (OAK) 270–1
United Kingdom (UK) **154**; action on financial instabililty 41; austerity 156–8, 161–2; budget deficit prior to the financial crisis 150–1; debt/GDP ratio 157; financial globalization, leadership usurpation by US–UK financial capital 13–14; fiscal policy after the global financial crisis 149–64; fiscal responses to the 2007 crisis 154–6, **154**, **155**; fiscal retrenchment 158–61; government action on the financial crisis 152–4; index-linked borrowing 160, **160**; Keynes's American gift proposal 54–6; Northern Rock crisis 152; public spending 157–8, *158*; quantitative easing policy 155–6

United Shipbuilding Corporation (OSK) 271
United States (US): bailout and early recovery of the megabanks 35; Dodd–Frank Act 21, 35–40; excessive issuance of dollars 243–4; family incomes 9; financial globalization, leadership usurpation by US-UK financial capital 13–14; financial liberalization - Glass–Steagall (GS) Act and Gramm–Leach–Bliley (GLB) Act 27–9; fiscal deficits 78–9; fiscal policy 20, 21; foreign direct investment (FDI) 174, **174**; GDP 168, **168**, **169**, 179–80; IT industry 11; net capital outflows **173**, 174; Obama's financial regulatory reform proposals 34; public sector net borrowing **155**; separation of commercial banking from investment banking 28; savings shortages and overspending 243; unfairness, growing perception of 35; *see also* US–Japanese economic relations 1980s and 1990s
US–Japanese economic relations 1980s and 1990s 184–200; car industry conflict 191; current account deficit/surplus 192–3, **192**, 194–7; economic policymaking, primary determinants 186–90; Japanese economic development, influence on US trade relations 190–1; lessons learned from the conflict 197–9; misguided public opinion 185–6; misunderstanding of the current account deficit/surplus 197–9; objective criteria 193–4; "Open Letter to President Clinton and Prime Minister Hosokawa" 196–7; public opinion 194–7; revisionist ideas 195–6, 198; semiconductor industry conflict 191–2; structural barriers 198; Structural Impediments Initiatives (SII) 193; Super 301 193; trade friction development 185–6, 190–4; voluntary export restraints 190, 191; voluntary import expansion (VIE) 192, 193, 196, 198

Vargas, Getúlio 205–6
Vedomosti 270
Vickers Report 41
Vines, D. 52
Virginia school of economists 187–8
Vneshekonombank (VEB) 269, 270
Volcker, Paul 36
Volcker Rule 36, 39–40
voluntary export restraints (VER) 190, 191
voluntary import substitution (VIS) 192, 193, 196, 198

wage labor 220
wages 122–3, 229
Wall Street Journal 195, 197
Wallerstein, Immanuel 220
Walters, B. 57
Wang, Jian 241
Warren, Elizabeth 37
Washington Consensus 47, 48–52, 57, 61, 80, 149
Wealth of Nations (Smith) 82
welfare state 116–17, 119
White, S. 259
Wicksell effect 73, 74
Williamson, John 51
Wolf, Martin 78
Wolferen, Karel von 195
workers' rights 123
World Bank 241
World Development Report 1987 241–2
World Economic Forum 165
World Trade Organization (WTO) 16, 238
Wray, Randall 89–114

Yamomoto, Takashi 167
Yeltsin, Boris 12, 14–15, 31, 271
Young, Allyn 72, 73, 74–5, 76, 81–2, 84n1
Yukos 262–4

Zhao, Zhiyand 241
Zhou, Xiaochuan 243–4